MAKING WOMEN'S HISTORIES

Making Women's Histories

Beyond National Perspectives

Edited by Pamela S. Nadell and Kate Haulman

NEW YORK UNIVERSITY PRESS
New York and London

NEW YORK UNIVERSITY PRESS
New York and London
www.nyupress.org

© 2013 by New York University
All rights reserved

References to Internet websites (URLs) were accurate at the time of writing. Neither the author nor New York University Press is responsible for URLs that may have expired or changed since the manuscript was prepared.

This book was published with the generous support of American University's Patrick Clendenen Fund for Women's and Gender History.

LIBRARY OF CONGRESS CATALOGING-IN-PUBLICATION DATA

Making women's histories : beyond national perspectives / edited by Pamela S. Nadell and Kate Haulman.

pages cm

Includes bibliographical references and index.

ISBN 978-0-8147-5890-8 (cloth : alkaline paper) — ISBN 978-0-8147-5891-5 (paper : alkaline paper) — ISBN 978-0-8147-5892-2 (ebook) — ISBN 978-0-8147-5922-6 (ebook)

1. Women—Historiography. 2. Sex role—Historiography. 3. World history—Historiography. 4. Historiography—Social aspects. 5. Historiography—Political aspects. 6. Women historians. I. Nadell, Pamela Susan. II. Haulman, Kate.

HQ1122.M345 2012

907.2'02—dc23

2012032444

New York University Press books are printed on acid-free paper, and their binding materials are chosen for strength and durability. We strive to use environmentally responsible suppliers and materials to the greatest extent possible in publishing our books.

Manufactured in the United States of America
10 9 8 7 6 5 4 3 2 1

In memory of Robert Griffith (1940–2011)

Contents

Acknowledgments — ix

Writing Women's History across Time and Space: Introduction — 1
Pamela S. Nadell and Kate Haulman

IMAGINING NEW HISTORIES:
LATE-TWENTIETH-CENTURY TRAJECTORIES

1. Women's Past and the Currents of U.S. History — 17
   Kathy Peiss

2. New Directions in Russian and Soviet Women's History — 38
   Barbara Alpern Engel

3. Putting the Political in Economy: African Women's and Gender History, 1992–2010 — 61
   Claire Robertson

4. Sexual Crises, Women's History, and the History of Sexuality in Europe — 91
   Anna Clark

ENGENDERING NATIONAL AND NATIONALIST PROJECTS

5. Gender and the Politics of Exceptionalism in the Writing of British Women's History — 115
   Arianne Chernock

6. Amateur Historians, the "Woman Question," and the Production of Modern History in Turn-of-the-Twentieth-Century Egypt — 137
   Lisa Pollard

7. Women's and Gender History in Modern India: Researching the Past, Reflecting on the Present — 161
   Mytheli Sreenivas

EXPLORING TRANSNATIONAL APPROACHES

8. World History Meets History of Masculinity
   in Latin American Studies   187
   Ulrike Strasser and Heidi Tinsman

9. Connecting Histories of Gender, Health, and U.S.-China Relations   211
   Cristina Zaccarini

10. A Happier Marriage? Feminist History Takes
    the Transnational Turn   237
    Jocelyn Olcott

   About the Contributors   259
   Index   263

Acknowledgments

Sometimes scholars cannot recall the precise origins of a project. That, however, is not the case with this volume. It was the spring of 2008, in the midst of the American University conference "'With Vision Flying': New Perspectives on Women's and Gender History," when the idea came to life. That such a conference ever happened, and that this book is now in your hands, is due in part to the efforts and encouragement of our colleague, friend, and then department chair, the late Professor Robert Griffith. When a fund created in the 1890s for the "education of young women alone," unexpectedly fell into his lap, Bob, with his characteristic grand vision, imagined a series of projects which would advance the field of women's and gender history now that the academy had long moved beyond the need to provide for the "education of young women alone." American University's Clendenen Fund for Women's and Gender History was born.

Making Women's Histories: Beyond National Perspectives has not collected the papers originally presented at "With Vision Flying" (which took its title from a work by the nineteenth-century poet Rachel Luzzatto Morpurgo). But the conversations that conference engendered caused us to imagine a book in which prominent scholars of women's history, trained in various national histories, would reflect on the intellectual and political production of women's and gender history. With that vision to guide us, we invited contributors; the result is this volume.

Our debts are many, and it gives us great pleasure to acknowledge them. First, we thank our contributors. (With the exception of one pair of authors who revised a previously published essay for our purposes, all wrote new chapters for this volume.) They distilled their considerable knowledge of the historiographies on women and gender in their particular fields into their chapters. With good cheer and collegiality, all of them—Arianne Chernock, Anna Clark, Barbara Alpern Engel, Jocelyn Olcott, Kathy Peiss, Lisa Pollard, Claire Robertson, Mytheli Sreenivas, Ulrike Strasser, Heidi Tinsman,

Cristina Zaccarini—met our deadlines, dialogued with us about our suggestions for revisions, and played major roles in shaping the book.

NYU Press's anonymous reviewers helped us to refine our original conception. As always, it is a special pleasure to thank NYU Press's editor extraordinaire Jennifer Hammer, justly famed both for the alacrity with which she responds to emails and more importantly for her wise vision about the making of books. We also thank Universiteit van Amsterdam Professor of History and Gender Studies Frances Gouda for her insights.

Conversations with our colleagues in American University's Department of History and across campus buoyed us. We are deeply grateful to American University's Clendenen Fund for Women's and Gender History, which has supported this project in multiple ways, and especially to our Dean Peter Starr and former Dean Kay Mussell, both of whom understood from the beginning how this project would advance the aims of the Clendenen Fund.

We thank our families for providing a different kind of joyous support and much needed distractions—Kate's husband Guy Nelson and son Thomas; Pam's husband Ed Farber, son Yoni, and daughter Orly. But we have dedicated other books to them already. This one we dedicate to the memory of Bob.

It may seem odd to dedicate a book, entirely written by women, about the production of women's history, to a man, but this dedication affirms what our book proves—the centrality and capaciousness of this field of intellectual production which has touched every sphere of the historical profession. Robert Griffith was a distinguished scholar, beloved teacher, and visionary administrator, and, with his loving wife Barbara and their family at his side, a remarkable human being. We remember Bob fondly, and his genuine enthusiasm for this book, which to our sorrow, he did not live to see in print. We were blessed to have had him in our lives for the time he spent among us.

Writing Women's History across Time and Space

Introduction

PAMELA S. NADELL AND KATE HAULMAN

"My commitment to women's history came out of my life, not out of my head," wrote the pioneering historian Gerda Lerner. As a graduate student, Lerner had encountered "a world of 'significant knowledge,'" in which women seemed not to exist.¹ She dedicated her career to the project of remaking that body of knowledge, demanding that it include the lives and experiences of women as well as of men.

This volume examines that world transformed by considering the intellectual and political production of women's history across time and space. In ten chapters, scholars, who have all published significant works in women's and gender history in diverse national, imperial, and geographic contexts, stand atop historiographically defined vantage points, including Tsarist Russia, the British empire in Egypt and India, Qing dynasty China, and the U.S. roiling through the 1960s. From these and other peaks they gaze out at the world around them, surveying trajectories in the intellectual production of women's histories in recent and distant pasts, reflecting upon the historical circumstances that gave rise to such narratives, and envisioning their futures in diverse settings. The authors were asked to consider the differences women's history made within their national fields of study. How did the wider historiographies integrate this new knowledge? What have been the accomplishments of women's and gender history within their geographic fields? What are its shortcomings? Perhaps most significantly, what is its future?

Behind these questions lay the conviction, growing out of conversations with colleagues over the years, that parallel circumstances in diverse settings had sparked the writing of women's and gender history by professional historians. We wanted to probe this insight by asking scholars to expand upon the threads of those serendipitous conversations out of which the larger patterns had burst forth. This book demonstrates that the writing of women's histories was chronologically deeper than first imagined, regionally specific even as its development was transnational and global, and driven by wider intellectual, social, political, and economic currents. The authors in this book discuss their discovery of women's histories, the multiple turns the field has taken, the historiographies produced, and how place has affected the course of this scholarship. Some contributors investigate precursors to the contemporary field of inquiry; others imagine new directions the field will take as other voices join the conversation.

This volume also enters into another conversation currently underway in the historical profession, that of "Globalizing Historiography."[2] The discipline of history has long been a deeply nationalist one. While students and scholars say that they write political, social, or gender history, they almost invariably do so within a single geographic setting, whose broad historiography they have also mastered. But, in an age which sees the impact of "globalization" from McDonald's on the Champs Elysee to Facebook's role in the 2011 Arab Spring, the academic profession has grown increasingly critical of the limitations of the national and is trying to imagine the writing of history in transnational and intercultural global contexts. Although the chapters in this volume, with a few important exceptions, are not internally transnational or comparative, when read together they generate transnational comparisons and contrasts which will prove illuminating not only to scholars and students of women's and gender history, no matter their national field, but also to those studying and teaching in courses in the burgeoning fields of transnational and global history.

These chapters affirm our initial observations: Certain themes resound across time and space. Around the world and in different eras, those writing women's history, whether as amateur or professional historians, addressed similar questions and advanced parallel objectives. Whether in the twenty-first century or in the eighteenth, writing women's history has had explicitly political purposes. This led to the development of a historiography deliberately intended to advance the status of women in society. But the literature of women's history has also entered into a tangle of debates at the core of the modern experience, writing women into history to advance a host of ideas about modernity. In colonial societies, history-making around the woman question became yet one more venue for the confrontation between colonialism and anticolonialism. Writing women's history also contributed to the project of imagining the nation-state. Consequently, the discourse engendered by this scholarship was deeply conflicted, complicated, and contradictory. As the chapters in this volume intersect with one another, as the contributors reflect upon the emergence of women's history—subsequently retitled women's and gender history—and its historiographies, their convergences affirm the transnational nature of this field whose themes crisscross and intersect around the globe and across the centuries. In the end, historiography on women and gender sustains the truism that all history is politics. After all, "remembering is not a neutral act."[3]

The first section of this book, "Imagining New Histories: Late-Twentieth-Century Trajectories," looks back to the fairly recent past. Here Kathy Peiss, Barbara Engel, Claire Robertson, and Anna Clark, historians of women and gender in the U.S., Europe, and Africa, stand out for more than their sweeping breadth. They trace the arc of their contemporary fields from the first glimmers within 1960s second-wave feminism down through the first decade of the twenty-first century. Moreover, each reflects explicitly on the ways in which the political and intellectual contexts of 1960s feminism and the historical consciousness it engendered led to the birth of fields of academic inquiry, which then seemed utterly new.

As graduate students, these scholars helped to pioneer the professional writing of women's history. Both Barbara Engel and Claire Robertson were in graduate school during those heady days, a time of exciting possibilities when, as Engel recalls, "women's history seemed part of a movement that might transform the world we knew."[4] All shared similar experiences: They took no courses in women's history because none was offered. In those years "women's studies was so new it was possible to read everything."[5] And read they did and not only history, but also the early literature of women's studies then being produced by anthropologists, sociologists, psychologists, and theorists—"anything that shed light on the situation of women."[6]

They ventured largely into the unknown with their first books. When Engel decided to write about the women of Russia's nineteenth-century intelligentsia, she knew neither Russian women's history nor women's history more generally.[7] Her work, Robertson's socioeconomic history of Ghanaian women,[8] Peiss's study of working-women's leisure in turn-of-the-twentieth-century New York,[9] and Clark's work on sexual violence in England during the Industrial Revolution and the rise of Victorianism[10] are models of historical scholarship resting on the discovery of new sources and carefully crafted arguments. But their scholarship, and the historiography which has flowed from it, the subject of their chapters here, came out of their personal encounters with the political. As Peiss observes: "This was heritage that supported and legitimized a social movement."[11] This research and writing represented their personal contributions to the making of second-wave feminism. But, even as each reflects personally and along parallel lines about the exciting challenges of pioneering what she thought was an utterly new field, history and geography dictated that nation and region would assert centrifugal forces which propelled the writing of women's history along different paths.

Peiss opens with the birth of professional women's and gender history in the U.S. out of the broader social, political, and intellectual currents of the 1960s. Writing women into history surfaced as a political project riding the crest of second-wave feminism. In its early days, the project even reflected some of the movement's internal divisions over tactics and goals. Because its early scholarship emphasized the lives of the ordinary, it fit right into the social history then current in the profession. Later, as Peiss observes, the shift to gender history helped move this new historiography "from periphery to center" in the field of U.S. history.[12]

For historians writing on women in the Russian empire and the Soviet Union, the Cold War, which limited access to archives and which emphasized politics, virtually mandated that political history would dominate the field at the outset. Hence scholars focused on female political activism among Russian and Soviet women. This emphasis on political history set this historiography apart from the way the field was developing elsewhere as women's-history-as-social-history. But the gender turn also opened up new approaches for Russian and Soviet historians just as the Soviet Union was collapsing. The prism of gender compelled inquiry into women's bodies as objects of control and into gendered relations and the exercise of power. The questions opened up by the gender turn became influential among Russian and Soviet historians, even among those who did not focus their research on women.

History-as-politics comes into view in Claire Robertson's sweeping assessment of multidisciplinary work on African women's and gender history since 1992. Robertson speaks with justifiable pride of her role in developing women's history. Making no bones about it, she calls this scholarship "histoire engagée," intellectual production in an explicitly activist vein meant to be of use to its subjects. But, because Western-style, second-wave feminism has not proven a workable model for African societies, "African feminism," developing in resistance to colonialism and to "Western hegemony," focuses on collective gains and "bread, butter, culture, and power" issues rather than on individual female autonomy.[13] Hence scholarship on African women emphasizes resistance to Western hegemony, and, as Robertson underscores, some of it is not particularly historicized. The popular women's studies topics of sex work, reproductive politics, and genital cutting do not seem to have applicable histories. There is, in her view, a collapsing of the present and the past that unhelpfully reifies the notion of a timeless, unchanging "Africa" through, in part, a focus on the bodies of women. Scholars, she seems to suggest, must heed the *histoire* in the *engagée*.

Anna Clark reiterates what Peiss, Engel, and Robertson have already observed—that the contemporary shapes each era's historical production. She turns her gaze to the historiography of sexualities, a field which she pioneered and which emerged alongside of and intersected with the new scholarship on women and gender. Clark considers sexual crises of the late nineteenth and early twentieth centuries when scandals over homosexuality and white slavery, coupled with concerns about the nation's mothers producing citizens fit to serve, revealed deep-rooted clashes within the body politic. The first historians of sexuality equated "sex (not yet broken down into sex, gender, and sexuality) as a central historical motive force."[14] They were deeply influenced by coming of age during the 1968 student movements and by Marxist materialist analysis, with its emphasis on economic power and coercive state authority. They assumed that "sexual desire was natural and biological," and "ascribed sexual repression to capitalism, religion, and the bourgeois family." But, as feminist activists around the globe turned to sexual issues like domestic violence, scholars in service to the feminist movement, as Kathy Peiss has already observed, began considering such subjects in historical perspective, much as Clark had done in her first book *Women's Silence, Men's Violence: Sexual Assault in England, 1770–1845*. Demonstrating how wider social, political, and legal currents shaped sexual practices, identities, and representations in the past, they influenced the present. These historians complicated the neat Marxist-inflected formulation of earlier work by arguing that sexuality was a "key means for the oppression of women" and "a central dynamic of history."[15]

Peiss, Engel, Robertson, and Clark are not the only authors in this volume to underscore that the writing of women's history is a deeply political project, demonstrating how relationships of power, broadly defined, intersect with politics more narrowly defined. While almost all contributors observe how their particular subfield of women's and gender historiography burst forth out of the influence of second-wave feminism, Arianne Chernock, in her chapter on eighteenth- and nineteenth-century historical production on British women, uncovers the political nature of this earlier body of work by analyzing the genre of women's history called "women worthies."

"Women worthies" were the female queens, warriors, saints, and sometimes villains, whose lives were so exceptional that, despite being female, they left their imprint on the past. The first professional women's historians had carefully distanced themselves from the amateurs who wrote about these lives. Gerda Lerner characterized this scholarship as the "first level," and hence least advanced, in the development of the field.[16] Chernock reminds us that "many historians of women and gender remain, to some extent, embarrassed by their field's origins."[17]

But she joins a group of contemporary scholars, among them Bonnie Smith in *The Gender of History: Men, Women, and Historical Practice*,[18] who have not only uncovered the long trail of "woman worthy" literature, but whose analyses of this oft-dismissed "exceptionalist" genre reveal political purposes and objectives, which are far more complex and of greater historical import than first imagined. Chernock finds that eighteenth- and nineteenth-century histories of British "women worthies" became key sites for advancing the debate over woman's capacity to learn and to exercise civic and political rights. These histories put forward exceptional women from the past as role models capable of removing from society "that vulgar prejudice of the supposed incapacity of the female sex." Consequently, an intriguing parallel emerges. The amateurs writing great women into the past and the late-twentieth-century professional scholars of women's and gender history were equally convinced that "to have the courage to act in the present, women needed to know that they were not alone in history."[19]

This book affirms that writing women's and gender histories started out and remains a deeply political project with aims beyond advancing the status of women in society. This field of intellectual production engaged in the past, informs the present, and enters into the future enmeshed within a tangle of transnational debates over the meanings and uses of modernity, colonialism and anticolonialism, the nation and nationalism.

If the nation was to become modern, its women too had to be propelled forward. Modernizing men and women harnessed the intellectual production of women's histories to their project. Modernity demanded change—education for girls and women everywhere, cleanliness and order in colonized households, new forms of medical care. Modernity also meant repudiating women-focused traditions deemed anathema to Enlightenment ideals of rationality—footbinding in China, sati (the self-immolation of a widow on her husband's funeral pyre) in India, the harem in Egypt. Both colonialists and nationalists critiqued these behaviors for yoking women to the past and hence limiting the nation, preventing it from taking its proper place in the modern world order. For colonizers, the necessity of such reforms justified their imperial "gendered civilizing mission," to borrow Barbara Engel's phrase.[20] But anticolonialists also embraced the project of modernizing women; they, not the colonials nor the imperial state, would take charge of "liberating" women and thus would advance their aim of freeing the nation. All used an emerging literature on women's history for explicitly political purposes. Nationalists, both in the empire and in the colony, used this intellectual production to define the nation. Thus, as Arianne Chernock notes, this scholarship reveals "myriad and often disruptive motives," as it served different masters.[21] The chapters grouped under "Engendering National and Nationalist Projects" in this volume examine these other political projects of this historiography.

While appreciating how the "woman worthy" genre offered an alternative model of British womanhood meant to raise women's consciousness and fuel debates about their status, Arianne Chernock finds that the eighteenth- and nineteenth-century women's histories she read were "a means of defining, defending, and distinguishing 'Britishness' from other national identities." For some writers the "women worthies" upheld Britain's historic greatness. Other amateur historians, however, deliberately contrasted the powers of great women of the past with the narrow prospects open to contemporary British women. Their writings advanced the modern, "far more democratic conception of national identity," one which would have significant implications not only for British women but for all marginalized British subjects. Chernock concludes with the bold claim: "to write the history of women *was* to write the history of the nation."[22]

Like Chernock, Lisa Pollard also examines the work of nineteenth-century amateur historians who took up the "woman question," but in Egypt. She finds this work a by-product of imagining the nation-state as it wrested itself away from Ottoman hegemony and contended with British occupation. "Civil servants, intellectuals, journalists, and educators" asserted competing arguments: Women either "embodied Egypt's backwardness or its potential for modernity." Even as colonizers used the "reform and rescue of Egypt's women" to justify British rule, arguing that, due to its poor treatment of females, Egypt "could not yet be defined as a nation," anticolonialist intellectuals contended that modernizing the domestic sphere would allow them to take back the nation.[23]

Pollard also observes a distinction between histories produced by men and those written by women. Male writers celebrated a mythic "Lady Egypt"—a composite of women from Egypt's Pharaonic, Greco-Roman, and Arab Islamic pasts. Female writers brought exceptional women out of the darkness of the past and into the light of their present to provide models of modern womanhood for their readers and to write women into the current political struggles. In the end, these women's histories asserted competing "versions of where the Egyptian people came from and where, as a nation, they ought to be headed."[24]

Mytheli Sreenivas poses the question of the gendered nature of modernity itself in the case of India, tracing the trajectory of late-twentieth-century

Indian women's historiography and its evaluation of the consequences of nationalism and national liberation movements. She investigates the claims and processes of both the British colonial regime and the movement for self-rule. Sreenivas makes a point similar to one emphasized by Barbara Engel in her chapter: politics drives the wider historiography. Consequently, these early histories of women in India centered on activists in social reform and political movements.

For India, Sreenivas shows, historians discovered disturbing continuities over how colonial and anticolonial forces took up the "woman question" and promised that their rule would bring about women's "liberation." Deploying the universal concept of "women"—and too often paying little attention to actual women, especially of the lower castes—both projects were informed by normative, middle-class politics and gender norms. They resulted, whether intentionally or not, in the modernization of patriarchy rather than its dismantling. Thus, the bourgeois nationalism of Indian liberation no more represented different women's voices and interests than had British colonialism. She concludes that "the historiography of women and gender in modern India offers a profound critique not only of women's oppression, but also of colonial and postcolonial modernity."[25]

Many of the authors in this volume nod toward the transnational turn. For example, Robertson and Sreenivas point to the fundamentally transnational nature of their regional specialties whose historiographies are produced both within the region and in the West, which naturally draws scholars around the globe into conversation. But several scholars in this volume are explicitly engaged in "Exploring Transnational Approaches." Through the prism of Latin American Studies, Ulrike Strasser and Heidi Tinsman join two distinct and rarely intersecting historiographies: world history and masculinity. Even as historians of gender and sexuality rarely write world history, "world history marches along merrily without paying much attention to gender and sexuality," either ignoring women entirely or circumscribing them as subjects. The culturalist orientation of the former and the materialist emphasis of the latter have kept the two apart. But a focus on masculinities—for example, constructions of the masculine natures of the conquered and the conqueror, the gendered division of labor, and the different masculinities constructed within labor systems—allows for understanding historical episodes with global reach, such as the colonial encounter between Europe and the Americas, through the history of masculinities. Making "masculinity... a terrain of power," historians of gender and sexuality enter into the writing of world history.[26] But Strasser and Tinsman are careful to caution that the prism of masculinities is but a starting point for "feminist world historical work." Such studies are fraught with the potential to erase men's power over women and reinscribe women's "traditional invisibility." Our authors emphasize: "Of course, world history needs to pay more attention to women."[27]

Cristina Zaccarini certainly agrees. She focuses instead on the intellectual production of women's history in nineteenth- and twentieth-century China and its contributions to the writing of the history of U.S.-China foreign relations. Westerners and Chinese elites alike asserted that the inferior status of Chinese women reflected problems endemic to the nation. Western missionaries and physicians as well as Chinese intent upon modernization sought to overturn coercive traditions limiting girls and women—female infanticide and the preference for sons, footbinding and female seclusion, and the Chinese custom of "Thrice Following," which dictated a woman's subordination first to her father, then to her husband, and in old age to her son. If China were to modernize and remedy its weaknesses vis-à-vis the West, then these practices must give way. Zaccarini claims that, in "grappling with the issues of modernization, including the modernization of gender roles, China, as a nation, was invented." She also argues that Chinese women blended Chinese and Western cultures to achieve something unique, "redefining modernity for China and for themselves."[28]

Considering the "recent union of transnational and feminist history," Jocelyn Olcott finds the two fields sharing a tradition of "troubl[ing] conventional narratives" and "decentering those actors and processes" at the heart of much historical writing. When joined together as "transnational feminist history," the field, "arguably a marriage of necessity precipitated by the need to understand the rapid intensification of transnational feminism," challenges assumptions about "periodization, place, identification, and infrastructures" not interrogated in each separate field. For example, questions raised by transnational feminist scholars about the marking of historical time prompted a rethinking of women's and gender histories' articulation of "waves" of feminism and its emphasis on linear progression. Much as Cristina Zaccarini shows in her discussion of mission work in China, transnational feminist history, Olcott argues, brings to the fore international organizations crossing borders which opened up spaces for women to develop feminist consciousness. Likening transnational feminist history to a marriage which might yield "connubial bliss" or end in acriminious divorce, Olcott does not speculate about the field's future; instead she affirms that the insights yielded to date "have repaid the arduous scholarly work that has gone into it."[29]

But other authors also look into the future making of women's and gender histories, and do so by looking back to the past. Kathy Peiss asks—and she is by no means the first to do so[30]—if, given how the gender turn became hegemonic in the field, is the writing of women's history "an unfinished feminist project"? Having spent so much time considering "women worthies," Arianne Chernock boldly refuses to dismiss the biographical approach to history. She dares to posit that the earlier historiographic project may be worthy of emulation. If popular tastes are any indication, she may well be on the right track.

* * * *

The geographic, temporal, and conceptual range of political projects making use of women's history is striking. Across the modern era men and women have sought to mobilize women's history to address actual and ostensible "women's issues" and spaces, like the home, and to deploy the idea of "woman" to serve diverse political agendas. It seems, then, that there is always women's history at the heart of political projects. Yet, important distinctions appear within these political agendas as we compare the making of women's history conducted in the name of women with work produced by women who have mobilized and spoken for themselves through historical writing. From colonialism and resistance around the globe (usually spearheaded by men), to nation-making and nationalism (involving men and women, but generally led by men), to professional women's history writing (usually accomplished by women), the strategic narration of the past has proven a critical lever of politics, broadly defined.

The most obvious forms of politics addressed in this collection are formal polities and the institutions of governance. Whether framed within colonialism, anticolonialism, or nation-making, contests over the place of actual women, discussions of ideas about women and gender, and consideration of sexual practices involving women's bodies have accompanied the writing of women's history (often the history of those very things) to legitimate sweeping political changes. To some degree, the "woman question" and particular accounts of women's past and present, have been central to nationalism because colonial imperialist projects focused so intently on "saving brown women from brown men," as Gayatri Spivak put it.[31] When colonial officials and their codes of law were not attempting to rescue women from the traditions of their indigenous societies, they busied themselves with managing the "intimacies" of empire—chiefly, regulating sex across the color line.[32] Thus, movements for independence and self-rule attempted to occupy, or recolonize, the same terrain.

On the whole, this book suggests that such political movements have not been especially beneficial for most women across time and space, no matter their claims. From securing "rights" in the modern sense to improving material status, statist political movements have been decidedly mixed in their outcomes despite (or perhaps due to) the participation of women. That this is the case has much to do with the perpetually conflicted, ambivalent discourses evident in the writing of women's history revealed in this volume. One axis of tension is competing (and ever-shifting) notions of tradition and modernity. Historically speaking, this book suggests, women have been cast as both the carriers of tradition and the emblems of the modern—a heavy weight to bear. The writing of women's history in the service of political projects has also, sometimes inadvertently or unconsciously, helped to maintain gendered labor and class hierarchies. In several historical contexts, from the United States to India, the production of women's history has helped to preserve the gentility of elite and middle-class women, even in the face of gender-based agitation for greater inclusion within the liberal state.

Despite its subtitle, *Beyond National Perspectives*, this volume suggests that many roads in women's history still lead to the nation. This should not surprise us since much of women's history has been written within the nation and as a result of its promises and pitfalls. If the case can be made that the professional, academic discipline of history, with its origins in the nineteenth century and emphasis on empiricism, is ontologically related to the era of the modern nation-state (and not merely its era, but to the creation, legitimization, and maintenance of nations themselves), what does that mean for the production of women's history? Scholars have used the history of women to interrogate the nation—both specific national origins and trajectories, and the broader concept of "nation" itself. Now they are examining ways in which the production of women's history has been intimately bound up with the nation. As scholars we are not yet beyond the nation; instead we are interrogating its products, and one of them is women's history.

Expanding geographic frames, from the oceanic to the transnational to the global, is the order of the day in contemporary historiography. Such approaches, meant to free us from national and nationalist boxes, generate new stories and analyses: the very stuff of history. But there may be interpretive costs, not necessarily unique to the practice of women's history, which lend a retrogressive cast to what is essentially a progressive project. If we embrace biography and the lives of individual, often exceptional, women as a way to write internationally, what happens to the experiences of ordinary women whose lives do not carry them across borders? If we employ masculinities as a way of rethinking political economy, do we risk recentering men at the core of the historical narrative? Where do different temporal frames fit in a world in which a broad and inclusive approach to place seems more pressing than an expansive sense of time? Just as it has been important for scholars to see the animating role of the nation in their narratives, so too we must acknowledge the influence of the digital age and globalization as more than a mere backdrop to the making of women's histories.

These are the questions this volume leaves us pondering. We know much about the historiographies of women and gender produced in diverse settings and the circumstances which led to their creation. We have seen the parallel new and yet different "turns" this scholarship took as it wound its way through various national and geographic settings. Finally, every author in this book has compelled us to consider the political uses of the intellectual production of women's and gender history. The professional field created to provide "a usable past" now serves as a guide to that recent past, yet does not forgo its commitment to the lives of its subjects. While we can speculate about the field's future directions, we are not seers but rather reclaimers of the past who acknowledge our very present concerns. Thus, even as this volume reclaims the past under the influence of the present, it dares to envision the future, confident that the writing of women's and gender history is here to stay.

NOTES

1. Gerda Lerner, "Women among the Professors of History: The Story of a Process of Transformation," in *Voices of Women Historians: The Personal, the Political, the Professional*, ed. Eileen Boris and Nupur Chaudhuri (Bloomington: Indiana University Press, 1999), 1.
2. This was the theme of the American Historical Association annual meeting in 2009.
3. Letty Cottin Pogrebin, *Deborah, Golda, and Me: Being Female and Jewish in America* (New York: Crown Publishers, 1991), 139.
4. Engel, 38, this volume; Both Engel and Robertson earned their Ph.D.s in 1974; Peiss earned hers in 1982.
5. The quote is from Engel, 39, this volume; cf. Peiss.
6. Engel, 39, this volume.
7. Barbara Alpern Engel, *Mothers and Daughters: Women of the Intelligentsia in Nineteenth-Century Russia* (Cambridge, New York: Cambridge University Press, 1983).
8. Claire C. Robertson, *Sharing the Same Bowl? A Socioeconomic History of Women and Class in Accra, Ghana* (Bloomington: Indiana University Press, 1984).
9. Kathy Lee Peiss, *Cheap Amusements: Working Women and Leisure in Turn-of-the-Century New York* (Philadelphia: Temple University Press, 1986).
10. Anna Clark, *Women's Silence, Men's Violence: Sexual Assault in England, 1770-1845* (London: Routledge Kegan Paul/Pandora, 1987).
11. Peiss, 18, this volume.
12. Peiss, 23, this volume.
13. Robertson, 65, this volume.
14. Clark, 95, this volume.
15. Clark, 94, 101, this volume.

16. Gerda Lerner, *The Majority Finds Its Past: Placing Women in History* (Oxford, New York: Oxford University Press, 1979), 145–59.
17. Chernock, 127, this volume.
18. Bonnie G. Smith, *The Gender of History: Men, Women, and Historical Practice* (Cambridge: Harvard University Press, 1998).
19. Chernock, 120, 127, this volume.
20. Engel, 53, this volume.
21. Chernock, 115, this volume.
22. Chernock, 121, 124, 131, this volume.
23. Pollard, 138, 144, 150, 155, this volume.
24. Pollard, 139, this volume.
25. Sreenivas, 162, this volume.
26. Strasser and Tinsman, 190, 197, this volume.
27. Strasser and Tinsman, 201, this volume.
28. Zaccarini, 214, 229, this volume.
29. Olcott, 237, 252, 238, this volume.
30. Alice Kessler-Harris, "Do We Still Need Women's History?" *Chronicle of Higher Education* 54, no. 15 (December 7, 2007).
31. Gayatri Chakravorty Spivak, *A Critique of Postcolonial Reason: Toward a History of the Vanishing Present* (Cambridge: Harvard University Press, 1999), 287.
32. For an examination of this process in different imperial and colonial contexts, see Ann Laura Stoler, "Tense and Tender Ties: The Politics of Comparison in North American History and (Post) Colonial Studies," *Journal of American History* 88, no. 3 (2001): 829–65.

Imagining New Histories

Late-Twentieth-Century Trajectories

1

Women's Past and the Currents of U.S. History

KATHY PEISS

Less than half a century ago, the subject of women and gender barely registered in the scholarship and teaching of American historians. In remarkably short order, uncovering women's past became a political imperative and intellectual passion, and then emerged as a legitimate area of professional inquiry and research. With some distance from its origins, it is now possible to consider women's and gender history as particular forms of knowledge production that grew out of broad intellectual, social, and political developments in the post-World War II period. This chapter focuses on four conceptual "turns" in the field, and how they have shaped the practices of American historians and the study of women: the rise of women's history; the change in subject from women to gender; the linkage between gender analysis, poststructuralism, and cultural studies; and the growing importance of transnational history. These approaches overlap and continue to inform the work of a new generation of scholars; their contours reflect intellectual agendas consciously pursued, but also unforeseen or underestimated developments that have affected the field.

The Emergence of Women's History

The emergence of women's history as an intellectual endeavor grew directly out of feminist political movements in the 1960s and 1970s. I discovered women's history when I entered graduate school in 1975. I never took a course on the subject, but I found myself continually writing seminar papers on women. I managed to learn women's history on the fly, as a teaching assistant one step ahead of her students. Indeed, there was hardly any historiography for me to master then. My reading list for Ph.D. orals included every piece of secondary literature on women's history, and that was the last moment I could truthfully say I had read everything. As I began to conceptualize my dissertation topic, a history of working women, leisure, and sexuality that would eventually become *Cheap Amusements*, my advisers wondered whether I would find any evidence. Combing through libraries and archives, I could see that the organization of knowledge itself reflected a belief that women were only marginally historical actors. Thus I had the sense of being present at the creation of an entirely new field of inquiry, of uncovering and revealing a past that had never even been considered the past, or so I thought then.

Joined to that, of course, was the sense of being part of a collective feminist movement, the belief that our intellectual project had a political meaning and purpose. The women's liberation movement had issued an assault on academic disciplines, and history offered a long-suppressed record of patriarchal misdeeds. The title of Sheila Rowbotham's 1973 book *Hidden from History* is often quoted, but its original subtitle in England has been forgotten—"300 years of women's oppression and the fight against it"—changed in the first U.S. edition to a less politically charged phrase, "rediscovering women in history from the 17th century to the present." For activists, history provided inspiration, role models, and a tradition of female resistance. Thus the neologism "herstory" countered history's master narrative; the term "second wave" expressed the inheritance of an earlier feminist tradition; and artist Judy Chicago created the *Dinner Party*, with its place settings honoring path-breaking women of the past, in the name of an essentialized sisterhood. This was heritage that supported and legitimized a social movement.[1]

Women's history did not originate in the 1960s, however, but rather dates back several hundred years: As Arianne Chernock and Lisa Pollard explain in this volume, British political writers and Egyptian historians, mainly men, explored women's past to assess women's rights and modernity. As Bonnie G. Smith and Julie Des Jardins have shown, women intellectuals and amateur researchers also found their own histories compelling. Educated women of the Enlightenment examined the lives of powerful queens, while amateur historians, fascinated with such quotidian subjects as foodways, clothing, and household manufacturing, wrote the earliest social histories. In the nineteenth century, activists documented women's history in the making, in such invaluable works as the multivolume *History of Woman's Suffrage*, compiled by Elizabeth Cady Stanton, Susan B. Anthony, and Matilda Joslyn Gage; African American educators, librarians, and reformers also preserved and wrote black women's history. Although women were largely marginalized in the historical profession, such women as Mary Beard and Lucy Maynard Salmon published scholarship that centered on women. The Berkshire Conference of Women Historians, founded in 1930, created a professional network, and some of these historians evinced an interest in women's past. The American Historical Association annual meeting in 1940 was the first to hold a session on the history of women, including a paper on the "nurturing of feminism in the United States" by Jeannette P. Nichols.[2]

Even more important were efforts beginning in the 1930s to establish repositories for women's history, where the documentary record of women's actions would be preserved and made available for future generations. Mary Beard was unsuccessful in creating a World Center for Women's Archives, but the Sophia Smith Collection at Smith College and the "women's archive" at Radcliffe College, later known as the Schlesinger Library, were both established during World War II. "No documents, no history," Mary Beard used as her motto. If historical consciousness was a mode of making sense of the world and of placing oneself within it, such archives would serve as crucial sites of identity formation and political solidarity.[3]

The questions animating historians of women, as the modern field emerged, were informed not only by the second-wave political critique of male domination in the U.S., but also by the divisions within the movement over the means and ends of feminist social change. Although much of the success of post-1960s feminism lay in its ability to claim inclusion, equality, and rights in the framework of American political liberalism, it was the more radical approaches, especially socialist feminism and radical feminism, which shaped the early endeavors in women's history. In hindsight, the close relationship between women's history and second-wave feminist politics is readily apparent. An influential 1970 manifesto of the feminist group Radicalesbians, "The Woman Identified Woman," de-eroticized lesbianism and expanded the spectrum of female-centered relationships. It provided the ideological foundation for Carroll Smith-Rosenberg's groundbreaking essay, "The Female World of Love and Ritual," even if Smith-Rosenberg did not acknowledge it; first presented as a paper at the 1974 Organization of American Historians meeting, it was published the following year in the inaugural issue of *Signs: Journal of Women in Culture and Society*. Ellen DuBois's pioneering *Feminism and Suffrage* traced the rise of an independent women's movement in the mid-nineteenth century. Exploring the fraught relationship of antebellum women's rights and abolitionism, and the growing consciousness of the particularities of women's oppression, this history bore a striking resemblance to the emergence of second-wave feminism in the 1960s out of the civil rights and antiwar movements, especially the view that women's liberation required an autonomous movement.[4]

Beyond the politics of feminism, the field's analytical frameworks and methods were shaped by developments in historical studies and, more broadly, academic currents of the post-World War II period. French and British scholarship on social history strongly influenced a generation of

American historians in the 1960s to explore "history from the bottom up" as an alternative to the traditional emphasis on politics and diplomacy, laying the foundation for much of the early work in women's history. In particular, the reworking of Marxist analysis to emphasize the role of culture in class relations and power became a crucial analytical framework.[5] These approaches gave feminist historians a tool to combat the governing modes of understanding gender (then termed "sex") that had come out of American social and behavioral science after World War II: an emphasis on normative concepts of masculinity and femininity rooted in biology and psychology. To feminists in the 1960s, scientific understandings of women's nature undergirded the social arrangements that relegated them to childrearing and the home, and rationalized their marginality in the public domain of work and politics. The discipline of psychology, in particular, directed women to understand their situation as one of individual adjustment, not as a social problem to be addressed collectively and politically.[6] Feminist history refuted such views, not only by drawing upon the concept of social construction and considering women a "sex class," but also by insisting that the practice of history itself undermined biological determinism.

Social history combined with the politics of second-wave feminism to place an emphasis on uncovering women's experiences and listening to women's voices. Many focused on understanding the "private sphere" of household, family, sexuality, and reproduction, to reveal the historical construction of this domain, not its natural, biological determination. Others examined the institutional structures of politics, the workplace, unions, academia, and organizations of civil society to trace the processes whereby women were excluded and marginalized. Even as they established the historicity of male domination, however, women's historians insisted on viewing women as agents of their lives; thus Nancy Cott's classic 1977 study *The Bonds of Womanhood* played with two meanings, bonds that constrained women and bonds that united them.[7] That concern with agency—understanding how and under what circumstances women might change history—flowered into studies both of women leaders, active in suffrage, reform, and welfare policy, and of ordinary women whose everyday lives shaped American culture and society.

The Gender Turn

The turn toward gender analysis in the 1980s seemed nearly as transformative as the initial advance of women's history, but it is worth remembering that early on an interest in gender marked the field. In the mid-1970s, Natalie Zemon Davis and Joan Kelly called for a history of the "social relations of the sexes." As Davis put it at the second Berkshire Conference on the History of Women in 1975:

> [W]e should not be working only on the subjected sex any more than an historian of class can focus exclusively on peasants. Our goal is to understand the significance of the *sexes,* of gender groups in the historical past. Our goal is to discover the range in sex roles and in sexual symbolism in different societies and periods, to find out what meaning they had and how they functioned to maintain the social order or to promote its change.

The term "gender" had not yet become the convention—that happened in the late 1970s, when "sex" became understood as a biological category and "gender" the socially determined construction of sex. This concept of gender was a sociological category. Many women's historians employed the term *gender role*, a revision of *sex role*, from the functionalist school of sociology dating back to the 1940s, in which there were distinct and complementary responsibilities and ideals associated with men and women.[8]

Others adopted "gender relations" as an analogue to Marxist-based concepts of class relations. In this view, gender was a formation built through the social relations of men and women, particularly in the areas of production (understood as both the workplace and home) and reproduction (understood as both biological and social). One strand of women's history, highly significant at the time but less recognized in the present, involved efforts to integrate class and gender relations in a socialist-feminist framework. If the midcentury social sciences had depoliticized gender, this approach perceived gender to be a domain of conflict and inequality, not unity and complementarity. Women typically remained the subject of these studies, but the relational approach situated their experience in a broader context of political and familial power.[9]

In women's studies, calls for an integrated, "intersectional" analysis that treated gender, class, and race as equal and interdependent variables also began to be heard in the 1980s, spearheaded by academic and activist women of color. Challenging universalist assumptions in women's studies that elided or ignored the specificity of race and class differences, they not only pointed to the primacy of middle-class white women in historical studies, but as important, showed how their experiences and perspectives—including their relative power—came out of affluence and the privileges of white skin color. Intersectional analysis has focused on structural determinants, material conditions, and political relations, but like the "gender relations" approach it became increasingly concerned with social and cultural identity and difference as well.[10]

When we think of the "gender turn," however, it is usually understood as the moment when women's history ran smack into poststructuralism in the mid-1980s, by then already influential in American literary studies. Joan Scott, in particular, presented a thorough critique of the social-historical analysis of women and laid out a poststructuralist approach to the history of gender in a series of articles. The most influential of these, "Gender: A Useful Category of Historical Analysis," appeared in the *American Historical Review* in 1986. In it, Scott argued that gender should be understood not as a social role or social relation, but rather as a *representation* of perceived biological differences. She emphasized the production of particular kinds of knowledge about men and women, the symbols, images, norms, and speech acts that made up discourses. These articulations, she argued, constructed masculine and feminine subjects, naturalized them as essential or given, and bracketed off alternatives. In this way, power was mobilized through the production of knowledge about gender, especially with respect to sexuality, reproduction, the body, and identity. Gender maintained boundaries between the sexes and regulated the behavior of each. Just as important, Scott argued, gender provided a tool for analyzing domains that were not, on their face, about men and women at all. Because gender typically operated as a pair or binary, making masculinity and femininity into opposites, it worked as a deceptively natural symbol for mobilizing power in such arenas as formal politics, the economy, the military, and foreign policy, arenas in which women were typically on the margins of historical interpretation.[11]

Behind Scott's strategically anodyne title, claiming "usefulness" for gender, was a far-reaching diagnosis of the problems of women's history and a challenge to historians everywhere. From the beginning, feminist scholars had wanted to move beyond a "great woman" view of history, based on the contributions of extraordinary women. Rather, they believed women's history would reshape all historical narratives and transform history as a discipline. This impetus underlay a set of historiographical questions: Did women have a Renaissance? How could the "age of Jackson" be celebrated as a democratic era? But transformation was not in the offing. Women had been rendered historical actors in their own right, but the result was too often an afterthought. There were women in the West, in the labor movement, in the earliest computing labs, but what did their presence mean for historical reinterpretations? If old conventions, like Jacksonian democracy or Turner's frontier thesis, seemed immune to women's history, so did many contemporary histories of labor, the city, and politics. Women's history—however it flourished as a subfield—had not been integrated into the main currents of American history.

Changing the subject from women to gender was a move from periphery to center. By arguing that everything is gendered—not only the relations of men and women, but all discourses, institutions, and group relationships—gender historians were staking a large claim to interpretive significance. Advocates of this kind of gender analysis believed in the radical potential of their stance: striking at the foundation of gender—if poststructuralist theory was correct—would be a transformative intellectual and political act. The battle lines were drawn not between left and right, however, but rather within the intellectual Left in the U.S.: through gender analysis, Scott aimed to challenge Marxist theory and its materialist, class-based metanarrative of history. Less visible than Scott's *AHR* article, but more revealing, was the debate that raged in the pages of the journal *International Labor and Working-Class History* in 1987, when Scott presented a poststructuralist critique of the "new" labor history. Although some of the respondents to her article grappled with ways of integrating discourse analysis with Marxist perspectives, Canadian labor historian Bryan Palmer attacked Scott head on. Real people, not representations, died in violent labor conflicts, he observed, a point he elaborated in his book *Descent into Discourse*, and real women could be integrated into the social histories of popular struggles, even if the particularities of their experiences were subordinate to class conflict.[12] Women's historians felt more ambivalent. The hostility of many male New Left historians seemed to be a replay of the 1960s, when feminists leveled charges of women's marginalization and invisibility in historical studies. Now that battle was being waged on a different theoretical terrain. Many retained a sense of history that derived from Marxism, even if in a more attenuated form, and perceived gender and class as equal determinants, inevitably intertwined. At the same time, they appreciated the analytical tools poststructuralism offered for exposing such naturalized categories as gender and race.[13]

What was difficult to see at the time of this internecine battle, but is more apparent in retrospect, was the broader intellectual and political context of the 1980s and 1990s in which the gender turn occurred. Although Marxism retained a presence in U.S. academic circles, its legitimacy as an intellectual and political framework grew increasingly attenuated. Broad political developments in the U.S. and abroad undercut the rhetoric and aims of radical social historians. The collapse of Communism, end of the Cold War, a renascent pro-business and neoliberal politics, and the decline of the labor movement made it ever more difficult to imagine class-based or socialist alternatives to capitalism. At the same time, identity politics became an increasingly important focus within feminism, gay and lesbian activism, and social movements of African Americans and other people of color. Whether the political aim was a liberal one of inclusion and equality, or a more liberationist stance, questions of subjectivity, representation, identification, and difference became central. By casting its opposition to feminism and gay rights in terms of natural, God-given, and normative identities, social conservatism reinforced the significance of gender and sexual identity for political action.

That was especially true in the academy, where women's studies and African American studies programs, taking off in the 1970s, were followed by a host of identity-based programs of inquiry and activism. Such programs were instituted after hard-fought battles with administrators and traditional departments, and often maintained their viability on limited budgets and volunteered faculty labor. Nevertheless, the rapidity with which women's studies spread in American universities and colleges is striking; an institutional base for the study of women arose in the late-twentieth-century U.S. that was replicated in few other places. These programs changed the academy by pushing for greater representation of women faculty and support for teaching and scholarship that, only two decades earlier, had not even been an academic subject. Women's studies programs mainstreamed this subject, in the sense that the study of women in all the disciplines flourished. Initially challenging the academy from the outside, they rapidly became incorporated into American institutions of higher education, as they branded themselves sites for fostering diversity and interdisciplinarity.[14]

In history departments, women's historians also experienced resistance to the field and to the presence of women, and these problems continue to the present. Still, the growth of women's and gender history in the U.S. has far outpaced all other areas of history in the last thirty years. According to the American Historical Association, the number of historians who specialize in the field "grew more than eight fold" from 1975 to 2005. The proportion of departments with at least one faculty member in the field grew from 18 percent in 1975 to over 50 percent in the 1980s, and then rose sharply to nearly 80 percent in the early 1990s, the very time of the gender turn.[15] In retrospect, gender analysis paradoxically might be seen as a radical intellectual move and prudent professional repositioning. It enabled senior scholars and a younger generation to move away from the marginality of the "subfield" of women's history and, through a revisionist focus on gender, established a standpoint for the reinterpretation of the main narratives of U.S. history. The relative openness of the American academic system and its centrality as a site of identity politics arguably contributed to this research agenda among American historians.

The Cultural Turn and Its Impact on Gender History

The call for gender analysis in history was part of a broader movement, first in the humanistic disciplines and then the social sciences, toward interpretive approaches, often referred to as the "cultural turn" or "linguistic turn." Asserting that it was only through systems of signs that social reality could be known, this scholarship placed the analysis of discourses, representations, and the production and circulation of cultural meaning in the foreground of critical inquiry. It rejected positivistic knowledge, unmediated facticity, and materially based analysis, and made culture not only its subject but, to a great extent, an overarching explanation of historical change.[16]

Merging interpretive approaches with the new commitment to studying gender crucially redefined the feminist project of women's history, and launched new and fruitful ways of thinking about women, men, and the past. Gender analysis raised questions about the naturalness of male identity. Studies of men and manhood had initially focused somewhat schematically on changing prescriptive ideals, or they charted periodic "crises" in masculinity that remained rooted in a psychoanalytical framework. Now historians examined more carefully the ways that manhood figured in other historical processes, particularly the making of racial identity and hierarchy. Gail Bederman analyzed how the turn-of-the-twentieth-century discourse of manliness and civilization could be articulated and deployed in contending ways, on the one hand, to support the "natural" leadership of a white male elite, and on the other, to call it to account. Martin Summers took the study of masculinity one step further, by examining the cultural practices and social institutions, such as African American Masonic lodges and fraternities, through which discourses of black middle-class masculinity were ritualized and affirmed. Even more sophisticated was George Chauncey's exemplary *Gay New York*, in which the male-female binary sorted out men who had sex with men into unremarkable "normal" men, on the one hand, and "fairies," who inverted their gender characteristics, on the other.[17]

Poststructuralist gender analysis was rapidly integrated into other areas of research emerging in the 1980s and 1990s. Historians of consumer culture increasingly examined the ways gender defined consumer markets, advertising campaigns, and selling strategies. They traced how notions of femininity and consumption were historically bound together in discourses on luxury, vanity, and frivolity, and changed over time to create the social role of "Mrs.

Consumer." Scholars also began to find a "hidden" history of male consumer desire.[18] The history of the body has developed as a field of inquiry, largely because scholars have used gender analysis to assert the body's historicity, against the view of it as a natural, timeless entity. Thomas Laqueur's *Making Sex* was a highly influential study that traced how discourses of gender established conceptions and experiences of embodiment in history: the premodern representation of gendered bodies as a "one-sex" model gave way to the dimorphic view of the body after 1800.[19] Work on the gendered history of beauty, dieting, body image, and physical disabilities opened up new insights into modern American society and culture. For example, Marie Griffith showed how evangelical religious beliefs shaped the "born again body," with a particular valence for women, while David Serlin considered how new technologies, including prosthetics and hormones, were deployed to reconstruct appropriately gendered bodies after World War II. My work on the cosmetics industry and the rise of an American beauty culture also built on these new interests; although my subject was women and beauty, the new attention to gender shaped how I interpreted the emergence of a consumerist concept of female beauty, simultaneously produced by and defining both women entrepreneurs and consumers. It also led me to ask an obvious question, why don't men wear makeup?—only to discover a quixotic effort to persuade them to do so as early as the 1920s.[20]

Modern U.S. historians also embraced gender analysis in studies of the American state, social policy, government institutions, and political culture. This scholarship established the role of women as players in a male-dominated public arena, even before they had gained voting and other civil rights, as reformers, social workers, lobbyists, fund-raisers, and advocates. A gender framework enabled Glenda Gilmore to reinterpret the early Jim Crow era; she uncovered the ways that white women could make a fragile and unequal alliance with African American middle-class women over temperance, yet quickly break those ties as white men—indeed their husbands—forcibly disenfranchised black men. Other historians revealed how much gender shaped American political solutions to the social problems of the late nineteenth and twentieth centuries. As Theda Skocpol, Linda Gordon, Alice Kessler-Harris, and others have shown, deep-seated ideological commitments to the nuclear family, featuring a male breadwinner, housewife and mother, and dependent children, governed the legal, policy, and political frameworks for social welfare, however inadequate that formulation was to social reality; such gendered social policy took a particular toll on poor women and children. Taken together, this literature shows how much gender undergirded American social welfare institutions and policies for decades.[21]

Transnational Histories of Women and Gender

If American gender historians offered new and compelling interpretations of U.S. politics and the nation-state, these traditional subjects of history were simultaneously destabilized by initiatives to foster transnational, comparative, and global histories. Here too gender analysis has played an important role since the 1990s in revisionist histories of American empire and foreign relations, once an area of history that seemed least open to feminist perspectives. Drawing inspiration from postcolonial studies of empire, particularly in South and Southeast Asia, this new work is termed the "new U.S. international history," or "the United States in the world," to distinguish it from the established concerns of diplomatic history with the politics and policies of nation-states. The scholarship of historical anthropologist Ann Stoler, who has explored the workings of imperial power through discourses and practices of intimate life, has directly challenged and inspired American historians to examine the interconnections between the domestic and foreign, with particular attention to the history of gender, race, and culture.[22]

Early American historians have been in the forefront of such work. For example, Kathleen Brown's *Foul Bodies* examines how changing ideas and practices of cleanliness constituted a "civilizing project" in the Atlantic World, in which body care constructed gendered, "raced," colonial, and national subjects; Jennifer Morgan's *Laboring Women* traces the centrality of gender, sexuality, and reproduction—and specifically African women— in the making of racial slavery in Britain's American colonies.[23] Historians of the nineteenth and twentieth centuries—the period of the postcolonial American nation-state—have been slower to adopt the comparative or transregional approach, but increasingly they analyze the role and effects of gender in transnational organizations, migrations, and networks. Studies of American missionaries in such places as China and the Middle East reveal "contact zones" in which gender ideals and rituals became essential aspects of norm-building and "civilizing," and a means of moral, social, and evolutionary ranking; they show as well how the subjects of such missionary work responded to this surveillance and the imposition of new rules, from accommodation and appropriation to resistance.

These studies enable us to see women's international endeavors in new ways. Although operating as non-state actors, they interacted with government officials and local populations. Their gendered identification with domestic and childrearing matters, as well as the growth of so-called "women's professions," including teaching, home economics, and nursing, enabled their involvement in public affairs in American colonies and territories. In a different vein, the rise of international women's rights activism brought American women into contact with feminists, nationalists, and anticolonialists from around the world; organizing around ideals of collective female advancement, in practice these organizations reflected deep economic and social inequities and often foundered on the differing diagnoses of women's oppression.[24]

Another group of studies examines transnational networks and flows, with a focus on gender. These include such works as Kristin Hoganson's *Consumers' Imperium*, which argues against the view that globalization meant Americanization. Focusing on middle-class women, she shows how international commerce and consumption of goods from Europe and Asia were brought into American domesticity and fostered a women's international imaginary, through interior design and travel clubs, in the late-nineteenth and early-twentieth-century United States. Other studies examine gendered labor and migration in a transnational context. Catherine Choy argues, for example, that the extensive migration of Filipino nurses to the United States, despite the need for health care workers in the Philippines, was not simply a matter of greater economic opportunities in the United States, but must be traced to the nurse training programs established as part of U.S. colonial rule in the early twentieth century. American immigration policies enforced national borders, identity, and security in part through the policing of non-normative sexuality and gender; Eithne Luibhéid, for example, shows how policies initially intended to prevent the entry of Chinese prostitutes expanded to restrict lesbians, pregnant unmarried women, and interracial couples.[25]

Methodologically, the studies that center upon gender—rather than women—frequently analyze texts, images, and practices as discursive fields that defined and shaped Americans' understanding of itself and the world. On the one hand, these works persuasively uncover the processes by which national ambitions were understood in gendered terms to reinforce notions of American exceptionalism: imperialism, militarism, and violence were rendered in the language of domestic and familial protection—in Amy Kaplan's terms, "manifest domesticity." The image of imperialism tamed and brought home was apparent during the Spanish-U.S. war and occupation of the Philippines beginning in 1898. As Laura Wexler shows, early women photojournalists—pursuing careers as New Women—helped create a domestic image of the war and American warriors; children's books and world's fair exhibits rendered Filipinos as childlike, racially backward, and in need of paternal protection.[26]

Often these studies focus on the relationship between men, masculinity, and power. They center on the ways that male government officials, military officers, servicemen, and citizens drew upon a gendered imaginary and their own deeply felt sense of manhood to understand world affairs and make foreign policy decisions. In *Taking Haiti*, a cultural study of U.S. intervention in Haiti in the early twentieth century, Mary Renda examines how a gendered and racialized discourse of white male paternalism underlay the views of men from Woodrow Wilson to the Marines on the ground, enabling them to legitimize military conquest and occupation as a civilizing mission. Robert Dean tracks how these earlier notions of "imperial manhood"—elite masculinity, fervent heterosexuality, and the militarist bonds between men—persisted into the Cold War era, and undergirded the American leadership that led the nation disastrously into the Vietnam War.[27]

At its best, this historical literature reveals how gender not only shaped Americans' perceptions of and policies toward the world, but also framed the responses of the peoples who were affected by these encounters. In *Reproducing Empire*, Laura Briggs shows how a public health and scientific discourse on prostitution, birth control, eugenics, and overpopulation underlay American efforts to govern the Puerto Rican population. The U.S. colonial government and Puerto Rican elites fixed on poor and working-class women's sexuality as both symbol and cause of the island's social disorder; such women found themselves increasingly the targets of surveillance and regulation, as well as subjects of pharmaceutical experiments on the birth control pill. Harvey Neptune's study of Trinidad during World War II offers a different picture of the uses of gender. A British crown colony, Trinidad had become an enormous military base for the United States during the war. At that time, poor Trinidadian youths—known as saga boys—were able to gain employment with the high-paying Americans and embraced the stylish attire of American zoot suiters. Performing a new masculine identity by appropriating American looks and gestures, they resisted their dependent status as British colonial subjects.[28]

Gender Analysis in the American Grain

From the first, many feminist historians expressed concerns and uneasiness about gender analysis and the logic of poststructuralism. Although antiessentialism had always been a foundation of post-1960s feminist thought, gender theorists believed that their critical analysis of discursive language and representation would expose essentialist ideologies and social arrangements in a way that women's history, by itself, could not. In this sense, it was a radical political as well as intellectual project. Others, however, believed that an emphasis on gender would depoliticize women's history, fearing that privileging representation over women's agency and abandoning the idea of a stable, unified, autonomous subject would displace or even erase "real women" as the subject of inquiry. Laura Lee Downs put the question sharply in a 1993 essay: "If 'Woman' Is Just an Empty Category, Then Why Am I Afraid to Walk Alone at Night?"[29]

Some of those tensions continue to the present. In a 2007 article in the *Chronicle of Higher Education*, Alice Kessler-Harris, while deeply appreciative of gender as an intellectual framework, expressed concern that the writing of women's history is an unfinished feminist project that is being neglected in favor of gender analysis. There is a widespread sense that the history of women is too narrow, partisan, and passé, and for younger scholars, gender analysis is women's history's other—broad, integrative, more objective. What scholarly journals choose to publish is also telling: the *Journal of American History* has welcomed analyses of masculinity in the political culture of the Cold War, with essays on, for example, the gendered sexual language of George Kennan and Arthur Schlesinger, Jr., but has never published an article on the lived experience or politics of lesbians. However inadvertently, the gender turn may have contributed to this sense that somehow we "know" about women's past, that the work has been done.[30]

By the late 1990s, Joan Scott herself reflected upon the way that gender analysis had lost its radical potential and *frisson* as it became a conventional category applied by historians and other scholars to the subject at hand.[31] Striking in retrospect is the way that academic gender theory became common currency beyond the world of higher education. Consider the mobilization of gender representations in the wake of 9/11, from burka-clad women whose freedom became a reason "why we fight," to the female soldiers in Iraq, such as Army Private Jessica Lynch, captured in an Iraqi ambush and freed by Special Forces, and Lynndie England, accomplice in the abuse of prisoners at Abu Ghraib. As historians have showed for earlier periods, we see gender working to support imperial intervention and to downplay larger political and institutional failures. What is distinctive, however, has been the rapidity with which such official gendered discourses are deconstructed, not only by antiwar activists and academics, but by the participants themselves: Lynch, for example, explicitly renounced the Pentagon's heroic narrative, accusing the media and military of turning her into a symbol of female valor for propaganda purposes. Academic feminism has so permeated politics, mass media, and popular culture, that we all deconstruct gender now.

Perhaps by now the debate over the politics of poststructuralism, gender analysis, and women's history has exhausted itself. The gender turn, for all the insightful work it produced in the 1990s and early 2000s, does seem less relevant, less in conversation with our times. That may be especially true in ongoing studies of identity, culture, and sexuality—all of them important subjects—but which often seem unmoored from institutional structures, formal politics and policymaking, labor and the economy. The revival of interest in political economy—both in a national and international context—may find new uses for a gender analysis less bound by the cultural or discursive domain.[32]

However, what has been less commented upon—but what comes out in the chapters in this volume—is the various and uneven application of gender analysis. It has been embraced in some areas of history, downplayed in many others. Just as important, there are differences in the ways historians of diverse regions and time periods have employed gender analysis. In modern U.S. history, scholars have maintained an ambivalence toward the poststructuralist approach to gender, embracing it more in cultural history, the history of sexuality, and histories in which identities are a primary concern. A number of works have been justly celebrated for highlighting the processes whereby certain kinds of knowledge about gender are produced, in ways that generate social hierarchies and power. Elizabeth Lunbeck's *The Psychiatric Persuasion*, for example, examines the discourses of behavioral science, professionalization, and institutionalization that created the subject positions and relations of male psychiatrists, female psychiatric social workers, and patients.[33]

Nevertheless, U.S. historians often use flattened and inconsistent concepts of gender, perhaps due in part to the very vagueness of the term itself. In her two-page piece in the *Chronicle*, for example, Kessler-Harris describes gender as a "lens through which to view the world," as an "explanatory agent," as a "ground for the exploration of subjects ... not ... restricted to one sex or the other," and as the "organization of relationships between men and women."[34] Here and elsewhere, gender can be a subject of study, a methodology, and an explanation.

In 2008, Jeanne Boydston criticized the way that gender analysis has come to have an undertow of essentialism: "although we have argued for 'gender' as a historical process, we have frequently treated that process as non-historically-contingent—that is, as unfolding in much the same way and in much the same terms in all societies." She found in her field of early American history a tendency to reify masculinity and femininity as dualistic, opposing categories, inadvertently naturalizing the binary between men and women, rather than decentering it. She pointed to scholarship in other time periods and geographical areas that offers a more complex mapping of gender identities and identifications.[35] Boydston's observations hold true for modern

American history as well, including the new gendered histories of politics and international relations. Despite their claims to historicize gender, these studies show markedly similar, if not uniform, conceptions of masculinity across time, which has the effect of essentializing male gender and its relationship to political leadership. The sense of masculinity being in crisis, of enervated men, and the need of manly revitalization, underlies studies of imperialists in the Philippines, African American Garveyites, Cold Warriors, and New Left *Fidelistas*.[36]

While paying obeisance to gender analysis, many feminist historians remain fundamentally interested in the reciprocal relationship between women's actions and perspectives on the one hand, and social, political, and cultural institutions on the other. Frequently, analysis of gendered discourse or representations goes hand in hand with rich empirical studies of women's activities, politics, and practices. The phrase "women's and gender history" erases an intellectual and political genealogy that for a time made the two at odds. In practice, however, this rubric captures where many in the field locate themselves today, and it is where some of the best work is being done.

Without embracing old ideas about American character, it is worth noting that this compromise, which overlooks the contradictions between women's history and gender history, seems very much rooted in deeply held assumptions that underlie American feminism, political ideology, and academia. As Heidi Tinsman insightfully argues, U.S. historians write about gender difference from a standpoint that assumes inclusion and universal rights. Liberal democracy has afforded them a claim to social and political participation that, however hard won (and incomplete), has profoundly shaped their experiences—especially those with access to higher education.[37] The production of women's and gender history has taken place in that context. Poststructuralism may require more from us than we are prepared to give—to recognize *ourselves* as subjects constituted in discourse, to be historians who are not autonomous agents creating narratives but who are, rather, effects of them. It is no wonder, then, that American feminist historians have remained committed to asserting and exploring women's agency, both personal and collective.

Conclusion

This overview raises some questions about the future of women's history and gender analysis. Gender may always be present and at work, but is it always explanatory? A look at the new, gendered U.S. international history, which treats decisions over politics and war by foregrounding gender and culture, suggests that we need to consider precisely when and in what ways gender is significant to a particular event or historical setting. We could also ask whether essentialism always needs to be the bête noire of feminist analysis, whether the intense interrogation of essentialism leads us away from other interesting and fruitful questions about the beliefs, practices, and politics of women and men. In a similar vein, one wonders about the ultimate end of destabilizing traditional modes of historical analysis, as the "turns" I have described have sought to do. Gender studies, along with studies of race and sexuality, have given us profound insight into the constructedness of categories and identities heretofore naturalized; the field has revealed the significance of the margins for challenging our understanding of the center. Still, the deconstructive moves have at times been in tension with another aim, one that was foundational to the work of feminist history: inclusion in the main currents of historical writing.

When I began work as a women's historian, we all promised each other a revolution. If the original goal was to write women into history, we have made amazing progress—from exclusion to inclusion, from private to public, from attention to "women worthies" to an extraordinary exploration of women from many different origins and all walks of life, in the United States and around the world. Women's activities, their politics, and their thoughts are part of the documentary record, and recognized as such; from the lonely institution building of the Sophia Smith Collection and Schlesinger Library, now many research libraries acquire and highlight their collections on women. Gender history also promised transformation. The poststructuralist mode has given us compelling insights into the ways that power works through cultural representation and gendered discourse; we are asking new questions and exploring new territory. It has also given us a greater self-awareness as historians, making us think more carefully about the production of the evidence we use, the nature of archives, and the use of classificatory schemes, all of which are in part products of gendered history. Now, women's history and gender analysis are shaping the comparative, transnational, and international histories that are beginning to revise anew how we understand the American past.

NOTES

1. Sheila Rowbotham, *Hidden from History: 300 Years of Women's Oppression and the Fight Against It* (London: Pluto Press, 1973); *Hidden from History: Rediscovering Women in History from the 17th Century to the Present* (New York: Pantheon, 1974). On feminist history as an invented tradition, see Maria Grever, "The Pantheon of Feminist Culture: Women's Movements and the Organization of Memory," *Gender and History* 9 (August 1997): 364–74.
2. Bonnie G. Smith, *The Gender of History: Men, Women, and Historical Practice* (Cambridge: Harvard University Press, 1998); Julie Des Jardins, *Women and the Historical Enterprise in America: Gender, Race, and the Politics of Memory, 1880–1945* (Chapel Hill:

University of North Carolina Press, 2003). See also Joan W. Scott, "American Women Historians, 1884—1984," in *Gender and the Politics of History* (1988; rev. ed. New York: Columbia University Press, 1999), 178-98; Jacqueline Goggin, "Challenging Sexual Discrimination in the Historical Profession: Women Historians and the American Historical Association, 1890-1940," *American Historical Review* 97 (June 1992): 769-802; Pero Gaglo Dagbovie, "Black Women Historians from the Late 19th Century to the Dawning of the Civil Rights Movement," *Journal of African American History* 89 (Summer 2004): 241-61. Alice Kessler-Harris, "Women's History: From Neglect to Prominence and to Integration," in Richard S. Kirkendall, ed., *The Organization of American Historians and the Writing and Teaching of American History* (New York: Oxford University Press, 2011), 188-97. On the 1940 AHA session, see Jesse Dunsmore Clarkson, "Escape to the Present," *American Historical Review* 46 (April 1941): 545.

3. Des Jardins, *Women and the Historical Enterprise in America*, 225-40. Anke Voss-Hubbard, "'No Document—No History': Mary Ritter Beard and the Early History of Women's Archives," *American Archivist* 58 (Winter 1995): 16-30. Amy E. Hague, "'Never ... Another Season of Silence': Laying the Foundation of the Sophia Smith Collection, 1942-1965," in *Revealing Women's Life Stories: Papers from the 50th Anniversary of the Sophia Smith Collection, Smith College, Northampton, Massachusetts, September 1992* (Smith College, 1993), 9-28, http://www.smith.edu/libraries/libs/ssc/about.html.

4. Radicalesbians, "The Woman Identified Woman" (Pittsburgh: Know Inc., 1970), reprinted in *Documents from the Women's Liberation Movement: An On-Line Archival Collection*, Special Collections Library, Duke University, http://scriptorium.lib.duke.edu/wlm/womid/. Carroll Smith-Rosenberg, "The Female World of Love and Ritual: Relations between Women in Nineteenth Century America," *Signs* 1 (Autumn 1975): 1-29. Ellen Carol DuBois, *Feminism and Suffrage: The Emergence of an Independent Women's Movement in America, 1848-1869* (rev. ed. 1999; Ithaca: Cornell University Press, 1978). For the governing interpretation of the origins of second-wave feminism at that time, see Sara Evans, *Personal Politics: The Roots of Women's Liberation in the Civil Rights Movement and the New Left* (New York: Knopf, 1979).

5. On these developments, see Georg G. Iggers, *Historiography in the Twentieth Century: From Scientific Objectivity to the Postmodern Challenge*, rev. ed. (Middletown: Wesleyan University Press, 2005); Peter Novick, *That Noble Dream: The "Objectivity Question" and the American Historical Profession* (Cambridge: Cambridge University Press, 1998), chapter 16; Geoff Eley, *A Crooked Line: From Cultural History to the History of Society* (Ann Arbor: University of Michigan Press, 2005).

6. See Mari Jo Buhle, *Feminism and Its Discontents: A Century of Struggle with Psychoanalysis* (Cambridge: Harvard University Press, 1998); Daniel Horowitz, *Betty Friedan and the Making of "The Feminine Mystique": The American Left, the Cold War, and Modern Feminism* (Amherst: University of Massachusetts Press, 2000).

7. Nancy F. Cott, *The Bonds of Womanhood: "Woman's Sphere" in New England, 1780-1835* (New Haven: Yale University Press, 1977).

8. Natalie Zemon Davis, quoted in Joan Kelly-Gadol, "The Social Relations of the Sexes: Methodological Implications of Women's History," *Signs* 1 (Summer 1976): 809-23 (quotation on 817). See also Joan Kelly, *Women, History and Theory: The Essays of Joan Kelly* (Chicago: University of Chicago Press, 1984); Natalie Zemon Davis, "'Women's History' in Transition: The European Case," *Feminist Studies* 3 (Spring-Summer 1976), 83-103. For an excellent discussion, see Joanne Meyerowitz, "A History of 'Gender,'" *American Historical Review* 113 (December 2008): 1346-56.

9. For an early overview, see Elizabeth Fox-Genovese, "Socialist-Feminist American Women's History," *Journal of Women's History* 1 (Winter 1990): 181-210.
10. See Patricia Hill Collins, *Black Feminist Thought: Knowledge, Consciousness, and the Politics of Empowerment*, rev. ed. (New York: Routledge, 2000); Tessie Liu, "Teaching the Differences among Women from a Historical Perspective: Rethinking Race and Gender as Social Categories," *Women's Studies International Forum* 14 (1991): 265-76; Leslie McCall, "The Complexity of Intersectionality," *Signs* 30 (Spring 2005): 1771-1800.
11. Joan W. Scott, "Gender: A Useful Category of Historical Analysis," *American Historical Review* 91 (December 1986): 1053-75. See also Scott, *Gender and the Politics of History*.
12. Joan W. Scott, "On Language, Gender, and Working-Class History," *International Labor and Working-Class History* 31 (March 1987): 1-13. Bryan D. Palmer, "Response to Joan Scott," *International Labor and Working-Class History* 31 (March 1987): 14-23; Bryan D. Palmer, *Descent into Discourse: The Reification of Language and the Writing of Social History* (Philadelphia: Temple University Press, 1990).
13. Christine Stansell, "A Response to Joan Scott," *International Labor and Working-Class History* 31 (March 1987): 24-29. See also Joan Scott and Linda Gordon's reviews of each other's books and responses in "Reviews," *Signs* 15 (Summer 1990): 848-60; Kathleen Canning, *Gender History in Practice: Historical Perspectives on Bodies, Class, and Citizenship* (Ithaca: Cornell University Press, 2006), chapters 1-2.
14. NORC at the University of Chicago (National Opinion Research Center), *A National Census of Women's and Gender Studies Programs in U.S. Institutions of Higher Education*, December 26, 2007, www.nwsa.org/PAD/database/downloads/NWSA_Data_Report_08.pdf.
15. Robert B. Townsend, "What's in a Label? Changing Patterns of Faculty Specialization since 1975," *Perspectives Online* (American Historical Association), January 2007, http://www.historians.org/perspectives/issues/2007/0701/0701new1.cfm. Elizabeth Lunbeck, *The Status of Women in the Historical Profession 2005* (Committee on Women Historians, American Historical Association, 2005), www.historians.org/governance/cwh/CWH-Report_5.20.05.pdf.
16. See Victoria E. Bonnell and Lynn Hunt, eds., *Beyond the Cultural Turn: New Directions in the Study of Society and Culture* (Berkeley: University of California Press, 1999), especially their introduction, 1-33; also useful is John Toews, "Intellectual History after the Linguistic Turn: The Autonomy of Meaning and the Irreducibility of Experience," *American Historical Review* 92 (1987): 879-907.
17. Gail Bederman, *Manliness and Civilization: A Cultural History of Gender and Race in the United States, 1880-1917* (Chicago: University of Chicago Press, 1995); Martin Summers, *Manliness and Its Discontents: The Black Middle Class and the Transformation of Masculinity, 1900-1930* (Chapel Hill: University of North Carolina Press, 2004); George Chauncey, *Gay New York: Gender, Urban Culture, and the Makings of the Gay Male World, 1890-1940* (New York: Basic Books, 1994).
18. See especially Victoria de Grazia's volume and section introductions in de Grazia with Ellen Furlough, eds., *The Sex of Things: Gender and Consumption in Historical Perspective* (Berkeley: University of California Press, 1996). See also Roger Horowitz and Arwen Mohun, eds., *His and Hers: Gender, Consumption, and Technology* (Charlottesville: University Press of Virginia, 1998); Jennifer Scanlon, ed., *The Gender and Consumer Culture Reader* (New York: NYU Press, 2000).
19. Thomas Laqueur, *Making Sex: Body and Gender from the Greeks to Freud* (Cambridge: Harvard University Press, 1990). See also Barbara Duden, *The Woman beneath the Skin:*

A Doctor's Patients in Eighteenth-Century Germany, trans. Thomas Dunlap (Cambridge: Harvard University Press, 1991).
20. Marie R. Griffith, *Born Again Bodies: Flesh and Spirit in American Christianity* (Berkeley: University of California Press, 2004); David Serlin, *Replaceable You: Engineering the Body in Postwar America* (Chicago: University of Chicago Press, 2004); Kathy Peiss, *Hope in a Jar: The Making of America's Beauty Culture* (New York: Metropolitan Books, 1998).
21. Glenda Elizabeth Gilmore, *Gender and Jim Crow: Women and the Politics of White Supremacy in North Carolina, 1896–1920* (Chapel Hill: University of North Carolina Press, 1996). Theda Skocpol, *Protecting Soldiers and Mothers: The Political Origins of Social Policy in the United States* (Cambridge: Harvard University Press, 1992); Linda Gordon, *Pitied But Not Entitled: Single Mothers and the History of Welfare, 1890–1935* (New York: Free Press, 1994); Alice Kessler-Harris, *In Pursuit of Equity: Women, Men, and the Quest for Economic Citizenship in 20th-Century America* (New York: Oxford University Press, 2001). For an early, path-breaking effort to understand women in a gendered political system, see Paula Baker, "The Domestication of Politics: Women and American Political Society, 1780–1920," *American Historical Review* 89 (June 1984): 620–47.
22. Ann Laura Stoler, "Tense and Tender Ties: The Politics of Comparison in North American History and (Post) Colonial Studies," *Journal of American History* 88 (2001): 829–65. This article led to a rich collection of essays by Americanists in Ann Laura Stoler, ed., *Haunted by Empire: Geographies of Intimacy in North America* (Durham: Duke University Press, 2006).
23. Kathleen M. Brown, *Foul Bodies: Cleanliness in Early America* (New Haven: Yale University Press, 2009); Jennifer L. Morgan, *Laboring Bodies: Reproduction and Gender in New World Slavery* (Philadelphia: University of Pennsylvania Press, 2004). See also Jennifer M. Spear, *Race, Sex, and Social Order in Early New Orleans* (Baltimore: Johns Hopkins University Press, 2009). See also the essays in Thomas A. Foster, ed., *New Men: Manliness in America* (New York: NYU Press, 2011).
24. Heather J. Sharkey, *American Evangelicals in Egypt: Missionary Encounters in an Age of Empire* (Princeton: Princeton University Press, 2008); Jane Hunter, *The Gospel of Gentility: American Women Missionaries in Turn-of-the-Century China* (New Haven: Yale University Press, 1984); Ian R. Tyrrell, *Women's World/Women's Empire: The Women's Christian Temperance Union in International Perspective, 1800–1930* (Chapel Hill: University of North Carolina Press, 1991). Leila J. Rupp, "Constructing Internationalism: The Case of Transnational Women's Organizations, 1888–1945," *American Historical Review* 99 (December 1994): 1571–1600; Leila J. Rupp, *Worlds of Women: The Making of an International Women's Movement* (Princeton: Princeton University Press, 1998). I am grateful to several current and former graduate students—Sarah Manekin, Anna Schatz, Jaffa Panken, and Winifred Connerton—whose work on American empire and international relations from a gender and/or cultural perspective has deepened my understanding.
25. Kristin L. Hoganson, *Consumer's Imperium: The Global Production of American Domesticity* (Chapel Hill: University of North Carolina Press, 2007). Catherine Ceniza Choy, *Empire of Care; Nursing and Migration in Filipino American History* (Durham: Duke University Press, 2003). Eithne Luibhéid, *Entry Denied: Controlling Sexuality at the Border* (Minneapolis: University of Minnesota Press, 2002); see also Margot Canaday, *The Straight State: Sexuality and Citizenship in Twentieth-Century America* (Princeton: Princeton University Press, 2009); Margot Canaday, "Thinking Sex in the Transnational Turn: An Introduction," *American Historical Review* 114 (December 2009), 1250–57.

26. Amy Kaplan, "Manifest Domesticity," *American Literature* 70 (1998): 581–606; Amy Kaplan, *The Anarchy of Empire in the Making of U.S. Culture* (Cambridge: Harvard University Press, 2005). Laura Wexler, *Tender Violence: Domestic Visions in an Age of U.S. Imperialism* (Chapel Hill: University of North Carolina Press, 2000). See also Brian Rouleau, "Childhood's Imperial Imagination: Edward Stratemeyer's Fiction Factory and the Valorization of American Empire," *Journal of the Gilded Age and the Progressive Era* 7 (October 2008): 479–512; Paul Kramer, "Making Concessions: Race and Empire Revisited at the Philippine Exposition, 1901–1905," *Radical History Review* 73 (1999): 74–114.
27. Mary Renda, *Taking Haiti: Military Occupation and the Culture of U.S. Imperialism* (Chapel Hill: University of North Carolina Press, 2001); Robert D. Dean, *Imperial Brotherhood: Gender and the Making of Cold War Foreign Policy* (Amherst: University of Massachusetts Press, 2001). See also Kristin L. Hoganson, *Fighting for American Manhood: How Gender Politics Provoked the Spanish-American and Philippine-American Wars* (New Haven: Yale University Press, 1998).
28. Laura Briggs, *Reproducing Empire: Race, Sex, Science, and U.S. Imperialism in Puerto Rico* (Berkeley: University of California Press, 2002); Harvey R. Neptune, *Caliban and the Yankees: Trinidad and the United States Occupation* (Chapel Hill: University of North Carolina Press, 2007).
29. Laura Lee Downs, "If 'Woman' Is Just an Empty Category, Then Why Am I Afraid to Walk Alone at Night? Identity Politics Meets the Postmodern Subject," *Comparative Studies in Society and History* 35 (April 1993): 414–37. For the controversy among historians, see Meyerowitz, "A History of 'Gender'"; for a helpful discussion of the varieties of feminist antiessentialism, see Alison Stone, "Essentialism and Anti-Essentialism in Feminist Philosophy," *Journal of Moral Philosophy* 1 (2004): 135–153; http://eprints.lancs.ac.uk/34/2/Microsoft_Word_-_E9130088.pdf.
30. Alice Kessler-Harris, "Do We Still Need Women's History?" *Chronicle of Higher Education*, December 7, 2007, B6–7. See also Kessler-Harris, "Women's History: From Neglect to Prominence and to Integration"; on the *Journal of American History*'s publishing history, see Kathy Peiss, "The History That Dare Not Speak Its Name," in Kirkendall, ed., *The Organization of American Historians and the Writing and Teaching of American History*, 217–27.
31. Joan Scott, "Preface to the Revised Edition," and "Some More Reflections on Gender and Politics," in *Gender and the Politics of History*, ix–xiv, 199–222.
32. See, e.g., Stephanie McCurry, *Confederate Reckoning: Power and Politics in the Civil War South* (Cambridge: Harvard University Press, 2010).
33. Elizabeth Lunbeck, *The Psychiatric Persuasion: Knowledge, Gender, and Power in Modern America* (Princeton: Princeton University Press, 1994).
34. Kessler-Harris, "Do We Still Need Women's History?"
35. Jeanne Boydston, "Gender as a Question of Historical Analysis," *Gender & History* 20 (November 2008): 558–83.
36. Hoganson, *Fighting for American Manhood*; Summers, *Manliness and Its Discontents*; Dean, *Imperial Brotherhood*; Van Gosse, *Where the Boys Are: Cuba, Cold War America, and the Making of the New Left* (New York: Verso, 1993). Bederman, in *Manliness and Civilization*, critiques the psychological framework undergirding the notion of a "crisis in masculinity."
37. Heidi Tinsman, "A Paradigm of Our Own: Joan Scott in Latin American History," *American Historical Review* 113 (December 2008): 1357–74.

2

New Directions in Russian and Soviet Women's History

BARBARA ALPERN ENGEL

A product of second-wave feminism, in the United States the field of Russian and Soviet women's history was also born under another and very different political star: the Cold War. For students of the imperial and modern periods of Russia's history, if not of earlier times, the impact of the Cold War was enormous, lingering even after 1991 and the end of the geopolitical divisions from which it had arisen. Only in the past ten or fifteen years have historians in the United States begun to free themselves from the intellectual paradigms necessitated, it once seemed, by the very existence of the Soviet Union. Colleagues in the former Soviet Union, whose contributions to the field of women's and gender history are now substantial, have been largely freed from their own version of those paradigms, but face new obstacles to making their scholarship known to its potential audiences not only abroad but at home.

The impact of the Cold War, it must be said, was far less palpable at the time than it is now, forty years later and in hindsight. In the heady atmosphere of the late 1960s, through the following decade, and even later, women's history seemed part of a movement that might transform the world we knew. My own lifelong involvement was inspired by the thrilling experience of marching down New York's Fifth Avenue on August 26, 1970, together with tens of thousands of other women, commemorating the fiftieth anniversary of the Women's Suffrage amendment. Then a graduate student at Columbia University, I took part in what became the birth of a field among professionalized historians. Neither at Columbia, nor, to my knowledge, anywhere else at that time, were there courses on Russia's women. There also existed neither current academic scholarship nor the possibility of presenting women's history as a field in one's comprehensive exams. When I undertook the study of Russian female radicalism in the nineteenth century, I had the approval of my supervisors, but knowledge neither of Russian women's history nor of women's history more generally.

My situation was identical to that of others in my generation of feminist academics. We learned as we went along, many of us learning together. In those days, women's studies was so new it was possible to read everything, not only history but anthropology, sociology, psychology, theory—anything that shed light on the situation of women, as Kathy Peiss also notes in her chapter in this volume. I participated in several of the informal and interdisciplinary feminist study circles, many with a Marxist orientation, which flourished in New York City, where I had the great good fortune to live at that time. Like other students of Russia's women, I benefited from the informal but invaluable mentorship of Richard Stites, who had defended a dissertation on the women's liberation movement in Russia in 1968. I also took part in regular, intense, and fruitful conversations with a handful of other colleagues in Russian and Soviet history, most importantly Rochelle Ruthchild, another historian of Russian women, and soaked up information and methods at the Berkshire conferences of women's history, the first of which took place in 1973. In those days, the Berks were relatively small, and as much like a pajama party as a scholarly conference. Scholarly papers were presented during the day; at night, we chatted in our rooms (only dormitory rooms in those years), sat on the lawns and sang folk songs, and attended women's dances. My own work, and likely that of others of my generation, profited immensely from, and still bears the impress of, the wide-ranging, deeply engaged conversations of those years.

Even if we remained largely unaware of it at the time, however, Cold War politics were as influential as second-wave feminism in the field of Russian and Soviet women's history. The influence can be discerned on a number of levels. Most obviously, hostilities between the United States and the U.S.S.R. severely limited the sources that we were able to consult. The Soviet Union was off-limits to U.S. scholars in the Stalinist era, and began to allow academic exchanges with the United States only in 1958. Those who participated braved notoriously difficult research and living conditions. Access to Soviet archives was restricted not only by political considerations (what you were permitted to see, what was off-limits), but also by the lack of access to lists of archival holdings. To know what documents to request, one scoured the footnotes of Soviet scholars or depended upon the choices of one's assigned research assistant. To be sure, scholars could and did make use of the rich holdings of libraries in Moscow and Leningrad, renamed St. Petersburg after 1991. But many preferred Helsinki, Finland. Once part of the Russian empire, Helsinki offered easy access to a treasure trove of prerevolutionary publications, and copying that was relatively straightforward, by contrast with the onerous process in the Soviet Union, where certain materials—statistics, even prerevolutionary statistics, for example—could not be copied at all, or at least not by me as late as 1985. The consequences were evident in our scholarship. Most of the first books and articles that treated the history of Russian and Soviet women drew primarily on published documents or on archives housed in Europe and the United States, and used Soviet archives to a limited degree or not at all.

Especially in the early years, politics influenced the development of Russian and Soviet women's history in the United States in a less obvious way as well. Political history played an inordinate role, distinguishing much of our work from that being published in other fields of women's history. The predominance of politics was largely the consequence of the revolutionary events of 1917 and Bolshevik seizure of power, which prompted a more or less teleological approach to the imperial period. Historians of imperial Russia tended to study either the autocracy and its institutions and policies, or the movements and individuals that opposed them. Whether it was even possible to study Soviet history, apart from political history and (largely thanks to Loren Graham, who pioneered the field) the history of science, remained a question until well into the 1970s and a source of considerable contention even later. The first two monographs treating Soviet women were the work of political scientists, not historians; of the seventeen contributors to the groundbreaking interdisciplinary collection, *Women in Russia*, most were social scientists, and only four, historians.[1]

But the prevalence of politics was also related to the prominence of women in Russia's radical movements, who offered rich subject matter to historians just embarking on their careers. While historians of the United States explored the origins of feminism, feminist politics, and the agency of women, and, increasingly, the historical importance of the "private sphere" of home and family, historians of Russia's women tended to focus on women of the radical intelligentsia and Bolshevik efforts to emancipate women.[2] Concerned as we were with the activities of women in public rather than their experiences in private, some of us also strove to broaden the understanding of "the political" by exploring the private experiences that helped to shape women's consciousness and the underlying social and cultural forces that enabled them to assume a public role.[3]

The "women worthies" we discovered, unlike the ladies discussed in Arianne Chernock's essay on British women's history, suited the radical cast of mind of many in our cohort, as well as the general political orientation of the field. In this early period, Alexandra Kollontai, the "Bolshevik Feminist," to borrow Barbara Clements's formulation, became the object of particular fascination, and not only in the United States. Kollontai was an organizer of women before the revolution, a prominent Bolshevik in 1917, and briefly, a leader of the Zhenotdel or Women's Bureau, which between 1919 and 1930 was charged with overseeing the emancipation of Soviet women. Kollontai was also a theorist who wrote articles, pamphlets, and books treating the situation of women in the past, present, and future. Pioneering in her effort to meld Marxism and feminism, Kollontai was also attentive to sexuality and sexual relations, and to women's inner lives as well as their material conditions. Indeed, as a result of her unorthodox sexual ideas and behavior, as well as her affiliation with groups that opposed Lenin's line, she fell into political disfavor after 1922. In the early 1970s, many of her works were translated from the Russian into a variety of languages and made available for the first time, almost simultaneously with the revival of Soviet interest in her ideas after an eclipse of close to half a century.[4] Biographies of her soon followed.[5]

Our political orientation also meant that historians of Russia turned to social history rather later than most, and historians of the Soviet Union, much later still.[6] Nevertheless, as the Soviet Union became more open and archival restrictions eased, the trickle of scholarship that sidestepped the radical political orientation of earlier studies gradually became a stream. The resulting scholarship on imperial Russia focused primarily on elite women and on educated women who participated in public life not as revolutionaries, but as reformers, some—but by no means all, of a feminist orientation. Offering new detail about such women's lives and the institutions they helped to build, this scholarship also played a role in challenging the ways we interpreted Russia's past by providing a more expansive view of the possibilities for civil action in the imperial period, if not of the existence of a genuine civil society.[7]

The process of discovery extended to women of the peasantry, the overwhelming majority of Russia's population. Here, too, politics was a factor: romanticized by some as the "true Russia," peasants were regarded by others as emblematic of Russia's backwardness.[8] Peasant women's illiteracy compounded the difficulty of unmediated access to their experiences and worldview. Historians adopted several approaches to this dilemma. One was demographic, reconstructing family patterns and the place of women within the peasant household, which yielded concrete results but also no sense of individual experience. [9] Another was to draw on ethnographic and folkloric sources, buttressed by the remains of cases from the peasants' own cantonal courts. Bringing the researcher far closer to the peasants' own values and worldview, and enabling her to re-create the world from a peasant perspective, such sources had the disadvantage of a kind of timeless quality that minimized the impact of economic and other sources of change on peasant life.[10] A third approach has been to draw critically on sources that reflect such women's interaction with the outsiders with whom they came into contact—professionals, reformers, agents of the tsarist state. Pioneering this approach in his study of the abandonment and fosterage of infants over the course of more than a century, David Ransel's account of the impact on peasant women of elites' modernizing agendas suggested peasant women's agency as well as victimization.[11]

If anything, political questions loomed even larger for the few of us who studied working-class women. The Bolshevik seizure of power in 1917 in the name of "conscious workers" made the categories of "consciousness" or "backwardness," characterizing those lacking in political consciousness, central to the work of historians in the field, who tended to privilege the "conscious" worker, invariably young, single, and generically male. The difficulties this posed for historians of women was vividly reflected in the title, "'Backward' Workers in Skirts?" of a paper on women factory workers that Rose Glickman presented at a 1982 Russian Labor History Conference. They also shaped the key arguments of her full-length study. Demonstrating the substantial proportion of women in the labor force and their extended labor history, Glickman challenged the prevalent dismissal of women workers as "backward," by exploring the circumstances that retarded working women's activism as well as highlighting the activism that others had overlooked. In my own study of the working and family lives of peasant women as they moved between village and city, I built on the foundation Glickman provided and struggled against the same conceptual categories. However, instead of trying to adapt women's experience to them, I sought to problematize the categories themselves by demonstrating their gendered nature, while also exploring the history they concealed, in particular the family economy and family relations that were so significant to the development of Russia's working class.[12]

Social history was slower to influence the field of Soviet history. British scholars played a leading role. Less constrained by Cold War paradigms, more comfortable with alternative views of socialism than were most of us in the United States, they also enjoyed more ready access to the Soviet Union. *Soviet Sisterhood*, an interdisciplinary, edited volume published by a collective of British feminists in 1985, heralded the shift away from politics, political movements, and political transformation to focus attention on the everyday and family lives of Soviet women, and the impact upon them of the policies of the Soviet state.[13] When historians of women in the United States followed their lead, they joined a "revisionist" cohort that challenged the prevailing "totalitarian," top-down model, according to which the Soviet state exercised near-total control over, and acted independently of, society. Drawing on the methods of social history, members of this cohort demonstrated varying degrees of popular engagement with, influence upon, and opposition to, the project of Soviet state building.

Only a handful of revisionist historians studied women, however. The relative paucity of work on the Soviet period was evident at the conference on women's history sponsored by the National Endowment for the Humanities, held in Akron, Ohio, in the summer of 1988. The majority of the papers given at that conference, like most that were subsequently published in an edited volume, were devoted to the early modern and imperial periods. The first full-length study of Soviet women from a revisionist perspective appeared in 1993. Its author, Wendy Goldman, rejected the then-dominant idea that the failure of early Soviet efforts to emancipate women was the result of either Bolshevik ideology or the lack of leadership commitment. Instead, she attributed it to the grim social and economic circumstances of the postrevolutionary years. She also drew attention to the social basis of the Stalinist retreat from revolutionary gender policies. Emphasizing women's agency, experience, and aspirations in addition to those of the party officials, legal experts, and others who endeavored without much success to reshape women's lives, she argued that, as a result of their difficult circumstances, working-class women themselves supported the conservative family policies introduced under Joseph Stalin in the mid-1930s.[14]

Offering new ways to think about power and its exercise, gender history began to transform our field in the 1990s. It was pioneered by Laura Engelstein, whose work breathed new and exciting life into the largely neglected subject of liberalism. Initially in a series of articles and then in a rich and multifaceted full-length work, Engelstein explored how sexual ideology shaped the efforts of liberal professionals to wrest political and cultural authority from a recalcitrant autocratic state, while also illuminating how Russia's liberal reformers differed from their counterparts in the Western countries that served them as models, at least until 1905. Although women occasionally figure in her work as activists and intellectuals, it is women's bodies as objects of disciplinary control, and women's powerlessness and the identification with that powerlessness by male professionals that are most salient to the arguments of her book.[15] It is difficult to exaggerate the enthusiasm with which the broader community of Russian historians welcomed the work, vividly illustrating Joan Scott's contention that gender history, unlike women's history, could avoid the label of feminine particularity.[16] Even as gender history deeply problematized the social-historical emphasis on autonomous agency and experience, it also opened up fresh approaches to Russian and even more so, to Soviet history. Gender history arrived on the scene at a very propitious moment, just as the collapse of the Soviet Union prompted a major paradigm shift in our field.

The Collapse of Old Paradigms

It is difficult to exaggerate the impact of the collapse of the Soviet Union on Russian and Soviet history. Archival access gradually eased, allowing historians for the first time to pursue their research in comparative freedom and in far-flung locations that had hitherto been off-limits to them. Now it became possible to consider the past virtually anew. Although scholarship in the 1970s and 1980s had already begun to challenge the implicitly teleological approach to Russia's past, that is, primarily as a forerunner to the revolution to come, the collapse of the Soviet Union gave the challenge fresh impetus. The collapse also called into question the notion of Russian exceptionalism often implicit in the teleological approach, with its assumption that Russia was somehow inherently different from other societies that had avoided its revolutionary upheavals. If the communist era was only a temporary phenomenon, however long-lived, perhaps the revolution was not the inevitable outcome of Russia's historical development but an aberration, a response to the particular circumstances of war and failures of leadership. Perhaps the Russian and even the Soviet past were not so dissimilar to those of other European nations, and much the same questions might be addressed to them.

Entirely new avenues of inquiry opened up. In particular, Russia's middling classes—like liberals, a group to whom historians had paid little or no attention—became objects of inquiry, as did their gendered practices, which, as in the capitalist West, played an important role in affirming social place and defining gender norms.[17] Studies of consumption drew attention to the impact on women of modernization and the proliferation of public venues such as stores, theaters, dance halls, and mass entertainments that offered new ways of conceiving the female self.[18] For the first time, historians began to explore masculinity, not only as social construct and experience, but also, significantly, as an important element in men's self-presentation and social authority.[19] The resulting work identified many ways that Russia resembled, rather than differed from, its neighbors to the West.

The end of the Cold War, coinciding as it did with the intensification of globalization, postcolonial challenges to Eurocentrism, and growing interest in transnational processes, also brought fresh attention to Russia's relationship with the rest of the world, Western Europe in particular, and to Russia's imperial character and relations with the myriad peoples who composed its empire. The result was very close to a rebirth of scholarship, as older questions concerning, for example, feminism and radicalism were reframed, and new ones asked.[20] Russian and Soviet history, including women's and gender history, came into its own, and not only for scholars in Western Europe and the United States, but also for our colleagues in Russia.

The rebirth of Russian-language scholarship has been particularly noteworthy. During the Soviet era, a hardy few had undertaken the study of women and the woman question within the highly politicized parameters of Soviet historiography.[21] After 1991, the number of historians of women and gender steadily increased, despite the formidable obstacles they still face. These include a paucity of outlets for their work and the absence of any centralized database from which scholars in Russia or elsewhere might learn of the work of others; their difficulty in accessing work in foreign languages, an especially severe problem for the many scholars who work outside of Moscow and St. Petersburg; the general lack of institutional support for, or even interest in, women and gender (with several important exceptions); and finally, the conservatism of the historical profession, or at least of its old guard, who were trained during, and practiced for much of their life within, the Soviet system. The work on women and gender written in Russian is now sufficiently sophisticated and varied that it is impossible to identify its key themes or approaches in a chapter of this length.[22]

Despite the very different circumstances in which scholars in the U.S., Western Europe, and Russia conduct their work, the remainder of this chapter will examine the new scholarship thematically, rather than by country of origin of its authors, and for the most part will treat work in English. It will focus on three themes: the nature of Russia's relationship with an imagined "West"; gender and the Soviet experience; and the role of gender in the Russian and Soviet Union empires. Selected for their relevance to contemporary scholarly concerns, these themes also highlight some of the ways that Russia's particular history and positioning—the periphery of Europe, stretching eastward into Asia—provide valuable comparative perspectives.

Russia and the West

Russia's complex relationship with Western Europe can usefully be approached as an early, and highly suggestive, example of the transnational process of cultural transfer, its adaptation to local circumstances, and its gendered consequences. Russia at the close of the seventeenth century remained almost entirely untouched by Renaissance humanism or the scientific revolution and the intellectual innovations to which they gave rise. Although by then some in aristocratic circles had already begun to experiment with ideas and objects of foreign origin, Tsar Peter the Great's (1689–1725) dramatic, sudden, and forcible imposition on noble elites of ideas, institutions, and models of behavior drawn from Western models converted voluntary experimentation into state-mandated adherence. Combined as they were with innovations in the military and other realms, they ensured Russia's attainment of imperial status.

Changes in Russia's elite gender order were central to the process. Tsar Peter forced noblewomen to exchange their body-concealing and loose-fitting caftans for form-fitting and revealing western dress that required corsets, and ended the practice of female seclusion, mandating that elite men and women socialize in evening parties.[23] To break open the traditional Russian family structure, the tsar changed the laws governing marriage to allow for somewhat greater individual autonomy, circumscribing although not ending the control of parents or guardians over the marriages of the young. These changes reflected not only his belief that marriage based on attraction would yield demographic benefits, but also his personal inclinations. As Nancy Shields Kollman has argued, Peter the Great's elaborately celebrated second marriage to a woman of his own choice introduced ideas of emotional reciprocity and expectations for emotional satisfaction into a marital culture where they had hitherto been absent.[24] In the decades that followed, Russia's elites gradually embraced the West as a model; by the late eighteenth century, in their dress and demeanor, the women and men of Russia's urban elites had become virtually indistinguishable from their Western European counterparts.

Peter's innovations in his own private life resonated as well. Fostered by the Enlightenment, the concept that marriage should be based solely on a couple's mutual attraction or romantic love gained far broader currency in the second half of the eighteenth century, at least among elites. Propounding the possibility of individual happiness on earth, the Enlightenment "rehabilitated the passions," among them romantic love and sexual desire, as elements essential to such felicity.[25] Belles-lettres introduced these ideas to Russia's reading and theater-going public. The challenges such ideas raised to family interests and the patriarchal order were played out on the Enlightenment stage, where romantic love and its defiance of patriarchal authority served as a major theme.[26] Some came to view the home itself as a domain of virtue, as John Randolph has demonstrated in the case of the Bakunin family.[27] Even the Russian Orthodox Church was affected. Having hitherto propounded an authoritarian view of marriage, toward the end of the eighteenth century the church began to affirm women's place as the family's moral center. It placed new emphasis on the affective ties of spouses and their reciprocal responsibilities, while downplaying, although not eradicating, the patriarchal character of gender relations.[28] Michelle Lamarche Marrese has found that by the early nineteenth century, noblewomen as well as men had become comfortable in both Russian and foreign cultural forms, and moved easily between them.[29]

At the same time, work on gender suggests the importance of local context: ideals and practices deriving from the West metamorphosed when they crossed the border, modified to suit local needs and customs. Especially revealing in this respect is the cult of domesticity, a "transnational, hegemonic discourse," in the words of historian Judith Walsh, which came to Russia at the end of the eighteenth century, and was adapted for its local context just as elsewhere.[30] Building on the long-standing idea that woman's sphere was "domestic," the cult transformed the definition and significance of domesticity, elaborating on and celebrating women's responsibilities for house, child, and husband care, and reducing but not eradicating the economic dimensions of the domestic role. Yet before 1861, when the serfs were emancipated, and arguably, even after, when the trickle of prescriptive literature propounding domesticity became a torrent, its impact was limited by Russia's particular circumstances.

At least until 1861, this was certainly the case for noblewomen, the social group most likely to be exposed to such ideas. Noblewomen's status in property law was unique in Europe. In the course of the eighteenth century, even as married women to the West lost their right to independent ownership and management of property, Russian women's property rights expanded. The Russian experience suggests that law can be a significant force in counteracting ideological imperatives, or so Michelle Lamarche Marrese has argued. Nobles took advantage of women's legal rights, dowering daughters with property in land and bequeathing property to them. By the mid-nineteenth century about a third of noble property was in the hands of women, many of them married, who bought and sold property on their own behalf. Devoting themselves to administering their assets, which included peasant serfs, many propertied noblewomen consigned the nurturing of children to others, despite the new emphasis on mothering.[31]

After 1861 and the emancipation of the serfs, the influence of the cult of domesticity became more palpable, even for noblewomen, and in some social circles at least, it became associated with middle-class status. Nevertheless, the idea that women's calling was exclusively domestic never gained full ascendancy among the "middling" classes in Russia. Until the end of the imperial period, it competed with alternative discourses which favored a public role for women, although by then the growth of industrial capitalism had created the conditions that favored domesticity in other national settings.[32]

The ideas that constituted "the woman question," another transnational—although, alas, not hegemonic—discourse, were similarly reconfigured in their passage across the border. This was largely due to Russia's political culture. Until the early twentieth century, the tsar monopolized all political authority and demanded unquestioning submission from his subjects. The authoritarian political order was reflected in and reinforced by patriarchal family laws that granted elders near-absolute power over the young and husbands near-absolute power over wives, that made divorce inaccessible for most, and that strictly forbade marital separation. The setting inflected Russians' interpretation of the "woman question." From its emergence in the mid-nineteenth century, it not only stimulated protofeminist efforts to improve women's status, initially by means of philanthropy and then through the establishment of higher educational opportunities for women; it also provided a language with which to challenge, indirectly, the political order itself. Beginning in the reign of tsar Alexander II (1855–81) and continuing thereafter, critiques of women's oppressed status in marriage and of "family despotism" comprised a central component of the liberal intelligentsia's assault on political "despotism"—that is, the arbitrary political authority that oppressed such men, too. One consequence was that at least until the revolution of 1905, while male anxieties about women in public existed in Russia, they were far less pervasive, at least among the educated and privileged, than in most of Western Europe.[33]

The gendered consequences of industrialization, when it came to Russia, likewise reflected the particularities of its context. Two factors are especially salient: first, the fact that Russia was an overwhelmingly peasant society where women labored outside the home as well as in it and made vital contributions to the family economy; and second, the comparative weakness of the ideology of separate spheres, which defined domesticity as women's only proper calling. Together, they influenced the reception of women's labor force participation. Although a division of labor very much stratified by sex figured among the "real life" constraints that structured women's labor choices and women's treatment at the workplace in Russia as everywhere else, the idea that women's "virtue" resided exclusively in motherhood or genteel behavior and precluded work outside the home never gained ascendancy.[34] Indeed, for the majority of the population—that is, peasants—work itself was a source of virtue, albeit in the case of unmarried women in particular, best performed in or near the home. In peasant villages, marriages customarily brought a worker (*rabotnitsa*) into the household, and the predominant images of femininity were those of mother and the worker.³⁵ As a result, working-class men appear to have felt far less ambivalence about women in the labor force than their counterparts in Western Europe and the U.S., although they were no less eager than their counterparts elsewhere to exclude women from their trades and, in the case of the unskilled, asserted a masculinity based on toughness and bonding practices from which women were pointedly excluded.³⁶

Moreover, and again by contrast with developments closer to the European heartland, educated elites were on the whole equally accepting of women's work outside the home. Even maternal and child welfare movements, which elsewhere in Europe and the United States tended to be dominated by maternalist rhetoric, in Russia emphasized women's participation in the workforce over their role as mothers. Imperial philanthropic agencies, too, based their policies on the belief that "poor women must and should earn their own living."³⁷ Thus, unlike their middle-class contemporaries in Western Europe and the United States, educated Russians might regard with approval the remunerative labor of women, even when the women were married, even when they were mothers.

It is likely that the local setting also affected the form that Marxist ideas about women's place assumed in the Russian context. The relative comfort with women in public and the absence of a hegemonic cult of domesticity that celebrated the home, as well as the hyper-masculinity of working-class culture, were all reflected in policies that affected women and the domestic sphere following the Bolshevik seizure of power in 1917, to be discussed in more detail below. In turn, this affected Russia's own contribution to transnational processes, that is, the Marxist-Leninist ideology and practice that became the template for socialist states elsewhere, with its valorization of the male worker, celebration of the public, and neglect of private life.³⁸ At the same time, the Russian model was itself transformed as it moved across borders, adapting to the economies, politics, and cultures of the places to which it migrated.

Gender and the Soviet Experience

The above discussion, devoted as it has been to transnational cultural transmission and local adaptation, made no distinction between work in social history that treats women, and scholarship that adopts a cultural or linguistic approach to explore the ways that gender structures and legitimates relations of power. I do so below. The focus here is on the first three decades of the Soviet experience: while significant work has begun to appear on the postwar period, it is not yet so rich and varied. This scholarship highlights the particular contributions that a gendered approach can bring to the study of the Soviet past. However, as noted below, it also underscores the limitations of an exclusively cultural focus, when it overlooks human experience, self-perception, and capacity for agency in interpreting the human past. I conclude this section with a brief survey of recent scholarship that addresses these limitations and suggests promising new ways to overcome them.

There can be no question that, since the 1990s, a gendered approach has brought the Soviet past into fresh and illuminating perspective. That the revolutionary government was the first in history to declare the equality of the sexes as its goal has long been a commonplace in our field, even as historians disagreed, sometimes fiercely, about the motivations of key actors, the commitment with which emancipation was carried out, and the consequences for Soviet women. What those who examined culture—literary scholars as well as historians—have demonstrated was how very central gendered rhetoric and practices were to the foundation and development of the new regime, to legitimating the postrevolutionary state and its authority, and to shaping the evolving cultural and social order.

What they offered was a picture of a revolutionary party and culture unremittingly masculinist in character. From the first, the party embraced—indeed, almost literally embodied—the "masculinist definition" of labor and politics that had dominated nineteenth-century socialist rhetoric, not only in Russia but also everywhere else in Europe, and it rendered that definition hegemonic.[39] Even as the new regime transformed Russia's patriarchal legal order, undermined the patriarchal family, opened new opportunities for women, and mobilized them to an unprecedented degree, it also reinscribed gender differences in a range of ways that ensured women's secondary status. Both rhetorically and in revolutionary iconography, the woman worker occupied the margins, not the center, of the new civic order. Often depicted as "backward" in contrast to the "conscious" male worker, she needed to prove her worthiness for membership in a new civic order to which he automatically belonged.[40] In the first decade following the revolution, the message was clear: a woman should become more like a man. The unprecedented attack on the domestic sphere and private life, unleashed by the Bolsheviks in the 1920s, reinforced that message, associating with "backward" women the home and all that was wrong with the prerevolutionary way of life.[41] Studies of scientific discourse inspired by the work of Michel Foucault likewise underscored the importance of gendered imagery to the new civil order. Thus, in their efforts to enforce social hygiene or gain control over procedures such as childbirth and mothering that had hitherto been in women's hands, male experts, mainly physicians and scientists, stigmatized only women—for example as child-endangering midwives, or as bearers of sexually transmitted disease, or of pathologies of sexual deviance.[42]

Stalin's assumption of dictatorial powers at the close of the 1920s brought significant changes to these gendered policies and practices. The emphasis, for good reason, has long been on the harm these changes brought to women. Laws that reinforced the family, now entitled the "new socialist family," replaced laws that undermined it. To promote a higher birthrate, abortion, legal since 1920 and the primary means of birth control, was outlawed in 1936. Divorce, easy to obtain in the 1920s, became far more difficult and expensive. The industrialization drive that did away with unemployment at the same time intentionally stratified the labor force according to sex.[43] Gendered representations changed to suit the new priorities: while masculinity remained constant, representations of the feminine became conventionally feminized, eliminating the "unsexed" (meaning androgynous or male) feminine ideal of the first postrevolutionary decade.

Cultural historians have identified a number of purposes served by the newly feminized woman, none of which advanced her own interests. Crucially, she was better suited than her predecessor to the intensified, and intensely pronatalist, emphasis on women's "natural" role of mother—part of an effort that resembled as well as differed from pronatalist policies undertaken by other authoritarian European states.[44] She also figured as emblem and agent of the state's new civilizing mission, as expressed in the term *kulturnost'* or culturedness, which in this period assumed great importance as a goal toward which Soviet people strove. The wife-activist movement, which emerged in 1936 with encouragement from above—the first time since the revolution that wives were celebrated as such—represented the quintessence of this trend, as well as, in the eyes of some historians, the emergence of a new middle or privileged class.[45] Finally, portraits of newly feminized women surrounding Stalin contributed to the visual constitution of his political power by naturalizing the relationship of society to the Stalinist state: society, feminized, adored Stalin, the mighty leader.[46]

Recently, however, the work of a cohort of mainly younger historians has begun to complicate this seemingly straightforward picture. Alert to the importance of cultural constructions of gender, this new work attends closely to the particular social and political contexts in which gender is structured and enacted, and raises questions about the impact on individual subjectivity, identity, and capacity for agency. Drawing both on newly available archival evidence and published materials that previous historians have either overlooked or dismissed, scholars have explored how individuals adapted and adopted for their own purposes the Stalinist gender order, and found complexity rather than singularity in gendered norms.

They have drawn attention, in particular, to the positive Soviet heroines of the 1930s and how they might inspire and empower women. Figuring prominently in celebrations of Stalinist achievements, in this period women ceased to exemplify backwardness and became symbols of Soviet modernity.[47] Images of the "modern" Soviet woman shaped the self-perceptions and aspirations of at least a portion of Soviet youth, the first generation to come of age in the postrevolutionary era. Some women found Soviet efforts to mobilize women and involve them in state-sponsored projects genuinely empowering, and regarded themselves as beneficiaries of the regime's stated goal of liberating women. They identified with the Soviet state, willingly participated in its campaigns, and took pride not only in their accomplishments but also in their newly emphasized "femininity" and even the domestic responsibilities that accompanied it.

Such women figure in Elena Shulman's account of the campaign to populate the Soviet Far East. Adaptable and energetic, able to overcome obstacles and take difficulties in stride even as others succumbed to them, they also envisioned themselves as enjoying family and domestic life while they continued to work outside the home, freed from the choice between one or the other that confronted activist women in the twenties. Such women are more prominent still in Anna Krylova's recent study of the tens of thousands of Soviet women who demanded the right to fight in World War II. Challenging the very concept of gender as a hierarchical binary, at least in the wartime Soviet context, she argues that her subjects embodied a new, militarized femininity. Encouraged by propaganda that recognized and celebrated women's military capacity and ability to shoot a gun, among other factors, her women soldiers combined without tension the violence of warfare with "feminine" concerns with appearance and the like.[48] Based as key portions are on a surprisingly uncritical reading of published personal documents, Krylova's argument occasionally overreaches. Nevertheless, combined with other recent work, it suggests how much more there is to learn not only about the nature and outcomes of the Soviet experiment in gender transformation, but also about the complex interaction between gendered representations, political power, and individual agency, and not only in Stalinist Russia.

Empire

Of the three categories I explore in this chapter, gender and empire is both the most promising and the least well developed. It is the most promising because it holds the potential to enrich and perhaps even to complicate existing interpretations, which take Western European overseas empires as the norm. Russia's was a contiguous rather than overseas empire, formed over the course of centuries by the incorporation of neighboring territories. By the late nineteenth century, it had come to consist of over a hundred different peoples, with widely varying economies, cultures, and ways of life. It survived the break of 1917 more or less intact, ending only with the collapse of the Soviet Union in 1991. More long lasting and more diverse than most, the Russian and the Soviet empires nevertheless shared with others many fundamental characteristics.

Work on the Russian empire has flourished since the fall of the Soviet Union; work on its gendered character, to a far lesser degree. Thus far, gendered analyses have concentrated almost exclusively on the regions to the South, East, and Northeast of the Russian heartland, rather than on areas to Russia's West and Southwest—Finland, say, or Poland or the Baltic states—whose stages of economic and social development were more or less similar to Russia's or even more advanced. The few works that treat gender in the latter regions focus either on movements for political autonomy or on Russia's Jewish minority, and frame them in terms other than gender and imperial policies.[49] Regions inhabited by peoples whom Russians deemed "backward" clearly remain more amenable to existing interpretive paradigms.

In those regions, a gendered civilizing mission that greatly resembled that of other colonizing empires provided a key rationale for Russian hegemony and interference in native affairs, starting in the late eighteenth century. As elsewhere, it was based upon the alleged superiority of Russians, as reflected, in part, in their treatment of women. This shaped the ways that the colonial project was presented to the broader public. As Susan Lawton has shown, tales of Russian men's exploits in exotic areas captured the public's imagination by celebrating the masculinity of the conqueror. In the early nineteenth century, readers—still a tiny minority of the Russian public—devoured sensational stories of love between Muslim women and Russian men that were set in the exotic Caucasus mountains, where Russians waged a war of conquest. Almost invariably, the Russian colonizer was a chivalrous and valiant man, and the "good" native a nurturing, sexually available, and ardent woman. The native men, by contrast, were savages, fanatical, and lustful brutes.[50] Similarly gendered imagery served to underwrite Russia's imperial mission in Central Asia as well.[51] In the second half of the nineteenth century, gendered representations of conquest reached a mass audience through the personality and publications of the explorer, naturalist, and author, Nikolai Przheval'skii. Celebrated in the popular press, Przheval'skii was aggressively virile, an exponent of "conquistador imperialism" who took pride in Russian superiority. Przheval'skii regarded the peoples of the East as passive and helpless, desirous of Russia's hegemony and protection.[52]

The alleged superiority of Russians also shaped the ways that the colonial project was realized in practice. Following the conquest of more "backward" regions, Russians assumed responsibility for improving native women's status as part of a broader effort to alter problematic native customs. Russian law served as an important means to that end, especially in the Muslim regions of the Caucasus and Central Asia. Newly created state courts offered Muslim women enhanced leverage in their relations with men. They defended women from abuse, helped them to safeguard their honor, and even eased their escape from unhappy marriages, while also extending state control into everyday life, much as they did among Jews in the Pale of Settlement, the region of Russia's Western borderlands where Jews were required to reside. However, in Muslim areas, late-nineteenth-century Russians additionally sought to end a range of customs they viewed as "backward," in particular the betrothal of widows to male in-laws, the payment of *kalym* or brideprice, and the marriage of female children and adolescents, which in the Russians' view infringed on the human rights of women.[53]

After the revolution of 1917, the state's transformative agenda grew still more ambitious and in Muslim regions such as Azerbaijan and Central Asia, gender became still more central to it, reflecting, in part, gender's significance to the revolutionary vision itself. Initially, law provided the primary means to bring about change, much as in the earlier period. But now the goals were more ambitious—to eliminate customary family practices such as polygamy, early marriage, and bride price—and the penalties became more serious. Those who violated new laws might be declared "enemies of the people." When legal change proved ineffective, direct action replaced it. In 1927, the regime launched an all-out campaign to transform women's place.

The foot soldiers of this campaign were often women, distinguishing the Soviet experience from comparable efforts elsewhere. In Azerbaijan, Azeri Bolshevik women took the lead. In Central Asia, activists were usually Russians, Armenians, or Jews who belonged to the Zhenotdel (Women's Bureau). Everywhere in the "backward" regions, they encouraged native women to speak at public meetings, attend school, and work outside the home. Where native women wore the veil, as in Uzbekistan, Tajikistan, and Azerbaijan, female outsiders played a leading role in the massive campaign to unveil them. The reaction was often violent. In Uzbekistan especially, thousands of women, primarily unveiled women and female activists, were killed or wounded. Although the violence forced the party to back off from the unveiling campaign, less dramatic and more gradual approaches continued. The focus became fostering women's education, initially primary education, expanding their access to professional health care, and bringing women into the labor force. By the outbreak of World War II, these efforts had made real, if still limited, inroads among the Muslim peoples of Central Asia and Azerbaijan.[54]

Historians' assessments of these efforts have varied as our field has evolved. Gregory Massell's pioneering study, written in 1974 when the Cold War still raged, presented the Communist party's approach to women as entirely instrumental: women would provide the spearhead of revolutionary transformation—a kind of "surrogate proletariat," in Massell's felicitous phrase—in a region where an indigenous proletariat or homegrown communist movement was lacking or weak. Their emancipation would undermine indigenous, patriarchal cultures and overcome resistance to Soviet rule.[55] Recent work, almost all of it influenced by postcolonial theory, thoroughly grounded in the literature of empire elsewhere, and based on local archival sources in native languages, has greatly enhanced our knowledge and also complicated this story.

Recently, indeed, historians of gender have begun to challenge the very notion that the Soviet Union was an empire, one of the core assumptions of Cold War scholarship. Douglas Northrup, for example, finds the Soviet Union to be a kind of hybrid. Offering on the one hand a classic example of colonialism in an empire that took pride in its own anticolonialism, on the other, it pursued policies more typical of modern or modernizing states that seek to build a modern polity with modern ideas of citizenship.[56] Recently, Adrienne Edgar has taken this second line of reasoning a step further, by placing the Soviet experience in its pan-Islamic context. Comparing the Soviet experience not only with the "classic" imperial policies of Great Britain and France, but also with the modernizing agendas of Muslim states such as Turkey and Iran under Reza Shah, she concludes that Soviet gender policies were in fact *more* similar to those of modernizing states than to those of empires. Nevertheless, she finds, because Soviet policies were *perceived* as an attempt at foreign domination, whether or not that was the intent, local people resisted them at least as fiercely as others did the efforts of more classically imperial polities.[57]

Conclusion

Freed from the Cold War paradigms that shaped the field in the early years, the history of Russia's women and of gender relations underwent a remarkable efflorescence following the collapse of the Soviet Union. So diverse has that scholarship been that it is literally impossible to do it justice in a brief chapter such as this. And in the United States, if not in Russia, it increasingly influences studies of other subjects—although as yet, rarely of Russia's empire—and is often incorporated into broader syntheses and textbooks, taught in graduate courses and the like. And yet beneath these dramatic changes continuities remain, even if they are not so obvious. Interest in the gendered consequences of state policy remains at the heart of much of our work on the Soviet period, while historians of the imperial period continue to grapple with the question of Russia's exceptionalism, in which gender now offers a crucial variable. A state of nations rather than a nation-state, an ambiguous empire located to the east of the European heartland and on the borderland where Europe becomes Asia, a late-comer to modernity as defined by Western European standards, Russia's particular history offers a valuable comparative perspective.

NOTES

1. Gregory Massell, *The Surrogate Proletariat: Moslem Women and Revolutionary Strategies in Soviet Central Asia* (Princeton: Princeton University Press, 1974); Gail Warshofsky Lapidus, *Women in Soviet Society: Equality, Development and Social Change* (Berkeley: University of California Press, 1977); Dorothy Atkinson, Alexander Dallin, and Gail Warshofsky Lapidus, eds., *Women in Russia* (Stanford: Stanford University Press, 1977).
2. Barbara Alpern Engel and Clifford Rosenthal, eds., *Five Sisters: Women against the Tsar* (New York: Knopf, 1975); Carol Eubanks Hayden, "The Zhenotdel and the Bolshevik Party," *Russian History* 3, no. 2 (1976): 150–73; Barbara Alpern Engel, "From Feminism to Socialism: A Case Study of Women of the Chaikovskii Circle," in Marilyn Boxer and Jean Quataert, eds., *Socialist Women* (New York: Elsevier Scientific Publishing Co., 1978), 51–75; Richard Stites, *The Women's Liberation Movement in Russia: Feminism, Nihilism and Bolshevism, 1860–1930* (Princeton: Princeton University Press, 1978); Amy Knight, "Female Terrorists in the Russian Social Revolutionary Party," *Russian Review* 38, no. 2 (1979): 139–59.
3. Barbara Evans Clements, *Bolshevik Feminist: The Life of Alexandra Kollontai* (Bloomington: Indiana University Press, 1979); Barbara Alpern Engel, *Mothers and Daughters: Women of the Intelligentsia in Nineteenth Century Russia* (New York: Cambridge University Press, 1983).
4. Alexandra Kollontai, *Red Love* (Westport, Conn.: Hyperion Press, 1973); Judith Stora-Sandor, ed., *Alexandra Kollontai: Marxisme et révolution sexuelle* (Paris: François Maspero, 1975); Alexandra Kollontai, *Die Situation der Frau in der gesellschaftlichen Entwicklung. Vierzehn Vorlesungen vor Arbeiterinnen und Bäuerinnen an der Sverdlov-Universitat 1921*, with afterword by Anne-Marie Troger (Frankfurt: Verlag Neue Kritik, 1975); Alix Holt, ed., *Alexandra Kollontai: Selected Writings* (London: Allison and Busby, 1977). For the Soviet Union, Aleksandra Kollontai, *Izbrannye stat'i i rechi* (Moscow: Politizdat, 1972), and *Iz moei zhizni i raboty. Gody i liudy* (Moscow: Sovetskaia Rossiia, 1974).

5. Clements, *Bolshevik Feminist*; Beatrice Farnsworth, *Alexandra Kollontai: Socialism, Feminism and the Bolshevik Revolution* (Stanford: Stanford University Press, 1980). On the English-language historiography, see Moira Donald, "'What Did You Do in the Revolution, Mother?' Image, Myth, and Prejudice in Western Writing on the Russian Revolution," *Gender and History* 7, no. 1 (April 1995): 85–99.
6. The shift was pioneered by David Ransel, ed., *The Family in Imperial Russia: New Lines of Historical Research* (Urbana: University of Illinois Press, 1978).
7. Ruth Dudgeon, "The Forgotten Minority: Women Students in Imperial Russia, 1872–1917," *Russian History* 9, pt. 1 (1982): 1–26; Linda Harriet Edmondson, *Feminism in Russia, 1900–1917* (Stanford: Stanford University Press, 1984); Christine Johanson, *Women's Struggle for Higher Education in Russia, 1855–1900* (Montreal: McGill-Queens University Press, 1987); Adele Lindenmeyr, "Public Life, Private Virtues: Women in Russian Charity, 1762–1914," *Signs* 2, no. 3 (Spring 1993): 562–91;Brenda Meehan, "From Contemplative Practice to Charitable Activity: Russian Women's Religious Communities and the Development of Charitable Work, 1861–1917," in Kathleen McCarthy, ed., *Lady Bountiful Revisited: Women, Philanthropy and Power* (New Brunswick: Rutgers University Press, 1990), 142–56; Christine Ruane, *Gender, Class and the Professionalization of Russian Village Teachers, 1860–1914* (Pittsburgh: University of Pittsburgh Press, 1994).
8. Cathy A. Frierson, *Peasant Icons: Representations of Rural People in Late Nineteenth Century Russia* (New York: Oxford University Press, 1993), chapter 8.
9. For example, Peter Czap, Jr., "Marriage and the Joint Family in the Era of Serfdom," in Ransel, ed., *The Family in Imperial Russia*, 103–124; Rodney D. Bohac, "Widows and the Russian Serf Community," in Barbara Evans Clements, Barbara Alpern Engel, and Christine D. Worobec, eds., *Russia's Women: Accommodation, Resistance, Transformation* (Berkeley: University of California Press, 1991), 95–112.
10. See, for example, Rose Glickman, "The Peasant Woman as Healer," in *Russia's Women*, 148–62; Barbara Alpern Engel, "Peasant Morality and Premarital Sexual Relations in Late Nineteenth Century Russia," *Journal of Social History* 23, no. 4 (Summer 1990): 695–714; Christine D. Worobec, *Peasant Russia: Family and Community in the Post-Emancipation Period* (Princeton: Princeton University Press, 1991).
11. David Ransel, *Mothers of Misery: Child Abandonment in Russia* (Princeton: Princeton University Press, 1988). See also Nancy Mandelker Frieden, "Child Care: Medical Reform in a Traditionalist Culture," in *The Family in Imperial Russia*, 236–59, and more recently, and reflecting the linguistic turn, Christine Worobec, *Possessed: Women, Witches and Demons in Imperial Russia* (DeKalb: Northern Illinois University Press, 2001).
12. Rose L. Glickman, *Russian Factory Women: Workplace and Society, 1880–1914* (Berkeley: University of California Press, 1984); Barbara Alpern Engel, *Between the Fields and the City: Women, Work and Family in Russia, 1861–1914* (New York: Cambridge University Press, 1994).
13. Barbara Holland, ed., *Soviet Sisterhood: British Feminists on Women in the USSR* (London: Fourth Estate, 1985). See also Elizabeth Waters, "Teaching Mothercraft in Post-Revolutionary Russia," *Australian Slavonic and East European Studies* 1, no. 2 (1987): 29–56; and Elizabeth Waters, "The Modernization of Soviet Motherhood, 1917–1937," *Soviet Studies* 44, no. 1(1992): 123–35.
14. *Russia's Women*; Wendy Z. Goldman, *Women, the State and Revolution: Soviet Family Policy and Social Life* (Cambridge: Cambridge University Press, 1993).

15. Laura Engelstein, *The Keys to Happiness: Sex and the Search for Modernity in Fin-de-Siecle Russia* (Ithaca: Cornell University Press, 1992). For a comparable argument, see William Wagner, *Marriage, Property and Law in Late Imperial Russia* (Oxford: Clarendon Press, 1994).
16. Joan Wallach Scott, "Gender: A Useful Category of Historical Analysis," *American Historical Review* 91, no. 5 (December 1986): 1053–75.
17. Catriona Kelly, *Refining Russia: Advice Literature, Polite Culture, and Gender from Catherine to Yeltsin* (Oxford: Oxford University Press, 2001); Catherine Evtukhov, "A. O. Karelin and Provincial Bourgeois Photography," in Valerie A. Kivelson and Joan Neuberger, eds., *Picturing Russia: Explorations in Visual Culture* (New Haven: Yale University Press, 2008), 113–18; Barbara Alpern Engel, *Breaking the Ties that Bound: The Politics of Marital Strife in Late Imperial Russia* (Ithaca: Cornell University Press, 2011).
18. Steve Smith and Catriona Kelly, "Commercial Culture and Consumerism," in Catriona Kelly and David Shepherd, eds., *Constructing Russian Culture in the Age of Revolution: 1881–1940* (New York: Oxford University Press, 1998), 106–55; Christine Ruane, *The Empire's New Clothes: A History of the Russian Fashion Industry* (New Haven: Yale University Press, 2009). On the liberating potential of commerce, see especially, Louise McReynolds, *Russia at Play: Leisure Activities at the End of the Tsarist Era* (Ithaca: Cornell University Press, 2003), 5–6, 113–31; and Louise McReynolds, "The 'Incomparable' Vial'tseva and the Culture of Personality," in Helena Goscilo and Beth Holmgren, eds., *Russia. Women. Culture* (Bloomington: Indiana University Press, 1996), 273–91.
19. Barbara Evans Clements, Rebecca Friedman, and Dan Healey, eds., *Russian Masculinities in History and Culture* (New York: Palgrave, 2002); Rebecca Friedman, *Masculinity, Autocracy and the Russian University* (New York: Palgrave Macmillan, 2005); Susan Reid, "Masters of the Earth: Gender and Destalinization in Soviet Reformist Painting of the Khrushchev Era," *Gender and History* 11, no. 2 (July 1999): 276–312.
20. For example, Ana Siljak, *Angel of Vengeance: "The Girl Assassin," the Governor of St. Petersburg and Russia's Revolutionary World* (New York: St. Martin's Press, 2008); Irina Iukina, *Russkii feminizm kak vyzov sovremennosti* (St. Petersburg: Aleteia, 2007); Rochelle Goldberg Ruthchild, *Equality and Revolution: Women's Rights in the Russian Empire, 1905–1917* (Pittsburgh: University of Pittsburgh Press, 2010).
21. Z. V. Grishina, "Dvizhenie za politicheskoe ravnopravie zhenshchin v gody pervoi russkoi revoliutsii," *Vestnik Moskovskogo universiteta*, seriia 8. *Istoriia*. 1982; G. A. Tishkin, *Zhenskii vopros v Rossii: 50-e—60-e gody XIX veka* (Leningrad: Izdatel'stvo Leningradskogo Universiteta, 1984).
22. The exceptionally valuable interdisciplinary bibliography prepared by Natalia Pushkareva cites scholarship in all languages through the year 2000, and is introduced with a comprehensive historiographical essay. See N. L. Pushkareva, *Russkaia zhenshchina: Istoriia i sovremennost'* (Moscow: Ladomir, 2002).
23. Lindsay Hughes, "'The Crown of Maidenly Honour and Virtue': Redefining Femininity in Peter I's Russia," in Wendy Rosslyn, ed., *Women and Gender in Eighteenth Century Russia* (Burlington, Vt.: Ashgate, 2003), 35–48.
24. Nancy Shields Kollman, "'What's Love Got to Do with It?': Changing Models of Masculinity in Muscovite and Petrine Russia," in *Russian Masculinities*, 15–32.
25. Cissie Fairchilds, "Women and the Family," in Samia I. Spencer, ed., *French Women and the Age of Enlightenment* (Bloomington: Indiana University Press, 1984), 98–99.
26. Liubov S. Artem'eva, "'Videnie vliublennogo': liubov i brak v kul'ture russkogo sentimentalizma," *Adam i Eva* 2 (2001): 268; Elise Kimerling Wirtschafter, *The Play of Ideas in Russian Enlightenment Theatre* (DeKalb: University of Northern Illinois Press, 2003), 56, 156.

27. John Randolph, *The House in the Garden: The Bakunin Family and the Romance of Russian Idealism* (Ithaca: Cornell University Press, 2007).
28. Wagner, *Marriage, Property and Law*, 73–76.
29. Michelle Lamarche Marrese, "'The Poetics of Everyday Behavior' Revisited: Lotman, Gender, and the Evolution of Russian Noble Identity," *Kritika* 11, no. 4 (Fall 2010): 701–39.
30. Judith E. Walsh, *Domesticity in Colonial India: What Women Learned When Men Gave Them Advice* (Lanham, Md.: Rowman and Littlefield, 2004), 2, 25–28.
31. Michelle Lamarche Marrese, *A Woman's Kingdom: Noblewomen and the Control of Property in Russia* (Ithaca: Cornell University Press, 2002).
32. *Classic Russian Cooking: Elena Molokhovets' A Gift to Young Housewives*, translated and introduced by Joyce Toomre (Bloomington: Indiana University Press, 1992), 11–12; Beth Holmgren, "Gendering the Icon: Marketing Women Writers in Fin-de-Siecle Russia," in *Russia. Women. Culture*, 321–46.
33. Engelstein, *Keys to Happiness*; Wagner, *Marriage, Property and Law*.
34. Alice Kessler-Harris, *Gendering Labor History* (Urbana: University of Illinois Press, 2007), 117–18.
35. T. G. Leont'eva, "Sel'skie zatvornitsy: zhenshchiny i baby v dorevoliutsionnoi derevne," in *Iz arkhiva tverskikh istorikov* 3 (2003): 110.
36. S. A. Smith, "Masculinity in Transition: Peasant Migrants to Late-Imperial St. Petersburg," in *Russian Masculinities*, 94–112.
37. Adele Lindenmeyr, "Maternalism and Child Welfare in Late Imperial Russia," *Journal of Women's History* 5, no. 2 (Fall 1993): 114, 116, 119.
38. Sonia Kruks, Rayna Rapp, and Marilyn Young, eds., *Promissory Notes: Women in the Transition to Socialism* (New York: Monthly Review Press, 1989).
39. Eric D. Weiz, "The Heroic Man and the Ever-Changing Woman: Gender and Politics in European Communism," in Laura L. Frader and Sonya O. Rose, eds., *Gender and Class in Modern Europe* (Ithaca: Cornell University Press, 1996), 311–52.
40. Elizabeth Wood, *The Baba and the Comrade: Gender and Politics in Revolutionary Russia* (Bloomington: Indiana University Press, 1997); Elizabeth Waters, "The Female Form in Soviet Political Iconography, 1917–1932," in *Russia's Women*, 225–42; Victoria Bonnell, *Iconography of Power: Soviet Political Posters under Lenin and Stalin* (Berkeley: University of California Press, 1999), 64–99.
41. Anne Gorsuch, "'A Woman Is Not a Man': The Culture of Gender and Generation in Soviet Russia, 1921–1928," *Slavic Review* 55, no. 3 (Fall 1996): 636–60.
42. Frances Lee Bernstein, *The Dictatorship of Sex: Lifestyle Advice for the Soviet Masses* (DeKalb: Northern Illinois University Press, 2007); Tricia Starks, *The Body Soviet: Hygiene, Propaganda and the Revolutionary State* (Madison: University of Wisconsin Press, 2008).
43. Wendy Goldman, *Women at the Gates: Gender and Industry in Stalin's Russia* (New York: Cambridge University Press, 2002).
44. David L. Hoffman, "Mothers in the Motherland: Stalinist Pronatalism in its Pan-European Context," *Journal of Social History* 34, no. 1 (Fall 2000): 35–54.
45. Sheila Fitzpatrick, "Becoming Cultured: Socialist Realism and the Representation of Privilege and Taste," in *The Cultural Front: Power and Culture in Revolutionary Russia* (Ithaca: Cornell University Press, 1992), 216–37.
46. Susan Reid, "All Stalin's Women: Gender and Power in the Soviet Art of the 1930s," *Slavic Review* 57, no. 1 (Spring 1998): 133–73.
47. Choi Chatterjee, "Soviet Heroines and the Language of Modernity, 1930–1939," in Melanie Ilic, ed., *Women in the Stalin Era* (Houndsmills, Basingstoke, U.K.: Palgrave, 2001), 49–68.

48. Elena Shulman, *Stalinism on the Frontier of Empire: Women and State Formation in the Soviet Far East* (New York: Cambridge University Press, 2008); Anna Krylova, *Soviet Women in Combat: A History of Violence on the Eastern Front* (New York: Cambridge University Press, 2010). See also Mary Buckley, *Mobilizing Soviet Peasants: Heroines and Heroes of Stalin's Fields* (Lanham, Md.: Rowman and Littlefield, 2006).
49. See, for example, Martha Bohachevsky-Chomiak, *Feminists Despite Themselves: Women in Ukrainian Community Life, 1884–1939* (Edmonton: Canadian Institute of Ukrainian Studies, 1998); Chae-Ran Y. Freeze, *Jewish Marriage and Divorce in Imperial Russia* (Hanover, N.H.: Brandeis University Press, 2002).
50. Susan Lawton, *Russian Literature and Empire* (New York: Cambridge University Press, 1994).
51. Douglas Northrup, "Nationalizing Backwardness: Gender, Empire and Uzbek Identity," in Ronald Grigor Suny and Terry Martin, eds., *A State of Nations: Empire and Nation-Building in the Age of Lenin and Stalin* (New York: Oxford University Press, 2001), 191–220.
52. David Schimmelpenninck van der Oye, *Towards the Rising Sun: Russian Ideologies of Empire and the War with Japan* (DeKalb: Northern Illinois University Press, 2001), 24–41.
53. Austin Jersild, *Orientalism and Empire: North Caucasus Mountain People and the Georgian Frontier, 1847–1917* (Montreal: McGill-Queens University Press, 2002), 102–05; 120–21; Robert D. Crews, "Empire and the Confessional State: Islam and Religious Politics in Nineteenth-Century Russia," *American Historical Review* 108, no. 1 (February 2003): 50–83. On policies in the Pale, see Freeze, *Jewish Marriage*.
54. Nayereh Tohidi, "Gender, Ethnicity, and Islam in Soviet and Post-Soviet Azerbaijan," *Nationalities Papers* 25, no. 1 (1997): 149; Douglas Northrup, *Veiled Empire: Gender and Power in Stalinist Central Asia* (Ithaca: Cornell University Press, 2004); Adrienne Edgar, *Tribal Nation: The Making of Modern Soviet Turkmenistan* (Princeton: Princeton University Press, 2004); Paula Michaels, "Medical Traditions, Kazak Women, and Soviet Medical Politics to 1941," *Nationalities Papers* 26, no. 3 (1998): 493–509.
55. Massell, *The Surrogate Proletariat*.
56. Northrup, *Veiled Empire*, 23–41.
57. Adrienne Edgar, "Bolshevism, Patriarchy and the Nation: The Soviet 'Emancipation' of Women in Pan-Islamic Perspective," *Slavic Review*, 65, no. 2 (Summer 2006): 252–72.

3

Putting the Political in Economy

African Women's and Gender History, 1992–2010

CLAIRE ROBERTSON

In the mid-1980s, my historiographical survey of scholarly works on African women revealed a focus on political economy, with emphases on women's highly productive and important economic activities and women's agency, moving away from the tendency either to ignore women entirely or treat them as passive victims. These attempts to rectify the gaps in the literature rebutted the stereotypical oversexualization of black women by whites and the related assumption that female slaves in Africa were mainly desired for biological reproduction, for instance.[1] Since then scholarship on African women and gender has multiplied to the point that any assessment of new historical works becomes a daunting task. Comprehensiveness is no longer possible; a work could be excellent and not cited in this thematic appraisal of over 150 randomly selected works. Shown here is that since about 1992 the political part of political economy is ascending. Women's power and political concerns have emerged as major foci of this literature in a continuing interdisciplinary scholarly tradition.

This chapter also addresses Oyèrónké Oyěwùmí's assertion in *The Invention of Women: Making an African Sense of Western Gender Discourses* that all "Western" women have a preset agenda in studying "African" women that derives from "Western" experiences and is neocolonialist and irrelevant to "African" women, who should set their own priorities for research regarding women and gender.[2] While the totalizing categories of "Western" and "African" women are deeply problematic, her main point is worth testing. It raises the question of identifying the priorities of an "African" research agenda on women and gender. The questions thus become: who has been primarily responsible for refocusing African women's and gender history on issues of power? Is this agenda shared by African and non-African scholars of Africa? This chapter seeks answers to these questions by assessing the historiography on African women and gender, its strengths and weaknesses, its contributions to the wider historical enterprise, and its trajectory from 1992 on, when the trend began that is still dominant of emphasizing power issues with regard to gender.

Some brief observations about African history's contributions to the wider historical enterprise are a good place to begin. African history began in the U.S. as a field separate from European imperial history in the 1960s. It has made at least three major contributions to the historical discipline, although these may not often be recognized by those in other fields. First, as with other non-Western fields, the chronology differs from that in Eurocentric history and by African polity. Second, Africanists use oral history creatively; some scholars have established important historical trends as far back as the sixteenth and seventeenth centuries.[3] Third, interdisciplinary perspectives, especially insights from anthropology, are integral to the work of most African historians. For instance, my graduate and postgraduate training included seven languages, four of them African; African history, my major field; and courses on African political science, anthropology, geography, literature, art history, and European history. I taught myself ethnobotany, cloth manufacture, Caribbean history, statistics, economics, Marxist and feminist theory, and even women's and gender studies, not then offered in graduate school. In its interdisciplinarity African history meshes well with women's and gender studies. African women's and gender history makes an important fourth contribution: the breaking of common stereotypes about Africa and women, the contestation of categories.

Here I will avoid a teleology that sees U.S. women's studies as determining goals for an international field. Many African scholars of women and gender have deliberately charted a course other than that set by U.S. feminist scholars. That distinction must be noted and valued, especially given the African colonial past. In the case of African history, especially women's and gender history, much of the scholarship is *histoire engagée*, meant to be of use to its subjects, scholars, and the wider community.

The Development of African Women's and Gender History

African women's and gender studies emerged in the 1960s with Niara Sudarkasa's pioneering study "Women, Trade and the Yoruba Family."[4] In the 1970s African women's history developed in the U.S., alongside women's studies (gender as a term was not in common use then). My 1974 dissertation might have been the first in the U.S. focusing primarily on African women's history.[5] The first American scholars to study African women's history include, among others: Margaret Strobel, Susan Geiger, Margaret Jean Hay, and Iris Berger, who published excellent studies of the diverse experiences of women in Kenya, Tanzania, Nigeria, and South Africa. In the 1985 survey I made a deliberate attempt to include studies by African and African American scholars, whose works had often been ignored.[6] Subsequently the deficit in numbers of African women scholars, an artifact of colonial and neocolonial thought and experiences chronicled by many cited here, has been substantially reduced.

The growing impact of African women's and gender studies on African studies in general is evident from the annual conference programs of the African Studies Association, the largest international group of Africa-related scholars in the world, whose membership now includes many Africans and African Americans, Euro-Americans and Europeans. As the ASA moved from a predominantly white male membership in the 1960s to its present diversity, the proportion of sessions that had in their title women or gender increased markedly. In 1981, 8 percent fell into that category; in 1995 more than 11 percent, and by 2009 almost 13 percent, while the rise in the number of other panels with at least one paper on women or gender went from 5.6 percent in 1981 to 11.1 percent in 1995 and 8 percent in 2009, demonstrating the further integration of women and gender studies within African studies.[7] Lest we become too optimistic, however, Tiyambe Zeleza provides a corrective in his survey of African history textbooks' coverage of women and/or gender. In eight general African histories authored by Americans, Britons, and Africans of various nationalities, he found that none adequately represented women and that female authors were rare. The few that did include materials on African women confined their commentary mainly to titles of illustrations and infantilized women by classifying them with slaves and children.[8] In African slavery studies the omission of women as slaves and slave owners largely continues, even though most slaves kept in Africa were female.[9]

Unlike most African studies journals, the *Journal of African History* (*JAH*), the oldest Anglophone journal on the subject that began in 1960, has never published a special issue on African women or gender. The first two women, both white, to publish in it were Margaret Priestley in its first issue, and Diana Wylie seventeen years later. The first article focusing on an African woman was in 1975 by Joseph Miller, on Queen Nzinga of Matamba. Keletso Atkins became the first woman of color to publish an article in the *JAH* in 1986. Not until 1997 did the first article focusing on women or gender by an African scholar appear: Tshidiso Maloka's "Khomo Lia Oela: Canteens, Brothels and Labour Migrancy in Colonial Lesotho, 1900–40." By the mid-1990s articles in the *JAH* about women and/or gender were common, authored by promising and established female and male scholars: Linzi Manicom, Colleen Kriger, Barbara Cooper, Marc Epprecht, Jean Allman, Susan Geiger, Julia Wells, Lisa Lindsay, Sean Hanretta, Judith Byfield, Helen

Bradford, Thaddeus Sunseri, Lynn Thomas, and Laura Fair, for instance. Yet the complete omission of African women scholars remains disturbingly evident.

A few final observations shed some light on this omission beyond any obvious discrimination. Some Africa-based academics have had to contend with deteriorating economic and political conditions that have made it particularly difficult to be productive scholars. Women are especially affected because they retain primary responsibility for sustaining families. African scholars receive less funding for research due to neocolonial economies, and also teach heavier course loads than their U.S. and European counterparts. Nonetheless, there is now a new generation of African women historians adding ably to the work pioneered by scholars such as Bolanle Awe, Kamene Okonjo, Achola Pala, and Maud Muntemba.

A good way to identify research priorities is to look at international conferences. The chief subject of the UN End of the Decade for Women conference in Nairobi, Kenya, in 1985 was women and development, spurred largely by continuing poverty afflicting African women. Beyond Nairobi, where persistent divisions between developed and developing countries were reflected in differing agendas, the eighth International Interdisciplinary Congress for Women in Kampala, Uganda, in July 2002 featured work by many African scholars led by the Women's and Gender Studies Program at Makerere University. Among the 482 papers presented with African content, nearly a third focused on economic topics, while fewer discussed violence and warfare, including domestic violence and genital cutting; politics and power; or education, health, and the AIDS crisis. Fewer than 1 percent of the Congress papers discussed African women's history, that is, focused on chronologically located change in any topic concerning women and gender. Does this distribution of topics represent a valid ranking of priorities for historical studies of African women and gender at present, and if so, for whom?

Politics on the Agenda: Current Historical
Studies of African Women and Gender

A promising literature on women's and gender history is developing in many of the fifty-five countries usually classified as African, including North Africa.[10] Anglophone countries with the most historical studies of women and gender include Nigeria, Kenya, South Africa, and Ghana, with promising progress coming from Lesotho, Uganda, and Botswana. Nigeria has the most elaborated historiography, to the point that Nkparom C. Ejituwu has done a regional historiographical survey of works on women and gender in Rivers and Bayelsa states in southeastern Nigeria, and Christopher E. Ukhun has edited *Critical Gender Discourse in Africa*.[11] In the latter volume Ayodele Ogundipe and Ukhun critique the buzzword "empowerment" of women haunting development circles and dismantle the moral justifications for female genital cutting. Francophone and Luzophone literature seems less developed, perhaps a casualty of available sources. Libya, Madagascar and other island nations, and Angola have produced comparatively little material. In this chapter instead of proceeding geographically or by nation, I will discuss the literature topically and will prioritize book-length efforts, including edited collections (a strong tradition in African women's/gender studies), especially those dating after 1992, when the newer trends emerged along with more historical engagement by African women scholars.

A random sample of historical works on African women and gender quickly illustrates that historians' research priorities were not consonant with the economic focus of the Kampala Congress. Instead, many writing history were concerned with politics and related topics like women's organizations, women's rights, and the law.[12] The political agenda set initially by African women scholars, with strong contributions by African American women scholars, has become dominant.[13] *Sisterhood, Feminisms and Power from Africa to the Diaspora*, edited by Obioma Nnaemeka, came out of the first Women of Africa and the African Diaspora (WAAD) conference in 1992, and is widely read.[14] Eva Evers Rosander edited a volume of papers given at a 1993 conference in Cameroon, *Transforming Female Identities: Women's Organizational Forms in West Africa*.[15] Politics, including feminisms and womanism, are at the core of both collections.

In 1997 Gwendolyn Mikell edited *African Feminism: The Politics of Survival in Sub-Saharan Africa*. Her introduction summarizes the different goals of Eurocentered or "Western" feminism and "African" feminism.

> African feminism owes its origins to different dynamics than those that generated Western feminism. It has largely been shaped by African women's resistance to Western hegemony and its legacy within African culture.... [T]he slowly emerging African feminism is distinctly heterosexual, pro-natal, and concerned with many "bread, butter, culture and power" issues. Until recently, the reference points for Western feminists and African women activists have been totally different, because Western women were emphasizing individual female autonomy, while African women have been emphasizing culturally linked forms of public participation.... African feminism has been the direct outcome of women's responses to political leaders ... [who] have retaliated on both symbolic

and explicit levels to recent female self-assertions.., [which] has pushed women toward greater boldness in addressing the economic and political elements that... affect their status in societies that have distinct cultural traditions and historical experiences.[16]

Almost half of *African Feminism*'s contributors are African women scholars. It focuses on family law, economic change, and political and economic crises and marked the transition from the early focus on political economy to scholarship emphasizing African women's agency and activism. In the volumes cited above, 58 percent of the thirty-two contributors are African, including four men.

A later volume edited by Valentine Moghadam, *From Patriarchy to Empowerment*, followed a 2002 conference focusing on North African and Middle Eastern women's political organizing; economic, social, and cultural participation; violence against women; peace and war; and women's rights.[17] This book demonstrates the geographical spread of interdisciplinary politicizing of African women's and gender history.

African Women's Diverse Roles in Precolonial, Colonial, and Current Politics

Literature before the 1990s on African women's precolonial political participation disagreed about the extent of their authority. Kamene Okonjo, Judith Van Allen, and others laid out a pattern of separate women's and men's authority structures, sometimes buttressed by substantial trading activities. West Africa near or on the coast, Igboland, the Yoruba polities, and other areas had dual-sex systems (Okonjo's term).[18] In 1984 in *Sharing the Same Bowl* I argued that among the precolonial Ga on the Gold Coast, age was more important than gender in determining who had authority.[19] Eugenia Herbert concurred in 1993 in her study of ironworking in African societies.[20] More recently, Oyěwùmí declared that age was more important than gender in determining power and authority in precolonial Africa as a whole and that precolonial elite Yoruba women had substantial power.[21] Dual-sex systems facilitated women organizing and leading revolts against colonial authority, sometimes against male collaborators, as with Igbo "warrant chiefs" who did not exist in the acephalous precolonial polity. The 1929 Igbo Women's War symbolized women's resistance to the loss of female power and authority under colonialism. This view superseded that of African women as universal victims or invisible.

Subsequent debate is more nuanced. While it is generally agreed that colonialism deprived women of political power, more research has elaborated on both the pervasiveness of women with power precolonially and that in many areas women were viewed as men's property and thus had little political power. In *When Men and Women Mattered*, Onaiwu Ogbomo contends that precolonial matriarchy existed in some areas of Nigeria, for example in Owan and with the queens of Daura circa 1000 C.E., but that it was overthrown by patriarchy in West Africa. Ogbomo demonstrates the consequences of the precolonial abandonment of matrilocality for women, and that matrilinearity ended up by being a disadvantage for women when an all-male governing structure developed precolonially and men used accusations of witchcraft as a social control mechanism.[22]

Emmanuel Konde in *African Women and Politics* focuses on late colonial and current politics in Cameroon, but a section entitled "Traditional Politics" documents a loss of power precolonially for women leaders of the Bavek, contrasted with the enduring dual-sex systems of the Bamileke and Bamoun.[23] He concludes that the very separateness of gender roles "gave men the upper hand," despite some women having direct and indirect political influence. These works critically reexamine women's precolonial formal and informal power and authority. Previous scholarship in some cases may have been too sanguine if even places like Cameroon, which had colonial protests by women in the form of *Anlu*, demonstrated a loss of power precolonially for women.

After my Ghanian research I still shared Oyĕwùmí's universalizing tendency, but my Kenyan research did not support it. Because Nairobi-area market women and agricultural workers staged a large colonial protest in 1922 (the Harry Thuku demonstration), I searched for evidence that these women had precolonial antecedents and authority for their actions, only to find that often these women were considered men's property.[24] It is not safe, then, to generalize even geographically about women's power in precolonial times; each situation warrants careful attention before drawing conclusions, even though the impact of the colonizers' restrictive Victorian notions on African women's gender roles is evident.

If the general picture is mixed, we now have available more biographies of precolonial African women leaders. Compensatory African women's history now includes, for instance, Flora Edouwaye S. Kaplan's edited *Queens, Queen Mothers, Priestesses, and Power*, a fine example of historical anthropology, which offers new perspectives on the often mystified category of the West African "queen mother" on market queens, and on the political mobility of female slaves.[25]

Studies by Edna Bay and Heidi Nast also address female slaves' upward political mobility. Bay's *Wives of the Leopard* chronicles the epigrammatic example of precolonial dual-sex authority in the Dahomean kingdom that employed doubling, or mirroring even by gender, the positions of persons in authority.[26] Women's power peaked in the mid-eighteenth century with co-rulership of the kingdom, but declined in the nineteenth century before the imposition of formal colonial rule. Nast in *Concubines and Power* also employed archival and oral sources, but as a geographer she examined spatial relationships to delineate the world of Kano royal concubines, who at times exercised real power and facilitated politically useful cross-cultural and territorial linkages.[27] Nast historicizes a category of women, previously essentialized in Western thought for their sexuality, as other slave and harem women are, by understanding their agency and political and economic value.

Biographies of women who became chiefs under colonial rule, led resistance to colonialism, and exercise current political leadership add new perspectives to the literature. Mary Wanyoike chronicles the rise and fall of Wangu wa Makeri, the only woman appointed a colonial "chief" in Kenya.[28] Nwando Achebe's *The Female King of Colonial Nigeria: Ahebi Ugbabe* uses oral sources to elaborate on the symbolic, ritual, and political roles of the only Nigerian woman appointed a colonial "chief."[29] These women problematize the construct of African women's powerlessness created by colonial rule, even as their exceptional status reinforces it.

Cheryl Johnson-Odim and Nina Emma Mba documented the life of Funmilayo Ransome-Kuti, one of the most prominent women leaders of the 1940s to 1970s, a suffragist, international activist, and the first woman to run for federal office in independent Nigeria.[30] Of equal interest is Wambui Waiyaki Otieno's life history, *Mau Mau's Daughter*.[31] Daughter of a Kikuyu chief who resisted British colonial rule and was murdered for it, Wambui Otieno became a guerrilla fighter for the Land and Resistance Army, and as a widow she resisted her husband's relatives' efforts to bury him on lineage land and disinherit her and their children. Micere Mugo's sapient piece critiquing hostile representations of Mau Mau women fighters also contributes to these biographical studies. She explores the distortions imposed by the fighters' own self-silencing as well as by colonizer representations, and compares their experiences to those of Zimbabwean ZANLA women fighters.[32] Recent autobiographical accounts by prominent women political figures, including those by Ugandan Miria Matembe, Liberian President Ellen Johnson Sirleaf, and South African Mamphela Ramphele, have added important dimensions to our understanding of African politics.[33]

Works about precolonial and colonial Lesotho form a useful example of the gendering of a national history by scholars such as Mary Nombuela Ntabeni, L. B. B. J. Machobane, and Marc Epprecht. Ntabeni looks at the negative consequences for ordinary Lesotho women of the war effort forced on them by British involvement in World War II, while Machobane documents the marital dynastic politics of the nation's founder, Moshoeshoe I, and their consequences for the Lesotho princess, Senate, and her son. Marc Epprecht offers an unromanticized take on the influential female regent Mantsebo and considers other women as agents in the history of Lesotho's gendered politics and economy.[34] In nearby Botswana, Yonah Hisbon Matemba's comparable study situates the recent appointment of female chiefs in Botswana in the precolonial past, when royal women could be quite influential.[35]

Elsewhere in Africa the political agenda continues with Elizabeth Schmidt's study of the changing role of women and gender in Guinean nationalist politics in the 1940s and 1950s, especially the Rassemblement Démocratique Africain, which work represents more than a geographical shift from her previous economic focus that reflected earlier trends.[36]

David Schoenbrun's *A Green Place, A Good Place* stands out for its creative interdisciplinary methodology drawn from archaeology, comparative and historical linguistics, environmental studies, ethnography, and women's studies. It examines political, social, and economic changes between 800 and 1500 C.E. in the Great Lakes region of Africa, without reference to contemporary borders established by colonialism.[37] While his discussions of women and gender remain speculative and are often general, he does consider the varying positions of the "queen mother," and is careful not to use the term "gender" as code for "women," since he also examines the masculinizing of power.

Other works of compensatory history include *Women in South African History*.[38] A third of its fifteen contributors are women of color. The volume examines identity alongside histories exploring women's activism in various venues such as work/unions, political uprisings, housing demolition, precolonial leadership, and peace and war. Finally, Heidi Gengenbach's "Naming the Past in a 'Scattered' Land" considers how changing women's self-naming practices during colonialism in Mozambique merged into a study of changing identities, the subject of this chapter's next section.[39]

Gender Identity, Sexuality, and the Politicizing
of Women's Roles: Women Organizing

With its focus on African perceptions and creative interpretations of colonial intents, representations of African women, and the reconfiguration and contestation of power, *Women in African Colonial Histories* edited by Jean Allman, Susan Geiger, and Nakanyike Musisi faithfully reflects and furthers contemporary historiographical trends. Including articles considering Buganda queen mothers' losing power under colonialism, marital power shifts among colonial Asante, southeastern Nigerian women's discourses about the Women's War of 1929, and female guerrilla fighters in Zimbabwe's liberation struggle,[40] it bears comparison to *Deep Histories*, a collection which also considers issues of representation and pays particular attention to ideologies of domesticity.[41] Lisa Lindsay's work on Nigerian railway workers examines the colonial creation of domesticity as well, but in the context of the remaking of masculinity.[42]

Studying slavery in gendered perspectives has added to the literature in evocative ways. In *Liberating the Family?* Pamela Scully moves away from more common economistic approaches to this topic. She contends:

> British slave emancipation reconfigured the relations between men and women, and individual and society ... because emancipation implied ... that slaves would be free to live as they pleased, that claims regarding the legitimacy of specific family, labor, gender, and sexual relations became central to the struggle by various colonial groups to shape post-emancipation society. For government officials the linkage of political economy to questions of cultural reproduction became a crucial component of the construction of colonial society in the mid-nineteenth century Cape colony.... The history of the ending of Cape slavery is inextricably entwined with a history of identity, or more accurately, with histories of identification [as freedpersons] ... situate[d] themselves along multiple and sometimes antithetical axes in relation to one another.[43]

This complicating of emancipation history rests upon cardinal principles of American women's history: a refusal to essentialize the subjects; close attention paid to cultural production and reproduction and gender employed as a constructed category; a reliance upon interdisciplinarity; and a discussion of identities. In this case freedwomen joined a deeply patriarchal white settler-dominated society in which all women were jural minors, and where the state allocated to itself the right to exercise strict control over slave and freed families and over women's sexuality. It promoted patriarchal families to assure a subordinate stable class of low-skilled workers defined by race.[44]

Similarities between the experiences of South African and U.S. blacks have prompted two excellent comparative volumes on black women's activism: *Boycotts, Buses and Passes*,[45] and *Stepping Forward*.[46] The latter includes perspectives from a number of settler colonies, including Liberia and Sierra Leone, but focuses on South Africa and the U.S. In it Sylvia

Ojukutu-Macauley considers how British colonial education policy in the nineteenth and twentieth centuries helped create gender inequality in Sierra Leone, and Sean Redding delineates gender tensions in the 1930s Transkei that surfaced in witchcraft accusations, a form of social control of women by (absent) men.[47]

The history of South African women's activism has moved beyond the hagiographic, although the moving photo essay *Women of South Africa: Their Fight for Freedom*[48] upholds that fine tradition pioneered by Ernest Cole in *House of Bondage*.[49] Anne Kelk Mager's *Gender and the Making of a South African Bantustan* explores the gendered history of a colonized space, the Ciskei, and how one of the political consequences of its creation was raised consciousness among its residents.[50] Moving to more current struggles, scholars have documented women's roles in the African National Congress (ANC) and South African constitution-making. The journal *Feminist Studies* devoted a special issue to contemporary South Africa: women's participation, gender representation, AIDS, masculinity, and women's poetry and art. Scholars consider women's organizing in South Africa and the problems of South Africa's Commission on Gender Equality and the difference between its rhetoric and the reality of the late 1990s.[51]

One of the best works on recent history and questions of identity is Tabitha Kanogo's *African Womanhood in Colonial Kenya 1900-1950*. Kanogo delineates shifts in Kenyan women's identity connected to socioeconomic controls imposed by colonial rulers and their local representatives vis-à-vis such central institutions as bridewealth, motherhood, clitoridectomy/initiation, laws, and marriage.

> By following the effects of the all-pervasive ideological shifts that colonialism produced in the lives of women, the study investigates the diverse ways in which a woman's personhood was enhanced, diminished, or placed in ambiguous predicaments by the consequences, intended and unintended, of colonial rule as administered by both the colonizers and the colonized.
>
> The study thus tries to historicize the reworkings of women's lives under colonial rule. The transformations that resulted from these reworkings involved the negotiation and redefinition of the meaning of individual liberties and of women's agency, along with the reconceptualization of kinship relations and of community.[52]

For example, Kanogo delineates the broader socioeconomic context for the controversial issue of female initiation/clitoridectomy, and explains why it became a highly charged political issue. "The abandonment of clitoridectomy put [procreation and economic production] in jeopardy."[53] Her study, with its interests in sexuality, violence, and the medicalization of maternity, relies largely on written records, which might privilege colonial ideology over local women's history, but she also derived much from oral sources.

Even though the eminent scholar, poet, and essayist Ifi Amadiume's formal training was as a social anthropologist, she frequently deals with historical subjects. Whereas in her first book *Male Daughters, Female Husbands*,[54] she examined genderbending, including woman-to-woman marriage among the Igbo, in *Re-Inventing Africa*[55] she critiqued the discipline of anthropology as imperialist and imbued with false notions of African women as passive, homebound members of nuclear families, who remain dominated by the legacy of a vicious colonial past and neocolonial present. In contrast, she called for a new social history recognizing the hidden "matriarchal" history of powerful African women.

In her 2000 work *Daughters of the Goddess*, which considers Nigerian women organizing, Amadiume produced yet another influential work that helped set the political agenda. She pays particular attention to the influences of Christianity and organizations like the Y.W.C.A., analyzes women's class-based roles in the reproduction of class relations, and critically considers such issues as organizational and government corruption and media images of women.[56] The book's title derives from what Amadiume sees as the struggle among women's groups between those dominated by grassroots African daughters of the goddess versus the elite, self-promoting daughters of imperialism who act only in their own class interest. Amadiume's endorsement of strong democratic state institutions demonstrates that African women's and gender history is always politically engaged.

Amadiume's work on genderbending in Africa deals largely with the positional aspect of African gender roles. Before colonial rule many African societies demonstrated that women could be classificatory males, female husbands, or rulers with all the prerogatives these roles entailed. Nineteenth-century European binary categories regarding proper female and male attire were sharply contested by contact with African societies such as the Tuareg, where young men wore long hair and makeup and were courted by women.

Some newer studies regarding sexuality, especially homosexuality, explore facets that for some African scholars are controversial and irrelevant to an African research agenda.[57] The collection *Boy-Wives and Female Husbands* intentionally inverts Amadiume's title and includes historical articles which analyze colonial writers' observations of African behavior.[58] Marc Epprecht's *Heterosexual Africa?* explores the genesis and progress of the false notion that Africans were/are only heterosexual.[59] Epprecht finds homosexual practices frequently coexisting with a high valuing of heterosexual marriage and reproduction. This book exposes inaccurate Western notions about African sexualities, and also analyzes literary and filmic representations of homosexuality by Africans, which portray bisexual practices rather than an established gay lifestyle centering around sexual preference. Sexual preference is therefore not necessarily connected to lifestyle, hence identity, in Africa, a finding commensurate with the work of anthropologist Rudolf Gaudio.[60]

Another collection, *Re-Thinking Sexualities in Africa* edited by Signe Arnfred, focuses on female sexualities, with some attention to masculinity.[61] With almost half of the articles by African women scholars, it represents the most attention devoted to the topic with significant African input (only one contributor to the *Boy-Wives* collection is African). Contributors deal with representation, diversity in sexual practices, HIV, female genital cutting, child bearing, prostitution, masculinity, feminist theory, and sexuality. Some observed widespread silence and silencing on the subject of sexuality. For example, anthropologist Heike Becker provides a historical perspective, asserting that there was no "break between the colonial past and the postcolonial present" in the continuance of negative representations of African sexuality. Becker observes:

> Some vocal Namibian feminist activists . . . have begun in the process of reclaiming their "roots" to question the hegemonic colonial assertions of a highly-patriarchal Owambo past. . . . The concurrence of silence and . . . public presence relates to past tensions of colonialism as well as current multiple identities in the postcolonial Namibian society.[62]

Issues of representation, as in Becker's work, are now common in much historical writing including Timothy Burke's, which looks at those surrounding consumption. In *Lifebuoy Men, Lux Women* he bridges the gap between older studies of political economy and the more recent focus on representation by considering the commodification of gender categories, the extension of colonial hygiene concerns into postindependence marketing by multinational corporations, consumption patterns, and the "commodity culture" of postliberation Zimbabwe. He demonstrates

> how white attitudes toward black bodies inspired institutions that remade practices of the body, domesticity, and manners. The bodily racism of settler society constantly lurked about the edges of the lives of those Africans whose social aspirations were most identified with "modernity," but

the shifting and loosely defined "hygienic ideals" of nineteenth-century Zimbabwean cultures also continuously reinvented and reproduced themselves in everyday life during the twentieth century.... Scholarly studies of the making of the colonial political economy are correct to identify the pivotal role of "new needs" in racial capitalism and settler rule.[63]

In *Creating the New Egyptian Woman*, Mona Russell explores twentieth-century urban consumption in Cairo among elite and middle-class women, who were exposed to Western consumer goods and ideology. She considers advertising and consumer culture, class differentiation, and women's formal education. She documents resistance to the influx of European goods as a nationalist reaction, concluding:

> Consumption of national goods... helped women to contribute to the larger effort of the country. Their identity was vested in the home and the marriage they created. By the same token, the economic boycott, or nonconsumption of British goods, was an active demonstration of their self-identification as Egyptian citizens.[64]

Shifting identities as they relate to the history of African dress have also drawn scholarly interest. *Fashioning Africa: Power and the Politics of Dress* is emblematic of the politicizing trend in addressing changing identity, nationalism, gender relations, sexuality, and globalization, without, however, input by Africa-based contributors.[65] Unfortunately, African scholars also played no role in *Clothing and Difference,* which collection has several pieces devoted to women in particular. Misty Bastian emphasizes the connections between cross-dressing and power, observing when 1980s Onitsha Igbo young women dressed as authoritative males, that

> the Nigerian reality of modernity that underlies these practices should be recognized [as] a thoroughly patriarchal one with decreasing space for female participation and a decreasing respect for female value. The dress of men is seen as the dress of power in southeastern Nigeria.[66]

Issues of visual representation of African women have also attracted scholars, especially in the case of Sara Baartman, the "Hottentot Venus," whose body became a circus display and whose bones were displayed in museums despite her expressed wish in early nineteenth-century Britain and France.[67] Fatima Fall finds more positive representations of African women in the Centre de recherches et de documentation du Senegal museum in

Saint Louis, a suburb of Dakar.⁶⁸ She describes the prominence and respect accorded Senegalese women in its exhibitions and observes its careful reinvention of women not as "traditional" but as important historical actors.

Violence and Control of Women and Their Bodies

One reason for the activist trend in African women's and gender history is because the subject embroils historians in contentious issues demanding political, social, and economic solutions. For instance, in the Kenya National Archives studying Nairobi area women's trade, I found evidence of colonial repressive measures taken against urban traders, while on the streets I was threatened with arrest for interviewing traders selling illegally and witnessed routinized extortion and arrests of women traders by police. It was obvious that colonial persecution of street traders continued and that addressing the neocolonial politics of persecution of traders was imperative.

Studying African women's and gender history reveals continentwide similarities regarding social control of women, not because patriarchy is universal but rather because of the unities of colonial policies, whatever the European power involved. The work of several scholars, including Kanogo and myself on Kenya, shows how colonial and colonized authorities instituted controls over women's mobility and that female traders and rebellious girls regularly contravened them. White settler colonies made great efforts to control women and their bodies. Recent works on Zimbabwe (Southern Rhodesia), Kenya, Swaziland, and South Africa⁶⁹ consider state intervention over women's bodies and physical mobility and redefinition of marriage and customary laws to disadvantage women. For instance, Lynette Jackson focused on Southern Rhodesian colonial controls over women's physical mobility and attendant compulsory venereal disease physical examinations imposed on African women urban and mine migrants.⁷⁰

Lynn Thomas's *Politics of the Womb* examines the close relationship between struggles over biological reproduction and the colonial and early postcolonial discursive construction of proper moral and political order in Meru. The book critiques the unswerving application of Foucault's idea of "bio-power" as a paradigm relevant to Africa but does find the Foucauldian notion of the body as a site of regulation and resistance relevant. Thomas concludes by setting her subject within contemporary gender politics: "In the twenty-first century... we need to understand how reproductive and sexual politics in Africa and elsewhere encompass struggles to accumulate material resources and fulfill moral ambitions, struggles that bind the global to the local."⁷¹

Paradoxically, in settler colonies colonial interventions sometimes offered women and girls new ways of exerting autonomy, while in areas where women's precolonial autonomy was already well established it was often the gerontocratic authority of senior women that was challenged, not just by the colonial authorities, but also by junior women. Caution is therefore imperative lest we overgeneralize about African women's history.

Nancy Rose Hunt in *A Colonial Lexicon of Birth* furthers the study of colonial medicine and women's bodies by examining the fetishized practices of colonial medicalized childbirth. Her focus is mainly discursive, with intense examinations of the local meanings and uses of botanical subjects, colonial objects, and representations. She also includes and analyzes her own fieldwork experiences.[72]

The vexed issue of African female genital cutting (FGC), an obsession within American feminist perspectives on African women, and often the only subject concerning African women taught in women's studies courses, has not generally been historicized. Instead it is described as "traditional," even though it is clear that FGC has a historical as well as a cultural context.[73] In our coedited collection *Transnational Sisterhood and Genital Cutting*, Stanlie James and I together with our contributors analyzed U.S. rhetoric surrounding FGC that reduces: Africa to one ahistorical place; all African women to the genitally mutilated woman; and all forms of genital cutting, no matter how minor, to the most severe, infibulation.[74] Ignorance of Africa's cultural and historical diversity is all too common, along with reluctance to respect African women's voices and leadership, scholarly or not. Both need remedying if progress on eradicating harmful procedures is to be made.

Violence and women, a topic prioritized at Kampala, is also an increasing focus of historical studies, but not always in the way featured in U.S. history. The discussion has not confined itself to African women as victims, but includes a growing literature on Dahomean women warriors and female guerrilla fighters in the Zimbabwe liberation war, while Muammar Khaddafi's crack bodyguard troops were female.[75] For instance, Josephine Nhongo-Simbanegavi's *Women and ZANLA in Zimbabwe's Liberation War*, enriched by materials from the ZANLA archives, takes a critical look at the much vaunted transformational power of women's strong role in fighting the Zimbabwe liberation war and concludes that, due to entrenched patriarchal values and widespread violence exercised against female participants, there was no enduring advance for women as a result of the war.[76] Much violence has been attributed to African women through witchcraft accusations, while throughout the colonial and independent periods senior African women often participate/d in demonstrations that have inflicted public shaming and sometimes property damage on men accused of antisocial behavior, such as: the Igbo Women's War; Anlu; the Thuku demonstration mentioned above; Takembeng in Cameroon;[77] as well as recent Chevron occupations in southern Nigeria. However, the authorities have normally perpetrated more violence against women than vice versa.

Violence against women began to receive much attention in the late 1990s. *What Women Do in Wartime*[78] deals primarily with women as survivors of warfare, not as combatants. The focus on past conflicts makes most of the pieces historical by implication. In *Gender Violence in Africa* December Green attempted an overview of different forms of violence against women, some of it historicized by analysis of past situations.[79] Studies also analyze whites' black peril fears of rape of white women by black men in the context of false accusations, and the colonial atmosphere conducive to South African white men raping black women.[80]

In some areas domestic violence was and is so pervasive that it goes unnoticed, as evidenced in Kenya in *Trouble Showed the Way* and *We Only Come Here to Struggle*, the life history of Berida Ndambuki I coauthored with her.[81] Berida described stunning incidents, including one in which her grandfather beat to death his daughter, who had gotten pregnant out of wedlock and refused to marry the husband selected for her. Life histories make good sources for recent history, and can contribute to historicizing violence against women.[82]

The Economics of the Political

The economizing trend of the 1980s that focused on women's work has taken new forms that conform to current trends. In 1994 *Cutting Down Trees: Gender, Nutrition, and Agricultural Change in the Northern Province of Zambia, 1890–1990*, Henrietta Moore and Megan Vaughan pioneered new modes of looking at the colonial construction of ecological knowledge, the gender politics of food and development, labor migration, land use, and changing household labor for rural women.[83] Miriam Goheen's 1996 work, *Men Own the Fields, Women Own the Crops: Gender and Power in the Cameroon Grassfields*, is primarily concerned with new forms of male hegemonic gender stratification that encourage pushback from ordinary young women who stay single and professional women who fight discrimination and violence against women. Goheen argues that women in the 1990s sharply contested new forms of male control intended to preserve men's power and status that rested mainly on control over women's productive and reproductive labor.[84] Grace Bantebya's and Marjorie Keniston McIntosh's history of Ugandan women's work focuses on the impact of changing ideology and education of women on women's work lives, including the British colonial "domestication of women" project.[85]

Commodity-centered histories respectively by Judith Byfield and myself trace both gendered symbolic and material aspects of women's production and trade in the indigo cloth-dying *adire* industry in Nigeria, and the dried staples trade in central Kenya.[86] There are substantial differences in the possibilities for women's empowerment through trade between areas where women were not jural minors and where they have been men's property, although a key element in both is the usual absence of communal property in marriage. Kathleen Sheldon looks at the impacts of changes in women's work imposed by urban garment factories, missionary education, and FRELIMO, the ruling party which led the armed resistance movement that achieved independence. Structural adjustment (SAPs), World Bank-mandated reforms, then reduced funding for social services, causing the usual privations for women.[87]

Barbara Cooper's *Marriage in Maradi*[88] and Kenda Mutongi's *Worries of the Heart*[89] share not only misleading titles but also a focus on community economics. Cooper looks at how the emancipation of slaves increased labor demands on both free and formerly enslaved women and considers women's property rights in relation to women's empowerment by French colonial enforcement of Maliki Islamic laws. She emphasizes the agency of rural Nigérien women who insisted on public participation in village-level decision making and looks at the positive implications of their proliferation of grassroots women's organizations.[90]

Kenda Mutongi studies land and inheritance rights, drought and famine, the impact of gold mining, and rising bridewealth in Maragoli in western Kenya. She begins with the impact of U.S. evangelical Quaker missionaries on local people before World War I and the effect of the increasing materialism of the mini–gold rush furthered by the missionaries. Mutongi documents the trend in the 1940s for young persons of both sexes to escape family control, thus producing the widows' "worries of the heart." Older women too became less tolerant of physical abuse by husbands, and were more likely to divorce and turn to colonial courts to air their complaints. She ends by looking at the contemporary political implications of her findings.

Mutongi's conclusion reflects her informants' forcing her to recognize, despite her prior assumptions about the negative effects of colonial rule, that in some ways it was better for Maragoli women than the greed, corruption, and incompetence of Kenyan neocolonialists. Both Cooper and Mutongi, then, document both negative and positive effects of colonialism on women, and Mutongi challenges her own assumptions—as I do when informants' priorities influence redesign of my research. Many scholars, but especially those engaged in oral history, must, as Mutongi observes, question their own biases and assumptions in order to be faithful to their subjects' voices and perspectives.

Gendering Symbolic Categories: Religion

A leading trend in African women's and gender history is scholarship focused on religion, omitted from many earlier studies and which in precolonial Africa was inextricably imbricated with politics. However, indigenous African religions have received less attention in the literature, which focuses mainly on Christianity and Islam.[91] Many authors mentioned above have focused on the "domestication" of women—how women's Christian mission education in Africa distorted and/or reinforced male dominance in attempting to create "housewives." Anthropologist Dorothy Hodgson in *The Church of Women* provides yet another example of unintended consequences and a nuanced description of the interaction of Christianity and indigenous religion when Catholic Spiritan missionaries in Tanzania began converting Maasai men, but by the mid-twentieth century, and not by design, attracted mostly Maasai women. Hodgson explains the shift in reference to gendered religious categories:

> Conversion was perceived as a rupture and threat to "being Maasai men," . . . [while] missionary interventions complemented and expanded the spiritual dimension of female roles in Maasailand . . . [which provided] women with an expanded spiritual platform . . . [that] enabled women to reaffirm and reinforce their claims to spiritual and moral superiority in opposition to the increasingly material interests of men.[92]

Maasai women's belief in their special relationship with their deity, Eng'ai, entailing a prophetic tradition, caused them to "cast men's historical usurpation of political and economic power [enabled by colonialism] as not just an affront to the privileges of Maasai women, but to the precepts and moral vision of Eng'ai."[93] Also relevant here is Nwando Achebe's study of Igbo women's prophetic traditions, which examines the interplay of charisma and the influence of absolutist Christian traditions in changing the pantheon permanently.[94]

Mirijke Steegstra considers missionaries' impact and ideas about gender and sexuality among the Krobo of the Gold Coast in the nineteenth century. The Basel Mission Society missionaries sought to replace female *dipo* initiation rites with Christian education, creating a situation similar to the frequently analyzed 1920s Scottish Mission girls' initiation rites crisis in central Kenya, which helped produce the Kikuyu independent schools' movement. The latter has received more attention because the *irua* initiation rites involved clitoridectomy.⁹⁵

If Hodgson's work shows how some African women could take advantage of certain Christian interventions, like mission education, and Achebe elaborates on the politico-religious space available to women during colonial rule, the most thorough revision of African women's and gender history, I would suggest, comes from studies of women, gender, and Islam in North and sub-Saharan Africa. For example, Sondra Hale's 1997 study, *Gender Politics in Sudan: Islamism, Socialism, and the State,* pioneered the examination of women's reconstruction of Islamic identities, in this case in northern Sudan in the midst of a power struggle among state, political, and religious interest groups, while the Islamist state banned women's organizations. She found that, contravening stereotypes, a women's political culture could generate both defiance and resistance and modify men's expectations of women, even within a nationalist fundamentalist Islamic matrix.⁹⁶

Other studies of Islamic women are contextualized historically, although they are not necessarily works of conventional history. Some scholars pay primary attention to identity. Eva Evers Rosander's *Women in a Borderland: Managing Muslim Identity* looks at Soza women inhabiting the area of Morocco next to Spain. Their identities are partly constructed in opposition to Spanish culture and especially in relation to men, who uphold notions of family honor that in the past required them to defend it by fighting other men, but now beat female relatives deemed to have betrayed it. She chronicles shifts in symbolic identity expressed in women's clothing—the full coverage of the *jellab* has now become "traditional," and spending on bridewealth, big weddings, and pilgrimages to Mecca has inflated, while women's networks have widened.⁹⁷ In the end, she sees identity as historically and culturally contingent, and refuses to essentialize Soza women and men.

Julia Clancy-Smith looks at the shifting nature of identities in her study of Algeria, but from an etic viewpoint—how the changing goals of colonialism affected European representations of Algerian/Arab women, a subject with a long history pioneered by Malek Alloula and Frantz Fanon. Clancy-Smith argues that "the construction of French Algeria was as much the forging of a gaze—or a spectrum of gazes fixed upon Muslim women—as it was the assembling of mechanisms for political and economic control."⁹⁸

Many scholars' assessments of Muslim women's actions in growing Islamist fundamentalist movements are most definitely *histoire engagée,* politically focused, concerned with improving women's status by presenting a usable history to validate women's activism.⁹⁹ Adeline Masquelier analyzes the impact of Malam Awal's Sufi reformism on a small town in Niger, looking at the "forms that this project of Islamic reform has taken, its costs and consequences, as well as the possibilities it has generated for women seeking to embrace, or alternatively, resist, Awal's vision of Islam." Not surprisingly, she finds the record mixed: the reform gave women more access to divorce and education, a better understanding of their rights, and enhanced identification with Islam internationally. Yet it also restricted their mobility and economic activities and regulated their fertility. In the end, it raised their consciousness, their critical faculties, and their self-awareness, all of which enable women's agency.[100]

Linguist Ousseina Alidou's tour de force, *Engaging Modernity: Muslim Women and the Politics of Agency in Postcolonial Niger*, looks at how women's agency is shaped by religion, ethnicity, class, education, and citizenship. She emphasizes that the possibilities for agency are constrained by the larger society, while also arguing that modernity is possible without westernization, an unusual distinction.[101] Alidou examines various epistemological traditions related to women's education from Hausa poetry to French colonial education, from female *madrasas* to Niger's most prominent female educator, Malama A'ishatu. She traces changes in the political economy of education from the precolonial introduction of literacy and seclusion for Islamic women, to colonial times when the French marginalized women's oral literature and discriminated against girls in education and employment, to the postcolonial continuing lack of formal education for girls, discriminatory gender stereotyping in a sex-segregated labor market, and control over female sexuality, especially through early marriage. Alidou's interdisciplinarity, then, is seamless and engaging at every level.[102]

A recent collection, *New Perspectives on Islam in Senegal*, demonstrates the new importance of women's and gender analysis in African Islamic studies. Half the contributors are female, although none are African women, and considerations of women and gender are well integrated throughout. Aly Dramé's piece historicizes marriage's role in converting precolonial women to Islam as key to its spread, while Beth Buggenhagen analyzes the political and material economy of women's exchanges which furthered the success of the Muridiyya.[103] In sum, the perpetual mobility of Islam in West Africa has evoked much current creative historical work on women and gender.

Conclusion

What, then, has African women's and gender history contributed to contemporary historical discourses? First, the problematizing of assumed categories is pervasive. The literature has disproved the assumption that women were an oppressed category throughout history. It debunks the notion that all women fall into one category and that patriarchy is and was universal. It has also deconstructed the meanings of Islam for women beyond the stereotype of "victim," and injected nuance and agency into African women's precolonial, colonial, and contemporary lives.

A common misperception among those unacquainted with African women's and gender history is that colonialism liberated African women. If the first generation of African women's historians definitively disproved that, more recent studies have made generalization about colonialism's impact more difficult, demonstrating mixed impacts, none of them, however, involving "liberating" women. If some women did take advantage of new opportunities, all too often colonial-induced economic privations drove them, and colonial and colonized men tried to impede their journeys. Studies of colonial representations of African women's bodies, women's education, and consumerism have demonstrated the enforcement of colonizer stereotypes on African women, also in the neocolonial context. Newer studies have examined violent acts by, as well as against, women, in wartime and at home. Scholars have historically contextualized FGC and not always seen it as violence against women. This scholarship has politicized women's economic history and undercut old assumptions about universal patriarchy, masculinity, and religious authority. We have long known that Africa is not one place, but we now know that most categories of analysis require deconstruction where African women and gender are concerned.

The overarching focus of this literature is power. A generalized politicization of historical studies of women and gender is evident, where, no matter the subject, most works examined power and authority. Increasingly this literature emanates from African female and male scholars. Whereas in my 1985 survey 15.5 percent of the scholars whose work was mentioned were African women and 1.5 percent African men (58 percent were white women of various nationalities, 5.7 percent were African American women, and 19 percent white men), in this review 26.2 percent are African women and 16.3 percent are African men (38.3 percent are white women, 9.3 percent are African American women, and 9.3 percent white men).

With regard to Oyěwùmí's presumption that "Western" and "African" female scholars have different and conflicting agendas, this literature that politicizes African women's and gender history does not demonstrate such a division. To the contrary, oral historians, of whatever origin, showed themselves willing to reflect accurately their informants' priorities, even when that meant abandoning dearly held scholarly assumptions. The community of scholars described here, whose writings delineate African women's and gender history, include men and women. While redistributing the world's resources more equitably is beyond the capacities of scholarship alone, greater cooperation between African and Africanist scholars is evident. The activist concern that African women's and gender history be accessible and engaged has continued and contributed to a pragmatic shared outlook that helps to explain its politicization.

The deliberate focus on women's power and agency is not just a response to reactionary government policies regarding women, but also to harsh realities in African women's lives negatively impact by "development" projects designed unilaterally that impoverish women further and increase their labor obligations; persecution of women traders, miniskirt wearers, and prostitutes; and political exclusion and fundamentalist attacks on women's rights from proponents of indigenous religions, Christianity, and Islam. Governments around the world ignore the misery of women and children in refugee camps and exacerbate the daily drudgery of women's lives with practices and policies inimical to women's well-being. African women bear much of the responsibility for feeding their children but lack the authority and resources to protect their interests. They do most of the agricultural labor, but a gendered division of labor and profits withholds rewards from women for their work. Given these disabling realities, historians find themselves compellingly drawn to questions of power and powerlessness, hoping that one way to reforge African women's identities is to establish their history of empowerment (and disempowerment), as so many of the works cited here do.

Despite the unity in diversity among scholars revealed here regarding issues surrounding women's power, certain differences are also evident. Studies of sexuality and sexual preference do seem to reflect non-African agendas; for this reason the study of homosexuality in Africa is still mostly compensatory history, showing little evidence of being taken up by many Africans studying women's and gender history. In 1985 I noted the paucity of African women historians and outsiders' difficulties with handling issues of "subjective consciousness," whereupon Philomena Okeke riposted justly that I had ignored embedded relations of power that inhibited African women's scholarship.[104] In this survey I have tried to take relationships of power into consideration, both within and outside the continent. An irony shown in this review is that studies of women's identity formation have, with sterling exceptions such as Kanogo's work, largely been carried out by non-African scholars, suggesting either that this is a new area for African exploration or not a priority for many.

What gaps are there in the literature? Domestic violence against women could use more historicization. I found only one study of aging and gender (in Zambia) that was not historical.[105] Yet oral historians often rely heavily on "elders" memories for information, without analyzing possible changes in their identities or positions. This deserves more historical attention; the shift from age to gender as primary criteria for assigning power and authority has had a monumental impact on women.

Another gap is related to the identity of researchers. One of the desirable characteristics of any research, but especially that incorporating oral history, should be reflexivity. One form involves researchers situating themselves with respect to their subjects in terms of status, identity, and the nature of their interactions with the community/ies or individuals studied, and detailing their efforts to overcome barriers dividing them from their subjects. Equally important is scholarly reflexivity, when research results are made available to its subjects in a form that is readily absorbed, at a point where they can effect changes. The latter form of reflexivity insures that the language used is widely comprehensible and enriches the research findings. If, for instance, large-scale surveys are involved, researchers can select certain representative individuals to test and amend the findings.

In this survey I found that historians of African women and gender do not usually situate themselves with respect to their subjects. Mutongi, Achebe, Hunt, and Alidou are exceptions to this rule, while as a white middle-class Midwestern American I have tried to acknowledge and account for any bias due to my subject position. There was also very little evidence of the second form of reflexivity in which manuscripts are translated if necessary into local languages and shared with the subjects of the research, giving them editorial authority. Having insufficient time and funds to return to a fieldwork site sometimes impedes this accomplishment. More common was the field practice of discussing points of disagreement among informants.

We all share the responsibility of situating ourselves with regard to the subjects of our research. It is time to problematize both insider and outsider as totalizing categories and reveal the particularities of the scholar's position not only by race and nationality but also by class, residence while doing research, language facility, and methods of research. Considering how informants view the researcher is imperative to this analysis, and can be illuminating for both scholars and readers.

In the end, the development of the dynamic field of African women's and gender history continues to inform history in innovative ways by rethinking categories, with African women assuming their rightful role in its perpetuation.

NOTES

1. Claire C. Robertson, "Developing Economic Awareness: Changing Perspectives in Studies of African Women, 1976–1985," *Feminist Studies* 13, no. 1 (Spring 1987): 97–136.

See also "Women's Importance in African Slave Systems," in *Women and Slavery in Africa*, eds. Claire C. Robertson and Martin A. Klein (Madison: University of Wisconsin Press, 1983), 3–25.

2. Oyèrónké Oyěwùmí, *The Invention of Women: Making an African Sense of Western Gender Discourses* (Minneapolis: University of Minnesota Press, 1997).
3. See works by Sandra Greene and Jan Vansina.
4. Gloria Marshall [later Niara Sudarkasa], "Women, Trade and the Yoruba Family," Ph.D. dissertation, University of Michigan, 1964.
5. Claire Cone Robertson, "A Socioeconomic History of Women and Class in Accra, Ghana," Ph.D. dissertation, University of Wisconsin, 1974.
6. Robertson, "Awareness." For early bibliography, see also the *Canadian Journal of African Studies*' special issue on women and gender: 22, no. 3 (1988).
7. Altogether the number of panels including material on women and gender studies rose from 9.1% to 25.9% in 1995, a high point, before leveling out at around 21% in 2009.
8. Paul Tiyambe Zeleza, "Gender Biases in African Historiography," in *African Gender Studies*, ed. Oyèrónké Oyěwùmí (New York: Palgrave Macmillan, 2005), 210, 232 n. 26.
9. David Northrup, ed., *The Atlantic Slave Trade* (New York: Houghton Mifflin, 2002). See Claire Robertson and Marsha Robinson, "Re-Modeling Slavery as If Women Mattered," in *Women and Slavery* (Athens: Ohio University Press, 2008), 253–83, for an analysis of why slavery literature and films ignore the experiences of women as slaves. Another work demonstrating an absence of African women in history and as authors is Joseph O. Vogel, ed., *Encyclopedia of Precolonial Africa: Archaeology, History, Languages, Cultures, and Environments* (London: Sage/AltaMira, 1997). In contrast, the authors in Susan Kent, ed., *Gender in African Prehistory* (Walnut Creek: AltaMira Press, 1998) prove that African archaeology can be informed by gendered perspectives.
10. Zeleza, "Gender Biases," 229 n. 5, discusses the racist roots that led to the division of North Africa from sub-Saharan "black" Africa.
11. Nkparom C. Ejituwu, "Towards a History of Niger Delta Women's Historiography," in *Women in Nigerian History: The Rivers and Bayelsa States Experience*, ed. N. C. Ejituwu and Amakievi O. I. Gabriel (Port Harcourt: Onyoma Research Publications, 2003), 103–20; Christopher E. Ukhun, ed., *Critical Gender Discourse in Africa* (Ibadan: Hope Publications, 2002).
12. See, for example, Johanna Bond, *Voices of African Women, Women's Rights in Ghana, Uganda and Tanzania* (Durham, N.C.: Carolina Academic Press, 2005); *Women and Law in West Africa: Gender Relations in the Family—A West African Perspective*, ed. Akua Kuenyehia (Accra: Yamens Press, 2003).
13. An earlier work that helped to set the agenda is Florence Abena Dolphyne, *The Emancipation of Women: An African Perspective* (Accra: Ghana Universities Press, 1991).
14. Trenton: Africa World Press, 1998.
15. Uppsala: Nordiska Afrikainstitutet, 1997.
16. Philadelphia: University of Pennsylvania Press, 1997, 4–5.
17. Subtitled *Women's Participation, Movements, and Rights in the Middle East, North Africa, and South Asia* (Syracuse: Syracuse University Press, 2007).
18. Kamene Okonjo, "The Dual Sex Political System in Operation: Igbo Women and Community Politics in Midwestern Nigeria," in *Women in Africa*, ed. Nancy Hafkin and Edna Bay (Stanford: Stanford University Press, 1974), 45–58.
19. Bloomington: Indiana University Press, 1984.
20. *Iron, Gender, and Power: Rituals of Transformation in African Societies* (Bloomington: Indiana University Press, 1993).

21. *Invention*.
22. Flexon Mizinga made the same point with regard to the history of Zambian matriliny under colonialism in "Marriage and Bridewealth in a Matrilineal Society: The Case of the Tonga of Southern Zambia, 1900–1996," *African Economic History* 28 (2000): 53–87, while Liazzat Bonate, "Matriliny, Islam and Gender in Northern Mozambique," *Journal of Religion in Africa* 36, no. 2 (2006): 139–64, chronicles the persistence of matriliny despite the incursions of Islam and colonial rule that furthered patriliny.
23. Subtitled *Knowledge, Gender, and Power in Male-Dominated Cameroon* (Lewiston, N.Y.: Edwin Mellen, 2005). Using "traditional" to describe the African past remains a problem besetting African history, implying a timeless African past, collapsing all of history into a vague ahistorical time before colonialism, and denying that any changes occurred in thousands of years of human experience on the continent. Sometimes even colonial-influenced practices are interpreted as "traditional" and deemed the source of women's current problems. See, for instance, Cikuru Batumike, *Femmes du Congo-Kinshasa* (Paris: l'Harmattan, 2009), and contributions by Patrice Bigombe Logo and Elise-Henriette Bikie, and Hussaina J. Abdullah and Ibrahim Hamza to *Women and Land in Africa: Culture, Religion and Realizing Women's Rights*, ed. L. Muthoni Wanyeki (London: Zed, 2003).
24. *Trouble Showed the Way: Women, Men and Trade in the Nairobi Area, 1890–1990* (Bloomington: Indiana University Press, 1997).
25. Subtitled *Case Studies in African Gender* (New York: New York Academy of Sciences, 1997).
26. Subtitled *Gender, Politics, in the Kingdom of Dahomey* (Charlottesville: University of Virginia Press, 1998).
27. Subtitled *Five Hundred Years in a Northern Nigerian Palace* (Minneapolis: University of Minnesota Press, 2005).
28. *Wangu wa Makeri* (Nairobi: East African Educational Publishers, 2002).
29. Bloomington: Indiana University Press, 2010.
30. *For Women and the Nation: Funmilayo Ransome-Kuti of Nigeria* (Urbana: University of Illinois Press, 1997).
31. Ed. Cora Presley (Boulder: Lynne Rienner, 1998).
32. *Muthoni wa Kirima, Mau Mau Woman Field Marshal: Interrogations of Silencing, Erasure and Manipulation of Female Combatants' Texts* (Harare: SAPES Books, 2004).
33. Matembe, with Nancy Dorsey, *Miria Matembe: Gender Politics and Constitution-Making in Uganda* (Kampala: Fountain Publishers, 2002); Sirleaf, *This Child Will Be Great: Memoir of a Remarkable Life* (New York: HarperCollins, 2009); Ramphele, *Across Boundaries The Journey of a South African Woman Leader* (Albany: SUNY Press, 1996).
34. *"This Matter of Women Is Getting Very Bad": Gender, Development and Politics in Colonial Lesotho* (Pietermaritzburg: University of Natal Press, 2000); Ntabeni, "The Impact of the Second World War on Basotho Women: Agricultural Subsistence and the War Effort"; Machobane, "Gender, Succession and Dynastic Politics: The Saga of Senate and Her Son Motšoene Molapo Moshoeshoe, 1858–1930," both in *Review of Southern African Studies* 4, no. 1 (June 2000): 1–18, and 19–41. This issue demonstrates the further strength of women's studies in Lesotho by including three more articles regarding development issues and women by Vusi Mashinini, H. Johnson Nenty and Thope Matobo, and Mokhantšo Makoae.
35. "A Chief Called 'Woman': Historical Perspectives on the Changing Face of *Bogosi* (Chieftainship) in Botswana, 1834–2004," *Jenda: A Journal of Culture and African Women Studies* 7 (2005): 1–15.

36. *Mobilizing the Masses: Gender, Ethnicity, and Class in the Nationalist Movement in Guinea, 1939–1958* (Portsmouth, N.H.: Heinemann, 2005); *Peasants, Traders and Wives: Shona Women in the History of Zimbabwe, 1870–1939* (Portsmouth, N.H.: Heinemann, 1992).
37. Subtitled *Agrarian Change, Gender, and Social Identity in the Great Lakes Region to the 15th Century* (Portsmouth, N.H.: Heinemann, 1998).
38. Subtitled *They Remove Boulders and Cross Rivers*, ed. Nombaniso Gasa (Cape Town: Human Sciences Research Council, 2007).
39. "Memory and the Powers of Women's Naming Practices in Southern Mozambique," Boston University African Studies Center Working Paper No. 234, 2000.
40. Bloomington: Indiana University Press, 2002.
41. Wendy Woodward, Patricia Hayes, and Gary Minkley, eds., subtitled *Gender and Colonialism in Southern Africa* (Amsterdam: Rodopi, 2002). This volume includes no contributions by African scholars.
42. "Domesticity and Difference: Male Breadwinners, Working Women, and Colonial Citizenship in the 1945 Nigerian General Strike," *American Historical Review* 104, 3 (1999): 783–812.
43. Subtitled *Gender and British Slave Emancipation in the Rural Western Cape, South Africa, 1823–1853* (Portsmouth, N.H.: Heinemann, 1997), 2–3.
44. Scully, *Liberating*, 3–4. See also Scully and Diana Paton, eds., *Gender and Slave Emancipation in the Atlantic World* (Durham: Duke University Press, 2005).
45. Pamela E. Brooks, subtitled *Black Women's Resistance in the U.S. South and South Africa* (Amherst: University of Massachusetts Press, 2008).
46. Subtitled *Black Women in Africa and the Americas*, eds. Catherine Higgs, Barbara A. Moss, and Earline Rae Ferguson (Athens: Ohio University Press, 2002).
47. Ojukutu-Macauley, "British Colonial Policy toward Education and the Roots of Gender Inequality in Sierra Leone, 1896–1961," 3–16; Redding, "Witchcraft, Women, and Taxes in the Transkei, South Africa, 1930–1963," 87–99.
48. Peter Magubane and Carol Lazar (Boston: Little, Brown, 1993).
49. N.Y.: Random House, 1967.
50. Subtitled *A Social History of the Ciskei* (Portsmouth, N.H.: Heinemann, 1999).
51. Shireen Hassim, *Women's Organizations and Democracy in South Africa: Contesting Authority* (Madison: University of Wisconsin Press, 2006); Gay Seidman, "Institutional Dilemmas: Representation versus Mobilization in the South African Gender Commission," *Feminist Studies* 29, no. 3 (Fall 2003): 541–60.
52. Athens: Ohio University Press, 2005, p. 1.
53. P. 98.
54. Subtitled *Gender and Sex in an African Society* (London: Zed, 1987).
55. Subtitled *Matriarchy, Religion and Culture* (London: Zed, 1997).
56. *Daughters of the Goddess, Daughters of Imperialism: African Women Struggle for Culture, Power and Democracy* (London: Zed, 2000).
57. In a new collection, edited by historians Toyin Falola and Bessie House-Soremekun, *Gender, Sexuality, and Mothering in Africa* (Trenton, N.J.: Africa World Press, 2011), only one article, by J. M. Ayuba, discusses African homosexuality with relation to the Hausa category of *'yan daudu*. It is based on the anthropological work of Rudolf Gaudio, *Allah Made Us: Sexual Outlaws in an Islamic African City* (Sussex: Wiley-Blackwell, 2009). Motherhood, a topic receiving more current interest, is the primary focus of the collection.
58. Ed. Stephen O. Murray and Will Roscoe (New York: St. Martin's, 1998).

59. Subtitled *The History of an Idea from the Age of Exploration to the Age of AIDS* (Athens/Scottsville: Ohio University Press/University of KwaZulu-Natal Press, 2008).
60. Gaudio, *Allah Made Us*.
61. Stockholm: Almqvist and Wiksell, 2004.
62. "*Efundula*: Women's Initiation, Gender and Sexual Identities in Colonial and Post-Colonial Northern Namibia" (35–56), quotation, 54.
63. Subtitled *Commodification, Consumption, and Cleanliness in Modern Zimbabwe* (Durham: Duke University Press, 1996), 215.
64. Subtitled *Consumerism, Education, and National Identity, 1863–1922* (New York: Palgrave Macmillan, 2004), 169.
65. Ed. Jean Allman (Bloomington: Indiana University Press, 2004).
66. In Hildi Hendrickson, ed. *Embodied Identities in Colonial and Post-Colonial Africa* (Durham: Duke University Press, 1996), 125.
67. Yvette Abrahams, "Images of Sara Bartman: Sexuality, Race, and Gender in Early Nineteenth Century Britain," in *Nation, Empire, Colony: Historicizing Gender and Race*, eds. Ruth Pierson and Nupur Chaudhuri (Bloomington: Indiana University Press, 1998), 220–36.
68. "The Place of Women in the Museum of Saint Louis," in *Museums and Urban Culture in West Africa*, eds. Alexis Adande and Emmanuel Arinze (Oxford: James Currey, 2002), 143–50.
69. Teresa Barnes, *"We Women Worked So Hard": Gender, Urbanization and Social Reproduction in Colonial Harare, Zimbabwe, 1930–1956* (Portsmouth, N.H.: Heinemann, 1999); Bret L. Shadle, *"Girl Cases": Marriage and Colonialism in Gusiiland, Kenya, 1890–1970* (Portsmouth, N.H.: Heinemann, 2006); Hamilton Sipho Simelane, "The State, Chiefs and the Control of Female Migration in Colonial Swaziland," *Journal of African History* 45 (2004): 103–24.
70. "'When in the White Man's Town': Zimbabwean Women Remember Chibeura," in *Women in African Colonial Histories*, eds. Allman et al., 191–215.
71. Subtitled *Women, Reproduction, and the State in Kenya* (Berkeley: University of California Press, 2003), 186. The recent draconian antigay legislation in Uganda instigated by American fundamentalist missionaries has a history worth exploration.
72. Subtitled *Ritual, Medicalization, and Mobility in the Congo* (Durham: Duke University Press, 1999).
73. See Mary Nyangweso Wangile, *Female Circumcision: The Interplay of Religion, Culture and Gender in Kenya* (Mayknoll, N.Y.: Orbis, 2007). For an attempt to historicize initiation and clitoridectomy, see Claire Robertson, "Grassroots in Kenya: Women, Genital Mutilation and Collective Action, 1920–1990," *Signs* 21, 3 (Spring 1996): 615–42.
74. Subtitled *Disputing U.S. Polemics* (Champaign: University of Illinois Press, 2002).
75. Robert Edgerton, *Warrior Women: The Amazons of Dahomey and the Nature of War* (Boulder: Westview, 2000); Tanya Lyons, *Guns and Guerilla Girls: Women in the Zimbabwean Liberation Struggle* (Trenton, N.J.: Africa World Press, 2004).
76. Harare: Weaver Press, 2000.
77. Susan Diduk, "The Civility of Incivility: Grassroots Political Activism, Female Farmers, and the Cameroon State," *African Studies Review* 47, 2 (September 2004): 27–54.
78. Meredeth Turshen and Clotilde Twagiramariya, eds., subtitled *Gender and Conflict in Africa* (London: Zed, 1998).
79. N.Y.: St. Martin, 1999.
80. "Rape, Race and Colonial Culture: The Sexual Politics of Identity in the Nineteenth-Century Cape Colony, South Africa," *American Historical Review* 100, 2 (1995): 335–359; Patricia

Hayes, "'Cocky Hahn and the 'Black Venus': The Making of a Native Commissioner in South West Africa, 1915–46," in *Gendered Colonialisms in African History*, eds. Nancy Rose Hunt, Tessie P. Liu, and Jean Quataert (Oxford: Blackwell, 1997), 42–70.
81. Subtitled *Stories from Berida's Lives* (Bloomington: Indiana University Press, 1999).
82. See, for instance, *Zulu Woman: The Life Story of Christine Sibiya*, a reissue of a 1930s life history written down by Rebecca Hourwich Reyher (New York: CUNY Feminist Press, 1999); *Mothers of the Revolution, The War Experiences of Thirty Zimbabwean Women*, ed. Irene Staunton (Bloomington: Indiana University Press, 1990); and Helena Halperin, *I Laugh So I Won't Cry: Kenya's Women Tell the Stories of Their Lives* (Trenton, N.J.: Africa World Press, 2005).
83. Portsmouth, N.H.: Heinemann, 1994.
84. Madison: University of Wisconsin Press, 1996.
85. *Women, Work and Domestic Virtue in Uganda 1900–2003* (Oxford: James Currey, 2006). See also McIntosh's *Yoruba Women, Work and Social Change* (Bloomington: Indiana University Press, 2009).
86. Byfield, *The Bluest Hands: A Social and Economic History of Women Dyers in Abeokuta (Nigeria), 1890–1940* (Portsmouth, N.H.: Heinemann, 2002); Robertson, *Trouble*. See also Gracia Clark, *Onions Are My Husband: Survival and Accumulation by West African Market Women* (Chicago: University of Chicago Press, 1994).
87. *Pounders of Grain: A History of Women, Work, and Politics in Mozambique* (Portsmouth, N.H.: Heinemann, 2002).
88. Subtitled *Gender and Culture in a Hausa Society in Niger, 1900–1989* (Portsmouth, N.H.: Heinemann, 1997).
89. Subtitled *Widows, Family, and Community in Kenya* (Chicago: University of Chicago Press, 2007).
90. A forthcoming volume entitled *The Power of Gender, the Gender of Power*, eds. Toyin Falola and Bridget Teboh, pays attention to symbolic and economic factors related to power.
91. Oyeronke Olajubu has analyzed Yoruba women's role in indigenous religion in *Women in the Yoruba Religious Sphere* (Albany: SUNY Press, 2003), while Karin Barber's many works on Yoruba drama have many implications for indigenous religious categories. See, e.g., *The Generation of Plays: Yorùbá Popular Life in Theater* (Bloomington: Indiana University Press, 2000); *The Anthropology of Texts; Persons and Publics: Oral and Written Culture in Africa and Beyond* (Cambridge: Cambridge University Press, 2007).
92. Subtitled *Gendered Encounters between Maasai and Missionaries* (Bloomington: Indiana University Press, 2005), 256–57.
93. Hodgson, *Church*, x.
94. "Igo Mma Ogo: The Adoro Goddess, Her Wives and Challengers—Influences on the Reconstruction of Alor-Uno, Northern Igboland, 1890–1994," *Journal of Women's History* 14, 4 (2003): 83–105.
95. "'A Mighty Obstacle to the Gospel': Basel Missionaries, Krobo Women, and Conflicting Ideas of Gender and Sexuality," *Journal of Religion in Africa* 32, 2 (2002): 200–29.
96. Boulder: Westview, 248.
97. *Stockholm Studies in Anthropology* 26, 1991.
98. "Islam, Gender, and Identities in the Making of French Algeria, 1830–1962," in *Domesticating the Empire: Race, Gender, and Family Life in French and Dutch Colonialism*, eds. Clancy-Smith and Frances Gouda (Charlottesville: University Press of Virginia, 1998), 154–74; Malek Alloula, *The Colonial Harem*, trans. Myrna Godzich and Wlad Godzich (Minneapolis: University of Minnesota Press, 1986).

99. Abdelkader Cheref, "Engendering Politics in Algeria? Salima Ghezali, Louisa Hanoune and Khalida Messaoudi," *Journal of Middle East Women's Studies* 2, 2 (2006): 61–85; Fatima Sadiqi, "The Impact of Islamization on Moroccan Feminisms," *Signs* 32, 1 (2006): 32–47.
100. *Women and Islamic Revival in a West African Town* (Bloomington: Indiana University Press, 2009), xiv.
101. Madison: University of Wisconsin Press, 2005. An unfortunate collapsing of modernity, modernization, and westernization has bedeviled some scholarship that seeks to be postmodern but instead ends up continuing the pre-1970s development model that conflated modernization and westernization.
102. For an examination of the feminist political implications of changing Islamic doctrines in Egypt, see Saba Mahmood, *Politics of Piety: The Islamic Revival and the Feminist Subject* (Princeton: Princeton University Press, 2005).
103. Aly Dramé, "Migration, Marriage, and Ethnicity: The Early Development of Islam in Precolonial Middle Casamance," 169–88; and Beth Buggenhagen, "Beyond Brotherhood: Gender, Religious Authority, and the Global Circuits of Senegalese Muridiyya," 189–210, both in *New Perspectives on Islam in Senegal: Conversion, Migration, Wealth, Power, and Femininity*, eds. Mamadou Diouf and Mara A. Leichtman (New York: Palgrave Macmillan, 2009).
104. Okeke, "Postmodern Feminism and Knowledge Production: The African Context," *Africa Today* 43, 3 (1996): 223–33, is still relevant. She finds restructuring "feminist relations" among white and black/African scholars more important than the "grand designs of postmodernism" (231), and cogently analyzes the issue of who can speak for whom in light of unequal power relations:

    > in terms of a shared intellectual space where different knowledge bases seek representation, we are positioned differently [as insiders and outsiders] and cannot deny the fact that relations of power mediate these positions (230).

105. Lisa Cliggett, *Grains from Grass: Aging, Gender, and Famine in Rural Africa* (Ithaca: Cornell University Press, 2005).

4

Sexual Crises, Women's History, and the History of Sexuality in Europe

ANNA CLARK

In 1916, Austrian feminist Grete Meisel-Hess proclaimed that a "sexual crisis" afflicted contemporary society. Sexual fulfillment was necessary for both men and women, she argued, but the capitalist order and men's selfishness prevented its flourishing, locking women into unhappy marriages or the sexless misery of spinsterhood.[1] Expanding on Meisel-Hess, I define a sexual crisis as a time of great social upheaval when two or more cultures of sexual morality clash, and when conflicts between men and women and debates over sexuality become political issues. In the late nineteenth century, women like Grete Meisel-Hess, who celebrated women's need for sexual pleasure, combated not only traditional moralists and new eugenicists but also social purity feminists who advocated male self-control more than female sexual freedom.

This chapter will explore how contemporary sexual crises shaped the way in which historians examined past sexual crises. Another sexual crisis roiled modern western society in the late 1960s and early 1970s. Sixties radicals mocked fifties sexual repression, feminists critiqued conventional marriage, and gay liberationists refused to accept the stigmatization of homosexuality. New forms of history emerged from these movements—women's history, the history of sexuality, gay and lesbian history, and queer history.

As political and intellectual contexts changed, so did understandings of power in these fields. At first, women's history used a materialist analysis to examine the powers that oppressed women: socialist feminists focused on social and economic structures and class, and radical feminists concentrated on physical force and sexual violence. In the early history of sexuality, gay rights activists and Freudian analysts influenced by Wilhelm Reich saw power as embedded in tradition and repression: homosexuals and other sexual "deviants" were thus oppressed by the stigma of traditional society. Gender and sexual identities were both seen as stable categories: "woman" and "man," "heterosexual" and "homosexual," or "gay and lesbian."

By the late seventies and eighties, changing theories, shifts in the politics of the academy, feminism, and the GBLTQ (Gay, Bisexual, Lesbian,

>> 91

Transgendered, Queer) movements transformed the history of sexuality and gender. Influenced by lesbian feminism and Michel Foucault, theorists began to challenge the notion of stable sexual identities, and even the coherence of the category "woman." Instead of focusing on the power of economic coercion and sexual oppression, scholars now analyzed power based on representations, discourses, and norms. Feminist scholars now focus on "gender" rather than the category "woman," defining gender as the system of social relations built on notions of masculinity and femininity. Gender is no longer seen as stable and binary, but rather contingent and complex; in some cultures and time periods, gender is modulated by hierarchies such as race and class so that there are several definitions of manhood and womanhood.

According to Michel Foucault, power is productive, creating desires, not repressing them. Foucault defined sexuality as a "great surface network in which the stimulation of bodies, the intensification of pleasures, the incitement to discourse, the formation of special knowledges, the strengthening of controls and resistances, are linked to one another."[2] His work concentrated on the creation of sexual identities as historically contingent rather than inborn. For both feminists and theorists of sexuality, power became somewhat abstract, although mainly expressed in discourses that tried to shape people into stable gender or sexual identities. However, this was an impossible task, since gender and sexuality were seen as much more fluid. Sexuality is therefore not just about identity, but about the broader set of sexual practices, desires, relationships, and acts, as they are constituted by culture. Furthermore, since most cultural images of sexuality in this broader sense concern non-normative behavior—prostitution, adultery, same-sex desires—the study of sexuality is a particularly productive way of getting at the instability of the gender system as well.

This chapter will concentrate on two sexual crises, around 1800 and around 1900, when definitions of sexuality and gender seemed especially unstable and contested. I will demonstrate how different political moments in women's history and the history of sexuality shaped the interpretation of these sexual crises. For instance, in the 1970s socialist feminists in Great Britain focused on the early nineteenth century, another time of sexual crisis in the age of the industrial revolution, the demographic revolution, and the French Revolution.

The Age of Revolutions

The French Revolution of 1789 was only the most dramatic and condensed example of challenges to traditional political and social structures during the late eighteenth and early nineteenth centuries. Two other social revolutions, the demographic and industrial revolutions, transformed society more gradually, but more profoundly. In the demographic revolution, the number of births rose sharply, both within and outside of wedlock. Moralists responded by fulminating against fornication, and political economist Thomas Malthus feared that population would outstrip the means of subsistence. The industrial revolution moved the population from rural to urban areas to work at wage labor in the new factories.

Attracted to revolutions, Marxist historians tried to understand all these phenomena with a materialist analysis—that is, based on the economic power of those owning the means of production—factories and mines—and the physical power of the state to coerce and imprison. They believed that Marxism provided a scientific way to analyze the larger social structures and dynamics which powered the motor of history. They expected that the classic factory proletariat should have fomented a socialist revolution. Most of these historians did not acknowledge women's history for several reasons: class struggle took precedence over feminism, housewives were not proletarians, and women workers were at best a distraction and at worst a division within the working class.

Emerging from this tradition, yet repudiating the notion of scientific Marxism, British historian E. P. Thompson emphasized cultural as well as material factors. He saw class as a relationship, not as a thing, and depicted the working class as agents in the making of their own culture. Yet Thompson did not incorporate gender as a system of power into his compelling story of the heroic rise to manhood of the working class; he celebrated male artisans rather than female factory workers.[3]

Thompson among others inspired the History Workshop movement that started in 1967 to focus on history from below; they met in pubs and working men's clubs to interview ordinary people in oral histories, discover labor traditions, and recover tales of community. This movement emerged from the ferment of the New Left that challenged the old Marxism, and inspired the student and antiwar movements. At this time, socialist women found themselves making love and cups of tea but not taken seriously as intellectuals. They organized themselves outside of the academy by meeting in shabby counterculture offices and pubs as the London Feminist History group. Feminist History Workshop historians at first asserted that in the last instance capitalism was the primary power relationship between men and women. For example, in a very early work, Catherine Hall's fascinating oral history of married women in Birmingham argued that the ideology of domesticity and women in the home benefited capitalism above all—she did not focus, at that time, on its benefit to men.⁴ When they weren't depicting women as workers, socialist feminists analyzed reproduction as parallel to production in the capitalist system. Women's labor in the home, producing children and feeding male workers, was seen as essential for the maintenance of the proletariat.

Unlike women's historians, the first historians of sexuality emerged from the academy. Nonetheless, the zeitgeist influenced them. While traditional labor organizing was often quite puritanical, the 1968 student movement asserted pleasure as a revolutionary force. Historians of sexuality ascribed sexual repression to capitalism, religion, and the bourgeois family. Similarly, academic historians of sexuality assumed that sexual desire was natural and biological: traditional mores repressed sexual drives, which were then sublimated—or exploded, as in Columbia professor Steven Marcus's *The Other Victorians* (1975).⁵ Princeton professor Lawrence Stone's *The Family, Sex and Marriage* (1977) argued that the early modern traditional, customary power of fathers to control marriages was challenged in the eighteenth century by new romantic, egalitarian ideals, and his student Randolph Trumbach made a similar more detailed argument in *The Rise of the Egalitarian Family* (1978). Both saw power as anchored in patriarchy (seen not as male domination but the power of older men over younger men), tradition, and religion, and as exercised by sexual repression.⁶

Edward Shorter used a similar perspective to explain the great rise in births out of wedlock starting in the mid-eighteenth century. He argued that factory girls were sexually liberated because their wages gave them the independence to defy parental and community control.⁷ In contrast, feminist historians such as Louise Tilly and Joan Scott drew on personal testimonies of unmarried mothers to show that they became pregnant because they were vulnerable, not because they sought independence, liberation, and pleasure. Young women worked to support their families, not just for their own ends. This reflected a notion of agency based not on the masculinist concept of individualism, as Stone and Shorter understood it, but rather on women and men acting as part of a community defending its way of life. Working people did not simply defy middle-class morality to accept a free-and-easy sexuality. Rather, they had long practiced a different kind of morality: plebeian (lower-class) men and women often had sex after a promise of marriage, waiting to save a dowry, inherit a farm, or learn a trade—or for pregnancy—to marry. If a young man would not marry his sweetheart, the community would come after him. But the instability associated with the capitalist economy disrupted the regulation of desire long practiced by communities. The new capitalist economy could bring high wages and flush times. But a boom might suddenly end, throwing whole factories and towns out of work. Men might have planned to marry their sweethearts, then found themselves unemployed and forced to wander far from home in search of work.[8]

When feminists began looking more deeply at intimate relationships between men and women, the fissures in working-class unity began to emerge. The wider feminist movement began to tackle domestic violence, and historians such as Nancy Tomes and Ellen Ross found that wife beating was common among working-class communities.[9] Barbara Taylor examined the sexual antagonism that caused the Owenite cooperative socialist movement of the 1830s and 1840s to founder. Owenites tried to organize men and women workers together, but male artisans resented the competition of low-waged female workers and struck against them. They attacked the hypocrisy of bourgeois morality and advocated free love, but women, who were too vulnerable to being left pregnant, rejected it.[10]

In the early 1980s, I and some other younger women in the London Feminist History group had become impatient with the convolutions necessary to demonstrate that sexual regulation and the oppression of women ultimately benefitted capitalism. Instead, we asserted the importance of male dominance as a primary motivator—and sexuality (along with reproduction and work) as a key means for the oppression of women. We collectively coedited a book entitled *The Sexual Dynamics of History: Men's Power, Women's Resistance*, deliberately equating sex (not yet broken down into sex, gender, and sexuality) as a central historical motive force akin to capitalism or class.[11] To be sure, the collective strenuously debated these issues, divided between hardline separatist feminists and those like myself torn between socialist feminism and radical feminism. In this context I wrote my first book, *Women's Silence, Men's Violence: Sexual Assault in England, 1775–1840*. I argued that sexual assault robbed women of their right to consent to sexual pleasure, but that for nineteenth-century authorities, such as employers and judges, it made little difference whether a woman said she was seduced or forced; she lost her chastity in either case. Although I approached this problem from a socialist feminist perspective, expecting to find widespread rape of servants by masters, I instead found that working-class women were most likely to be assaulted by working-class men.[12]

In my next book, *The Struggle for the Breeches: Gender and the Making of the British Working Class* (1995) I built on the insights of Tilly and Scott, and Barbara Taylor. I described the late eighteenth and early nineteenth century as a time of sexual crisis because middle-class ideals of women's domestic role and sexual morality clashed with the traditional plebeian importance of female labor and premarital courtship. Now, I would call this a crisis of gender and sexuality, acknowledging the social construction of both concepts, but nonetheless in that book I was following the new trend of gender history to examine masculinity. I also identified divisions among the working class, between different cultures of masculinity—such as artisans and factory workers. Some men, especially in the textile trades where men and women worked together, tried to have a more collaborative, companionate relationship with women, and criticized violence against women, whereas other men, especially in artisan trades organized around male bonding in apprenticeship, and threatened by female labor, had a more hard-edged kind of masculinity, which was somewhat more accepting of violence against women. My analysis of power was based on both capitalism and male dominance. Like E. P. Thompson, I saw working people as making their own culture, but unlike Thompson, I saw the working class as tragically divided by gender and sexual antagonism.

Historians influenced by socialism and social history also played a role in critiquing the notion of an exclusive, essential homosexual identity. In an important article that he began to write around 1979, John D'Emilio explored the links between capitalism and gay identity. He insisted that "homosexuals" had not always existed—rather, changing socioeconomic circumstances made possible the emergence of subcultures of men who had sex with other men. As capitalist wage labor undermined the link between the family and the economy, men were able to live on their own in cities, finding other men for sex and companionship and associating in cafés and pubs. Capitalism, therefore, could be a productive power dynamic. Social historians such as Randolph Trumbach and Jeffrey Merrick began to explore the subcultures of men who had sex with other men that arose in Europe's burgeoning cities in the eighteenth century.[13]

Interestingly, lesbian feminists were among the first to criticize the notion of a distinct, essential homosexual identity. Sheila Jeffreys and others in the movement did not necessarily see lesbianism as an inner essence that women could discover in finding their true selves and sexuality. Rather they defined lesbianism as a political choice, and movement supporters wore buttons saying "Any Woman can be a lesbian." Lesbian feminists interpreted desire as a means of the oppression of women, and women's desire for men as something that could be changed. Lesbian separatists challenged the association of desire with heterosexuality—and indeed with genital sexuality too. The poet Adrienne Rich came up with the notion of a lesbian continuum, which could begin with women's friendship and affection and extend to passionate romantic love between women. Historian Carroll Smith-Rosenberg wrote about the female world of love and ritual in nineteenth-century America as a place where romantic love between women was celebrated but not recognized or even expressed as sexual. However, at that time Rich and Smith-Rosenberg still relied on an essentialist notion of women as nurturing, asexual, and emotional rather than seeking their own pleasure. More recently, Judith Bennett claims that even if some women in the past did not fit a modern lesbian identity, they could be regarded as "lesbian-like." By using "lesbian-like" as an adjective rather than the noun "lesbian," she tries to avoid the notion of an essential sexual identity.[14]

The decoding of Anne Lister's diaries, containing explicit accounts of her sexual adventures, challenged the assumption that nineteenth-century women in intense female friendships did not have sex with each other.[15] More recently, Sharon Marcus has provocatively argued (extending Carroll Smith-Rosenberg's original thesis) that intense female friendships, even "female marriages" (lifelong, openly acknowledged partnerships between women) did not undermine, but instead strengthened, Victorian marriages between men and women.[16]

In examining the late eighteenth and early nineteenth centuries, historians also began to turn away from social history toward discerning the larger symbolic structures of gender—the social construction of masculinity and femininity—by claiming that our binary notion of gender was not based on biology, but in fact invented around the eighteenth century. Historian Thomas Laqueur posited a shift from a one-sex model, in which women were seen as inferior versions of men—their genitals like men's, only inside out, composed of the same substances in different balances—to a two-sex model, in which women were seen as radically different from men in every part of their bodies and personalities.[17] Randolph Trumbach hypothesized a shift from a model of sexuality from two sexes to three genders, from one in which men could have sex with younger men, to one in the eighteenth century in which the exclusive roles of heterosexual, sodomite, and sapphist arose.[18] For Dror Wahrman, this contributed along with political turmoil to a late-eighteenth-century crisis in the representations of gender identity.[19]

Psychoanalysis was another source for the cultural turn.[20] Modern psychoanalytically oriented history did not try to analyze individuals; rather, they examined the subconscious conflicts of the psyche as manifested in discourses. Lynn Hunt used psychoanalytic understandings of gender and sexuality to analyze political rhetoric in *The Family Romance of the French Revolution*. Instead of addressing the debate about whether the French Revolution advanced or worsened the status of "woman" seen as a stable category, she demonstrated that metaphors of sexuality and gender infused political debates on a conscious and unconscious level. The crisis of the French

Revolution was not just one of the political order or the social structure, but a psychic crisis. Obscene caricatures desacralized the bodies of the French king and queen by portraying them as engaged in lurid, pansexual, incestuous orgies. The power of the king as father was therefore dissolved; celebrating fraternity, the revolutionaries saw themselves as a band of brothers toppling the father.[21]

Hunt's psychoanalytical, discursive approach contributed to the turn away from social history toward cultural history, what has been turned the "linguistic turn." While primarily stemming from intellectual developments, political shifts may have also influenced working class and feminist history by the 1980s and early 1990s. The great mass protests in the streets of the peace movement, of the labor movement, had failed, revolutionary potential seemed dead, and conservative politics triumphed in Britain and the United States. Repudiating a notion of class power based on relationships to the means of production, many historians began to see discourse as the primary way power is exercised. Discourses can include political rhetoric, medical texts, psychological examinations, sociological investigations, all the words and images that shape the way people think. Oppressive power structures were much more difficult to conquer than we had earlier thought, since they did not just constrain people's actions, but also shaped their minds. Historians and theorists focused on examining the structures of power in thought and culture, rather than the face-to-face relationships of revolutions, strikes, and personal relationships. Furthermore, by this time, most socialist and feminist historians had joined the academy as professionals, since it was too difficult to make a living agitating and community organizing. Since academics create discourses, it is not surprising that we began to see them as all-powerful.

Joan Scott herself had shifted from the Marxist labor and social history approach characteristic of her early work as a pioneer in feminist history to a heavy emphasis on discourse. She renounced any attempt to reclaim experiences, arguing that the notion of an authentic experience was illusory, since it was always filtered through discourse.[22] Although she recounted the actions of women workers in the revolutionary era of the 1840s, she swiftly moved toward an analysis of how political economists depicted women workers. She rejected notions of gender based on sexual antagonism, which seemed to imply a hopeless, eternal conflict. Instead, her analysis of gender depended largely on representation and discourses, since it "involves four interrelated elements: first, culturally available symbols ...; second, normative conceptions ... expressed in doctrines"; third, politics and social institutions and organizations, and fourth, "subjective identity."[23] These symbolic structures legitimate understandings of gender. But furthermore, as Scott famously stated, gender is a metaphor for wider structures of power.

The Late Nineteenth and Early Twentieth Centuries as a Time of Sexual Crisis

Sexuality itself was often at the heart of scandals and conflicts in the long fin-de-siècle period marking the turn from the nineteenth to the twentieth century. Europeans viewed homosexuality as a sign of the degeneration of national populations during a time of war, conceived as a social Darwinist struggle for survival. Authorities were preoccupied with the venereal disease prostitutes passed onto soldiers, weakening their forces. In the late nineteenth century, authorities were especially concerned with producing more citizens as mothers, laborers, and soldiers to maintain and expand the strength of the nation. Eugenics, the pseudo-science of human breeding, claimed that middle-class women were producing too few children and poor women too many.[24]

At the same time, radical social movements and new trends in thought challenged these assumptions and fomented scandals such as the White Slavery scandal of the 1880s when journalists alleged that evil foreign pimps trafficked young girls into prostitution. Conversely, conservative authorities fought back against these radical trends with censorship and regulation. These conflicts reflect wider political tensions over the role of the state, the monarchy, and socialism versus authoritarianism. As in the earlier period, they also reflected deep-rooted clashes between different views of sexual morality: social purity versus the tolerance of hidden prostitution, social purity versus the radical sexologists and socialists, traditional female roles as wives and mothers versus the emancipated and independent New Woman. Evolutionary thought rejected the notion of marriage as an elevated spiritual state and exposed it as a social arrangement meant to harness biological instincts.[25]

The late nineteenth century was also the epicenter of the discursive changes identified by Michel Foucault. Foucault did not see these radical movements as overthrowing repression. Rather, this was a time of an explosion of discourses about sex and the invention of new categories. For Foucault, the most powerful discourses in terms of regulating sexuality were those of sexologists and other so-called experts, who defined and examined the masturbating child, the hysterical woman, the prostitute, the contraceptive couple, and the homosexual. Their discourses became materialized in institutions such as psychiatric hospitals which defined, regulated, treated, and often confined those defined as deviant, who did not fit the norm.²⁶ Sexologists such as Richard von Krafft-Ebing, author of *Psychopathia Sexualis*, first published in 1885, exemplified the creators of these discourses.²⁷

Judith Walkowitz, my adviser, was one of the first feminists to quickly absorb the insights of Michel Foucault's *History of Sexuality, Volume I* in her 1980 book *Prostitution in Victorian Society: Sex, Class and State*.²⁸ As the subtitle demonstrates, she still held onto socialist feminist notions of power and resistance embedded in class and state, but she also saw power as exercised through discourses, forms of representation, and regulation that became institutionalized. For instance, the writings of experts such as Dr. William Acton became enshrined in the Contagious Diseases Acts, which mandated that women suspected of selling sex be registered as prostitutes and subjected to forcible examination, and confined in Lock Hospitals for treatment. Walkowitz was a pioneer in demonstrating that these institutional structures controlled the lives of many other working-class women.²⁹

While Foucault mentioned the possibility of resistance in his theory of reverse discourse—the subjects of sexological discourses, for instance, could turn it to their own ends—Walkowitz focused on resistance in much more detail. This was not only the traditional form of resistance through public associations such as the Ladies' National Association which called for the repeal of the Contagious Diseases Acts, but also the everyday actions of women and their neighbors on the streets of Plymouth and Portsmouth. Walkowitz did not see the sex workers she studied simply as case studies defined by the discourses of William Acton and other experts on prostitution—nor were they just victims of male violence. Instead, she emphasized that they were often enterprising actors, simultaneously defiant and impatient of authority, in rather appealing ways.

In the early 1980s, the late-nineteenth-century debates over sexology, prostitution, and homosexuality became the subject of contemporary debates among socialist and radical feminists. For both factions, sexuality now took center stage in the dynamics of women's oppression. From the point of view of radical feminists such as Sheila Jeffreys in Britain and Catharine Mackinnon and Andrea Dworkin in the United States, sexuality was the essential means of male domination, played out in pornography, prostitution, and rape. Mackinnon declared that "Sexuality is to feminism what work is to Marxism." To unpack this sentence, Marxists saw work—as exemplified in the question of who owed the means of production, and who had to work at wages—as the central question of capitalism. For Mackinnon, sexuality was the central question for feminism, since she saw male sexual power over women as the central element of their oppression.³⁰ Radical feminists identified male power over women as expressed in the discourses of pornography and sexology as the problem. They campaigned to allow women to sue pornographers for assault, seeing sexualized images as a form of violence against women, and prostitution as the sexualized exploitation of women.

Many of those who originated from socialist feminism now began to see sexuality as a central dynamic of history, as distinct from gender and from capitalism (although still interrelated). Theorist Gayle Rubin, in a pathbreaking article, "The Traffic in Women," had originally argued that the "sex/gender system" fused gender and sexuality.[31] However, influenced by Foucault, she moved on to insisting that sexuality had to be understood as distinct from gender as a vector of power. She regarded sexuality as socially constructed, and espoused the Foucauldian dynamic of a transition from a focus on sexual acts to a notion of sexuality as an identity under the pressure of late-nineteenth-century discourses such as sexology. But she emphasized that the subjects of these discourses also created their own communities. In turn, these communities and individuals were stigmatized by new political discourses and persecuted by the state. This article was published in a book, *Pleasure and Danger*, that came out of an explosive 1982 conference at Barnard College where feminist activists and academics came together to debate sexuality.[32] In emotional and angry clashes, radical feminists contended with self-described "sex-positive" feminists over such issues as prostitution and pornography. This led to a long-running controversy known as the "sex wars" that simmered primarily in activist feminist circles.[33] For "sex-positive" feminists, power—seen in psychic and discursive terms—was inescapable in sexual relationships. However, women could also assert power through sex; domination and submission were not seen as traits of biological masculinity and femininity, but rather as roles anyone could take on.

Late-nineteenth-century feminist campaigns against child sexual abuse and prostitution were often cited in these debates. Sheila Jeffreys claimed in her book, *The Spinster and Her Enemies* (1985), that the late-nineteenth-century feminist suffrage movement defended women against exploitative and abusive male sexuality. She was inspired by the contemporary radical feminists who had recently exposed the reality of incest and the sexual abuse of children, denied by Freudians for much of the twentieth century. Drawing parallels with this movement, Jeffreys justified the campaign in 1885 to raise the age of consent to sex for girls from 13 to 16 for attacking the sexual privileges of upper-class men. Even more radically, Jeffreys followed her nineteenth-century predecessors in arguing that heterosexual sex itself was harmful to women. She celebrated the social-purity feminists of the late nineteenth century, such as Ellice Hopkins, for protecting victimized women, and endorsed suffragette Christabel Pankhurst's slogan "Votes for Women and Chastity for Men," who claimed that 80 percent of British men were infected with venereal disease. Jeffreys also repudiated male sexologists for imposing a Darwinian notion of sexuality on women which compelled them into sexual services and reproduction, and excused male violence against women. Male sexuality, then, was seen as a form of power over women, as expressed through physical power, coercion, and exploitation.[34]

Socialist feminists were uncomfortable with this harsh focus on male violence and separatism. They argued that the censorship of pornography fed into right-wing morality, and they feared that Jeffreys and her allies were hostile to sexual pleasure in general. Sex-positive feminists critiqued the lesbian separatist movement and anti–violence against women activists for denying the complexities of sexuality and for facilitating the regulation of women by trying to protect them.

Walkowitz, whose work was cited by Gayle Rubin, drew out the similarities between the late-nineteenth-century social purity movement and the twentieth-century feminist antipornography movement. After the suspension of the Contagious Disease Acts, the social purity movement led by Ellice Hopkins began to rival the repeal movement. Instead of criticizing the acts as unjust and immoral, Hopkins argued that it was more important to rescue and reform prostitutes, and even to prevent prostitution by educating children in social purity. Walkowitz pointed out that Ellice Hopkins's efforts, and the campaign against child prostitution, actually contributed to the passage of a whole series of acts, culminating in the Criminal Law Amendment Act of 1885, that allowed police to remove children from dwellings reputed to be brothels, and put them into industrial homes and reformatories. Instead of helping sexually abused children, these reformatories imprisoned and stigmatized them. For Walkowitz, this was a cautionary tale of the perils of overemphasizing the danger of sexuality, and of making alliances with right-wing moralists in order to "protect" women from male violence.[35]

Similarly, historians demonstrated that the German feminist movement at the turn of the twentieth century was divided between bourgeois feminists, who often wanted to control prostitution, and the radical feminists of the Bund für Mutturschutz, an organization which defended single mothers and celebrated female sexual pleasure. Some historians have depicted the former as maternalist feminists; they could be seen as protecting younger and working-class women, or as controlling and confining them with their class power.[36] More recently, Yvonne Svanstrom placed the late-nineteenth-century Swedish feminist campaign against the regulation of prostitution in the context of contemporary efforts to criminalize male customers of prostitutes in Sweden.

Male experts, she argues, justified prostitution by claiming it was necessary to fulfill male sexual needs, but the most radical of the late-nineteenth-century feminists repudiated this notion and refused to stigmatize women engaged in sex work. However, other scholars have argued that the Swedish criminalization of "johns" is still part of a repressive system that harms and stigmatizes prostitutes for violating the boundaries of Swedish society.[37]

At the same time, this debate was much more complicated than the nineteenth-century struggle between those exploring sexual pleasure and those advocating social purity. Women of color began to point out that the assumption that "woman" was a unified category subjected to oppression by men did not take race into account.[38] As class politics faded in Europe, and as questions of multiculturalism, racism, and postcolonialism came to the fore, feminist historians began to focus on imperialism more than the working class. Antoinette Burton portrayed British feminists as using claims to protect Indian women in order to assert their own right to political participation.[39] Philippa Levine extended the study of the Contagious Diseases Acts to the colonies.[40] The work of Ann Stoler, among others, has demonstrated that controlling sexuality was a central task of imperial power, for interracial sex threatened the boundaries of race and the legitimacy of empire. Interracial sex symbolized dangers to empire, but at the same time it could never really be controlled as a practice; discourses of sexuality insisted on racial purity while always evidencing anxiety about its impossibility.[41]

It was not just a matter of imperial impositions, but of conflicts within colonized societies. For instance, over the course of the nineteenth century some British officials tried to change Indian religious customs concerning marriage, banning sati (widow burning) in 1829, allowing widow remarriage in 1856, and raising the Age of Consent in 1891. The Subaltern Studies movement, in addressing these issues, had moved beyond its earlier social history and somewhat Marxist focus to concentrate on the power of discourses. Partha Chatterjee argued that during the late nineteenth century, Indian men, disenfranchised politically, began to see the material world as controlled by colonialists, while the home was the pure realm of the essence of Indian nation and religion. However, they were not trying to preserve traditional patriarchy, he asserts, but to reform it. Indian men could be modern individuals, while preserving Indian customs and communal values in the home.[42] But for feminist critic Himani Bannerji, Chatterjee inaccurately conflates conservative Hindu ideologies with Indian nationalism as a whole and refuses to see the oppressive nature of Hindu patriarchy.[43]

The Age of Consent debate in 1891 brought these questions to a head. A coalition of some Indian reformers, such as Benjamin Malabari, and British feminists and missionaries pressured the British government in India to abolish the custom of consummation of marriage involving very young girls.[44] British feminists were obviously trying to extend the age of consent effort in Britain to India, but this was a very different task. Instead of criminalizing behavior generally acknowledged as deviant—the prostitution of young girls—it attacked normative marriage in India. While Indian men asserted their citizenship by protesting the Act, they also used patriarchal masculinity to justify their own claims to political authority and to criticize British imperialism, as Tanika Sarkar argues.[45] Minralini Sinha points out that the Indian opponents of the bill "represented the defense of orthodox Hindu patriarchy in a more universal patriarchal language of the 'natural rights' of all husbands."[46] Sinha and Sarkar both use the tools of social history and discourse analysis to return to an emphasis on male power and patriarchy.

The late nineteenth century has also been seen as a key moment for the history of homosexuality. Indeed, the Labouchère amendment which criminalized "indecent acts" between men was passed in the same year as the White Slave scandal, as part of the Criminal Law Amendment Act of 1885 in Britain, which had raised the age of consent. Ten years later, Oscar Wilde was prosecuted and imprisoned under the Act, and became a martyr in the history of homosexuality.

But Michel Foucault famously argued that before the late nineteenth century authorities did not conceptualize the "homosexual" as a personality; rather, they focused on punishing the crime or sin of sex between males. Psychiatrists and sexologists in the late nineteenth century then invented the idea of homosexuality as defining a personality. For Foucault, power was exercised not by repression and incarceration, but by shaping people's understandings of themselves through surveillance and discourses. For instance, the new sexological and legal discourses, argues Jeffrey Weeks, created a homosexual identity: "It seems likely that the new forms of legal regulation, whatever their vagaries in application, had the effect of forcing home to many the fact of their difference and thus creating a new community of knowledge, if not of life and feeling, amongst many men with homosexual leanings."[47] Lesbian feminists such as Sheila Jeffreys, however, condemned sexologists for stigmatizing female friendships and creating the image of the perverted mannish lesbian.

In examining the emergence of these discourses in the context of the late-nineteenth-century sexual crisis, historians have also shown that sexology played a more dynamic and positive role.[48] Early historian of sexuality Esther Newton declared that Radclyffe Hall, author of the lesbian classic *The Well of Loneliness* (1929) used sexology in order to develop and justify her own identity as a mannish lesbian.[49] Harry Oosterhuis has further challenged the assumption that sexologists imposed a notion of homosexual identity on men and women who could not otherwise conceive of it. Through a close analysis of the writings and correspondence of psychologist and sexologist Richard Krafft-Ebing, Oosterhuis found that he did not simply create a notion of a homosexual identity which was then taken up by men who were attracted to other men. Rather, Krafft-Ebing corresponded with men who had sex with men, even borrowing the term "urning" from activist Hans Ulrich. He changed his own attitude toward homosexuality in dialogues with such men (and some women).[50] But in his *London and the Culture of Homosexuality, 1885–1914* Matt Cook downplays the influence of sexology on notions and practices of same-sex desire, instead emphasizing the idealization of Greek culture and the persistence of the imperative of silence.[51]

Historians have also demonstrated that the sexual scandals from the 1890s and early 1900s did not only produce moral panics against homosexuality, they also stimulated defenses of homosexuality. Havelock Ellis's sympathetic sexological work, *Sexual Inversion*, for instance, was censored by British authorities in 1897. However, two years later German sexologist Magnus Hirschfeld established the first organized movement for homosexual emancipation, agitating for the repeal of Paragraph 175, the law which banned homosexual acts between men.[52] This was part of a larger ferment and discussion in which the conservative social purity efforts around sexology were challenged by socialists and feminists interested in sexual liberation. Conservatives saw homosexuality as symbolic of the "degeneration" they feared that society faced, fomenting a "moral panic," but some heterosexual sexologists became more sympathetic to homosexuality as part of their larger critique of conventional sexual morality. Both socialists and conservatives could use homosexual scandals to discredit their enemies, for instance in the 1908 Eulenberg scandal when the same-sex proclivities of many high-ranking aristocrats in Kaiser Wilhelm II's government were exposed.[53] A homosexual scandal soon erupted in the Swedish press, which had followed the Eulenberg affair closely. In both Germany and Sweden, sexologists and activists used the crisis as the occasion to call for the repeal of laws criminalizing homosexuality.[54]

As in the fin-de-siècle, the 1980s and early 1990s witnessed a backlash against gay culture fueled by fears of disease and degeneracy. The rise of the new right with its moral crusades endangered gay rights in both the United States and in Britain. Clause 28 of Margaret Thatcher's 1988 education bill forbade teachers and schools from discussing homosexuality in any sort of positive way, and police in Europe and the U.S. harassed gay people on the streets. The AIDS crisis further stoked this backlash. Reclaiming the past of gay communities seemed more urgent than ever before. As scholars and activists rushed to produce more gay histories, this sexual crisis also facilitated important changes in the field.

The AIDS crisis further undercut the notion of an exclusive sexual identity. Activists realized that in trying to combat the spread of AIDS, it was not enough to educate men who thought of themselves as gay. Many men, especially in communities of color and in the global South, did not define themselves as gay, and had sex with women as well as men. In looking back on western history as well, historians recognized the prevalence of this pattern. More recently, in *Queer London*, Matt Houlbrook demonstrates that even as "queer" subcultures were emerging among middle-class Britons in the 1920s, some working-class men persisted in having sex with other men, taking the dominant role, without thinking of themselves as homosexual or viewing their masculinity as compromised.[55]

Building on the earlier work on urban subcultures, historians also began to challenge the centrality of sexual crises and moral panics in the history of same-sex desire. H. G. Cocks in his book *Nameless Offenses: Homosexual Desire in the Late Nineteenth Century* (2003), argues that the late nineteenth century, and in particular the Labouchère amendment of 1885, did not represent a significant break in the codification and criminalization of homosexuality. Throughout the nineteenth century the police prosecuted men who had sex with men in London on charges of indecency. Labouchère's Amendment therefore just codified an existing practice into law, and Oscar Wilde's prosecution did not significantly change the rate of prosecutions during the 1890s. Although the police surveilled and harassed men who had sex with other men, they often did so quietly, not wanting to create publicity about the offense the law said was "not to be named among Christians."[56] Anjali Arondekar has also stressed the role of silence in efforts to regulate same-sex desire. In India, the British felt confident that they could know and regulate prostitutes (even when women constantly evaded such regulation) but they found it very difficult to define and regulate sex between men because they were rather confused by the hijras, who were people born male or intersex who became or were regarded as eunuchs and dressed as women. Some experts in medical jurisprudence tried to claim that such a person who wore women's clothes, whose anus showed evidence of sodomy, and who had venereal disease, should be punished as a habitual sodomite, but judges refused to do so, wanting to punish only on evidence of actual acts.[57]

Some in the gay movement had responded to AIDS by emphasizing monogamy and respectability as a way to prevent the spread of disease. But others found new insights in the tragedy; activists also criticized the move toward monogamy for sapping the movement of its subversive energy, turning gay men (and lesbians) into mirrors of heterosexuals. Inspired by Foucault, scholar activists such as Michael Warner developed the notion of "heteronormativity" as a means of control, arguing that it was not only that people were pressured into being heterosexual, but they were also supposed to conform to norms of white, middle-class monogamy.[58] In this context, power is exercised through the norm. As Karma Lochrie and other thinkers, including Foucault, have pointed out, the notion of the "norm" as the average, regular, and natural was invented in the nineteenth century by such disciplines as sexology, biology, and statistics.[59] The norm is a different sort of power than the materialist explanations favored by earlier radical or socialist feminists—it is disembodied, somewhat abstract, although embedded in institutions and discourses. The norm functions by constructing and regulating people's understandings of themselves as natural. For Judith Butler, the norm is what makes people intelligible, for instance as male or female—what enables them to be "read" or understood by the state and in social relations. This differs from a juridical model of power. Norms actually create desires, and create our notions of ourselves, for instance as masculine or feminine. It is not only a matter of discovering how homosexuals and other "deviants" were subject to regulation, but to show how the "norm" subjected all men and women to social construction.[60]

Historians such as Jonathan Ned Katz argued that not only homosexuality but also heterosexuality was an invented category.[61] They attribute its invention to the work of marriage advisers and sexologists in the late nineteenth century, who developed the notion in opposition to homosexuality. Darwinianism forced a re-creation of relations between men and women and a valorization of sex, as sexual selection and competition was seen as essential for evolution. But as Joan Scott pointed out, gender (and by implication heteronormativity) is never constructed as stable. It is constantly undermined by fantasies, by desires, by fears, and must be constantly challenged and reconstructed.[62] Queer theorists, often coming from a background in literary criticism, have shown that the norm of heterosexuality is constantly undermined by queer desires. Queerness, therefore, is not an identity belonging to a separate and distinct class of individuals, but a kind of transgressive desire that destabilizes all identity.

If we understand the late nineteenth century as a time of sexual crisis, it becomes clear that the heterosexual "norm" was highly unstable, not only because of the threat of same-sex desire, but in addition because of its own internal conflicts. Indeed, historian Edward Ross Dickinson has published an article on the perceived "impossibility of heterosexual love" in late imperial Germany.⁶³ The feminist movement criticized the double standard which allowed men to go to prostitutes and punished women who had sexual affairs. Like many at the time, Grete Meisel-Hess, with whom I began this chapter, thought that marriage was in crisis: marriages were too unhappy, there were not enough men to marry because of the expense of supporting a wife, and women were so financially dependent they could not choose whom to marry. Both the sexologists and some feminists saw men as motivated mainly by lust, and women by love and the need to reproduce. For sexologists, this was normal, and for feminists, it was a tragedy. As Dickinson argues, men and women seemed to be on two sides of a great chasm; yet he suggests that there was a way out. Some radicals, inspired by the homosexual rights movement, argued that men and women were not utterly different— people had different balances of masculinity and femininity in them. By the early twentieth century, some sexologists took up the ideas of feminists who argued for women's sexual pleasure and began to explore the ways in which mutual sexual pleasure might strengthen conventional marriages.⁶⁴ Heterosexuality had been reconstructed, but this was a fragile truce.⁶⁵

Conclusion

By putting the crisis in heterosexuality and the contests over homosexuality in the late nineteenth century and early twentieth century in the same frame, we can productively bring together the two fields of the history of sexuality and women's history. As we have seen, the insights of queer history have helped undermine the notion of gender as a stable category. At the same time, the feminist analyses of historian Edward Dickinson and early-twentieth-century activist Grete Meisel-Hess reveal that not only queer desires, but the power dynamics of men and women made gender relations unstable.

But we should not fall prey to a teleological model in which historians of gender and sexuality have moved beyond the materialist analysis of stable categories to a more sophisticated understanding of discursive power and fluid identities. First, this shift itself was conditioned by changing material conditions of feminists and gay activists in the academy. As this survey has shown, the way in which historians understand past sexual crises is profoundly influenced by the way they live out their present confusion. Certain moments are particularly key in shaping historiographical change: the sixties/early seventies, the sex wars of the 1980s.

Second, by analyzing both gender and sexuality as a set of practices, rather than identities (whether fluid or stable) the insights of both materialist and discursive analyses can flourish. After all, Grete Meisel-Hess blamed both the oppressive discourses of femininity and the capitalist order for the sexual crisis under which she suffered. Sexual crises are a productive way of discerning the instability inherent in gender and sexuality systems, because they reveal the fractures at their heart.

NOTES

1. Grete Meisel-Hess, *The Sexual Crisis; a Critique of Our Sex Life*, trans. Eden Paul and Cedar Paul (New York: The Critic and Guide Company, 1917), 17.
2. Michel Foucault, *The History of Sexuality: An Introduction*, trans. Robert Hurley (New York: Vintage Books, 1990), 105–06.
3. E. P. Thompson, *The Making of the English Working Class* (New York: Pantheon Books, 1964).
4. Catherine Hall, "Married Women at Home in Birmingham in the 1920s and 1930s," *Oral History* V (1977): 62–83.
5. Steven Marcus, *The Other Victorians: A Study of Sexuality and Pornography in Mid-Nineteenth-Century England* (New York: Norton, 1975).
6. Lawrence Stone, *The Family, Sex and Marriage in England, 1500–1800*, abridged ed. (New York: Harper & Row, 1979); Randolph Trumbach, *The Rise of the Egalitarian Family: Aristocratic Kinship and Domestic Relations in Eighteenth-Century England*, Studies in Social Discontinuity (New York: Academic Press, 1978), 679.
7. Edward Shorter, "Female Emancipation, Birth Control, and Fertility in European History," *American Historical Review* 78, no. 3 (June 1973): 605–40.
8. Joan Wallach Scott and Louise Tilly, *Women, Work, and Family* (New York: Methuen, 1987), 39, 97.
9. Ellen Ross, "'Fierce Questions and Taunts': Married Life in Working-Class London, 1870–1914," *Feminist Studies* 8, no. 3 (Autumn 1982): 575–602; Nancy Tomes, "A 'Torrent of Abuse': Crimes of Violence between Working-Class Men and Women in London, 1840–1875," *Journal of Social History* 11, no. 3 (Spring 1978): 328–45.
10. Barbara Taylor, *Eve and the New Jerusalem: Socialism and Feminism in the Nineteenth Century* (New York: Pantheon Books, 1983).
11. London Feminist History Group, *The Sexual Dynamics of History: Men's Power, Women's Resistance* (London: Pluto Press, 1983).
12. Anna Clark, *Women's Silence, Men's Violence: Sexual Assault in England 1780–1845* (London: Pandora, 1987).
13. John D'Emilio, "Capitalism and Gay Identity," in *The Lesbian and Gay Studies Reader* (New York: Routledge, 1993), 470–71; Randolph Trumbach, "London's Sodomites: Homosexual Behavior and Western Culture in the Eighteenth Century," *Journal of Social History* 11, no. 1 (1977): 1–33; for a later work, see Jeffrey Merrick, "Sodomitical Inclination in Early Eighteenth-Century Paris," *Eighteenth-Century Studies* 30, no. 3 (1997): 289–95.
14. Adrienne Rich, "Compulsory Heterosexuality and the *Lesbian Continuum*," *Signs* 5 (1980): 631–60; Carroll Smith-Rosenberg, "The Female World of Love and Ritual," *Signs* 1, no. 1 (1975): 1–29; Judith Bennett, *History Matters: Patriarchy and the Challenge of Feminism* (Philadelphia: University of Pennsylvania Press, 2006), 110.
15. Anna Clark, "Anne Lister's Construction of Lesbian Identity," *Journal of the History of Sexuality* 7, no. 1 (July 1996): 23–50. For more on Anne Lister, see Helena Whitbread, ed., *No*

Priest but Love: The Journals of Anne Lister from 1824–1826 (Otley, W. Yorks: Smith Settle, 1992) and Jill Liddington, *Female Fortune: Land, Gender, and Authority: The Anne Lister Diaries and Other Writings, 1833–36* (London: Rivers Oram, 1998).

16. Sharon Marcus, *Between Women: Friendship, Desire, and Marriage in Victorian England* (Princeton: Princeton University Press, 2007), 193–204.
17. Thomas Laqueur, *Making Sex: Body and Gender from the Greeks to Freud* (Cambridge: Harvard University Press, 1990).
18. Randolph Trumbach, *Heterosexuality and the Third Gender in Enlightenment London, vol. 1: Sex and the Gender Revolution* (Chicago: University of Chicago Press, 1998), 427.
19. Dror Wahrman, *The Making of the Modern Self: Identity and Culture in Eighteenth Century England* (New Haven: Yale University Press, 2004), 263.
20. Sally Alexander, "Feminist History and Psychoanalysis," *History Workshop* 32 (Autumn 1991): 128–33.
21. Lynn Hunt, *The Family Romance of the French Revolution* (Berkeley: University of California Press, 1992). In my book *Scandal: The Sexual Politics of the British Constitution* (Princeton: Princeton University Press, 2004), I also examined the sexual symbolism of political rhetoric, without the psychoanalytic approach.
22. Joan W. Scott, "The Evidence of Experience," *Critical Inquiry* 17 (1991): 773–97.
23. Joan Wallach Scott, "Gender: A Useful Category of Historical Analysis," *American Historical Review* 91, no. 5 (December 1986): 95.
24. Anna Clark, *Desire: A History of Sexuality in Europe* (London: Routledge, 2008), 142–62.
25. Max Nordau, *Degeneration*, 2nd ed. (Lincoln: University of Nebraska Press, 1993); Daniel Pick, "The Degenerating Genius," *History Today* 42, no. 4 (1992): 17–23.
26. Michel Foucault, *The History of Sexuality, vol. I* (New York: Vintage Books, 1980).
27. Richard von Krafft-Ebing, *Psychopathia Sexualis, with Especial Reference to the Antipathic Sexual Instinct; a Medico-Forensic Study* (New York: Bell, 1965).
28. Judith R. Walkowitz, *Prostitution and Victorian Society: Women, Class, and the State* (Cambridge: Cambridge University Press, 1980).
29. Alain Corbin, *Women for Hire: Prostitution and Sexuality in France after 1850* (Cambridge: Harvard University Press, 1990); Mary Gibson, *Prostitution and the State in Italy, 1860–1915*, 2nd ed. (Columbus: Ohio State University Press, 1999); Jolanta Sikorska-Kulesza and Agnieszka Kreczmar, "Prostitution in Congress Poland," *Acta Poloniae Historica* (2001): 123–33.
30. Catherine Mackinnon, "Feminism, Marxism, Method and the State: An Agenda for Theory," *Signs* 7, no. 3 (1982): 55–56.
31. Gayle Rubin, "The Traffic in Women: Notes on the 'Political Economy' of Sex," in Rayna Reiter, ed., *Toward an Anthropology of Women* (New York: Monthly Review Press, 1975), 157–67.
32. Gayle Rubin, "Thinking Sex: Notes for a Radical Theory of Sexuality," in Carole S. Vance, ed., *Pleasure and Danger: Exploring Female Sexuality* (New York: Routledge, 1984), 293, 307.
33. Elizabeth Wilson, "The Context of 'Between Pleasure and Danger': The Barnard Conference on Sexuality," *Feminist Review* 13 (Spring 1983): 35–41.
34. Sheila Jeffreys, *The Spinster and Her Enemies: Feminism and Sexuality, 1880–1930* (London: Pandora Press, 1985).
35. Judith Walkowitz, "Male Vice and Feminist Virtue: Feminists and the Politics of Prostitution," in *Powers of Desire*, ed. Ann Snitow et al. (New York: Monthly Review Press, 1983).

36. Ann Taylor Allen, "Feminism, Venereal Diseases, and the State in Germany, 1890–1918," *Journal of the History of Sexuality* 4, no. 3 (1993): 35, and *Feminism and Motherhood in Western Europe 1890–1970* (New York: Palgrave Macmillan, 2005), 117.
37. Yvonne Svanström, "Through the Prism of Prostitution: Conceptions of Women and Sexuality in Sweden at Two Fins-De-Siècle," *Nora, Nordic Journal of Women's Studies* 13 (2005): 48–58; Elizabeth Bernstein, *Temporarily Yours: Intimacy, Authenticity, and the Commerce of Sex* (Chicago: University of Chicago Press, 2007), 145–56, 163–66; Don Kulick, "Sex in the New Europe: The Criminalization of Clients and Swedish Fear of Penetration," *Anthropological Theory* 3, no. 2 (2003): 199–218.
38. See articles in *Pleasure and Danger*, and Gloria Anzaldua, *This Bridge Called My Back: Writings by Radical Women of Color*, 1st ed. (Watertown: Persephone Press, 1981).
39. Antoinette Burton, *Burdens of History: British Feminists, Indian Women, and Imperial Culture, 1865–1915* (Chapel Hill: University of North Carolina Press, 1994).
40. Philippa Levine, *Prostitution, Race, and Politics: Policing Venereal Disease in the British Empire* (New York: Routledge, 2003).
41. Ann Laura Stoler, *Carnal Knowledge and Imperial Power: Race and the Intimate in Colonial Rule* (Berkeley: University of California Press, 2002).
42. Partha Chatterjee, *The Nation and Its Fragments: Colonial and Postcolonial Histories* (Princeton: Princeton University Press, 1993), 107.
43. Himani Bannerji, "Projects of Hegemony: Towards a Critique of Subaltern Studies' 'Resolution of the Women's Question,'"*Economic and Political Weekly* (March 11, 2000): 911. See also critique by Kamala Visweswaran, "Small Speeches, Subaltern Gender: Nationalist Ideology and Its Historiography," *Subaltern Studies* 9 (1996): 83–125, and by Inderpal Grewal, *Home and Harem: Nation, Gender, Empire and the Cultures of Travel* (Durham: Duke University Press, 1996), 55.
44. Grewal, 147, 211.
45. Tanika Sarkar, "A Prehistory of Rights: The Age of Consent Debate in Colonial Bengal," *Feminist Studies* 26, no. 3 (Fall 2000): 601–22.
46. Mrinilini Sinha, *Colonial Masculinity: The "Manly Englishman" and the "Effeminate Bengali"* (Manchester: Manchester University Press, 1995), 140.
47. Jeffrey Weeks, *Sex, Politics and Society* (London: Longman, 1989, 2nd ed.), 1083.
48. For more on the interchange between feminism and sexology, see Lesley Hall, "Hauling Down the Double Standard: Feminism, Social Purity and Sexual Science in Late Nineteenth-Century Britain," *Gender & History* 16, no. 1 (April 2004): 36–56.
49. Esther Newton, "The Mythic Mannish Lesbian: Radclyffe Hall and the New Woman," *Signs* 9, no. 4, *The Lesbian Issue* (Summer 1984): 557–75. For another, later example, see "Anna Ruling: A Problematic Foremother of Lesbian Herstory," *Journal of the History of Sexuality* 13 (2004): 477–99, and Anna Rueling, "What Interest Does the Women's Movement Have in the Homosexual Question?" in *Lesbians in Germany 1890s–1920s*, ed. Lilian Faderman and Brigitta Eriksson (Tallahassee: Naiad Press, 1990), 89.
50. Harry Oosterhuis, *Stepchildren of Nature: Krafft-Ebing, Psychiatry, and the Making of Sexual Identity* (Chicago: University of Chicago Press, 2000).
51. Matt Cook, *London and the Culture of Homosexuality, 1885–1914* (Cambridge: Cambridge University Press, 2003), 145. For a useful survey, see Joseph Bristow, "Remapping the Sites of Gay History: Legal Reform, Medico-Legal Thought, Sexual Scandal, Erotic Geography," *Journal of British Studies* 46 (2007): 116–42.

52. John C. Fout, "Sexual Politics in Wilhelmine Germany: The Male Gender Crisis, Moral Purity, and Homophobia," *Journal of the History of Sexuality* 2 (1992): 328–41.
53. James Steakley, "Iconography of a Scandal: Political Cartoons and the Eulenburg Affair in Wilhelmine Germany," in *Hidden from History: Reclaiming the Gay & Lesbian Past*, eds. Martin Duberman et al. (New York: Meridian, 1989), 233–63.
54. Jens Rydström, "Sweden 1864–1878: Beasts and Beauties," in *Criminally Queer: Homosexuality and Criminal Law in Scandinavia 1842–1999*, eds. Jens Rydström and Kati Mustola (Amsterdam: Aksant, 2007), 164; Jens Rydström, *Sinners and Citizens: Homosexuality and Bestiality in Sweden* (Chicago: University of Chicago Press, 2004), 50.
55. Matt Houlbrook, *Queer London: Perils and Pleasures in the Sexual Metropolis, 1918–1957* (Chicago: University of Chicago Press, 2005).
56. H. G. Cocks, *Nameless Offenses: Homosexual Desire in the Late Nineteenth Century* (London: I. B. Tauris and Co., 2003).
57. Anjali Arondekar, *For the Record: On Sexuality and the Colonial Archive* (Durham: Duke University Press, 2009), 27–96.
58. Michael Warner, *The Trouble with Normal* (New York: Free Press, 1999).
59. Karma Lochrie, *Heterosyncrasies: Female Sexuality When Normal Wasn't* (Minneapolis: University of Minnesota Press, 2005), 6.
60. Judith Butler, *Gender Trouble: Feminism and the Subversion of Identity* (New York: Routledge, 1990).
61. Jonathan Ned Katz, *The Invention of Heterosexuality* (New York: Dutton, 1995).
62. Joan Scott, *Gender and the Politics of History* (New York: Columbia University Press, 1999, revised ed.), 204.
63. Edward Ross Dickinson, "'A Dark, Impenetrable Wall of Complete Incomprehension': The Impossibility of Heterosexual Love in Imperial Germany," *Central European History* 40, no. 3 (September 2007): 467–97.
64. See also Carolyn Burdett, "The Hidden Romance of Sexual Science: Eugenics, the Nation and the Making of Modern Feminism," in *Sexology in Culture*, ed. Lucy Bland and Laura Doan (London: Routledge, 1998), 44–59; in their introduction to the volume, Bland and Doan also discuss the more positive aspects of sexology.
65. Carolyn J. Dean, *The Frail Social Body: Pornography, Homosexuality, and Other Fantasies in Interwar France* (Berkeley: University of California Press, 2000), 170.

Engendering National and Nationalist Projects

5

Gender and the Politics of Exceptionalism in the Writing of British Women's History

ARIANNE CHERNOCK

In 1793, a Norfolk surgeon named Richard Dinmore published the controversial tract, *A Brief Account of the Moral and Political Acts of the Kings and Queens of England from William the Conqueror to the Revolution in the Year 1688*. A political radical with close ties to "Jacobin" circles in nearby Norwich, Dinmore revisited the history of the reigning kings and queens of England in order to underscore the need for parliamentary reform. Dinmore was particularly interested in chronicling the history of queens regnant, because it was here that he found the most evidence of an unjust and illogical political arrangement. Surveying the reign of Queen Elizabeth I, for example, Dinmore congratulated early modern Britons for refusing to adopt the Salic Law, a law passed in fifteenth-century France barring women from the throne. At the same time, though, he wondered why a nation that allowed women to serve as heads of state balked at the idea of female political representation. "The want of this right [women's right to vote]," Dinmore observed, "is peculiarly absurd in this kingdom, where a woman may reign, though not vote for a Member of Parliament."[1]

Dinmore's strategic invocation of queenship bears consideration in any discussion of trends and trajectories in the "engendering" of British women's history. For his *Brief Account* reminds us that some of the earliest historians of women's pasts in Britain approached their admittedly elitist subjects with myriad and often disruptive motives. Not all of Dinmore's contemporaries, to be sure, had such radical goals in mind when they decided to explore the histories of women "worthies"—that is, those various female monarchs, warriors, saints, and savants distinguished by their rank, talent, piety, or otherwise noteworthy contributions. There was good reason why Mary Wollstonecraft, that leading proponent of the "rights of women" in 1790s Britain, professed so little interest in the history of female "worthies." "I have been led to imagine," she explained in her 1792 *Vindication of the Rights of Woman*, "that the few extraordinary women who have rushed in eccentrical directions out of the orbit prescribed to their sex, were male spirited, confined by

>> 115

mistake in a female frame."² For Wollstonecraft, the history of women "worthies" was not the history of women at all. Rather, it was the history of those select "masculine" few who made a mockery of "the sex" for their inability to transcend their circumstances.

But the project of reconstructing the lives of "worthy" women was contested terrain, and the very exceptionalism of the subjects explored could provide interpreters with rich and sometimes deeply unsettling material. This chapter, then, drawing on the most recent scholarship in this field, traces the range of motives and objectives underlying the "woman worthy" genre as it developed in Britain. Focusing on the mid-eighteenth to mid-nineteenth centuries, when this approach to the writing of women's history in Britain was ascendant, I will map the genre's surprising complexity and capaciousness. Writers found in the "woman worthy," I will argue, a means not only of forging alternative and often inspirational models of womanhood, but also of thinking more broadly and critically about the status and rights of women in their nation, and about the politics of "Britishness" more generally. By way of conclusion, I will reflect on the implications and legacies of this genre for approaches to the writing of women's and gender history in the present. As I will suggest, these early British histories, and the men and women who wrote them, have important lessons to impart to us—about the kind of knowledge that can be gleaned from "exceptional" subjects, about the collaborative dimensions of women's history writing, and about the intimate links between the intellectual production of women's history and national identity formation.

"Women Worthies" and the Politics of History

Historians of women and gender have long acknowledged that queens, warriors, and other female "worthies" were the first of their sex to command significant historical attention, not just in Britain but on the Continent and in America as well—a point made in passing by Kathy Peiss in her contribution to this volume.³ Beginning in classical antiquity and then continuing through the Renaissance and early modern periods, and accelerating during the Age of Enlightenment, conjectural philosophers, scholars, and essayists—more often men than women, at least initially—devoted significant effort to documenting the lives of "exceptional" women, usually in the forms of "catalogs" or compendia. While such compendia could be damning in their assessments of their subjects, they tended by the mid-eighteenth century to be preoccupied with portraying their "ladies" in a flattering light.⁴ Artemisia, the Queen of Sheba, Boadicea, Joan of Arc, Elizabeth I—these women representing diverse cultures, periods, backgrounds, and accomplishments came to serve in texts, ranging from Thomas Heywood's 1624 *Gynaikeion or Nine Books of Various History Concerning Women* to Fortunée Briquet's 1804 *Dictionnaire historique, littéraire et bibliographique des Françaises*, as shining examples of what women, or at least *certain* women, might accomplish in the public arena.[5]

That "worthies" were the first women to enter history, then, is a fairly incontrovertible point. What to make of this genre, however, has been a subject of intense debate. For some time, scholars tended to adopt a tone of condescension in their treatments of these early forays into the female past, in large part because the modern discipline of women's history, as pioneered during the 1970s, was overwhelmingly concerned with recovering middle- and lower-class women's collective experiences. From this perspective, the earlier preference for documenting "exceptional" women—that is, those women, most often of privileged circumstances, who had succeeded *in spite* of the limitations placed on their sex—seemed more to undermine than to serve the field's larger, solidarity-oriented and politically inflected purposes. The lack of nuance in many early practitioners' treatment of women "worthies" also produced some consternation, especially for those eager to forge a subfield founded on more discerning methods. Then, too, the fact that an overwhelming number of these early histories had been authored by men made them less compelling as subjects of "women's history," as the field was then being constituted.

As a result, these early compendia were often disavowed or at least represented as motivated by antiquated impulses. Writing in 1976, for example, Natalie Zemon Davis acknowledged the genre's "polemical purposes," but dwelled on the limits of the "woman worthy" genre, even urging her readers to shift their focus from "women worthies to a worthier craft."[6] Almost a decade later, Bonnie G. Smith likewise proclaimed the "great women" approach to history "naïve," though she too conceded that the "woman worthy" had "played a crucial role ... in organizing memories of the female past, in laying claim to historic personality, and in challenging or enriching traditional accounts of accomplishment and influence."[7] Even as the 1980s saw a move away from "women" and toward "gender" as a "useful category of historical analysis," these early histories of exceptional women continued to receive little scholarly attention.[8]

In roughly the past decade, though, the tenor of this conversation has decidedly shifted. While fully attuned to the criticisms leveled by Davis and others, scholars are now casting fresh eyes on the nascent stages of women's history writing. In the process, they are calling attention to the complexities of the "exceptionalist" genre, both in its form and content, and urging that these texts no longer be "[l]umped together . . . rarely examined and readily dismissed."[9] This shift in perspective has produced some dramatic reassessments. Philip Hicks, for example, has argued that histories of "female worthies" played the "most important" role in "shap[ing]" eighteenth-century women's "political consciousness."[10] Mary Spongberg has claimed in her synoptic account of women's history since the Renaissance that "women worthy" histories "provided a record of female activity in the past and strong role models, and were often written to plead for the rights of women." On these grounds, Spongberg suggests that "Histories of 'women worthies' served as important precursors to feminist approaches to women's history."[11]

Certainly, close scrutiny of the actual texts under discussion bears out Hicks, Spongberg, and others' findings. After all, Richard Dinmore's *Brief Account* of 1793, with which I opened this chapter, would be difficult to label as elitist in its approach or unsophisticated in its methodologies. The *Brief Account* chronicles the history of queens regnant, but Dinmore chose to focus on women "above their sex" in large part because he wished to link the "right of women to the throne" to the "rights of women" more generally. Nor does Dinmore's sex seem to be satisfactory grounds for excluding his work from consideration. As historians are now increasingly committed to demonstrating, the history of women *is* the history of men and women in conversation.[12]

The case against "lumping" and "dismissing" the history of "women worthies" takes on particular meaning in a British context. For here we gain an especially clear perspective on how the act of cataloguing female accomplishments could promote intense, even if at times oblique, sexual and political contestation. Perhaps more than any other people, Britons of the eighteenth and nineteenth centuries refused to treat the past as a foreign country. Theirs was a culture characterized by the triumph of Common Law, the persistence of the "ancient" constitution, and the veneration of Anglo-Saxon customs and traditions, in which to consider the past was to evaluate and even shape the present. History was construed as a form of advocacy, and often unabashedly so. "[T]he didactic dimension of history," observes Paulina Kewes, "was endlessly exploited, reviewed, and debated."[13] This is why "commonwealthmen" of the seventeenth and eighteenth centuries peppered their critiques of the state with references to the "ancient common law" and the "ancient right to petition." The policies and practices adopted by the Anglo-Saxons could be interpreted as potent signs of Britain's democratic tendencies.[14]

In a nation that prided itself on continuities, in other words, how one narrated history by choosing which characters, dates, disputes, and practices to highlight, had everything to do with one's perspective on the models which British subjects, and the nation more generally, should strive to emulate. The past had an immediacy for late-eighteenth- and early-nineteenth-century subjects that is difficult for us to grasp today, with our emphasis on the importance of alterity and critical distance. As Karen O'Brien, Margaret Ezell, Philip Hicks, Mark Phillips, and Jane Rendall, amongst others, have stressed, the "historical culture" of this period "can be characterized ... as one of deepening interest in the imaginative, affective and experiential aspects of history," with "renewed interest in the individual life both as historical exemplum and as a point of imaginative mediation between the present and the past."[15] Within this context, in which interpreting the past, and especially past lives, was regarded as a fundamentally instructive and even interventionist act, what one wrote about women of the classical, ancient, and early modern periods, however "exceptional" their lives may have been, could also serve as a referendum on women in the present. Indeed, as Rendall has suggested, "the past history of British women" offered a key "site for debate in late eighteenth-century Britain."[16]

The Antiquarian Impulse

Some of the earliest British chroniclers of "exceptional" women, of course, would not necessarily have acknowledged their histories as interventions in contemporary debates about the status of women. Rather, mid-eighteenth-century practitioners—George Ballard, John Duncombe, George Colman, Bonnell Thornton, Thomas Amory, and the anonymous author of the 1766 *Biographium Faemineum*, among others—seem to have been drawn to the "history of famous women" genre primarily because they identified women's pasts as uncharted terrain, ripe for investigation. For these men, many of whom were enamored by antiquarianism, it was the desire to recuperate, rather than to advocate, which first compelled them to document female accomplishment. Telling in this regard is the title of the writer Thomas Amory's *Memoirs of Several Ladies of Great Britain, Interspersed with Literary Reflexions, and Accounts of Antiquities and Curious Things* (1755), which calls direct attention to the ways in which "worthy" women were initially construed more as objects of fascination, cultural oddities, than as subjects with important lessons to impart to eighteenth-century audiences.[17]

This impulse is particularly apparent in the antiquarian George Ballard's *Memoirs of Several Ladies of Great Britain* (1752), an ambitious and pioneering text that chronicled the lives and (mostly literary) contributions of sixty-four British "worthies," and which remains "a central source of information about women of the sixteenth, seventeenth, and eighteenth centuries."[18] Ballard clearly relished the challenge of unearthing material that had previously been overlooked, and devoted fifteen years to researching this project, with the considerable assistance of the Saxon scholar Elizabeth Elstob.[19] As Ruth Perry observes in her astute introduction to the *Memoirs*, Ballard's antiquarian "orientation" defined the project, both in its preparation and execution. "He is," she explains, "a collector and does not show much interest in the charms of exegesis or analysis. He obviously felt he was a compiler, not an interpreter."[20]

Yet history's didactic function would not have been entirely lost even on these initial "compilers." Although they rarely injected direct analysis into their texts, they would have recognized that there was something relevant, and perhaps even radical, about their findings—that their undertakings were necessarily "concerned with pointing out what was worthy of emulation."[21] Ballard, for example, at one point explicitly states that the goal of his *Memoirs* is to "remove" "that vulgar prejudice of the supposed incapacity of the female sex."[22] Here he also acknowledges that the goal of biography is "to inform us of those particulars" in the "lives and manners" of others "which best deserve our imitation."[23] John Duncombe, meanwhile, opened his celebratory poem *The Feminiad* (1754) by demanding whether "lordly man" shall "[b]y *Salic* law the female right deny,/ And view their genius with regardless eye?"[24] In the preface to their *Poems by Eminent Ladies* (1755), the writers George Colman and Bonnell Thornton similarly forwarded the claim that the material included in their book offered proof of female intellect. "These volumes are perhaps the most solid compliment that can possibly be paid to the Fair Sex," they explained, adding that the "ladies" chosen were "proof that great abilities are not confined to the men, and that genius often glows with equal warmth, and perhaps with more delicacy, in the breast of a female."[25]

These prefatory remarks were often further fleshed out in the exposition that followed. That Mary Sydney, Countess of Pembroke, was able to master the Hebrew language, for instance, served for Ballard as evidence that "the female sex are as capable of learning this as any other language."[26] Where Ballard appears most outspoken on this subject, however, comes in his extensive treatment of Dorothy Pakington, whom he believed to be the author of the anonymously-published *The Whole Duty of Man* (1658). "It has been very surprising to me," Ballard wrote, "to hear the many shifts and evasions which have been made use of on this occasion by several gentlemen, in order to deprive this lady and the fair sex, of the honour of those excellent performances."[27]

Such commentary would have provided significant ammunition for those seeking to counter the widespread claim that women possessed a different, and decidedly inferior "mental organization," a popular charge in the prolonged *querelle des femmes*. In fact, simply by showcasing those exceptional women who "were volunteers in the cause of learning, dedicated to letters, scholarship, and the pursuit of their own arcane versions of the truth," Ballard and others implicitly weighed in on the question of intellectual equality, "the burning issue of his day."[28] This was a point not lost on their peers, many of whom ridiculed the "woman worthy" project. "Many are the Attacks I have met with from a great variety of Gentlemen," Ballard once reported, ruefully adding that "to be reproached by those who have long labour'd in the Republic of Letters, & who consequently ought to have imbib'd better & more generous Principles, is like receiving Wounds in the Houses of ones Friends."[29] However cautiously Ballard may have framed his exposition, the *Memoirs* provided empirical ballast for egalitarian arguments.

Then, too, there is something highly suggestive about the fact that even these initial "compilers" weighed in not just on female intellectual capabilities, but also on the links between these capabilities and the meaning of "Britishness" in a broader sense. That is to say, their compendia sought to some extent not only to recover female exceptionalism but also to use this exceptionalism to make a larger point about the nation's distinctive qualities. This is why the subjects of mid-eighteenth-century "worthy" histories in Britain were so often culled from the nation's own past. Ballard, for example, took pains to show in his *Memoirs* that he had chosen his subjects as "ornaments" of both "sex" *and* "nation," even manipulating women's biographies so as to be able to claim his sixty-four "worthies" as specifically British subjects.[30] One of his goals was to illustrate how Britain had surpassed its rivals in producing "famous women" during this period. "[I]t is pretty certain," Ballard boasts in his preface, "that England hath produced more women famous for literary accomplishments, than any other nation in Europe."[31] Duncombe, Colman, Thornton, and others too followed Ballard's lead, framing their histories of notable women as patriotic endeavors, with "British nymphs" serving as markers both of national greatness and of the distance between Britain and other polities. Colman and Thornton, for example, made clear that the "ladies" included in their *Poems* were intended to "honour" "their sex" as well as "their native-country."[32]

In this respect, charting the history of women "worthies" could also serve as a means of defining, defending, and distinguishing "Britishness" from other national identities, a central preoccupation of eighteenth-century Britons, especially following the Act of Union with Scotland in 1707.[33] Just as a "cult of origins" was "linked to nation building," so women's "exceptional" pasts suggested to some extent what was specific and special about Britain's own inheritance, particularly in contradistinction to its Continental rivals.[34] The sheer number of women "worthies" in Britain's history reflected the nation's civility, morality, and "genius."[35] Mid-eighteenth-century "compilers" were eager to call out these tendencies. Where they became more tentative, however, was in explaining what these tendencies might mean for women in the present, and especially for those women *of* their sex rather than *above* it.

From Compilation to Advocacy

This reticence would change by the late eighteenth century. The latent radicalism of Ballard and other midcentury "compilers" would be exploded by many of the men and few women—Mary Scott, John Bristed, Thomas Garnett, Benjamin Heath Malkin, Richard Dinmore, T. S. Norgate, and William Enfield, among others—working in this genre in the years leading up to and during the Age of Revolution, when history took on only more charged and affective meanings. Immersed in the wider debates about the rights of man and woman spawned by the American and French Revolutions, several authors of "women worthy" literature became much more explicitly combative and used their texts to tout women's intellectual capabilities and to underscore their nation's continuing obligation to serve and promote women's interests. In their hands, "exceptional" women often became potent weapons in the multifaceted reformist attack on irrationality and privilege.

No longer hesitant, many of these late-eighteenth-century authors made clear that their "celebrated ladies" serve as examples of what women in general might be able to achieve. Shedding all pretenses of antiquarian preoccupation, they came forward instead to proclaim the "woman worthy" as evidence of female potential, especially in the intellectual arena, and frequently invoked her as a means of destabilizing long-standing theories of sexual difference.[36] Rebuffing those critics who insisted that the "appearances" of "masculine" women were "too uncommon to support the notion *of a general equality in the natural powers of mind*"—or what one smug reviewer in the *Monthly Magazine* described as the fact that there was not as yet "a Female Homer, or Virgil, or Bacon, or Newton"—they identified a host of women "worthies," including figures as diverse as Queen Elizabeth I, the Tory philosopher Mary Astell, and the classicist Elizabeth Carter, as women whose accomplishments reflected the broader capabilities of the female mind.[37] The poet Mary Scott, for example, used her 1774 *The Female Advocate,* which celebrated the contributions of fifty early modern British women, to draw out the implicit arguments of John Duncombe's earlier *Feminiad* about female capabilities, insistent that "facts have a powerful tendency to convince the understanding."³⁸ Another writer who adopted this approach was reform-minded historian Benjamin Heath Malkin, who proclaimed in his *Essays on Subjects Connected with Civilization* (1795), citing the accomplishments of women "worthies," that: "[T]he occasional display of female heroism" indicated that "mental inferiority is only the consequence of untoward circumstances."³⁹

A handful of late-eighteenth-century reformers even invoked "exceptional" females as a means of securing the "rights of women," a leap that would have been almost unthinkable just decades earlier. One "Calidore," for example, likely the Scotch reverend-turned-writer Andrew Macdonald, wrote a letter in 1788 to *The Gentleman's Magazine,* wherein which he grounded his bold argument for women's political rights in close readings of Boadicea, and queens Elizabeth and Anne. In his words, they were "heroines" who showed that the "leading maxims of feminine empire are to rouze men from ignorance and barbarism, and to diffuse among them arts and literature," a particularly interesting use of "worthies" in that "Calidore" drew profoundly egalitarian claims from his observations about distinctly "feminine" ways of ruling.⁴⁰ "Calidore's" treatment of Boadicea especially marked a significant departure from earlier characterizations of this "British queen of the Iceni tribe," who had long troubled British chroniclers with her demonstrations of "native savagery and resistance to Roman rule." What had struck early modern chroniclers as "savage excess" was recast in "Calidore's" text as passionate and unwavering commitment.⁴¹

During the 1790s, several other reformers followed "Calidore's" lead, invoking selected "heroines" to make bold claims for the "rights of women." Richard Dinmore, for example, discussed at length at the start of this chapter, used his *Brief Account* (1793) to flesh out how specific queens, and the succession policies that enabled their rule, underscored the need to incorporate women into the modern political system. Thomas Starling Norgate, another Norwich-based essayist and acquaintance of Dinmore, also found in the "woman worthy" a useful means of advancing his claims for women's rights. In the first part of his lengthy essay "On the Rights of Women," inspired by the writings of Mary Wollstonecraft and published in 1794–95 in the local periodical *The Cabinet,* Norgate turned to "exceptional" women from both the classical and early modern periods to demonstrate that women and men had the same capacity for reason and for marshaling what he described as the "masculine virtues," and thus were equally deserving of shared civil and political rights. "Can we maintain that females are unfit for councils, when Artemisia, queen of Halicarnassus, before the battle of Salamis, saved, by her advice, the mighty army of Xerxes," Norgate demanded. "[O]r shall we say that they are unfit to govern, when the ability with which Semiramis swayed the scepter of Assyria, induced Plato to maintain 'that women as well as men ought to be instructed with the government of states, and the conduct of military operations?'"[42] Norgate also heaped ample praise on Elizabeth I, devoting a separate essay to defending her "great and splendid" abilities.[43] To the extent that these women remained atypical, moreover, Norgate held culture rather than nature responsible. Once Britons committed themselves to providing women with the "power of education," he explained, the "woman worthy" would cease to be exceptional.[44]

As with authors working in this genre in the mid-eighteenth century, however, there was for many of these writers also a strongly nationalist dimension to their line of argumentation. The goal was never simply to call attention to untapped female potential, but also to use the figure of the "woman worthy" to make specific claims about the British nation. Yet in this case, the nationalist rhetoric was far more controversial than it had been in earlier texts such as Ballard's, where the sheer numbers of talented women were treated as useful tools for measuring the perspicacity of the nation. Here, reformers were often less interested in using the "woman worthy" to jockey for space on the European stage than in using her to vaunt an oppositional politics, one highly critical of contemporary practices.

In transforming the "worthy" into a potent source of critique, writers such as "Calidore," Norgate, and Dinmore departed from the earlier, celebratory mode of invoking "exceptional" women. Instead of linking women's aggregate accomplishments to national greatness, they instead rewrote the "worthy" as a symbol of an alternative, and far more democratic conception of national identity, one with roots in the nation's own "ancient" past. For them, "exceptional" women were not just "proof" of British "genius"; they were also vessels harboring the nation's own deep-seated, albeit somewhat dissipated and disrupted egalitarian instincts—instincts, that is, very much in need of recovery. Drawing on the works of Tacitus and Dio Cassius who, already in the second and third centuries had commented on the egalitariansim of early Britons (in terms often discomfiting to subsequent readers), as well as on the path-breaking revelations offered by such early-eighteenth-century antiquarians as George Hickes, author of a *Thesaurus* (1703–05) outlining Anglo-Saxon culture and politics, these writers frequently cast "women worthies" as emblems of Britain's democratic past. For them, this past was most fully realized under the Anglo-Saxons; their texts include lengthy expositions regarding how their "Saxon ancestors" had "looked up to the female sex as imbued with a superior intelligence, and deliberated with them in national emergencies."[45]

According to their interpretations, in fact, it was only following the Norman invasion of 1066 that women's position in Britain had begun to deteriorate, a process that had continued, albeit unevenly, through the eighteenth century. These were grave charges in a culture that placed heightened emphasis on the linear progression of "civilization" through discrete "stages" of history.[46] Those few "exceptional" women who had subsequently achieved prominence on the national stage reflected these earlier and increasingly elusive pro-Woman traditions. This is why, for instance, Dinmore and Norgate dwelled at such great length on Elizabeth I's reign. The very fact that she had been able to rule reflected these homegrown egalitarian impulses. It was now time, they urged, to restore these impulses—impulses that, once trained on the modern polity, would have significant implications not just for Britain's women, but also for all those subjects currently marginalized or disenfranchised.

The "Woman Worthy" in the Nineteenth Century

This invocation of the "woman worthy" as an oppositional figure would decline in Britain in the first decades of the nineteenth century. The rise of Napoleon and threat of French invasion, coupled with increasingly coordinated anti-Revolutionary activity at home, contributed to an atmosphere of quietism, with implications both for feminist activity and for reformist efforts more generally. The radical universalism that had characterized feminist discourses of the 1790s ceded to a new emphasis on men and women's "separate spheres" and the reinscription of sexual difference.[47] History, meanwhile, continued to serve a didactic purpose, but its goals proved increasingly conciliatory rather than combative.

As a result of these crucial shifts, most writers working in the "worthy" tradition once again became more hesitant in their attempts to link their subjects to women's rights or to a critical, albeit still patriotic politics. Of course, there were some exceptions to these tendencies. Writing shortly after the Peterloo Massacre in 1819 (a violent confrontation in the northern city of Manchester which pitted cavalry against parliamentary reformers and in which females played a large role), the radical Samuel Ferrand Waddington penned a "Vindication of Female Political Interference." He urged his readers to see the "lovely female sex of Manchester" not as "novel" in their willingness to enter into political and military skirmishes. Rather, he narrated a history of women "above their sex" to make his point that women had "possessed *coequal power*" at various moments in history, and especially in British history. "We should not . . . forget that our Queen Boadicea headed our troops, and made the last great effort against Roman tyranny," Waddington reminded his readers.[48]

Yet overall, the trend pointed away from this kind of aggressive use of "worthies." More often than not, authors chose instead to frame their inquiries as moral rather than expressly political investigations, with the goal of highlighting the ultimately "feminine" attributes of those "characters remarkable for some extraordinary deviation from the generality of the sex."[49] Thus, for example, Agnes Strickland's unabashed emphasis on Queen Elizabeth I's penchant for needlework in *The Lives of the Queens of England* (1840–48), coauthored with her sister Elizabeth.

Even in this more repressive climate, though, authors continued to use "worthies" to make important and often controversial claims about female capabilities. Their tendency to adopt the language of "separate spheres" and reluctance to engage explicitly with women's rights tenets should not be confused with apoliticism or conservatism. The present and future of British women weighed heavily on the minds of Mary Hays, William Boyd, Lucy Aikin, Elizabeth Benger, John Doran, John Heneage Jesse, Agnes and Elizabeth Strickland, Anna Jameson, Mary Anne Everett Green, Hannah Lawrance, and Mrs. Matthew Hall, to name just a few of the writers working in this increasingly popular and feminized genre—changes wrought by the rise of "professional" history and the expansion of the literary marketplace, and also by Queen Victoria's own coronation in 1838, which sparked a public demand for "worthy" texts while simultaneously authorizing women to write them.[50] These writers in different ways and to different degrees indicated that their "exceptional" subjects, an overwhelming number of whom were now, not surprisingly, queens and other female royalty, were meant to inspire the "fair sex," and perhaps even compel them to alter their circumstances.

In part, of course, nineteenth-century authors gravitated toward "women worthies," and especially female royalty, for pragmatic reasons. In a moment in which the discipline of professional—or as the reformer Mary Hays once put it, "scholarly"—history was beginning to crystallize, amateur historians often struggled to gain access to primary sources. Royalty therefore offered amateurs the opportunity to write history even if they lacked access to private collections. In many cases, in fact, apart from family histories, this was the only kind of history that amateurs *could* feasibly write. That compendia of "women worthies" also tended to be commercially successful, especially in the years following Queen Victoria's ascension, when the nation craved means of comprehending (and to some extent normalizing) female rule, also made the genre highly appealing. Agnes and Elizabeth Strickland proved particularly adept at churning out best-selling "worthy" histories that enabled the sisters to live by their pens.

Yet as Karen O'Brien and others have provocatively suggested, there were also political reasons for undertaking "woman worthy" histories in the first decades of the nineteenth century. The subjects typically under discussion— queens, princesses, and other "great ladies"—also enabled "a productive," even if highly mediated "means of exploring women's relationship to public culture and of articulating their aspirations for greater female prestige, education, and rights."[51] That is to say, a focus on elite women allowed many authors a way not just of writing history, but also of "writing about publicly significant female lives without the need to generalize their case as feminist argument."[52] The "appealing ambiguity" of powerful women's position, "at once public (by virtue of their rank) and private (by virtue of their gender)," made them rich subjects for inquiry, especially during this period of heightened conservatism.[53] Indeed, many late Georgian and early Victorian commentators recognized the queen's potential power to disrupt. As one journalist remarked in 1833, "We think those anomalous beings called maiden queens, and celebrated mistresses, even those that had their heads cut off, deserve no sympathy at present. The less that is said of them the better."[54]

Mary Hays's *Female Biography; or Memoirs of Illustrious and Celebrated Women of All Ages and Countries*, first published in 1803 and intended "for women, and not for scholars," in many respects set the agenda for this new approach to "women worthy" history.[55] Although often described as a project that removed Hays from the fray (during the 1790s, Hays, an associate of Wollstonecraft, had weighed in vehemently on a number of thorny political subjects), her *Female Biography* was not conceived as a form of "retreat."[56] Although "women's rights" are nowhere near as central in this text as they had been in her earlier *Appeal to the Men of Great Britain in Behalf of Women* (1798), Hays recognized that female emancipation would depend on creating a more dynamic and inspirational past, which women could aspire to "emulate."[57] For Hays, the two projects were mutually constitutive; to have the courage to act in the present, women needed to know that they were not alone in history. Already in her *Appeal*, Hays had begun to build a case for the importance of women's history as a means of informing women of their duties and rights. For these purposes, Hays identified the history of "women worthies," and especially of queens and other female royalty, as particularly valuable.[58] "Let it not be said," Hays insisted in her *Appeal*, "that crowned heads are too much out of the common road, to be brought forward for examples; for as they are neither more nor less than men and women, they come quite within our sphere."[59]

Drawing on the work of Ballard and other pioneers of the genre, Hays therefore explicitly seized on the didactic function of history to catalog the accomplishments of 288 women, with a heavy emphasis on queens and other royalty. Perhaps even more telling than her choice of royal subjects, however, was Hays's approach to writing their lives. In her *Female Biography*, Hays wanted to portray her "worthies" as "flawed characters, subject to human frailty, rather than merely exemplary human beings."[60] It was through creating nuanced character studies, Hays insisted, that the "emulative" functions of history would be best served. Not surprisingly, savvy critics quickly cottoned on to Hays's agenda. "In these volumes," proclaimed one reviewer for the *Monthly Review*, "we contemplate the laudable and successful exertions of a female to rescue her sex from the charges of being endued [*sic*] with inferior powers of mind."[61] These themes would only be further drawn out in Hays's *Memoirs of Queens* (1821), which she framed as an effort to advance "the moral rights and intellectual advancement of *woman*."[62]

In the months and years immediately following the publication of *Female Biography*, Hays was joined by a number of other authors interested in using royal women to promote female progress. William Boyd's *Eccentric Biography; or Memoirs of Remarkable Female Characters*, for example, published the same year as Hays's text, also examined the lives of "remarkable" women from a range of times and places, though with a heavy emphasis on British subjects, including Boadicea, Aphra Behn, Angelica Kauffmann, and Mary Wollstonecraft (to whom, given the cultural climate, Boyd extended surprisingly lavish praise).[63] Tellingly, Boyd also insisted that his study not be limited to the perfect and the pious, and laid great stress on the range of ways in which women had "distinguished themselves." The goal was to show women just how wide a sphere it was in which their sex has historically moved, and also the range of ways in which "femininity" could be expressed.[64] Lucy Aikin's *Epistles on Women, Exemplifying Their Character and Condition in Various Ages and Nations* (1810) also fleshed out some of these themes, drawing attention to the complexity both of women's characters and their contributions, and using what she described as the "impartial voice of history" to show how women could be "the worthy associates . . . of the best of men" and that "souls have no sex."[65]

Like their predecessors, these early-nineteenth-century authors also continued to link their inquiries to larger claims about the nation and national identity, and about women's participation in the construction of that identity. Even as some authors, most notably Hays and Boyd, experimented with moving beyond exclusively national frameworks, the nation remained a central and animating force in their narratives. For these authors, the "woman worthy" offered a way to explore not only female accomplishments but also these accomplishments in relation to the construction of a broader "British" national culture. Writers routinely underscored how their "exceptional" subjects had intervened at key moments in the nation's history, often in ways that were undervalued or overlooked in subsequent narratives, precisely because their interventions had been moral rather than political.

It is a fear of forgetting what women had done for the nation, in fact, which appears again and again in nineteenth-century "worthy" texts. The prolific writer Hannah Lawrance, for example, fretted in her *Historical Memoirs of the Queens of England* (1838–40) that "the queens of England still remain almost unknown."[66] Five years later, she would express similar sentiments in her *History of Woman in England* (1843). Lawrance's resolute goal, then, was to reveal just how much women had contributed to the nation, especially during the medieval period when, or so Lawrance believed, women had been accorded more opportunities for rational instruction.[67] Her "heroines" included Queen Margaret and Queen Maude, women "connected not only to the progress of English liberty and commerce, but also to cultural advancement."[68] (In this respect, Lawrance distinguished herself from many of her contemporaries, who either, in the tradition of Norgate and other eighteenth-century authors, looked to the Anglo-Saxon period for inspiration, or, in the mode of the Strickland sisters, concentrated their efforts on Tudor-Stuart England.) Mary Anne Everett Green, meanwhile, lamented how little her peers knew of what English princesses had done for the nation.[69]

By calling attention to women's often special role in the nation-building process, of course, these historians were offering a means, however subtle, of advocating a reconsideration of women's status and rights in the present, and perhaps even a means of legitimating—at least for those women working in this genre—their own authorial aspirations. "A formal recognition of women's presence and importance, in both the national community and the nation's historical record," writes Rosemary Mitchell, "was essential before new ideas on their role could evolve, or old ones be challenged."[70] We must remember that theirs was a culture preoccupied by the immediacy of history, in which narrating the past almost always served a didactic purpose.

But these writers also invoked the nation as a means of registering their concerns with the ways in which the discipline of history itself was emerging. Contesting the content privileged by the new "scholarly" histories, with their overwhelming focus on the public acts of great men, historians of "women worthies" questioned what Mary Spongberg has described as "masculinist generic conventions."[71] As Agnes Strickland explained in *The Queens of England*, "History, separated from the companionship of her sister biography, is an inexplicable riddle; for in the individual characters of rulers and princes... can alone be traced the springs of the outward and visible actions, which history records."[72] In this respect, many nineteenth-century historians of "exceptional" women construed their biographies as critical supplements to the professional histories in circulation—supplements which not only helped to create a more balanced assessment of the nation's past but which also called the very premises of "scholarly" history into question.

A Worthy Legacy?

Given the complexity and dynamism of the "women worthy" genre in eighteenth- and nineteenth-century Britain, how are we to assess these histories' legacies? Despite the recent reappraisals of this mode of historical writing, many historians of women and gender remain, to some extent, embarrassed by their field's origins. For indications of this discomfort, one only has to turn to Judith Bennett's recent *History Matters,* which worries, given the preponderance of "books, articles and dissertations... adopting a biographical approach" to the female past, whether women's history is "in danger of tilting... too far back toward women worthies?"[73] Yet I would argue that such anxieties are misplaced. Not only have practitioners come too far to revert completely to an older style of scholarship, but the older style itself, as I have mapped here, is also far more worthy of analysis and to some extent perhaps even of emulation. I will conclude by briefly elaborating on the lessons we might learn from this particular "biographical approach" to women's pasts.

First, examination of the multiple ways in which historians of women in Britain seized on and manipulated the "woman worthy" genre reveals the potential benefits to be accrued by directing more critical energy at the study of "exceptional" women. Many in our discipline continue to express profound skepticism toward research focused on "women on top." Still there remains much to be learned about "anomalous" women of the past, first in terms of how such women fostered and negotiated their own exceptionalism. But much can also be learned from how others, historians included, responded to, recovered, and recorded these elites' special status, a dynamic that played no small role in shaping attitudes toward women over time and in different cultural and historical moments. This is especially true in the British instance, where "women on top" have long played a decisive role in shaping the broader culture. As Clarissa Campbell Orr explains, in urging scholars to engage more seriously with the subject of British queenship, "Studies of British womanhood have, with valuable exceptions... tended to focus on women of middling or lower social rank... Yet much is to be gained for women's history and feminist history by looking at women at the social apex, including their roles, representations and symbolic importance for other men and women."[74]

Second, even a brief survey of eighteenth- and nineteenth-century approaches to the "women worthy" genre in Britain indicates something telling about the collaborative dimensions of early women's history writing. Despite occasionally willful attempts to narrate the history of women's history as a prolonged gender struggle—with beleaguered women battling to overcome various obstacles in uncovering the female past—the gendered dynamics in play in the early production of women's history were, in fact, much more complex than this dominant narrative suggests. For various reasons, which I have begun to sketch here, men as much as women were drawn to the writing of women's history, and it is perhaps more difficult than might be expected to tease out male versus female approaches to their subject matter. In fact, as detailed earlier, some of the most radical articulations of "women worthy" history were penned by male reformers of the 1790s. Well into the nineteenth century, men, including John Heneage Jesse and John Doran, continued to take pride in women's past accomplishments, as was most evident in Jesse's extended poem, *Mary, Queen of Scots* (1829). This is not to suggest that gender strife played no role in the writing of women's history. Certainly, women faced specific challenges in trying to gain access to records, as well as in their encounters with sometimes hostile male publishers and critics. But early women's history was by no means the exclusive provenance of women. It would behoove us to remember this in reflecting on the future of women's history and its evolving relationship to and positioning within the broader historical discipline.

Finally, this line of inquiry opens up important questions about the intersections between women's history and the history of the nation. Though placed in a collection that aims to situate women's history within comparative, transnational, and even global frameworks—highly laudable projects—this chapter simultaneously reminds us that we are not yet finished with the "nation" as a critical category of analysis, especially vis-à-vis the intellectual production of women's history. There is still much more work to be done on the process by which women's history and "British" history emerged in ways that were mutually constitutive. Indeed, as this survey suggests, late-eighteenth- and early-nineteenth-century histories of gender and nation appeared not just alongside each other but also *with* each other, even if at times in ways that placed them in tension. During this period, to write the history of women *was* to write the history of the nation, however variously the "nation" was understood. Given these early entanglements, it may prove impossible to ever fully move beyond the nation in writing the history of women.

NOTES
1. For this intriguing argument, see Richard Dinmore, *A Brief Account of the Moral and Political Acts of the Kings and Queens of England, from William the Conqueror to the Revolution in the Year 1688* (London: H. D. Symonds, 1793), 178–79. On the history of the elaboration of the Salic Law in France, see Sarah Hanley, "The Family, the State, and the Law in Seventeenth- and Eighteenth-Century France: The Political Ideology of Male Right versus an Early Theory of Natural Rights," *Journal of Modern History* 78, 2 (2006).
2. Mary Wollstonecraft, *A Vindication of the Rights of Woman* (London: J. Johnson, 1792), 68. See also Mary Spongberg, *Writing Women's History since the Renaissance* (New York: Palgrave, 2002), 35.
3. On this point, see also Natalie Zemon Davis, "'Women's History' in Transition: The European Case," *Feminist Studies* 3, 3/4 (Spring–Summer 1976): 83.

> The genre of women's history is no newcomer on the scene. In one form it goes back to Plutarch, who composed little biographies of virtuous women, intended to show that the female sex could and should profit by education. Taken up again by Boccaccio in the fourteenth century, the collective memorials of 'Women Worthies' continued in an unbroken line—from the City of Ladies of Christine de Pisan through Madam Briquet's 1804 Dictionary... of French Women... known for their Writings; from the seventeenth-century Gynaikeion of Thomas Heywood to the eighteenth-century British Ladies... Celebrated for their Writings of George Ballard. Sometimes the subjects had talents in many fields; other times they were all religious, as in Osbern Bokenham's medieval *Legends of Hooly Wommen*; or all literary; or all political, as in the *Lives of the Queens of England* by the Victorian Strickland sisters.

> For a list of "early examples" of collective female biographies, see also Alison Booth's important bibliography in *How to Make It as a Woman: Collective Biographical History from Victoria to the Present* (Chicago: University of Chicago Press, 2004), 348–51. While this is only a partial list, it conveys the range of participants in this project.

4. On the earlier tradition of celebrating/denigrating "women worthies," see Spongberg, *Writing Women's History*; Glenda McLeod, *Virtue and Venom: Catalogs of Women from Antiquity to the Renaissance* (Ann Arbor: University of Michigan, 1991); Miriam Elizabeth Burstein, "Women worthies," in Mary Spongberg, Barbara Caine, and Ann Curthoys, eds, *Companion to Women's Historical Writing* (New York: Palgrave, 2005); and Sarah Gwyneth Ross, *The Birth of Feminism: Women as Intellect in Renaissance Italy and England* (Cambridge: Harvard University Press, 2009), esp. Chapter 3 on "The Biographical Tradition." Jodi Mikalachki, *The Legacy of Boadicea: Gender and Nation in Early Modern England* (New York: Routledge, 1998), is also excellent on the castigation of "women worthies," especially from the Roman period, in early modern British historiography. See especially p. 12: "Disrupting social hierarchies, resisting civility and dragging the native race into ruin, the savagery of ancient British women consistently thwarted early modern attempts to merge national history with the masculine order of Rome."

5. On Thomas Heywood as a "found]ing" contributor to this genre in England, see D.R. Woolf, "A Feminine Past? Gender, Genre and Historical Knowledge in England, 1500-1800," *The American Historical Review* 102, 3 (June 1997): 645-679. On Briquet, see Carla Hesse, *The Other Enlightenment: How French Women Became Modern* (Princeton: Princeton University Press, 2001).
6. See Davis, "'Women's History' in Transition," p. 93. For more on the "polemical purposes" of this genre, see Davis's statement, p. 83, about its ability "to disclose the range of female capacity, to provide exemplars, to argue from what some women had done to what women could do, if given the chance and education." For a different, but no less critical assessment, see Gerda Lerner, "Placing Women in History: A 1975 Perspective," in Berenice Carroll, ed *Liberating Women's History: Theoretical and Critical Essays* (Urbana: University of Illinois Press, 1976). As Lerner writes, p. 357, "The history of notable women is the history of exceptional, even deviant women, and does not describe the experience and history of the mass of women."
7. See Bonnie G. Smith, "The Contribution of Women to Modern Historiography in Great Britain, France and the United States, 1750–1940," *American Historical Review* 89, 3 (1984): 717–18.
8. On gender as a category of historical analysis, see Joan Wallach Scott, "Gender: A Useful Category of Historical Analysis," *American Historical Review* 91, 5 (1986): 1053–75. Of course, there are some notable exceptions to these trends. See especially Ruth Perry's largely positive assessment of George Ballard's approach to the writing of "women worthy" history in her "Introduction" to George Ballard, *Memoirs of Several Ladies of Great Britain*, ed. Ruth Perry (Detroit: Wayne State University Press, 1985), 12–48. Greg Kucich also expressed concern in 1993 that "as much as the contemporary project of feminist historical revisionism has reconfigured the traditional contours or 'man's truth,' it has paid only limited attention to its own eighteenth and early nineteenth-century precursors who were vigorously engaged in a critical endeavor." See Greg Kucich, "Romanticism and Feminist Historiography," *Wordsworth Circle* 24, 3 (Summer 1993): 134. Note, however, that Kucich is not exclusively interested in "women worthy" histories, though these are included in his discussion.
9. See Spongberg, *Writing Women's History*, 2.
10. See Philip Hicks, "Portia and Marcia: Female Political Identity and the Historical Imagination, 1770–1800," *William and Mary Quarterly* 62, 2 (April 2005), par 3. 15, accessed Dec. 2010 <http://www.historycooperative.org/journals/wm/62.2/hicks.html>.
11. See Spongberg, *Writing Women's History*, 110. Spongberg further elaborates on this point elsewhere in the book.
12. See especially my claim in *Men and the Making of Modern British Feminism* (Stanford: Stanford University Press, 2010), that "the link between sex and feminism needs to be denaturalized" (6).
13. See Paulina Kewes, "History and Its Uses," in *The Uses of History in Early Modern England*, ed. Paulina Kewes (San Marino, Calif.: Huntington Library, 2006), 1.
14. For more on the uses of the "ancient constitution," see J. G. A. Pocock, *The Ancient Constitution and the Feudal Law: A Study of English Historical Thought in the Seventeenth Century* (Cambridge: Cambridge University Press, 1957), and James Epstein, *Radical Expression: Political Language, Ritual, and Symbol in England, 1790–1850* (New York: Oxford University Press, 1994).
15. Karen O'Brien, *Women and Enlightenment in Eighteenth-Century Britain* (Cambridge: Cambridge University Press, 2009), 204. See also Margaret Ezell, *Writing Women's Literary History* (Baltimore: Johns Hopkins University Press, 1993); Philip Hicks, "Portia and Marcia"; Mark Phillips, *Society and Sentiment: Genres of Historical Writing in Britain, 1740–1820* (Princeton: Princeton University Press, 2000); and Jane Rendall, "Tacitus Engendered:

'Gothic Feminism' and British Histories, c. 1750–1800," in Geoffrey Cubitt, ed., *Imagining Nations* (Manchester: Manchester University Press, 1998).

16. See Rendall, "Tacitus Engendered," 69. It should be noted, however, that Rendall is interested not just in the uses of "women worthies," but also, centrally, in the uses of women as a broader social category in the new conjectural or "stadial" histories that were beginning to be produced, largely by Scotch authors, from the mid- to late eighteenth century.
17. See Thomas Amory, *Memoirs of Several Ladies of Great Britain, Interspersed with Literary Reflexions, and Accounts of Antiquities and Curious Things* (London: John Noon, 1755).
18. See Perry, "Introduction" to *Memoirs of Several Ladies*, 12.
19. See Perry's discussion of Elstob's influence on Ballard in her "Introduction" to *Memoirs of Several Ladies*, 24: "Elstob's story influenced Ballard profoundly. He, who reverenced learning above all else, was horrified at how her fortunes had fallen when her brother died. It must have made him think about how many other learned women, stymied by circumstance, shared her fate and were living out silent martyrdoms, unknown to the world. And it must have made him wonder about intellectual women in the past, buried in history, their stories forgotten."
20. See Perry, "Introduction" to *Memoirs of Several Ladies*, 26–27.
21. Ezell, *Writing Women's Literary History*, 69.
22. See Ballard, *Memoirs of Several Ladies of Great Britain* (Oxford: W. Jackson, 1752), 321.
23. Ballard, *Memoirs*, v.
24. John Duncombe, *The Feminiad: A Poem* (London: M. Cooper, 1754), 5.
25. George Colman and Bonnell Thornton, *Poems by Eminent Ladies*, 2 vols. (London: R. Baldwin, 1755), vol. I, iii.
26. Ballard, *Memoirs*, 261.
27. Ballard, *Memoirs*, 320. As Perry notes in her "Introduction" to Ballard's text, such commentary was only more prevalent in the draft version of his manuscript: "Wherever Ballard corrected his original manuscript, he usually toned down his feminist polemic and omitted his heartfelt editorializing.... What one discovers when examining some of the excised passages is that Ballard was really more of a crusader for women's rights than would appear from the rather formal writing of the published version" (35).
28. Perry, "Introduction" to *Memoirs of Several Ladies*, 13 and 32.
29. Ballard, April 25, 1747, Stowe MSS, 753–75, British Library, cited in Perry, "Introduction" to *Memoirs of Several Ladies*, 37.
30. Ballard, *Memoirs*, vi. For further elaboration on this point, see Harriet Guest, *Small Change: Women, Learning, Patriotism, 1750–1810* (Chicago: University of Chicago Press, 2000), 57: "The distinctive feature of his work lay in his editorial policy, his principles of selection: the emphasis on national and gendered character, at the expense of differences between those memorialized. Ballard perceived his project specifically as a matter of competition with other European nations. In order to swell the numbers of learned women that 'England hath produced,' he introduces those of Ireland and Scotland, and includes women who lived on the Continent, but whom he believed could be claimed as British as a result of their birth, or knowledge of the language."
31. Ballard, *Memoirs*, vi.
32. Colman and Thornton, *Poems*, iii.
33. On the construction of "Britishness" in opposition to other nationalities, and especially to Catholic France, see the now classic formulation offered by Linda Colley in *Britons: Forging the Nation, 1707–1837* (New Haven: Yale University Press, 1992).

34. See Moira Ferguson, *Eighteenth-Century Women Poets: Nation, Class and Gender* (Albany: SUNY Press, 1995), 29. Miriam Elizabeth Burstein draws similar conclusions in her *Narrating Women's History in Britain, 1770–1902* (Burlington, Vt.: Ashgate, 2004), especially p. 16: "Writing about women's history has always been a convenient way of really writing about something else." For elaboration on this theme, see also Ross, *The Birth of Modern Feminism*. Ross describes Ballard's project as motivated by a desire to assign Britain "its rightful place in the pan-European world of letters" (129).
35. See Guest, *Small Change*, 49–50. On this point, see also Ferguson, *Eighteenth-Century Women Poets*, especially 29.
36. On this late-eighteenth-century reorientation, see Karen O'Brien, *Women and Enlightenment in Eighteenth-Century Britain*: "[M]any found the writing of history a productive means of exploring women's relationship to public culture and of articulating their aspirations for greater female prestige, education and rights" (203).
37. See respectively, John Bristed, *A Pedestrian Tour*, 2 vols. (London: J. Wallis, 1803), vol. 1, 356, and "Letter from A. B," *Monthly Magazine* (May 1796), 289–90.
38. Mary Scott, *The Female Advocate* (London: J. Johnson, 1774), vii. For background on Scott's contribution, see Ferguson, *Eighteenth-Century Women Poets*, especially chapter 3. As Ferguson explains, "Mary Scott composed *The Female Advocate*, partly inspired by this male outburst of gynocentric [midcentury] commendation" (29).
39. Benjamin Heath Malkin, *Essays on Subjects Connected with Civilization* (London: C. Dilly, 1795), 257–58.
40. See "Calidore," *The Gentleman's Magazine*, 58 (1788), 101.
41. See Mikalachki, *The Legacy of Boadicea*, especially 11–12.
42. T. S. Norgate, "On the Rights of Women, part 1st," *The Cabinet* (Norwich: J. March, 1794–95), 180–81.
43. See T. S. Norgate, "Observations on the Reign and Character of Queen Elizabeth," *Essays, Tales, and Poems* (Norwich: J. March, 1795), 142–43.
44. T. S. Norgate, "On the Rights of Women, part 1st," *The Cabinet*, 179.
45. "Calidore," *The Gentleman's Magazine*, 100.
46. On this point, see again Rendall, "Tacitus Engendered."
47. On this shift in feminist orientation, see Mary Spongberg, "The Ghost of Marie Antoinette: A Prehistory of Victorian Royal Lives," in Lynette Felber, ed., *Clio's Daughters: British Women Making History, 1790–1899* (Newark: University of Delaware Press, 2007), 71–96.
48. See Samuel Ferrand Waddington, "Vindication of Female Political Interference," in *The Republican*, 1, 3 (September 10, 1819), 45. Italics Waddington's.
49. William Boyd, *Eccentric Biography* (London: T. Hurst, 1803), iii–iv.
50. See again Burstein, "Women Worthies," in *Companion to Women's Historical Writing*, 595.
51. O'Brien, *Women and Enlightenment*, 203.
52. O'Brien, *Women and Enlightenment*, 218. On this point, see also Rosemary Mitchell, *Picturing the Past: English History in Text and Image 1830–1870* (Oxford: Clarendon Press, 2000), 141; and Spongberg, "The Ghost of Marie Antoinette," especially 74: "[W]omen writers . . . came to view biographies of royal women as an acceptable space where they could discuss the condition of women under patriarchy and make suggestions regarding its amelioration."
53. Mitchell, *Picturing the Past*, 142.
54. *Monthly Review*, New Series, vol. 2 (London: 1833), 285.
55. Mary Hays, "Preface" to *Female Biography*, 6 vols. (London: R. Phillips, 1803).

56. On Hays's *Female Biography* as a "retreat," see, for example, D. R. Woolf, "A Feminine Past?": "[*Female Biography* was] something of a retreat for this erstwhile radical" (676). One of the main reasons why Hays's *Female Biography* has been treated as a "retreat" from her earlier work is that Hays omitted Wollstonecraft from the text. Yet, as Gina Luria Walker has convincingly argued, Hays had already published a piece entitled "Memoirs of Mary Wollstonecraft" in the *Annual Necrology* for 1797–98 (London: R. Phillips, 1800). This piece, Walker argues, was "intended" "as the first entry" for her *Female Biography*. For an elaboration of this argument, see Gina Luria Walker, *Mary Hays (1759–1843): The Growth of a Woman's Mind* (Burlington, Vt.: Ashgate, 2006), and her "Women's Voices," in *The Cambridge Companion to British Literature of the French Revolution in the 1790s*, ed. Pamela Clemit (Cambridge: Cambridge University Press, 2011). I would like to thank Gina for sharing this piece with me in advance of publication.
57. See Spongberg, *Writing Women's History*, 117.
58. See Spongberg, "The Ghost of Marie Antoinette," 88.
59. See Hays, *Appeal to the Men of Great Britain in Behalf of Women* (London: J. Johnson, 1798), 36.
60. Spongberg, *Writing Women's History*, 118.
61. See the review of Mary Hays's *Female Biography* in the *Monthly Review* 15, 103 (July 28, 1803), p. 622.
62. See Mary Hays, "Preface," *Memoirs of Queens* (London: T. and J. Allman, 1821), italics Hays's, cited in Gina Luria Walker, ed., *The Idea of Being Free: A Mary Hays Reader* (Peterborough, Ontario: Broadview, 2006), 290.
63. On Wollstonecraft, see especially Boyd, *Eccentric Biography*, 138–42.
64. On *Eccentric Biography* as offering a challenge to a "monolithic representation of femininity," see Julian North, *The Domestication of Genius: Biography and the Romantic Poet* (New York: Oxford University Press, 2009), 20.
65. Lucy Aikin, *Epistles on Women* (Boston: W. Wells and T. B. Wait and Co., 1810). For fuller discussion of Aikin's project, see Rendall, "Tacitus Engendered."
66. Hannah Lawrance, *Historical Memoirs of the Queens of England* (London: E. Moxon, 1838), iii.
67. On Hannah Lawrance's approach to writing women's past, see Benjamin Dabby, "Hannah Lawrance and the Claims of Women's History in Nineteenth-Century England," *Historical Journal* 53, 3 (September 2010): 699–722. As Dabby argues, 710, "The connections Lawrance drew among education, women, and the march of civilization was the defining feature of these volumes and explains why Lawrance chose to locate her olden times in the medieval period."
68. Again, see Dabby, "Hannah Lawrance," 709.
69. For elaboration on these points, see Mitchell, *Picturing the Past*, 150.
70. Mitchell, *Picturing the Past*, 143.
71. See Spongberg, "The Ghost of Marie Antoinette," 74. On this point, see also Mitchell, *Picturing the Past*, 150.
72. Agnes and Elizabeth Strickland, *The Lives of the Queens of England*, 6 vols. (London: Bell and Daldy, 1864 [1840–48]), vol. 2, 540.
73. Judith Bennett, *History Matters: Patriarchy and the Challenge of Feminism* (Philadelphia: University of Pennsylvania Press, 2006), 24.
74. Clarissa Campbell Orr, ed., *Queenship in Britain 1660–1837: Royal Patronage, Court Culture and Dynastic Politics* (Manchester: Manchester University Press, 2002), 7.

6

Amateur Historians, the "Woman Question," and the Production of Modern History in Turn-of-the-Twentieth-Century Egypt

LISA POLLARD

Egyptian women only recently played critical roles in the eighteen days of protests that toppled Mohammed Husni Mubarak's thirty-year presidency on February 11, 2011.[1] Photographs of the demonstrations revealed women marching in the streets, confronting both the military and the Egyptian riot police, and tending to the sick and wounded in Tahrir Square. Similarly, video clips, recorded and released just prior to the outbreak of demonstrations on January 25, 2011, showed women openly discussing their behind-the-scenes roles in organizing the protests via social networks such as Twitter and Facebook.[2] For Western observers, such images of Egyptian women fighting for political change stood in stark contrast to the depictions of passive and sequestered Muslim women that have dominated the media since September 11, 2001. For Egyptians, however, the presence of women in the streets linked the revolution of 2011 to a century of protests and revolutions in which women have been active participants.

The role of women in political uprisings has been the source of Egyptian pride since women took to the streets against the British in 1919. Indeed, each March, the Egyptian press commemorates International Women's Day with photographs of women-led demonstrations from March 1919. Those photographs illustrate the critical roles women played in guaranteeing the birth of an independent Egyptian nation-state. It is difficult to find a historical account of 1919 that does not include a discussion of the roles women played in the revolution, engaging in activities that looked much like those their great-granddaughters would play in 2011.

While Egyptian enthusiasm for women's role in gaining their nation's independence is almost a century old, the mainstream academic production of women's history in Egypt is of relatively recent occurrence. Egyptian universities have housed history departments since the early decades of the twentieth century. Yet not until 1945, when the noted Egyptian feminist Doria Shafiq (1908–75), Sorbonne Ph.D. in hand, teamed up with Ibrahim ʿAbduh of Cairo University to pen *The Development of the Women's Awakening in*

Egypt between the time of Mohammed ʿAli and that of King Faruq, did the first text on the topic appear from within the Egyptian academy. The pair, working together again in 1955, published a history of Egyptian women from the Pharaonic era to the present.[3] It would take another generation before the Egyptian academy began producing a body of work specifically about Egyptian women's history.[4]

This seeming marginalization of Egyptian women's history within Egypt's universities has led to the development of the field elsewhere.[5] Outside Egypt, Egyptian and non-Egyptian historians working in North America and Europe have advanced the fields of women's and gender history in studies that have focused especially on women and the rise of the Egyptian nation-state, on Orientalist portrayals of Egyptian women, and on the gender politics of British colonial rule.[6] In Egypt, the American University of Cairo's School of Global Affairs and Public Policy houses the Cynthia Nelson Institute for Gender and Women's Studies. The Institute, which is both a research center and a graduate teaching center, is home to some of Egypt's finest scholars of women's and gender history and to students from around the globe, and encourages the transnational and interdisciplinary study of women's lived experiences, past and present.[7] Also in Egypt, the Cairo-based Women and Memory Forum, founded in 1995 by Egyptian academics, researchers, and activists trained in both Egypt and the West has done much to promote the study of women's history in Egypt. The group holds frequent workshops, dedicated to the articulation of new methodologies for the study of women's history. Additionally, the group's website and its substantial publications—including reprints of texts authored by Egypt's pioneering feminists—encourage interest in Egyptian women's historical legacy, and promote the replacement of negative stereotypes of Egyptian women with more accurate portrayals.[8]

The slowness with which the Egyptian academy embraced and promoted women's history as a formal program, however, belies the central role that debates about women played in producing the field of modern history in Egypt. Indeed, from the mid-nineteenth century onward, as the practice of modern historical writing saw its rise in Egypt, debates about such topics as religion, veiling, marriage, and the "proper" roles of women inside and outside their homes served as vehicles through which Egyptian civil servants, British colonial administrators, and Egyptian nationalists defined the territory that they called Egypt and began to narrate a specifically Egyptian history. By 1900 "the woman question" had emerged as the most common vehicle through which an emerging cast of amateur historians—civil servants, intellectuals, journalists, and educators—narrated and debated the origins, as well as the destiny, of the Egyptian people. The "woman question" remains a common vehicle through which nonacademic history—what historian Anthony Gorman calls "history in the streets"—is articulated, as journalists, intellectuals, and historians not allied with the academy use women as symbols through which to assert their versions of where the Egyptian people came from and where, as a nation, they ought to be headed.[9]

This chapter examines the nexus of the rise of the state, debates about women, and the emergence of a modern historical practice in nineteenth- and turn-of-the-twentieth-century Egypt. Its focus is on amateur historians whose work formed the basis of what would become a profession after World War I. The legacy of those nonprofessionals' concern with "the woman question" was not the immediate mainstream production of women's history from within the academy. Rather, amateur historians' attention to women as symbols for narrating history resulted in a popular historical practice, in which "Lady Egypt," the gendered-feminine embodiment of Egypt that emerged from turn-of-the-twentieth-century historical debates, continues to define Egyptians' commentaries about the state of their nation.[10]

Amateur historians in the nineteenth and early twentieth centuries were a mixed lot, ranging from Egyptian civil servants to British colonial officials. What each group had in common was a concern with defining modern Egypt. Beginning with an examination of literature produced in the nineteenth century by state officials, this chapter illustrates how Egyptians first came to understand Egypt as a distinct territory through attention to domestic practices. This literature created both gendered-feminine views of Egypt and linked women's domestic behavior to the modernization process.[11] European travel writers and the administrators who oversaw the British colonial state after 1882 furthered discussions about the relationship between Egyptian domestic practices and modernity by making the opposite argument: that the position of women in Egyptian society hampered its ability to be modern. The colonial officials who also wrote histories of what they called "modern" Egypt attributed British-authored reforms related to women to Egypt's first steps toward modernity. Their histories joined those of an increasing number of amateur Egyptian "bureaucrat historians" who made similar arguments, but who attributed reform and modernization to efforts made by the Egyptian state.[12]

This emerging body of history about the state and its reform programs linked "the woman question" to Egyptian modernity in ways pursued by yet another group of amateur historians: male and female nationalists who used the Egyptian press, beginning in the 1890s, to argue for their readiness for self-rule. Their debates about "the woman question" created a symbolic

"Lady Egypt"—a composite of women from Egypt's Pharaonic, Greco-Roman, and Arab Islamic pasts. In each case, debates about "Lady Egypt" allowed for the narration of the Egyptian past, and for commentary about the nation's future.

Domestic Dirt: The Construction of Modern Landscapes and Modern Histories

The linking of women to an emerging vision of Egypt as a distinct territory, and to the practice of modern historical narration, has its roots in the birth of Egypt's modern state. The emergence of that state infrastructure was the result of the efforts of an Ottoman military official, Mehmet ʿAli Pasha (1769–1848), who gained nominal suzerainty over the Ottoman province of Egypt by centralizing and modernizing it. To do so, he inaugurated a number of institutions which, in turn, gave rise to a cadre of civil servants who began imagining and writing about Egypt in new ways. Those state functionaries produced literature that depicted the modernization process not only as the acquisition and implementation of new governing tactics and industrial technologies by a ruler, but also as the adoption of new states of mind and the cultivation of new habits by his or her subjects. In a body of state-sponsored travel literature, history, and geography, published from the 1820s through the late nineteenth century, Egyptian civil servants ascribed the success of the state-building projects of modern rulers to the domestic habits of the men and women who inhabited their realms. Thus, as a new class of civil servants worked to modernize a territory that they referred to, with ever-increasing frequency, as distinctly Egyptian, they gestured toward women and the domestic realm as that which guaranteed (or, by contrast, inhibited) the modern nation's success.

Mehmet Ali's school of translation, for example, which opened in the early 1820s, produced graduates who could translate Western texts about political, economic, and military institutions (and apparatuses) into Arabic and Turkish for the use of Mehmet ʿAli's modernizing elite. The texts about accounting, medicine, civil administration, and arms building, which the graduates of the school of translation produced and published at the viceroy's request, served as instruction manuals for the implementation of his modernization programs. At the same time, translated European history and geography books introduced a second set of instructions about modernity. Historical accounts of modern rulers, for example, Jean-Henri Castéra's history of Catherine the Great and Voltaire's histories of Charles XII of Sweden and Peter the Great, among others, exposed Egyptian civil servants to accounts of great men (and women) who had modernized their domains.¹³ In those accounts, the success of reforming monarchs was measured by such things as the reorganization of their militaries, the rationalization of their bureaucracies, and their implementation of public works. Castéra and Voltaire also attributed these rulers' success in the public realm to their personal habits, marital practices, and domestic behaviors.

The French-German historian Georges-Bernard Depping made a similar connection between the political and the personal in his *Aperçu historique sur les moeurs et coutumes des nations*, in which he exposed Egyptian readers to a logic that would become common to literature produced by "bureaucrat historians" over the course of the nineteenth century. Depping opened his text by cataloguing nations in terms of their houses and of the customs practiced in them. Depping used his discussions of domestic practices as a yardstick for measuring a nation's political success, as he considered the condition of the body politic to be a reflection of household affairs.¹⁴ The Egyptian state functionaries who read history thus experienced state building as a kind of ethnography in which modernization was understood and charted through the habits and customs of those who undertook it.¹⁵ To be modern meant not only to wield power successfully but also to live and behave in certain ways.

In a similar vein, the substantial number of European-produced geography books that Egyptians translated in the 1830s linked modernity to domestic behavior. The Danish-French geographer Conrad Malte-Brun's *Précis de la géographie universelle*, which made its appearance in Cairo in 1838, organized the world's nations according to their levels of modernity, a condition that Malte-Brun characterized as beginning in the home and spreading outward to the body politic. Domestic "dirt," that is, poor hygiene and sexual licentiousness, produced despotism and corruption; advanced nations kept house in such a way as to produce well-mannered citizens and well-ordered governments. Malte-Brun's cartography rendered the world's boundaries both fixed and fluid, as nations were catalogued not only according to their longitude and latitude, but by their potential to be modern. Malte-Brun's system suggested that nations could move closer to modernity when rulers attended to reform, beginning with the domicile.¹⁶

While the school of translation allowed Mehmet ʿAli to bring the kind of modernity he sought to Egypt, the viceroy also sent Egyptian civil servants to Europe. Those Egyptians who studied abroad produced travel accounts that also linked the success of the modern European states to the domestic habits of their citizens. Rifaʿa Rafiʿ al-Tahtawi (1801–73), for example, the best known of the Egyptians selected to travel to Europe, returned to Cairo in 1835 after a nine-year stay in France to serve the nascent Egyptian state as an energetic translator, editor, educator, and administrator. His most substantial contribution to the modernizing project, however, was the published account of his stay in France, *A Refinement of Gold in the Summary of Paris* (*takhlis al-ibriz fi talkhis bariz*). While *A Refinement of Gold* was concerned with the study of France, the book inaugurated a literary genre in which Egyptian writers increasingly defined Egypt—both as a distinct territorial entity and as a modern nation (*watan*)—through an "inside" look at its public and domestic spaces.[17] That "show and tell" genre influenced several generations of journalists, polemicists, educators, and budding nationalists who used "tours" through Egyptian institutions as a means of commenting on Egypt's position relative to other modern nations.

A Refinement of Gold was the first Egyptian-produced comprehensive account of European society and culture. Published in 1834 by order of Mehmet ʿAli, the book's goal was to educate Egyptians about the West through a study of Western society and culture.[18] Yet while *A Refinement of Gold* was a personal account of al-Tahtawi's impressions and experiences in France, the work in many senses conforms to the conventions observed in works like those of Depping and Malte-Brun. Al-Tahtawi placed special emphasis on the physical location of Europe and on France's position relative to the other modern European nations.[19] He used tours of French institutions—libraries, academies, and houses of government—to make his case for France's modernity. Al-Tahtawi also linked modern Frenchmen's successes in the political and scientific realms to their domestic behavior; chapters on "The Habits of Parisians in the Homes" and "The Clothing That Parisians Wear" preceded his accounts of public spaces. He presented modern French home life through depictions of spatial arrangements, décor, table manners, and relationships between men and women. He took his compatriots on a tour through French living rooms, dining rooms, and bedrooms, commenting on their love of reading, their refined table manners, and their sleeping habits. He observed that men and women shared domestic quarters, and that they mingled freely together both at home and in public.

Women and their behavior were not objects of undue concern for al-Tahtawi. He did, however, attribute the relatively high levels of education among French women to two phenomena without which, he claimed, modernity could not be achieved. The first was order and cleanliness in middle- and upper-class homes. The second was a love of reading and inquiry, cultivated in the orderly home and then transported into the world outside. If, as al-Tahtawi claimed, domestic behavior distinguished the French from other European nations, what made them distinctly modern was the sound effect of their home life on the public realm.[20]

In 1872, al-Tahtawi applied this equation between domestic affairs and modernity specifically to Egypt in a pedagogical text entitled *An Honest Guide for Training Boys and Girls (al-murshid al-amin fi tarbiyyat al-banat wal-banin)*. In *An Honest Guide*, al-Tahtawi made explicit connections between modernity, the nation-state, and the behavior of Egyptians. The generations of Egyptian schoolchildren who read the book learned that their home life had a bearing on the nation's success, and that modernity was learned and practiced in the home and then transported to the public realm.[21]

Al-Tahtawi also tried his hand at writing history, publishing *Courses for Egyptian Minds in the Joys of Contemporary Manners (manahij al-albab al-misriyya fi mabahij al-adab al-ʿasiriyya)* in 1869. The text has been referred to as a treatise on Egypt's progress, and as a "haphazard history." Gorman notes, however, that what gave the text coherence was al-Tahtawi's use of the nation-state as an organizational trope. By doing so, he was making a case for the role of state-driven modernizing activities in advancing the nation.[22]

Al-Tahtawi's contribution to the development of Egyptian history was mirrored by that of his contemporary, ʿAli Mubarak (1823–93). Like al-Tahtawi, Mubarak studied in France before returning to Egypt to serve the state in a number of high-ranking positions, including Minister of Education. In 1882, he published *ʿAlam al-Din*, which was a fictional account of Europe and the Europeans written as a series of conversations between an Egyptian and an English Orientalist as the two toured Europe together.[23] Like *A Refinement of Gold*, Mubarak's text used tours to "expose" Europe to Egyptian readers.[24] Mubarak's greatest contribution to historiography, however, came with the publication, beginning in 1888, of his twenty-volume encyclopedic portrayal of Egypt's landscape, including the transformations brought to it as the result of the state's accomplishments. Six volumes focused on Cairo, and one on Alexandria; the remainder arranged Egypt's towns and villages alphabetically. The texts helped to define Egypt as a territorial space, and to situate the state as the architect of that territory's modernization.[25]

Gorman calls both al-Tahtawi and Mubarak prototypical amateur historians of the mid- and late nineteenth century. They wrote at the Egyptian state's request, and produced literature that was designed to celebrate Mehmet ʿAli and his successors' continued tasks of modernization and centralization. Whether or not his employer intended al-Tahtawi to define Egypt as a nation (*watan*), a term that al-Tahtawi is credited with having coined, is impossible to know.[26] What is clear in al-Tahtawi's oeuvre, like that of ʿAli Mubarak, is the emergence of Egypt as a modern historical subject, and the state as a subject of historical investigation. Historian Yoav Di-Capua has suggested that al-Tahtawi and his disciples marked the first generation of Egyptian thinkers to let ideology shape their understanding of the relationship between the past and the present.[27] If al-Tahtawi and Mubarak indeed possessed an ideology, it was the idea that state-mandated transformations, in technology, landscapes, and personal habits, brought both the modern nation and its citizens into being.

Domestic Debauchery: Harem Fantasies and the Construction of Colonial History

European sojourners also characterized Egypt as a place defined by its interior spaces. The Europeans who began arriving in nineteenth-century Egypt in ever-increasing numbers, as travelers, fortune seekers, and specialists employed by an ever-growing and expanding Egyptian state, also shared a fascination with Egypt's inner spaces. Unlike the Egyptians who traveled to Europe in the same period, however, European travelers to Egypt were not looking to uncover the ways in which Egypt was modern. Rather, Europeans journeyed to Egypt in search of the ancient and the exotic. While their fascination with Egyptian women also served to define Egypt as a distinct territorial entity, Europeans claimed that Egypt could not yet be defined as a nation because the treatment of women there rendered it backward.

European travelers displayed an obsession with uncovering and revealing Egypt's ancient history. Nineteenth-century Europeans were fascinated with Pharaonic history, and it was therefore the ancient monuments that litter the Egyptian landscape that received the lion's share of their attention. As travelers climbed on and descended into pyramids, tombs, and temples, they seemed determined to get inside the past that those monuments contained:

> Climb the Great Pyramid, spend a day with Abou on the summit, come down, penetrate into its recesses . . . is it not tangible in this hot vastness of incorruptible death? Creep, like the surreptitious midget you feel yourself to be, up those long and steep inclines of polished stone. . . . Now you know the great Pyramid. . . . *It is familiar to you*.[28]

Those travelers also seemed determined to find Cleopatra inside the ancient monuments and to compare her to modern Egyptian women. Indeed, a common trope in nineteenth-century travel literature was the comparison of modern Egyptians with the ancients whose images appeared on temple walls. Wrote one French traveler: "Egyptians . . . have preserved the same delicate profile, the same elongated eyes, as mark the old goddesses carved in bas-relief on the Pharaonic walls . . . they would only have to do their hair in tiny braids in order to resemble Hofert Hari or Isenophé."[29]

This conflation of Egypt with its ancient past had ramifications for nineteenth-century Egyptians. The first was the idea that modern Egypt had slipped from earlier periods of greatness. Nineteenth-century Egypt appears in travel literature as a shabby stand-in for a formerly great civilization and evokes the need for its reform and resuscitation. Additionally, the idea that Egypt's past could be discovered inside its ancient monuments led to the practice of looking for its present inside more modern Egyptian buildings, especially its houses. In a rush to know Egypt by getting inside it that was only matched by their quest to penetrate ancient monuments, European travelers made their way to the harems of the Egyptian elites and the hovels of the peasantry. Even when those spaces were inaccessible to them—it is quite unlikely that harem doors were thrown open for European examination—travel writers produced descriptions of domestic space that resembled their depictions of ancient monuments:

> Let us enter one of these harems. . . . Here is the Eunuch at the door. . . . Here we are in the entrance which is like ours but more open and with more light. There are many couches, a small round inlaid table, a chandelier, a few small tables laden with ashtrays and cigarettes—these are the classic furnishings. This is where one receives guests during the summer, and where the family prefers to gather.[30]

Westerners largely depicted what they found in Egyptians' domestic spaces as bizarre and depraved. Europeans portrayed harem women as the victims of seclusion and polygamy, as imprisoned illiterates whose daily existence consisted of little more than gossip, indolence, and the sexual gratification of their husbands. Similarly, peasant women emerged from travel literature as lazy, lascivious, and immoral, preferring, for example, to be naked than to wear clothing. The frequently sexually charged descriptions through which the West came to know nineteenth-century Egypt and its domestic spaces eclipsed the harsh realities of Egyptian peasant women's labor and the demands of their domestic responsibilities. Similarly, images of the ignorant harem inmate belied elite women's literacy, overlooking what historian Afaf Marsot has called the "executive" duties that women performed from inside the harem.[31]

Thus, nineteenth-century European travel literature created a conflation of Egypt, past and present, with the imaginary specter of womanhood that inhabited its domestic spaces and was etched into its monuments. While travel writers based this feminization of Egypt's landscape largely in fantasy, their writings nonetheless produced a vision in which Egypt's past glories and present debaucheries were embodied in its women and the spaces they occupied.

Such a vision of Egypt was central to the governing strategies of the British elite who governed Egypt after the occupation in 1882. Indeed, the officials who oversaw the occupation of Egypt seemed to understand Egypt—as a territory, a set of institutions, and a race of people—through its women. Evelyn Baring (1841–1917, known as Lord Cromer after 1892), who served as occupied Egypt's first consul general between 1883 and 1907, understood Egyptian women to embody the ills of a decrepit race. Over the course of his administration, Cromer maintained a preoccupation with Egyptian women and their position in Egyptian society. He wrote energetically about the plight of Egyptian females of all classes, and linked his understanding of "the Egypt question" that he had been sent to solve with "the woman question" that seemed to trouble him. The result was an administrative platform that connected the position of women in Egyptian society to the alleged ills of the Egyptian political realm from which those women were wholly absent.

Cromer recorded his musings about Egypt, and published them as *Modern Egypt* just after his tenure as consul general ended in 1907.[32] Di-Capua reminds us that a handful of the British colonial elite were also amateur historians.[33] Indeed, Cromer shared his fondness for writing history with his contemporary Alfred Milner (1854–1925), undersecretary of state for finance between 1890 and 1892, and author of *England in Egypt* (1892). Like travel writers, Milner and Cromer linked contemporary Egyptians to the ancient past. Cromer described Egyptian peasants, for example, as "The small, thick-lipped man with dreamy eyes, who has a faraway look of one of the bas reliefs of an ancient Egyptian tomb."[34] Unlike travel writers, however, Cromer and Milner advanced the platform that what made Egypt modern was Britain's efforts to reform it.[35] This sort of logic is evident in Milner's opening passages of *England in Egypt*, in which he assesses the relationship between British reforms and Egypt's slow progress toward modernity: "Egypt is still far enough off even now for anything like an ideal standard of civilization or administrative excellence; but the difference between Egypt now and Egypt in the latter days of Isma'il is as the difference between light and darkness."[36]

Milner structured *England in Egypt* so as to illustrate for the reader the general state of decline and backwardness in which England found Egypt in the early 1880s. His accounts of Britain's guiding hand in the amelioration of Egypt's agriculture, its military, its educational and legal systems, and its infrastructure followed vivid descriptions of ineffective political and economic institutions. The result of British rule, according to Milner, was better Egyptian rulers, more functional institutions, and an increasingly prosperous and governable Egyptian populace.

Where Cromer departed from Milner was in his attention to the crucial role that Egyptian women were to play in hastening Egypt's modernity, making the reform of women the linchpin of Egypt's transformation. "There can be no doubt that a real advance has been made in the material progress of this country.... Whether any moral progress is possible in a country where polygamy... blights the whole social system is another question." While Egyptian women were thus not participants in the political and economic realms that were placed under British tutelage in 1882, Cromer linked them to an open-ended occupation the end of which would be determined by their reform.

Cromer described the position of women in Egyptian society in language that evoked travel literature from the period, including a keen focus on polygamy, veiling, and the harem.[37] Cromer then linked the allegedly wretched condition of Egyptian women to the inability of Egyptian men to run the nation. He connected the sexual and marital habits of the Egyptian khedives to despotism and to financial mismanagement, for example, concluding that if Isma'il Pasha (r. 1863–79), the ruler whose bankruptcy precipitated the occupation, had been unfit for rule, it was in large measure due to his harem childhood, his wont for polygamy, and his taste for extramarital affairs. Cromer argued that the resuscitation of Egypt could only be accomplished via the thorough reform of its ruling elite, a process that would have to begin with the release and reform of the harem "inmate." Indeed, Cromer's strategy for reforming Egypt rested on the idea that the emancipation of women from the harem, along with their education, would, in addition to rescuing Egyptian womanhood, produce a generation of monogamous men. Once British reform had produced educated wives, and mothers whose sons preferred monogamy over harem life, Egypt could be handed over to its rightful rulers.

Domesticating Egypt: Nationalist Accounts of Home, Women, and Nation

When, in the 1890s, a rapidly expanding Egyptian press opened the floodgates for responses to such ideas about Egypt and plans for its reform, Egyptian intellectuals used a similar logic about reform, modernity, and women to shape their own understandings of "the Egypt question." During that decade, the Egyptian press grew by leaps and bounds. A small handful of Ottoman-Turkish and French-language periodicals joined a burgeoning Arabic-language press, edited and published by men and women alike, in Egypt's two largest cities, Cairo and Alexandria. In these periodicals, a milieu of educated Egyptians articulated and circulated their own ideas about what it meant to be a modern Egyptian. Their discussions reflected the tropes used by both Egyptian civil servants and Europeans to describe Egypt, as the press was full of debates about domestic and marital habits. Nationalists' discussions also reflected the idea that Egypt's advance toward modern political practices could be measured in the behavior of its elite classes, and determined by the reform of those classes. Until 1907, at which point the British allowed Egyptians to form political parties, the press served as the most visible arena for shaping nationalist sentiment and for articulating platforms against the occupation. By the eve of World War I, at which point 144 locally produced journals shaped public opinion, the idea that women and the management of their behavior was synonymous with the nation's progress had become commonplace for the literate elite.

A staple in both the male- and female-authored press circa 1900 was columns about home economics (*tadbir al-manzil*). While Egyptians had already been using domestic tropes to shape their observations about modernity and about Egypt's position relative to Europe prior to the British occupation, columns on home economics seemed to offer powerful ripostes to European claims about Egyptian backwardness.[38] On the one hand, the logic of such columns mirrored nineteenth-century travel literature's most common motif: that Egyptian interior space was most reflective of the Egyptians' political condition. On the other hand, Egyptians would use their home economics columns to illustrate Egypt's potential to be modernized, demonstrating the various ways in which, for example, an ever-expanding rank of educated Egyptian women tended to their households in ways that would make their Victorian counterparts proud.

Often "home economics" columns used history to make powerful points about Egypt's future by referring to the greatness of its past. In early 1895, for example, the editors of the popular journal *al-Muqtataf* ran a cover story called "the future of civilization," which appraised the political systems of Western Europe and the United States and provided commentary about the kinds of people, institutions, and relationships that characterized modern politics in those nations. "The future of civilization," a translation of an article by the American essayist Henry George, was serialized over several editions of the journal; the May edition ran the article next to its home economics column on the front page. The topic of the column was "cleanliness." The anonymous author of "The Secret of Cleanliness" asked how it was that Egyptians had gotten so dirty and what might be done about it. The author insisted that Egyptians had once been "cleaner," saying:

If a high priest from the Pharaonic era, one who witnessed the days when the ancient Egyptians like Ramses the Great ruled the earth, when naked and barefoot women washed and drank from the Nile and its canals, water that in those days was not polluted, saw what the Nile has become, he would cry. After witnessing how the ancients worshipped the Nile... he would be horrified to see... the sewers of the cities and villages that regularly empty into it. He would prefer to go back to living in the land of the dead.[39]

The author of this column did not know how Egypt and the Egyptians had become so dirty. He claimed, however, that because modernity was characterized by cleanliness, Egyptians would have to "clean up" if they wanted to imitate their great ancestors. His solution to the problem was thus quite scientific: he described the kinds of alkaline solutions that properly trained Egyptian women could use to wash clothes, lingering in his attention to the proper applications of both soap and hot water. As per European literature about Egypt, the ancients appear as markers of Egypt's past. In Egyptian literature, however, modernized, educated women and the activities of their domestic spaces appeared as indicators of Egyptians' ability to "clean up" and, therefore, to be modern.

A handful of those who used the press to challenge the British occupation also tried their hand at writing history. The bourgeois intellectuals (lawyers, journalists, bureaucrats) who came of age a decade after the British occupation were both the products of Egyptian state secondary schools and graduates of European universities. They had likely read al-Tahtawi, and would have had some exposure to Egyptian and European history in Egyptian schools. The interests and techniques of this group of intellectuals reflected both those of al-Tahtawi (a focus on Egypt as a defined territory and as a historical subject) and of their European contemporaries: an emerging preoccupation with time (modern Egypt as distinct from the Ottoman era that preceded it) and an interest in the roots of the Egyptian nation with its Pharaonic, Greco-Roman, Arab, and Ottoman pasts.[40] This group of amateur historians also shared an interest in the efforts and activities of the nation-state. In this milieu of nationalists' claims for Egyptian modernity, however, it was not British reforms that had advanced the nation they struggled to liberate; rather, it was the series of modernization programs inaugurated by Mehmet ʿAli that had brought modern Egypt into existence. The Syrian émigré to Egypt Jurji Zaydan (1861–1914), for example, who edited the widely read monthly journal *al-Hilal* (*The Crescent*) published *A Modern History of Egypt* (*tarikh misr al-hadith*) in 1899. The text narrated the history of Egypt from the time of the Pharaohs, using Egypt's succession of rulers and dynasties as its organizing trope.[41] His text joined those of other emerging nationalists and government officials whose goal was to account for the activities of the Egyptian state. In 1892, for example, *A Concise History of Ancient and Modern Egypt* (*khulusat tarikh misr al-qadim wal-hadith*) was published by Mohammed Diyab `Abd al-Hakim, who was an official in the Egyptian Ministry of Education.[42]

Often, "the woman question" that so dominated the popular press at the turn of the twentieth century provided this group of amateur historians with a vehicle through which they could define the Egyptian people at various stages of their historical development, chart the state's contributions to women's reform (or, by contrast, lament its negligence), and forecast the future based on women's past achievements. There was no more high-profile blending of history and "the Woman Question" in turn-of-the twentieth-century discussions about Egypt's destiny than that produced by the French-trained lawyer and intellectual Qasim Amin (1865–1908) with the publication of *Tahrir al-Mara'* (*The Liberation of Women*, 1899) and *al-Mara' al-Jadida* (*The New Woman*, 1901). As the result of Amin's call for women's education, reform of divorce laws, and rethinking of the use of *hijab* in Egyptian society, both feminist and nationalist scholars have claimed Amin as the father of the Egyptian feminist movement. Amin's texts produced intense reactions among Egyptian intellectuals of all persuasions, resulting in the outbreak of great debates in the press and in a proliferation of books countering his position. Whether they were for Amin's positions or against them, writers agreed that women embodied Egypt's backwardness or its potential for modernity.

In his body of writings, however, Amin appeared far less concerned with improving living conditions for the elite Egyptian women about whom he wrote than he was with using women as rhetorical devices through which he could narrate his vision of history and of progress. Like Cromer, Amin believed that it was reform that moved a nation from backwardness to modernity. Amin linked progress to a society's willingness to renounce its traditions and to replace them with customs better suited to the modernizing process. Knowing its past allowed what Amin called an "emerging" society like Egypt to become acquainted with the customs that had hindered its advancement. Between 1895 and 1898, just prior to the publication of his two famous texts, Amin used the pages of a Cairene periodical to advance this idea, in the series "Reasons and Results" ("asbab wa nata'ij"). He wrote:

> When a society knows where it has come from it will know where it is going and how to get there. Change comes from no other source, not from

the will of one person or a hundred people, not from the issuing of one law or hundreds of them. It comes only from history.⁴³

Amin asserted that knowing the history of a nation's customs pertaining to women provided the reader with an insight into that nation. For him, societies passed through four stages, each of which could be left behind only through a thorough reform of its domestic institutions. Indeed, in *The New Woman*, Amin placed the heart of historical development in the family and in familial structures, arguing that it was the reform of the family, undertaken at the hands of the state, which would advance the nation:

> Women lived freely during the first periods of history, while humanity was at its infancy. With the formation of the institution of the family, women fell into real slavery. When humanity began its journey on the road to civilization, women started gaining some of their dues. . . As human civilization reached its climax, women received their complete freedom and most of the rights that men have. These are the four phases that reflect women's changing status in our world's civilization. Egyptian women are still in the third stage of that historical development.⁴⁴

At the fourth and most advanced stage, families and governments resembled one another: France, England, and America, he argued, saw family life as democracy writ small. To get Egypt from its current position at stage three, in which its families and its government were despotic, its family life would have to be transformed. "Women are slaves to men, and men are slaves to rulers. Egyptian men are oppressors in the home and oppressed outside of it."⁴⁵ If education produced women who could be partners to men, savvy homemakers and competent mothers, he argued, Egypt's households would begin to produce the kind of democracy that Amin and others ultimately envisioned. The male products of these reformed households would, in turn, inaugurate further reforms, such that Egypt's progress toward modernity would proceed apace.

Thus, reading history, according to Amin, was of substantial consequence for the educated members of a modernizing society. Knowing the history of customs pertaining to women would serve as a road map for navigating away from the past. Amin was especially keen to have Egypt's newest generation of women read history so that they too would have an understanding of how their behavior would shape the future.⁴⁶

Amin's fans as well as his detractors advanced similar arguments about the relationship between women's position in society and society's ability to advance. His best-known critic, Mohammed Talaat Harb (1867–1941), for example, joined Amin in calling for the reform of Egyptian women, recommending increased education as a way of improving the status of women and that of Egyptian society. Like Amin, Harb advanced the argument that a thorough reform of Egyptian social institutions would hasten the occupation's end. Where he parted from Amin, however, was in his choice of the kinds of reforms that were suited to Egypt, and which models modern Egyptian women should emulate. Whereas Amin encouraged westernization and provided readers with North American and European models, Harb encouraged an emulation of the Islamic past. Harb circulated stories about women from the time of the Prophet Mohammed, arguing that emulating those women would steer Egyptian history back to its roots.[47] While the debate between Amin and Harb is typically remembered for their disagreements over the *hijab*—Amin called for the elimination of the *hijab* while Harb enjoined Egyptian women to continue wearing it—at the heart of their disputes lay the struggle to define Egypt's past.[48]

Many Egyptians became literate in the early decades of the twentieth century via texts about "the woman question." Lessons about home economics and the connection of domestic behavior to Egypt's past and future alike shaped literacy for schoolchildren who came of age in the years leading up to the Egyptian revolution. Textbooks circa 1900 reflected the same kind of thinking that was being peddled by Cromer, Amin, and Harb: namely, that reform was the motor behind historical development, and that reform was to begin in the home.

It was often in textbooks designed to shape Egyptian schoolchildren's manners, or to teach them the basics of home economics, that Egyptian youth learned the equation between their personal behavior, the greatness of the Egyptian past, and the potential of contemporary Egyptians to re-create that greatness through the nationalist movement. Often, textbooks on the domestic sciences provided Egyptian children with their only encounter with history, as the study of that subject was highly contested in occupied Egypt. Beginning in the 1890s, battles waged between nationalists and the British over curriculum, and history was a subject over which the two contended. Cromer determined that the study of ancient and modern history was unnecessary for elementary school students; he wanted their education limited to reading, writing, arithmetic, and manners. Similarly, Cromer saw history as superfluous to Egyptian secondary school education which was designed to prepare students for the civil service. Even the most superior state schools were limited in the number of hours they could offer history each week.[49]

And yet, the kinds of history lessons that circulated in the nationalist press about the relationship between contemporary home life, women's domestic behavior, and the renaissance of ancient Egypt circulated in courses which, on the surface, had little at all to do with history. Boys and girls alike learned to be like their ancestors from textbooks used in reading and grammar classes, in courses on manners and morals, and—in the case of young girls—in courses on home economics. Children of both sexes took away a series of lessons about the past, the most important of which seemed to be that the polygamy that had accompanied the age of Isma'il had been detrimental to the nation. At the same time, Egyptian textbooks peddled the idea that a transformed home life—which must include monogamy, Victorian models for domestic relations, and scientifically educated housewives and mothers—would move Egypt closer to modernity and independence.[50]

If circa 1900 Egyptian men used the press to circulate stories about American and European women or, by contrast, about women from early Islamic history, to produce an idealized female symbol of the Egyptian nation's aspiration, Egyptian women similarly used the pages of nationalist periodicals to circulate stories about praiseworthy women from the past. Female biographers' use of the past seemed to have a different goal than that of men; women wrote about the past neither to idealize Egyptian womanhood nor to illustrate the nation's potential. Rather, the biography gave literate, elite women examples of how their predecessors had faced challenges and resolved dilemmas; they became examples of lived experiences rather than amorphous models. Like their male counterparts, female biographers drew on history. Unlike men, however, the women, who used women's journals to circulate stories about the past, drew on the past in order to write women into the present, to validate and commend their lived experiences, rather than to forecast the future. While the women's awakening that they hoped to fuel certainly had nationalist overtones, women used journals to serve other women in addition to commenting on the national experience.[51]

Journals edited by women and targeted at a female audience were similar to male-authored journals in that they used discussions about idealized women and idealized home life to comment on Egypt's struggle for liberation and to offer women guidelines for self-improvement. In other words, the same "Lady Egypt" who had appeared as the gendered, female stand-in for the nation in the male press also began to adorn the pages of the women's press.[52] At the same time, however, women's journals departed from the male-authored press by including biographies of notable female historical figures.[53]

The inclusion of biographies in women's journals accomplished a number of goals. To begin with, journals offered literate women a forum in which to write. Women who wrote biographies penned a kind of history. The production of that history drew on traditional Arabic-language biographical forms and provided innovations on those forms. At the same time, biographical studies of "great women" served to historicize "the woman question," placing turn-of-the-twentieth-century Egypt within the context of both Western and Islamic historical trajectories. Finally, biographies served to take "the woman question" debate out of the realm of the abstract, and to provide concrete examples of real women for literate women in Egypt to emulate at a time of substantial social and cultural change. Marilyn Booth has called the early-twentieth-century biography a literature of exemplarity, noting the genre's contribution to discussions about Egyptian modernity through its "construction of a certain kind of life narrative."[54]

When the Syrian immigrant to Egypt Maryam Nahhas Nawfal (1856–88) published the first female-authored biographical dictionary about women in 1879, *The Fine Woman's Exhibition of Biographies of Famous Women*, she drew on a well-established male-authored genre. Nawfal, and the women who followed her lead, innovated with the genre not simply because they were female authors working in a historically male terrain, but also because they employed rhetorical styles suggestive of their acquaintance with the *Female Worthies*, "a book of women's lives so popular in the West that its title came to label a genre."[55] Booth tells us that by 1910 at least four female-authored biographical dictionaries had been published by women and about women in Egypt. Those biographies were frequently serialized in journals both in Cairo and in Alexandria, Egypt's second-largest city, in columns aptly titled "Famous Women."

The subjects of women's biographies were both contemporary and historical. Contemporary female subjects were feminists and literary figures like 'Aisha Taymur (1860–1902). Taymur was a popular poet in Cairo, and her erotic *ghazals* were—perhaps—as shocking to local readers as were her calls for equality between men and women. Historical subjects of female-authored biographies included ancient Egyptian women, pre-Islamic Egyptian Christian women, Arab Muslim and Turkish Muslim women, as well as Europeans and Americans. Female biographers depicted women not in their relationships to men, nor in their alleged "women's spheres," but rather as "seekers and transmitters of knowledge, vocal participants in public life, actors in the economy."[56] The number of women's journals publishing biographies expanded as the nationalist struggle against Great Britain intensified, giving the wives and daughters of the nationalist elite concrete examples of exemplary women to pattern themselves after as liberal notions of citizen and citizenship began to take concrete form among Egypt's literate population.

The kinds of women whose stories were told in the women's press were in every sense reflective of the various visions that male and female nationalists had for Egypt's future. Whether they saw Egypt's identity as reflecting its Pharaonic heritage, as a stage in Arab-Islamic history, as a continuation of Ottoman imperial history, or as an episode in Western history, readers of biographies could anchor their present circumstances within a specific past. The stories of "great women" thus served as models after which readers in places like Alexandria and Cairo might fashion themselves, making "the woman question" less an abstract debate than a conversation about real-life issues past and present.

EPILOGUE

The great epistolatory flurry that was the by-product of the building of a central state in the early nineteenth century, an increased European presence in Egypt over the course of the nineteenth century, the British occupation of 1882, and an emerging nationalist movement served to write modern Egypt into existence, both as a territory and as a modern historical field. Amateur historians, whose ranks circa 1900 included Egyptian civil servants, European travel writers, British colonial officials, and budding male and female Egyptian nationalists, engaged in debates about women and narrated their histories as part of a quest to define Egypt, to exult or defile its past, and to imagine and shape its future. Employees of the early state produced texts in which nations were imagined and understood through the habits and cultures of their inhabitants. European travel writers imagined both ancient and contemporary Egypt through their encounters with its interior spaces, including the allegedly depraved spaces of elite harems and peasant hovels. Similarly, the British colonial elite attributed what they saw as Egypt's decay to the marital and domestic practices of its elite class. They used the reform and rescue of Egypt's women to make a case for their occupation. In turn, nationalists used domestic space to define Egypt, and to begin educating a new generation of Egyptians who, it was hoped, would use reformed domestic behavior to wrestle their nation back from the British. Male and female nationalists used debates about women to shape their responses to colonial discourse. In nationalist literature, "Lady Egypt" held pride of place in emerging historical-national narratives about Egypt's triumphant Pharaonic and Islamic pasts. Egyptian women writers began to break away from "the woman question" by authoring biographies about real women; nonetheless, their work also resulted in a conflation of women's behavior with the past that it was meant to evoke. In each case, women, their habits, behavior, and living conditions defined Egypt as a nation and a historical subject.

While women served as useful vehicles for writing histories, which varied in genre from travel literature to lessons on manners and morals, the conflation of women and the nation in turn-of-the-twentieth-century historical literature produced substantial tension between national gendered ideals and the talents and aspirations of the real women around whom the woman question swirled. Discussions about women's education, for example, which had been ongoing since the 1880s, resulted in the expansion of educational opportunities for Egyptian girls. By the turn of the twentieth century, Egypt could boast of a growing number of educated women. Many of those women aspired to roles greater than just those of housewives and mothers. One such woman, Nabawiyya Musa (1886–1951), who was among the first graduates of Egyptian state schools for girls, taught courses on women in ancient and modern Egypt in the country's first experiment with university education, the private Egyptian University. The university opened its doors in 1908, and included a women's section, to which Musa lectured, in 1909. Musa's audience included several dozen women, a few of whom were Egyptian. The university closed down its women's section in 1912 because of public protests stemming from ongoing debates over women's position in Egyptian society, and whether or not they should receive higher education.[57]

Similarly, while "Lady Egypt" was made symbolic of the nation and its struggles, Egyptian women's determination to contribute to the nation's struggle for independence from the British in 1919 achieved mixed results. That revolution attached great symbolic importance to women, and male and female nationalists alike used images of reformed houses, savvy housewives, and educated mothers to herald Egypt's readiness for self-rule.[58] At the same time, elite women, many of them the wives of the exiled leaders of Egypt's independence movement, involved themselves in organizing and fund-raising activities in their husbands' absence, gaining substantial experience in the process. They left the safety of their homes and took to the streets in demonstrations against the British. When the revolution was over, and Egypt had gained nominal independence from the British, elite women, such as Hoda Sha'arawi (1879–1947), sought to turn their revolutionary experiences into political enfranchisement. Male politicians rebuffed them, however, claiming, despite the prominent role that "Lady Egypt" had played in defining the nation, that women were not yet ready to participate in politics. While women were applauded for their skills and courage, they would not be granted suffrage until 1956.[59]

Women have worked outside the home, in ever increasing numbers, since the revolution of 1919. But the ideals of that revolution, that women be dedicated wives, housekeepers, and mothers, have placed pressure on women to succeed in both their homes and in the workplace. Domestic space is still used by commentators about the nation to gauge Egypt's success, and national crises continue to be measured in women's attention to their familial duties.[60] In Egyptian popular culture, marriage remains an arbiter of patriotism, and pundits see failure to marry and set up house in ways that evoke turn-of-the-twentieth-century standards as a challenge to both cultural and national ideals.

Finally, while "Lady Egypt" has changed guises over the course of the decades, reflecting ongoing debates about Egypt's national identity (she was secular Pharaonic in 1919, for example), the pressures on women to conform to the ideals of "Lady Egypt" circa 1900 continue to be high. Nasser crafted his own spin on "the woman question" to serve the needs of his Arab, socialist agendas. While the "Lady Egypt" of Nasser's era was "Arab" rather than "Pharaonic" in appearance, the discourse about her during his tenure as Egypt's president evoked that of an earlier age. Nasser encouraged women to take part in the labor force, but he also perpetuated a public commentary that encouraged women's dedication to the domicile.[61] Currently, debates over veiling, engaged in by those who wish to challenge the secular nature of the regime, frequently suggest that women's place has, historically, been the home.

The conflation of women and the nation has also produced tension between amateur and academic historians. Zaydan, often considered to be a founding father of the modern historical profession in Egypt, did not include women in his *Modern History of Egypt*. As if to presage the later split between professional historians' limited attention to women and amateurs' overreliance on "the woman question" to narrate their agendas, Zaydan used his popular monthly journal *al-Hilal* to discuss the woman question. The journal contained a column called "*hadith al-ma'ida*," or "table talk." The column's alleged purpose was to "give healthy advice on food and drink and other household tasks."[62] In reality, it mixed "table talk" with history, the woman question, and politics.[63] What Zaydan's semiprofessional *Modern History* failed to include was taken up in the popular press—a split that continues in contemporary Egypt.

As the academy, both in Egypt and elsewhere, and groups like the Women and Memory Forum continue apace to write women into history, they may succeed in mainstreaming a body of literature that favors women as subjects. The Women and Memory Forum's recent publication of texts on the relationship between feminism and history, and on the female pioneers of the twentieth century portend the increased availability of alternative models for writing about women, and critical rereadings of women's contributions to nationalism, education, and state-building.⁶⁴ Such texts, and others like them, may do much to match "woman question" debates with historical studies.

Similarly, the recent reorganization of the Egyptian National Archives, and the concomitant availability of previously unexamined documents, will increase possibilities for the production of social history. New documents, as well as innovative new approaches to previously mined archives, such as legal court archives, promise new insights into the lived experiences of real Egyptian women. As the visibility of women's history increases, the long shadow of "Lady Egypt" might well begin to diminish. Out of that shadow, Egyptian women will continue to emerge as full subjects of historical examination.

NOTES

1. This chapter is not about the state of the field of Egyptian gender historiography. Readers with an interest in this increasingly rich field would find the following recently published titles useful: Hanan Kholousy, *For Better or Worse: The Marriage Crisis That Made Modern Egypt* (Stanford: Stanford University Press, 2010); Wilson Chako Jacob, *Working Out Egypt: Effendi Masculinity and Subject Formation in Colonial Modernity, 1870–1940* (Durham: Duke University Press, 2010); Laura Bier, *Revolutionary Womanhood: Feminisms, Modernity and the State in Nasser's Egypt* (Stanford: Stanford University Press, 2011); Nancy Reynolds, *A City Consumed: Urban Commerce, the Cairo Fire and the Politics of Decolonization in Egypt* (Stanford: Stanford University Press, 2012).
2. See iamjan25.com
3. Ibrahim Abduh and Doria Shafiq, *tatawwur al nahda al-nisa'iyya fi misr min `ahd mohammed `ali ila `ahd al-faruq* (Cairo: matba`at al-tawakul, 1946); Ibrahim `Abduh and Doria Shafiq, *al-mar'a al-misriyya min al-fara`ina ila al-yawm* (Cairo: Maktabat misr, 1955).
4. Anthony Gorman, *Historians, State and Politics in Twentieth-Century Egypt: Contesting the Nation* (London: Routledge, 2003), 106. Relative exceptions to this have been accounts of women's participation in Egypt's 1919 Revolution against the British.
5. Gorman, *Historians, State and Politics in Twentieth-Century Egypt*, 106.
6. Pioneer works in the field include those written by Afaf Marsot, Juan Cole, Judith Tucker, Margot Badran, and Amira Sonbol. Recent contributors include Mona Russell, Beth Baron, Hanan Kholousy, Hibba Abugideiri, and Laura Bier. For an overview of the field in North America, see Nikki R. Keddie, *Women in the Middle East, Past and Present* (Princeton: Princeton University Press, 2006).
7. http://www.aucegypt.edu/GAPP/IGWS/Pages
8. www.wmf.org.eg
9. Gorman, *Historians, State and Politics*, chapter 3, "History in Street: The Non-Academic Historian," and 138–44, "Women and Nation: Symbolic Supplement or Dissonant Distaff."
10. Beth Baron, *Egypt as a Woman: Nationalism, Gender and Politics* (Berkeley: University of California Press, 2005).
11. This is the argument of my *Nurturing the Nation: The Family Politics of Modernizing, Colonizing and Liberating Egypt, 1805–1923* (Berkeley: University of California Press, 2005).
12. This is expression in Gorman's. See *Historians, State and Politics*, 11.

13. Jean-Henri Castéra, *Vie de Catherine II, impératrice de Russie* (Paris: F. Buisson, 1798); Voltaire, *Histoire de Charles XII, roi de Suède* (Basle: Christophe Revis, 1731), and *Histoire de l'empire Russie sous Pierre le Grand* (Paris: F. Didot Frères, 1841).
14. Georges-Bernard Depping, *Aperçu historique sur les moeurs et coutumes des nations* (Paris: Mairet et Fournier, 1821).
15. John and Jean Camoroff, "Of Totemism and Ethnicity," in *Ethnography and the Historical Imagination* (Boulder, Colo.: Westview Press, 1992).
16. Conrad Malte-Brun, *Précis de la gégraphie universelle; ou description de toutes les parties du monde sur un plan nouveau* (Brussels: Berthot, Ode et Wooton, 1829).
17. Roger Allen, *The Arabic Novel: An Historical and Critical Introduction* (Syracuse: Syracuse University Press, 1982).
18. Rifa'a Al-Tahtawi, *al-`Amal al-Kamila li Rifa`a Rafi al-Tahtawi*, ed. Mohammed `Imara (Beirut: Al-Mu'assasah al-`Arabiyya lil Dirasa wal-Nashr, 1973), vol. 2, p. 4, cited in Pollard, *Nurturing the Nation*, 34.
19. Daniel L. Newman, *An Imam in Paris, Al-Tahtawi's Visit to France (1826–1831)* (London: SAQI Books, 2004), 83–84.
20. Pollard, *Nurturing the Nation*, 32–39.
21. Mona Russell, *Creating the New Egyptian Woman: Consumerism, Education and National Identity, 1863–1922* (New York: Palgrave Press, 2004), 127.
22. Jamal Mohammed Ahmed, *The Intellectual Origins of Egyptian Nationalism* (London: Oxford University Press, 1960), 13; and Gorman, *Historians, State and Politics*, 13.
23. `Ali Mubarak, `*Alam al-Din* (Alexandria: Matba`at Jaridat al-Mahrusa, 1882).
24. In *The Arabic Novel*, Allen refers to both texts as grand tour literature.
25. Gorman, *Historians, State and Politics*, 13–14; Yoav Di-Capua, *Gatekeepers of the Arab Past: Historians and History Writing in Twentieth-Century Egypt* (Berkeley: University of California Press, 2009), 48–51.
26. Gorman, *Historians, State and Politics*, 11 and 13.
27. Di-Capua, *Gatekeepers of the Arab Past*, 7.
28. Robert Smythe Hichens, *Egypt and Its Monuments* (New York: The Century Co., 1908), 14. My emphasis.
29. Jeanne Fahmy-Bey, *l'Egypte Eternelle* (Paris: Renaissance du livre, 1863), 46. Madame Jeanne was a Frenchwoman writing under an Egyptian nom de plume.
30. Riya Salima, *Harems et musulmanes d'Egypte* (Paris: F. Juven, 1900), 6. Salima was a Frenchwoman writing under an assumed name.
31. Afaf Marsot, "The Revolutionary Gentlewoman in Egypt," in Lois Beck and Nikki Keddie, eds., *Women in the Muslim World* (Cambridge: Harvard University Press, 1978), 261–78.
32. Lord Cromer (Evelyn Baring), *Modern Egypt*, 2 vols. (London: Macmillan, 1908).
33. Di-Capua, *Gatekeepers of the Arab Past*, 78–79.
34. Cromer, *Modern Egypt*, vol. 2, 127.
35. Di-Capua, *Gatekeepers of the Arab Past*, 78–79.
36. Alfred Milner, *England in Egypt* (New York: Howard Fertig, 1970, thirteenth edition), 5–6.
37. Cromer admitted that he had drawn on travel literature in his assessment of the Egyptian ruling elite. In the draft of his *Modern Egypt* (1907), held in the British National Archives, he quotes Nassau William Senior's *Conversations and Journals in Egypt and Malta in Two Volumes* (London: S. Low, 1882) when writing about Isma`il Pasha, the Egyptian khedive. Cromer was keen to point out that he did not doubt Senior's accurate portrayal of Isma`il. See Pollard, *Nurturing the Nation*, 88 and fn 49.

38. Pollard, *Nurturing the Nation*, chapter 1. On the women's press in Egypt, see also Beth Baron, *The Women's Awakening in Egypt: Culture, Society and the Press* (New Haven: Yale University Press, 1994), and Russell, *Creating the New Egyptian Woman*.
39. *Al-Muqtataf*, May 1, 1895.
40. Di-Capua, *Gatekeepers of the Arab Past*, pp. 19–36.
41. Di-Capua, *Gatekeepers of the Arab Past*, p. 38.
42. Di-Capua, *Gatekeepers of the Arab Past*, 43.
43. Qasim Amin, "Reasons and Results," cited in Pollard, *Nurturing the Nation*, 155.
44. Qasim Amin, *The Liberation of Women*; Qasim Amin, *The New Woman: Documents in the History of Egyptian Feminism*, Samiha Sidhom Peterson, translator (Cairo: American University of Cairo Press, 2000), 126. This quote is from *The New Woman*.
45. Amin, *The New Woman*, 121.
46. Amin, *The Liberation of Women*, 12.
47. Mohammed Tala`at Harb, *tarbiyyat al-mar'a wal hijab wa huwa rad `ala da`a muharriri al-mar`a* (Riyadh, Saudi Arabia: Dawa'at al-salaf, 1999). See, for example, chapter 2, "wazifat al-mar'a" ("Women's Work.")
48. On Harb and women, see Leila Ahmed, *Women and Gender in Islam: Historical Roots of a Modern Debate* (New Haven: Yale University Press, 1992).
49. Pollard, *Nurturing the Nation*, 116–18.
50. Pollard, *Nurturing the Nation*, chapter 4; Russell, *Creating the New Egyptian Woman*, chapters 6 to 8.
51. Baron, *The Women's Awakening in Egypt*, 39–40.
52. Baron, *The Women's Awakening* and *Egypt as a Woman*.
53. Some male-authored journals in fact carried biographies, but columns on famous women were largely the lot of the women's press. See Marilyn Booth, *May Her Likes Be Multiplied: Biography and Gender Politics in Egypt* (Berkeley: University of California Press, 2001).
54. Booth, *May Her Likes Be Multiplied*, xiv.
55. Booth, *May Her Likes Be Multiplied*, 3.
56. Booth, *May Her Likes Be Multiplied*, 12.
57. For an excellent discussion of Musa and of women's education, see Russell, *Creating the New Egyptian Woman*, chapter 7.
58. Pollard, *Nurturing the Nation*, chapter 5.
59. Margot Badran, *Feminists, Islam and Nation: Gender and the Making of Modern Egypt* (Princeton: Princeton University Press, 1995).
60. Hanan Kholousy, *For Better, For Worse: The Marriage Crisis That Made Modern Egypt* (Stanford: Stanford University Press, 2004); Ghada abdel Aal, *I Want to Get Married*, trans. Nora al-Tahawy (Austin: University of Texas Press, 2009).
61. Laura Bier, *Revolutionary Womanhood: Feminisms, Modernity and the State in Nasser's Egypt* (Stanford: Stanford University Press, 2011).
62. *Al-Hilal*, September 8, 1900.
63. Pollard, *Nurturing the Nation*, chapter 5.
64. Hoda al-Sadda, *al-niswiyya wal-tarikh* (Feminism and History) (Cairo: The Women and Memory Forum, 2009).

7

Women's and Gender History in Modern India

Researching the Past, Reflecting on the Present

MYTHELI SREENIVAS

One might argue that historians always write, Janus-faced, with a view toward both the past and the present. Certainly, attention to these dual temporalities—to both the historical past and the contemporary context—helps us to understand the trajectories of research in Indian women's history from its professionalization in the 1970s and 1980s onward. Questions about the postcolonial present, most specifically about the ongoing oppression of women in independent India despite the promises of anticolonial nationalism to liberate all its subjects, have echoed across the writing of historians devoted to exploring women's lives and experiences. This chapter investigates these complex intersections between historical pasts and contemporary contexts as they have shaped the historiography of women and gender in modern India.[1]

To interrogate both past and present, historians have employed a variety of approaches, many of which resonate with the historiography of women in other times and places. Early attempts concentrated on a task of recovery, seeking to make known the voices and experiences of women who lived during the colonial era. However, developments within the field of South Asian history, as well as in the emerging fields of subaltern studies, cultural studies, and especially postcolonial feminism, called the politics of recovery into question. Some feminist historians instead outlined a more recuperative project, suggesting that women's voices were not simply lodged in dusty archives waiting to be heard. Rather, due to the violence of colonialism and modernity, evidence of women's subjectivity and agency was available to us only in fragmented, contingent form. Highlighting the task of interpretation, this research did not disavow the scholarly and activist impetus to know more about women's histories, but forced historians to reflect more critically on the kinds of evidence about women that could be recuperated from patriarchal pasts.

At the same time, ongoing inequalities in postcolonial India prompted historians to rethink the adequacy of women's history for a comprehensive understanding of either the past or the present. Calling attention to gender as a critical axis of power relations, historians writing from the late 1980s onward have considerably expanded the scope of scholarship to raise questions about the patriarchal underpinnings of both colonial rule and various forms of Indian nationalism. Here, the focus is sometimes women, but the research is more frequently attuned to the production of gendered difference and its relationship to the transformations of politics, culture, society, and economy during the nineteenth and twentieth centuries. Concerned at base with the staying power of patriarchal institutions and ideologies in modern India, this scholarship has been shaped by shifting postcolonial contexts of women's activism, the rise of right-wing religious nationalism, and most recently, the liberalization of the Indian economy. These dynamics are at work across much of South Asia. Prior to 1947, of course, "India" included what are now Pakistan and Bangladesh, and thus extended beyond the current boundaries of the nation-state. Scholarship on pre-1947 history quite rightly disregards these contemporary boundaries, and my analysis does likewise. However, in situating the intellectual, political, and activist context of history writing in the postcolonial era, I limit my analysis to India.[2]

Taken together, the historiography of women and gender in modern India offers a profound critique not only of women's oppression, but also of colonial and postcolonial modernity.[3] The careful work of numerous historians has documented how the gendered ideologies and institutions of colonial rule were not overthrown by dominant forms of Indian nationalism, but that instead, nationalist discourse and policy further solidified patriarchal relations in some contexts. The norms and practices that informed the construction of postcolonial India were thus deeply implicated in their colonial pasts. Yet the forms of women's oppression—and of their subjectivity and resistance—have not remained unchanging as we advance into the seventh decade of Indian independence. While aware of colonial legacies, scholars have tentatively begun examining postcolonial India with a historical lens, an important project if we are to continue the tasks of recovery, recuperation, and antipatriarchal critique that have characterized the field.

Colonizing and Decolonizing Women's History

The writing of Indian women's history has, from its outset, been deeply entangled in both British colonialism and anticolonial nationalism. Both Europeans and Indians turned toward the past to make sense of their present. Uncovering what they termed the "status of women" in ancient India played an important role in these investigations. Whereas nineteenth-century

European Orientalist historians recovered an ancient Indian "golden age," by contrast their Anglicist and Utilitarian counterparts wrote histories to demonstrate "the peculiarities of Hindu civilization and the barbaric practices pertaining to women."[4] Drawing from the latter view, the British rulers of India—as in other colonies—claimed to liberate colonized women from their patriarchal histories, marking this liberation as an instance of their broader colonial "civilizing mission." In a pithy encapsulation of the race and gender politics implicit in such a claim, Gayatri Spivak has deemed this a rhetoric about "white men saving brown women from brown men," that underlay British defenses of their colonial project in India. Indian nationalists countered these colonial claims in two distinct, albeit related, rhetorical modes. First, turning again to history, many nationalists (including both men and women) asserted that Indian women had held greater rights in the precolonial past than in the colonial present; women's oppression was thus seen as a deviation from a more "pure" and originary Hindu-Indian tradition to which Indians had to "return." Second, nationalists claimed that Indian nationalism itself—and not British colonial rule—would liberate women. Nationalist support for various sociolegal reforms concerning women, often in the face of colonial ambivalence, helped to bolster these claims.

Debate on the "women's question" took a different turn with the development of an all-India women's movement in the early twentieth century. During the 1920s and 1930s, women began to organize on an India-wide basis, bringing together largely middle-class activists to agitate for political, legal, and social reforms. Addressing issues including women's franchise, greater property rights, marriage reform, as well as legislation supporting the rights of women workers, the all-India women's movement forcefully brought women into greater visibility in Indian politics. Women's active involvement in anticolonial struggle further increased this visibility, while also firmly linking the all-India women's movement to Indian nationalism, especially as represented by the Indian National Congress. These alliances at once furthered nationalist claims to represent all Indians, including women, and supported the women's movement's assertion that it represented all women within the nation, across potential divides of religion, caste, or class.

With the end of colonial rule in 1947, Indian nationalist narratives about women acquired even greater legitimacy, and the achievement of political freedom was seen as a first step toward challenging a range of social inequalities, including not only gender, but caste and class as well. Despite the human tragedies that accompanied the partition of the subcontinent into India and Pakistan, women's activists shared with the nationalist movement a hope that political freedom was the harbinger of thoroughgoing change in all aspects of Indian society, including in women's lives. The implementation of a new Constitution for the Republic of India in 1950 gave women key rights that, without fulfilling all activist demands, brought women closer to legal equality with men. Meanwhile, several former leaders of the women's movement took up prominent positions within the independent Indian government. In this context, the largely middle-class women's movement shifted away from the agitational politics that had shaped its relation to the colonial regime, and directed its attention to "constructive work" that would support the development efforts of the newly independent Indian state.

Although the narrative of national progress was questioned and challenged by various social movements in the first decades after independence, the economic and political ferment of the 1970s marked a critical shift in this public optimism about postcolonial India. More specifically, for scholars and activists interested in women, the publication in 1974 of *Towards Equality: Report of the Committee on the Status of Women in India*, gave new focus to a growing unease about the unfulfilled promises of national freedom and development. Commissioned by the Indian government, the report concluded that "large masses of women in this country have remained unaffected by the rights guaranteed to them by the Constitution and the laws enacted since Independence." Not only had postcolonial Indian society not developed new gender norms to reflect women's improved legal status, but even more disturbingly, various indicators pointed to a "process of regression from some of the norms developed during the Freedom Movement."[5] If indeed women were on a march "towards equality" they had a very long way to go, and perhaps even had to change direction. The publication of *Towards Equality* helped to catalyze a new wave of research seeking to document why, despite the promises of both nationalism and the women's movement, there had not been more improvement—in some areas there was even a decline—in women's status after 1947. In the wake of the report, the Indian Council of Social Science Research established an advisory committee on Women's Studies, which in turn sponsored research extending and deepening the issues raised in *Towards Equality*. Several institutions took up these questions, including notably the Research Center for Women's Studies at SNDT Women's University in Mumbai.[6] Much of the scholarship produced in these centers during the 1970s and early 1980s was based in the social sciences—particularly in sociology, anthropology, and economics—rather than in the historical discipline.[7] Increasing academic and policy attention to women resonated with a growing activism in the field as well. A new women's movement, distinct from earlier waves of activism during the colonial era, began to take shape in India. Focusing attention especially on violence against women—both in public and in more intimate spaces—new organizations questioned earlier narratives that national independence would bring about women's liberation.

By the 1980s, we find the emergence and development of South Asian women's history as a distinct field of inquiry. Specialists in South Asian history based in Western institutions increasingly turned their attention toward women, and together with colleagues in India produced a first generation of professional research on modern Indian women's history. From the outset, therefore, this scholarship has been a transnational enterprise, with ongoing conversations among scholars based within and outside India. This wave of interest in Indian women's history resonated with feminist activism and its by-product, the professional writing of women's history, around the world. In the case of India, historians contextualized postcolonial patriarchies by investigating the impact of colonialism on women's lives. In this way, historical scholarship joined with the social sciences in asking why women had not moved closer "towards equality" in modern India.

Documenting Women's Voices and Women's Lives

Women's historians writing in the 1980s looked to recover women's voices as a way to document their lives and experiences during the colonial era. For example, Meredith Borthwick's *The Changing Role of Women in Bengal*, examined nineteenth-century women's magazines, private papers, and memoirs to investigate the "interdependence between practical and ideological change" among women of the English-educated Bengali professional class.[8] In identifying shifts in domestic practices, education, and family, Borthwick sought to uncover information about women usually absent from more conventional historical sources or narratives. The book concludes with a series of biographical notes about nineteenth-century women, attesting to the importance of making women's lives and experiences visible in the historical record. Other historians also took up this task of documenting women's experiences, among them the pioneering women's historian Geraldine Forbes, who has recovered, edited, and published the memoirs of several Indian women. The first was the memoir of Shudha Mazumdar, who writes about the first decades of the twentieth century from her perspective as a Bengali middle-class woman not directly involved in politics, but who nevertheless was "aware of and interested in the events happening around her."[9]

Historians during this period also uncovered women who were more direct participants and leaders in social reform and political movements. Gail Minault's important edited volume *The Extended Family: Women and*

Political Participation in India and Pakistan not only demonstrated that women had played important roles in a number of movements, but also asked about the intersection between nationalism, feminism, and sociopolitical reform. Geraldine Forbes's essay in the volume considers the "compatibility of women's and nationalist aims" by examining women's organizations in the decades before Indian independence.[10] Gail Minault's essay raises similar questions about the All-India Muslim Ladies' Conference and Indian nationalism. Barbara Ramusack's contribution, one of many articles she has authored on the relationship between British and Indian women, considers whether British feminists were "catalysts or helpers" in the struggles of Indian women and Indian nationalists.[11] Written amidst new waves of women's activism in the 1970s and 1980s in India and in the West, these historical studies raised critical questions about the ideological content, the tactical strategies, and indeed the critical consciousness of women's movements in the past.

A different investigation of women's consciousness is documented in *"We Were Making History": Life Stories of Women in the Telengana People's Struggle,* authored by the collective, Stree Shakti Sanghatana.[12] Members of the collective recorded the life stories of women involved in a peasant struggle (1948–51) against their oppressors in the princely state of Hyderabad, a struggle which eventually led them to face the Indian army. The work of the Stree Shakti Sanghatana expanded the archive of women's history beyond conventional reliance on written sources, and simultaneously called attention to the gendered consciousness of women whose caste and class background rendered them outside the largely middle-class women's movement of their time.

This focus on women's experience and consciousness continued into the 1990s. For instance, in *A Comparison between Women and Men,* Rosalind O'Hanlon translated and introduced a remarkable nineteenth-century critique of patriarchal culture by the previously little-known writer, Tarabai Shinde.[13] Shinde's critique, a polemical essay whose wide-ranging analysis encompasses everything from religious tradition to colonized cultures, suggests the extent to which at least some nineteenth-century women both recognized and overtly challenged patriarchal norms and practices. Another landmark documenting women's voices was the publication of the two-volume *Women Writing in India, 600 B.C. to the Present.*[14] Translating into English the work of many previously unknown writers, the editors, literary scholars Susie Tharu and K. Lalitha, vastly expanded the range of women's voices, writing in numerous languages, that historians could use to reconstruct a history of women in India.[15]

Geraldine Forbes's *Women in Modern India*, published in the prominent Cambridge New History of India Series in 1996, signaled that Indian women's history had arrived as a subfield within South Asian historiography.[16] Drawing both from existing scholarship and from her own very substantial efforts to uncover new sources and voices in women's history, Forbes developed a narrative of the nineteenth century to the present by using "women's materials to the greatest extent possible to demonstrate that Indian women have not been as silent as some accounts would have us believe."[17] Her survey covered not only social reform, nationalist, and feminist movements—which had been the topics of some historical research already—but also women's work and women laborers, subjects which had hitherto received less historiographical attention.

Colonialism, Nationalism, and Patriarchy

Women's history took a new direction with the publication of *Recasting Women: Essays in Indian Colonial History*, edited by Kumkum Sangari and Sudesh Vaid (1989). The editors highlighted their "need as academics and activists to understand the historical processes which reconstitute patriarchy in colonial India," especially since the implications of this reconstitution "bear significantly upon the present."[18] To study these processes, essays in the volume not only investigated women's experiences, but also raised critical questions about the gendered inequalities implicit in various modernizing projects in colonial India. Modernity—its institutions, ideologies, and assumptions—did not represent a liberating progress for Indian women, but rather "recast" them to suit the needs of a modern patriarchy. In making these claims, *Recasting Women* vastly expanded the scope and the relevance of women's history to make it central to how historians understand modernity and its gendered implications. As a turning point in the historiography, the volume reoriented the field toward examining gender and power to understand colonial rule and its postcolonial aftermath.

This turn in the field toward gender and power had much in common with shifts in women's historiography globally. However, in their introductory essay Sangari and Vaid also emphasized that Indian sociopolitical contexts in the 1970s and 1980s necessitated this shift. The research and social movements of this period had "shattered the post-colonial complacency about the improving status of women," and with it, undermined the "legitimacy of nationalist models of reform and 'development.'"[19] Sangari and Vaid thus at once questioned the colonial past and the postcolonial present. For if indeed colonialism had already been rejected, and (bourgeois) nationalism offered no antipatriarchal answers to the situation of Indian women, but was instead deeply implicated in patriarchal systems, what new alternatives could challenge modern Indian patriarchies? Addressing these questions required a new approach which recognized that "both tradition and modernity have been, in India, carriers of patriarchal ideology." Rather than relying on a dichotomous opposition between the two, feminists must recognize that as commonly understood, tradition and modernity are "eminently colonial constructs" and that neither provides a solution to the problem of women's oppression.[20]

From this premise, the essay charts an agenda for feminist historical research. Sangari and Vaid argue, first, that such feminist research need not focus solely on women, but rather must be "able to think of gender difference as both structuring and structured by the wide set of social relations,"[21] especially class, both because patriarchies are class differentiated, and because "defining gender seems to be crucial to the formation of classes and dominant ideologies."[22] This research agenda must attend to discourse and ideology, as well as materiality and lived experience; indeed, a critical question for women's history is to explore the interconnections among these domains. Consequently, the essays in the volume "either attempt to construe the lived culture or social relations of a particular time and place . . . or to show the making of a selective tradition through discursive and political processes."[23]

Essays documenting "selective tradition" focus on patriarchy as a site of intersection between colonialism and nationalism. Uma Chakravarti's "Whatever Happened to the Vedic *Dasi*?" recounts the systematic erasure of lower-caste women from nationalist narratives about ancient India.[24] Over the grounds of this erasure, nationalism countered colonial claims about the degradation of women in Indian civilization by proferring the chaste, upper-caste wife as the exemplar of Hindu-Indian tradition. The result was that the "Vedic dasi"—the lower-caste woman—lost any place in Indian nationalist understandings of the past. As Chakravarti notes, this nationalist construction of womanhood was implicitly upper caste and premised upon the disavowal of the lives and experiences of the majority of women.

Essays by Partha Chatterjee and Lata Mani also investigate the figuration of "woman" and "tradition" at the intersections of colonialism and nationalism. According to Chatterjee, the history of Indian nationalism began not with its contest against colonial rule, but with a more intimate assertion of authority over women and the domestic sphere.[25] By rejecting colonial attempts to intervene in domestic arenas, nationalism secured its status as arbiter over the "home"—a space supposedly uncorrupted by the depredations of colonial rule. In this domestic space, marked as uniquely Indian, women embodied and represented Indian identity. Only after consolidating authority over the "home-nation" did Indian nationalists turn to more explicit political confrontations with the colonial regime.

Lata Mani examines this contest between colonialism and nationalism by investigating the colonial discourse of sati (immolation by a widow on her husband's funeral pyre). The legal abolition of sati by Lord William Bentinck in 1829 was typically seen as a high point of colonial rule, and some mark it a starting point for the legal recognition of women's rights in India. The debates leading to the abolition had been understood as a contest between orthodox Hindus who wanted to preserve sati and British and Hindu reformers who sought to end the practice. However, as Mani argues, it would be a mistake to suppose that the sati debate was actually a confrontation between reformers and traditionalists over women's rights. Instead, the debates about sati primarily focused on competing interpretations of Hindu scriptures. As the orthodox mobilized scriptural support for sati, sati's opponents likewise turned to scripture to demonstrate that its proper interpretation advocated the abolition of sati. In the process, "women ... became the site on which tradition was debated and reformulated. What was at stake was not women but tradition."[26] As a result, women—their lives, their voices, their experiences—were completely removed from the terms of debate. In Mani's terms, "women are neither subjects, nor objects, but rather the ground of discourse on sati."[27] Hence for Mani, no history of sati can be truly recuperative; the colonial record will not reveal the history of the sati (or the woman) as a subject. Historians must instead untangle the gendered assumptions upon which our understanding of both "tradition" and "modernity" are premised.

Several essays directly address Sangari and Vaid's first objective, to evaluate Indian women's lived culture and social relations in specific places and times. For example, Nirmala Banerjee's "Working Women in Colonial Bengal: Modernization and Marginalization" investigates why and how the modernization of the Bengali economy via industrialization did not lead to women's increased entry into the industrial labor force or the service economy, as was the case with British industrialization, but instead pushed women into agricultural occupations. Examining a wide range of sources from labor statistics to Bengali folk songs, Banerjee suggests that although women were displaced from traditional occupations because of industrialization, social restraints on "their mobility between regions and occupations"[28] made it impossible for them to access the limited new opportunities created. And perhaps even more importantly, the industrial sector ultimately offered far fewer employment prospects than the older forms of employment it displaced, leaving women with few options outside agriculture. Prem

Chowdhry's essay, "Customs in a Peasant Economy: Women in Colonial Haryana," also examines the intersections of culture and economy. Chowdhry investigates the relationship between social customs among Jat caste peasants and the colonial economy in Haryana, arguing that the colonial state's selective enforcement of Jat "custom" became "responsible for lowering the status of women during the colonial period."[29]

Taken as a whole, *Recasting Women* both deconstructed assumptions about tradition and modernity underlying colonial Indian patriarchies, and also sought to reconstruct women's lived experiences within those patriarchal systems.[30] As a watershed in the field, the volume shifted the theoretical and methodological orientation of scholarship, and the text is still referenced by historians and other feminist scholars even two decades later. However, in the years since *Recasting Women*, it has been the deconstructive project, more than the reconstructive one, that gained increasing purchase in Indian women's history. Part of the reason for this emphasis is sources. Despite some brilliant and creative unearthing of alternative sources by women's historians in this period, state archives remained a critical site for documenting Indian history. Women's writing in the form of letters and diaries—so crucial in the writing of women's history in Western contexts—were not entirely absent for the modern era, but given high rates of illiteracy and the vagaries of record preservation, they are hard to find in large numbers. The kinds of sources which fueled a wave of social history and women's history writing in the West—parish registers, birth and death records, and the like—are almost entirely lacking in a South Asian context. Consequently, the records of the colonial state emerged as a site where women were at least talked *about*, albeit in limited ways, even though they were not figured as the subject of discourse or, typically, as the authors of texts. These factors, perhaps, encouraged a deconstructive turn toward the colonial archive and an attempt to unpack the historical production of "woman" as a category. This deconstructive turn would also make women's and gender history critical to the new interdisciplinary field of postcolonial studies as it developed in the late 1980s and 1990s.

Postcolonial, Subaltern, and Modern Subjects

Postcolonial theorists, some of whom were also women's and gender historians, engaged in a broad-ranging critique of national modernity, that is, they problematized nationalist visions of what constituted modernizing progress within the space of the nation-state. While interrogating the promises of Indian nationalism, they simultaneously raised questions about the liberatory possibilities of the nation-state as a form. This line of thinking was developed, in part, by Partha Chatterjee, one of the contributors to *Recasting Women*. In two widely influential books, Chatterjee argued that the forms of Indian nationalist thought remained unable to think outside the categories of colonial discourse, and further, that any alternatives to a (patriarchal) national modernity emerged only in fragmented form.[31] As Chatterjee suggested, these limitations of nationalism were not confined to India, but were characteristic of all colonial modernities which had uncritically accepted the universalities of European Enlightenment thought. The problem, in Chatterjee's terms, was that "even as it challenged the colonial claim to political domination," nationalism "also accepted the very intellectual premises of 'modernity' on which colonial domination was based."[32] A number of historians have subsequently sought to deconstruct these intellectual premises by historicizing the categories of colonial discourse.

This scholarship calls attention to colonial constructions of sexuality, race, and class in various imperial contexts, as historians interrogate the production of colonial difference. Differences between colonizers and their colonized subjects were neither self-evident nor neutral, but were actively produced and managed to serve the interests of colonial regimes. A preeminent example of this scholarship is Mrinalini Sinha's *Colonial Masculinity*. She documents how the distinctions between British rulers and their "native" subjects hinged on the active construction of masculinities contrasting the "manly Englishman" with the "effeminate Bengali." Investigating the production and contestation of these modes of colonial masculinity, Sinha argues, "simultaneously exposes the patriarchal politics of nationalism and the limits of the anti-colonial claims made on behalf of such patriarchal politics."[33] Within this framework, gender history holds the potential for unraveling the patriarchal collusions that have sustained both colonial and nationalist categories of thought, and possibly even suggests alternatives for the future.

Taking a related approach, some scholars have focused on colonial institutions, in particular colonial law. Janaki Nair's *Women and Law in Colonial India* broadly surveys nineteenth- and twentieth-century legal changes affecting women. Her study is underpinned by the central "recognition that the edifice of legal justice in India is more or less wholly constructed, interpreted, and administered by men, and its underlying concern is primarily the protection of patriarchal privilege." Tracing these patriarchal ideologies and practices to specific conjunctions of society, economy, and politics during the colonial era, Nair nevertheless maintains that "a wholesale rejection of the legal juridical framework would only be counterproductive in the long run."[34] Consequently, and in conversation with feminist legal studies,

Nair documents a "social history of the law" which lays bare its hierarchical underpinnings and marks fissures and spaces where legal and social activism has brought, and can continue to bring, positive change. Examining how gendered assumptions shaped legislation on labor and female workers, on women's franchise, on sexuality, and on the personal laws governing marriage, inheritance, property, and divorce, Nair suggests that women's activism is essential to creating the conditions of social transformation necessary to challenge oppressive legal structures and by extension the structures of patriarchal modernity, both colonial and nationalist.

Indian women's and gender history also resonated with a series of historical questions about elite versus nonelite subjects that were being raised by the Subaltern Studies school of historians of India. Arguing that existing studies of nationalism were limited to elite forms and subjects, Subaltern Studies scholars uncover a "politics of the people . . . in which the principal actors . . . [were] the subaltern classes and groups constituting the mass of the laboring population and the intermediate strata."[35] According to Ranajit Guha, a founder of the Subaltern Studies group, this subaltern class failed to take the nationalist movement away from its bourgeois roots toward a "full-fledged struggle for national liberation," and thus, "it is the study of this failure which constitutes the central problematic of the historiography of colonial India."[36] As in the case of *Recasting Women*, the early volumes in Subaltern Studies offered the possibility of simultaneously deconstructing elite nationalism while recuperating alternative voices and consciousnesses. Through painstaking archival work, Subaltern Studies research often brilliantly documents the histories of subjects configured as "subaltern" within the colonial political economy, and then uses these histories to deconstruct the dominant assumptions of both colonialism and nationalism. Also, as in the case of women's and gender history, Subaltern Studies scholars questioned the limitations of Indian nationalism and its liberatory promises. But even while Subaltern Studies frameworks and conclusions became immensely important to the field of South Asian history during the 1980s and 1990s, with few exceptions, both gender ideologies and women as historical subjects were largely ignored in early Subaltern Studies.[37]

Nevertheless, the coming together of these postcolonial and Subaltern Studies critiques of colonialism and nationalism posed a critical epistemological question for women's historians, as for all scholars interested in studying populations whose voices are marginalized in the historical record. Given the erasures that accompany a colonial politics of knowledge, is it ever possible to hear the voices of subaltern subjects? The literary critic Gayatri Spivak who, in addition to her own investigations of subaltern subjects, played an important role in bringing Subaltern Studies into closer conversation with the Western academy, poses this question. In several essays, she demonstrates the epistemological impossibility of accessing the consciousness of subaltern women. For Spivak, the Indian colonized woman became a paradigm for the erasure of the subaltern subject in colonialism's structures of knowledge. Consequently, searching the archive for women's voices would offer no solution to the feminist scholar, since the archive was premised upon the exclusion of the subaltern, and any voices found there were irretrievably marked by the conditions of this exclusion. Spivak's work thus problematized the notion that subaltern, or women's, consciousness could simply be recuperated and then expressed by the postcolonial feminist scholar. Instead, the researcher had the more "circumscribed task" of calling attention to the epistemic violence that constituted colonial knowledge.[38] Spivak's claims, taken up by postcolonial feminist theory, have not been ignored by historians for whom the task of recuperation persists, sometimes uneasily, alongside deconstructive critiques. Thus, within the field of Indian women's and gender history, engagements with postcolonial theory and Subaltern Studies have fostered a more critical approach to the colonial archive, rather than a turn away from archival sources. Historians have read archival texts not simply for what they reveal about women's lives, but also to examine the gendered assumptions that underpin colonial and nationalist epistemologies.

Women's History, "Hindu" History

In addition to the theoretical and methodological challenges posed by postcolonial and Subaltern Studies, women's and gender history has also grappled with shifts in the Indian political context during the 1980s and 1990s. This includes, most notably, the rise of forms of Hindu nationalism, or Hindutva (literally "Hinduness") as a major ideological and political force in Indian public discourse. The origins of Hindu nationalism can be traced back to the colonial era, but the late twentieth century witnessed the resurgence of Hindutva groups. In brief, Hindutva ideologies emphasize that, despite the presence of many religious minorities, India is essentially a Hindu nation and consequently a Hindu "ethos" must shape its political culture, law, and social life. Hindutva organizations vary in size and influence, from small localized groups to one of India's major political parties, the Bharatiya Janata Party (BJP), and their activities range from parliamentary politics to the violent suppression of non-Hindu (especially Muslim) populations. As Hindutva made political inroads in India during the 1980s and 1990s, Indian history became a critical site of contestation. India's pluralist heritage—long documented by historians—was called into question by Hindutva proponents who sought evidence of a "purer" Hindu past. They especially targeted historians of medieval and ancient India because their work had the potential to unsettle a retelling of Indian history that highlighted exclusively "Hindu" origins and contributions. The writing of women's history could not remain unaffected by this context.

A number of women's and gender historians refuted Hindutva's claims upon history, and, in particular, critiqued its patriarchal interpretations of Hindu "tradition." One critical site for this work in the late 1980s and early 1990s was sati. Although sati is extremely rare in postcolonial India, the immolation of eighteen-year-old Roop Kanwar in Rajasthan in 1987 on the funeral pyre of her twenty-four-year-old husband, shocked many and galvanized a broad range of feminist, activist, and scholarly responses.[39] Some in the Hindu nationalist right glorified her death as exemplary of Hindu "tradition" in terms eerily echoing the nineteenth-century rhetoric examined by Lata Mani. Indian women's groups rejected the glorification of sati that followed, and many historians sought to challenge the notion of a Hindu "tradition" upon which sati was based. The renowned historian of ancient India Romila Thapar carefully reconstructed the material and ideological contexts of sati throughout Indian history to show that its practice was not an unchanging element of an all-encompassing Hinduism. Instead, as she argues, "the particular social groups supporting sati have changed over time and this change has had to do with the role, function, and rights of women in social relations, property relations, and rituals." The glorification of sati following Roop Kanwar's death, she implies, was embedded in the contemporary context of Rajasthan's Rajput community, which sought "legitimation from the past."[40]

Sudesh Vaid and Kumkum Sangari similarly questioned the "traditional" status of sati by investigating more closely the Shekhawati region of Rajasthan where Roop Kanwar's death occurred. They maintained that the "specific constellation of social, religious, and cultural meanings which are presently being attached to widow immolation" were not simply the result of undifferentiated, homogeneous Hindu "tradition."[41] Rather, based on extensive fieldwork, Vaid and Sangari delineated the role of various elite castes in propagating a patriarchal cultural politics that favored sati, with the result that the Shekhawati region had witnessed the preponderance of sati incidents recorded in Rajasthan. Vaid and Sangari also pointed to the role of the state in failing to intervene in sati and stop its subsequent glorification. Other scholars took this critique further to argue that the state's treatment of Roop Kanwar's case was one example of a broader failure of the government to uphold secular values, and that instead "the state has succumbed to the temptations of revivalism."[42] Since this religious revivalism was built upon the rearticulation of women's rights and status in the present in order to conform to a uniformly patriarchal religious "tradition" of the imagined Hindu-Indian past, the task for feminist historians became both to reject contemporary patriarchal practices while challenging the historical validity of revivalist interpretations. In contrast to colonial era debates about tradition and modernity, feminist scholars sought also to theorize the subjectivity of the sati, and consider its implications for a broader feminist understanding of women's consciousness and agency.[43]

For scholars of women and gender, as for historians generally, the rise of Hindutva and its patriarchal and revivalist interpretations of the past changed the scholarly context within which historical knowledge was produced. Especially for scholars based in India, it raised the stakes of interpreting and interrogating both Hindu and Islamic traditions in the subcontinent. Some scholars have responded to this challenge by examining the historical roots of Hindutva itself. In a series of articles and book chapters Tanika Sarkar, a prominent women's historian, has sought to delineate a genealogy of Hindutva politics that outlines the relationship between its patriarchal ideologies and its socioeconomic contexts. Tracing the origins of "militant Hindu chauvinism" to a broader crisis in the late nineteenth and early twentieth centuries that stoked upper-caste worries about their declining hegemony in Indian society, Sarkar argues that "the upper-caste Hindu began to develop an explanatory system that held the Muslim—rather than his own caste privileges—responsible" for his precarious position.[44] Upper-caste Hindu women figured within this discourse on several levels: as the personification of the vulnerability of the putative Hindu nation from attack by Muslims; as marginal figures within the Hindu community who, like lower castes, were needed to generate active consent to these new forms of politics; and as mothers responsible for reproducing the Hindu nation.[45]

Sarkar has asked why such a politics—which neither critiques patriarchy nor espouses gender justice—has been so appealing for some women. Based on research about prominent female leaders and rank and file women active in Hindu right-wing organizations, Sarkar exposes ideologies and organizational structures that incorporate women without challenging existing caste, gender, or age-based hierarchies.[46] Several other scholars, most especially sociologists and political scientists, writing during the 1990s, asked related questions about the mobilization of women within Hindutva organizations. Among them is Amrita Basu, a professor of political science and women's and gender studies, whose work offers a detailed ethnographic analysis of women's participation in these organizations, and also situates scholarship on Hindutva in wider feminist conversations about the growing presence of women within right-wing organizations globally. In *Appropriating Gender: Women's Activism and Politicized Religion in South Asia*, Basu and her coeditor, sociologist Patricia Jeffery, situate Hindutva movements alongside Islamist movements in Pakistan, Bangladesh, and India to investigate both gender ideology and women's agency via participation and/or resistance to forms of politicized religion. Her scholarship has contributed to a transnational conversation among feminist scholars about women not only as victims of, but also as leaders and participants in, right-wing movements in many parts of the world.[47]

New Directions

Women's and gender history has continued to develop in new directions into the twenty-first century. As before, the contexts in which historians write influence their choice of topics and research. Questions about India's pluralist heritage and the challenge of Hindutva—expressed most dramatically in horrific violence against Muslims in Gujarat in 2002—continue to shape the political context in which Indian history is written. At the same time, scholars and activists are increasingly concerned about India's skewed sex ratio, which in some Indian states is among the most disparate in the world. While feminists have long been aware of the disparity, the recent national census, which notes the worsening sex ratio among young children, has further catalyzed concern that, as India moves toward a lower fertility rate, new reproductive technologies are increasingly being used to prevent the birth of female children. Historical work has great potential to inform these debates. Veena Talwar Oldenburg remains one of few women's historians who have studied the patriarchal practices that put the very lives of girls and women at stake. Her *Dowry Murder: The Imperial Origins of a Cultural Crime* historicizes violence against girls and women, including infanticide, neglect, and domestic assaults, in relation to a broader masculinizing of economic relations during the last two centuries. Although social scientists have also addressed this violence, there remains a great need to develop a better historical understanding of the multiple and intersecting processes that have contributed to devaluing female life in contemporary India.

Meanwhile, the liberalization of the Indian economy begun in the 1990s has accelerated in the decade since 2000. Unraveling years of economic planning that emphasized state control over key industries, liberalization in India—as elsewhere in the world—has meant the privatization of state resources and the dismantling of the public sector. While this has facilitated the rise of a new middle class whose increasing disposable incomes have attracted the attention of corporations seeking new markets, it has also produced new social tensions and intensified inequalities. Even as the Indian state seeks to match its growing economic might with increasing political prominence on the world stage, India remains low in estimations of human development, and is still quite far from meeting the United Nations' Millennium Development Goals. Thus, even as India's arrival as an emerging power is celebrated by its elites, some of the questions that have haunted the nation since independence still remain. Are women on a march "towards equality," or do they need to change direction? Does it even make sense—theoretically and politically—to continue talking about "women" when the divides among them are so stark? What are we to make of the decades-old promise of national liberation—for women and other oppressed groups—in the era of accelerating neoliberal forms of globalization?

In this political and economic context, a range of social movements have powerfully confronted the new global and the new Indian order, and women have played a critical role in many of these movements. For example, they have been very visible in agitation that has confronted environmental degradation, state-sanctioned and police violence (including against women), the forced displacement of poor and indigenous peoples, and the abuse of new reproductive technologies to harm the life prospects of girls and women. The development of new theories and activism around Dalit ("lower"-caste) feminism has highlighted the multiple hierarchies that constitute women's subjectivity, and at the same time has questioned the implicit erasure of lower-caste consciousness and experience in scholarly and activist engagements with "women."[48] While the intersections of caste and gender have received scholarly attention before, recent work is given further impetus by Dalit feminist theory and activism, which offers the possibilities of rethinking the caste basis of patriarchy in India.

Within this broader context, historical work on the nineteenth and twentieth centuries continues to deconstruct patriarchal norms and practices in untangling the history of colonialism, nationalism, and modernity. Tanika Sarkar's analysis of the patriarchal genealogies of Hindu nationalism is an important example of this kind of research. In one series of essays, Sarkar examines controversial debates about the marriage of girls prior to puberty, so-called "child marriage," during the 1890s, a practice then common among some Hindu castes, although typically consummation was postponed until after puberty. Reform activists in Bengal and elsewhere made child marriage a focus and called for a legal minimum age of consent to sexual intercourse.

However, when in 1891 the colonial administration sought to institute a legal age of consent for girls—thus potentially banning prepuberty marriage—a vocal movement arose in opposition. A fierce debate ensued, in the course of which supporters of prepuberty marriage developed a radical "cultural nationalist" opposition to colonial rule that far exceeded the more sedate politics espoused by the Indian National Congress established in 1885.

Several historians have examined this controversy, but Sarkar takes us in new directions by asking how claims and assumptions about gender helped to structure the terms of Bengali modernity in sometimes paradoxical ways. On the one hand, during the course of debate "consent" to sexual intercourse became biologized to figure only as a function of girls' chronological age and bodily maturity; even among reformers, there was a foreclosure of women's agency and subjectivity in favor of evidence read upon the body. Supporters of child marriage refused the notion that girls and women needed to consent to marriage or sexual intercourse at all; instead, "consent" came from a Hindu tradition that purportedly mandated prepuberty marriage to secure the continuity of the patrilineage. Yet in the course of the 1890s debates, Sarkar argues, this foreclosure of women's consent was fissured by the implicit acknowledgment that women had, indeed, a right not to be put to death by their "community," and that, if prepuberty marriage risked the death of a child-wife through violent rape by her husband, then it could be opposed. Supporters of child marriage were ultimately unable to refute this argument. Once female consent was admitted as a principle in marriage—albeit in a limited, circumscribed, and attenuated fashion—"it would inevitably open the door to more radical demands, as indeed it did."[49] Sarkar's analysis shows us the relevance of women's and gender history for a reconceptualization of dominant historical trajectories in modern India. In the case of child marriage, a gendered analysis sustains a reexamination of the relationship among individual legal rights, community norms, and citizenship rights as they were configured under colonial rule.

The relationship between women, community, and national citizenship comes in for further questioning in Mrinalini Sinha's *Specters of Mother India*. Focused on American journalist Katherine Mayo's notorious book *Mother India* (1927) and the controversies in India, Britain, and the United States that resulted from the book's publication, Sinha argues that the interwar period witnessed a "global restructuring of empire" that had significant implications for feminism, liberalism, and nationalism. Whereas claims to women's rights had hitherto been mediated by conceptions of community, Sinha suggests that the controversies surrounding *Mother India* opened a space for feminist groups to develop and lay claim to liberal notions of women's rights. Their citizenship was not mediated by community belonging or responsibility, but appealed directly to a developing Indian nationalism. One result was the passage of a marriage law in 1929 that applied to all women, regardless of their religious affiliation. The broader consequence, Sinha argues, was a realignment between social and political spheres in colonial India.[50]

Scholarship on sexuality has also investigated the complex relationship between social and political spheres, as mediated by colonialism, postcolonial politics, and the nation-state. Mary E. John and Janaki Nair's foundational edited volume *A Question of Silence? The Sexual Economies of Modern India* puts forward an agenda for the study of Indian sexualities. While sexuality has often been assumed to be silenced in modern India, John and Nair suggest that it has in fact been elaborated in numerous contexts. Not all of these are analogous with Western sites of incitement to discourse. Thus it is not "the confessional couch or the hystericised woman that generated knowledge and anxieties about sexuality in modern India," so much as anxieties of colonial governance on the one hand and the nationalist imperative to define its citizens/subjects on the other.[51] From this beginning, John and Nair suggest that studying law, anthropology, demography, political movements, cinema and media, and alternative sexualities constitute an archive for their "overwhelming desire to address our *present* and its history."[52]

This concern with genealogies of the Indian present—and thus of Indian "tradition" as well as "modernity"—surfaces in other work exploring the intersections of sexuality and gender. Ruth Vanita and Saleem Kidwai's collection, *Same-Sex Love in India: Readings from Literature and History*, brings together an extraordinary collection of texts from all periods of Indian history.[53] *Queering India*, also edited by Ruth Vanita, develops a historically informed scholarly discussion of same-sex love,[54] which, like earlier directions in women's history, seeks to recover and make visible historical spaces and consciousnesses formerly rendered invisible in both colonial and nationalist frameworks of knowledge. However, feminist scholars have also been attuned to the politics and epistemological assumptions underlying this kind of knowledge production, as suggested in Anjali Arondekar's recent analysis of the relationship between sexuality and the colonial archive.[55]

Other historians have also questioned the politics of the archive while exploring alternate sources for writing women's and gender history. Antoinette Burton's *Dwelling in the Archive* focuses on three colonial Indian women's texts to show how they each "made use of memories of home in order to claim a place in history at the intersection of the private and the public, the personal and the political, the national and the postcolonial."[56] She thus reads the home both as a "material archive for history" and as offering a site and language for the reconfiguration of women's subjectivity. Through this process, Burton suggests, sources that were hitherto neglected by historians, or even more significantly, dismissed as lacking a historical consciousness, can be reread to offer new insights into the history of colonial India. Indrani Chatterjee is another historian whose work, although written from a somewhat different perspective, forces us to reinvestigate the "home" as a historical site. Both in a monograph and an edited volume, Chatterjee demonstrates that households have been a critical site for the rearticulation of power relationships that included not only biologically related kin but also a host of other household members.[57] By thus bringing into history a space and a network of relationships formerly either ignored or dismissed by scholars, Chatterjee's work encourages women's and gender historians to treat home/household as an archive of political, social, and cultural history.

Ramya Sreenivasan expands archives in yet another direction by investigating the relationship between history and memory in the multiple (re)tellings of the legend of Padmini, a medieval Rajput queen. Considering narratives about Padmini dating from the sixteenth to the early twentieth centuries in a variety of genres, Sreenivasan asks how "reconstructions of memory and the reforming of gender relations" were important to the construction of various political collectivities prior to the emergence of the nation-state.[58] This approach offers one way to engage with sources conventionally assumed to be nonhistorical and thus implicitly of little interest to empiricist historiography. The possibilities for a women's and gender history that engages such new sources may lead to an exciting expansion of the field.

Finally, historians of women and gender are only just beginning to study independent India. Within the field of South Asian studies, research on the post-1947 era has typically been confined to social scientists, and historians have rarely crossed the colonial/postcolonial divide. With few exceptions, women's and gender history has largely followed these trends. Although several scholars have written chapters in larger works on some aspects of postcolonial history, there have been few attempts to conceptualize the key themes or questions arising from historical research on women and gender after 1947.

The result of this relative silence among historians is somewhat paradoxical. On the one hand, women's and gender history forcefully demonstrates the patriarchal collusions linking colonialism and nationalism, suggesting that postcolonial Indian modernity remains deeply marked by this intersection. On the other hand, by not engaging with the previous six decades of postcolonial history, the scholarship risks reifying the divide between colonial and postcolonial that it has sought to dismantle by calling attention to the continuities that characterize gendered discourses in the modern era. The fiftieth, and then the sixtieth, anniversaries of Indian independence have prompted greater scrutiny by historians of the postindependence decades, and this seems to be the case for scholarship focused on women and gender too. A growing number of researchers are crossing the boundaries that have long separated our study of colonial society from its postcolonial successor. This is an encouraging development indeed, for without engaging Indian history after 1947, the historiography of the modern era risks its own obsolescence, unable to speak to the ongoing inequalities and hierarchies that mark women's lives and experiences.

NOTES

1. By "modern" India, I follow the conventions of South Asian history to include roughly the eighteenth century to the present, but scholarship on women and gender has tended to focus more narrowly on the latter half of the nineteenth century and the first half of the twentieth. I do not address the substantial scholarship on pre-eighteenth century women's and gender history.
2. I focus as well on scholarship produced in English, which remains the dominant language of scholarly discourse in the subcontinent.
3. To my knowledge, there have been few attempts by historians to evaluate the scope and directions of the field of South Asian women's history. An important early article is: Barbara Ramusack, "From Symbol to Diversity: The Historical Literature on Women in India," *South Asia Research* 10, no. 2 (November 1990): 139–57.
4. Uma Chakravarti, "Whatever Happened to the Vedic *Dasi*? Orientalism, Nationalism, and a Script for the Past," *Recasting Women: Essays in Indian Colonial History*, ed. Kumkum Sangari and Sudesh Vaid (New Brunswick: Rutgers University Press), 34.
5. Committee on the Status of Women in India, *Towards Equality: Report of the Committee on the Status of Women in India* (New Delhi: Government of India, Ministry of Education and Social Welfare, 1974), 359.
6. Geraldine Forbes, *Women in Modern India*, pt. 4, vol. 2 of *The New Cambridge History of India* (Cambridge: Cambridge University Press, 1998), 228.
7. There were occasional exceptions to this trend. One important, historically informed volume on women emerging from this period is B. R. Nanda, ed., *Indian Women: From Purdah to Modernity* (New Delhi: Vikas Publishing House, 1976).
8. Meredith Borthwick, *The Changing Role of Women in Bengal, 1849–1905* (Princeton: Princeton University Press, 1984), 357.
9. Geraldine Forbes, "Introduction," in *A Pattern of a Life: Memoirs of an Indian Woman* by Shudha Mazumdar, edited by Geraldine Forbes (Columbia, Mo.: South Asia Books, 1977), xi.
10. Geraldine Forbes, "The Indian Women's Movement: A Struggle for Women's Rights or National Liberation?" in *The Extended Family: Women and Political Participation in India and Pakistan*, ed. Gail Minault (Delhi: Chanakya Publications, 1981): 49–82; quote on 49.
11. Gail Minault, "Sisterhood or Separatism: The All-India Muslim Ladies Conference and the Nationalist Movement," in *The Extended Family*, 83–108; Barbara N. Ramusack, "Catalysts

or Helpers? British Feminists, Indian Women's Rights, and Indian Independence," in *The Extended Family*, 109–50.
12. Stree Shakti Sanghatana, *"We Were Making History": Life Stories of Women in the Telengana People's Struggle* (London: Zed Books, 1989).
13. Rosalind O'Hanlon, *A Comparison between Women and Men: Tarabai Shinde and the Critique of Gender Relations in Colonial India* (Madras: Oxford University Press, 1994).
14. Susie Tharu and K. Lalita, eds. *Women Writing in India, 600 B.C. to the Early Twentieth Century*, vols. 1 and 2 (Delhi: Oxford University Press, 1991).
15. A related vein of scholarship has called attention to male writing about women which was not in English, and remained largely outside the colonial archive. For example: Barbara Metcalf, *Perfecting Women: Maulana Ashraf 'Ali Thanawi's Bihishti Zewar* (Berkeley: University of California Press, 1990).
16. Forbes, *Women in Modern India*, 228.
17. Forbes, *Women in Modern India*, 4.
18. Kumkum Sangari and Sudesh Vaid, "Recasting Women: An Introduction," in *Recasting Women: Essays in Indian Colonial History*, ed. Sangari and Vaid (New Brunswick: Rutgers University Press, 1990), 1.
19. Sangari and Vaid, 2.
20. Sangari and Vaid, 17.
21. Sangari and Vaid, 3.
22. Sangari and Vaid, 5.
23. Sangari and Vaid, 4.
24. Uma Chakravarti, "Whatever Happened to the Vedic *Dasi*? Orientalism, Nationalism, and a Script for the Past," in *Recasting Women*.
25. Partha Chatterjee, "The Nationalist Resolution of the Women's Question," in *Recasting Women*.
26. Lata Mani, "Contentious Traditions: The Debate on *Sati* in Colonial India," in *Recasting Women*, 118.
27. Mani, 117.
28. Nirmala Banerjee, "Working Women in Colonial Bengal: Modernization and Marginalization," in *Recasting Women*, 297.
29. Prem Chowdhry, "Customs in a Peasant Economy: Women in Colonial Haryana," in *Recasting Women*, 327.
30. It is important to note that the essays in this volume focused on Bengal and northern India. Other historians have noted the significant differences that characterized gender politics in other parts of the subcontinent, especially in the context of anti-caste movements and alternative nationalisms. For example: S. Anandhi, "Women's Question in the Dravidian Movement," *Social Scientist* 19, nos. 5–6 (May–June 1991): 24–41; Rosalind O'Hanlon, "Issues of Widowhood: Gender and Resistance in Colonial Western India," in *Contesting Power: Resistance and Everyday Social Relations in South Asia*, eds. Douglas Haynes and Gyan Prakash (Berkeley: University of California Press, 1992).
31. Partha Chatterjee, *Nationalist Thought and the Colonial World: A Derivative Discourse* (London: Zed Books, 1986); *The Nation and Its Fragments* (Princeton: Princeton University Press, 1993).
32. Chatterjee, *Nationalist Thought and the Colonial World*, 30.
33. Mrinalini Sinha, *Colonial Masculinity: The "Manly Englishman" and the "Effeminate Bengali" in the Late Nineteenth Century* (Manchester: Manchester University Press, 1995), 181.

34. Janaki Nair, *Women and Law in Colonial India: A Social History* (New Delhi: Kali for Women, 1996), 5. 6.
35. Ranajit Guha, "On Some Aspects of the Historiography of Colonial India," in *Subaltern Studies*, vol. 1, ed. Ranajit Guha (New Delhi: Oxford University Press, 1982): 1–8; quote on 1.
36. Guha, 6 and 7.
37. An important exception is Ranajit Guha, "Chandra's Death," in *Subaltern Studies*, vol. V (New Delhi: Oxford University Press, 1987).
38. Gayatri Spivak, "Can the Subaltern Speak?" in *Marxism and the Interpretation of Culture*, ed. Cary Nelson and Lawrence Grossberg (Urbana: University of Illinois Press, 1988), 308.
39. Veena Oldenburg, "The Roop Kanwar Case: Feminist Responses," in John Stratton Hawley, ed., *Sati: The Blessing and the Curse* (New York: Oxford University Press, 1994): 101–30.
40. Romila Thapar, "In History," *Seminar* 342 (February 1988): 14–19; quotes on 19 and 15.
41. Sudesh Vaid and Kumkum Sangari, "Institutions, Beliefs, Ideologies: Widow Immolation in Contemporary Rajasthan," *Economic and Political Weekly*, vol. 26, no. 17 (April 27, 1991): WS2–WS18; quote on WS3.
42. Imrana Qadeer and Zoya Hasan, "Deadly Politics of the State and Its Apologists," *Economic and Political Weekly*, 22, no. 46 (Nov. 14, 1987): 1946–1949; quote on 1947.
43. Rajeswari Sunder Rajan, *Real and Imagined Women: Gender, Culture, and Postcolonialism* (New York: Routledge, 1993).
44. Tanika Sarkar, "Woman, Community, and Nation: A Historical Trajectory for Hindu Identity Politics," in *Appropriating Gender: Women's Activism and Politicized Religion in South Asia*, ed. Patricia Jeffery and Amrita Basu (New York: Routledge, 1997), 91.
45. Sarkar, "Woman, Community, and Nation," 91.
46. Tanika Sarkar, "Aspects of Contemporary Hindutva Theology: The Voice of Sadhvi Rithambara," in *Hindu Wife, Hindu Nation: Community, Religion, and Cultural Nationalism* (Bloomington, Ind.: Indiana University Press, 2001); Tanika Sarkar, "Heroic Women, Mother Goddesses: Family and Organization in Hindutva Politics," in *Women and Right-Wing Movements: Indian Experiences*, ed. Tanika Sarkar and Urvashi Butaliat (London: Zed Books, 1995): 181–215.
47. Amrita Basu, "Hindu Women's Activism in India and the Questions It Raises," in *Appropriating Gender*. See also her "Feminism Inverted: The Gendered Imagery and Real Women of Hindu Nationalism," in *Women and Right-Wing Movements*.
48. Sharmila Rege, *Writing Caste, Writing Gender: Narrating Dalit Women's Testimonies* (New Delhi: Zubaan, 2006). See also Uma Chakravarti, *Gendering Caste through a Feminist Lens* (Calcutta: Stree, 2003); Gail Omvedt, *Dalit Visions: The Anti-Caste Movement and the Construction of an Indian Identity* (Hyderabad: Orient Longman, 2006 rev. ed.)
49. Sarkar, *Hindu Wife, Hindu Nation*, 245.
50. Mrinalini Sinha, *Specters of Mother India: The Global Restructuring of an Empire* (Durham: Duke University Press, 2006).
51. Mary John and Janaki Nair, "Introduction," in *A Question of Silence? The Sexual Economies of Modern India* (London: Zed Books, 1998), 19.
52. John and Nair, "Introduction," 37. More recently, Nivedita Menon's edited volume, *Sexualities*, includes several historically informed articles that expand the realm of sexuality studies further, to include domains of desire and pleasure (London: Zed Books, 2007).
53. Ruth Vanita and Saleem Kidwai, eds., *Same-Sex Love in India: Readings from Literature and History* (New York: St. Martin's Press, 2000).
54. Ruth Vanita, ed., *Queering India: Same-Sex Love and Eroticism in Indian Culture and Society* (New York: Routledge, 2002).

55. Anjali Arondekar, *For the Record: On Sexuality and the Colonial Archive in India* (Durham: Duke University Press, 2009).
56. Antoinette Burton, *Dwelling in the Archive: Women Writing House, Home, and History in Late Colonial India* (New York: Oxford University Press, 2003), 4.
57. Indrani Chatterjee, *Gender, Slavery and Law in Colonial India* (New York: Oxford University Press, 1999); Indrani Chatterjee, ed., *Unfamiliar Relations: Family and History in South Asia* (New Brunswick: Rutgers University Press, 2004).
58. Ramya Sreenivasan, *The Many Lives of a Rajput Queen: Heroic Pasts in India, c. 1500–1900* (Seattle: University of Washington Press, 2007), 14.

Exploring Transnational Approaches

8

World History Meets History of Masculinity in Latin American Studies[1]

ULRIKE STRASSER AND HEIDI TINSMAN

A transnational turn is certainly afoot in the discipline of history. While world history as a field is hardly new, it has usually played second-fiddle to the histories of particular nation-states and the regions carved out by area studies. But recently almost every national history field and regional field has recognized the need for a gaze that looks across hallowed borders and oceans with fresh eyes.[2] As the forces of globalization have simultaneously produced an astonishing degree of connection and an acute deepening of socioeconomic and political divisions, globalization's casualties and challenges command urgent attention. Even historians, forever leery of the analytical sin of presentism, have felt compelled to enter en masse the debate about globalization and its discontents. Given how much scholarly discussion on the subject has been generated disproportionately within other fields and often without a nuanced historical sensibility, this is a welcome intervention indeed.

But while historians as a group are only beginning to enter the fray, individual historians and various subfields of course are anything but new to discussions of inequality between peoples and uneven developments on a transregional or even global scale. This chapter concerns itself primarily with two particularly vibrant approaches: world history and historical studies of masculinity. Both have been profoundly committed to exploring issues of domination and difference, and they each have developed vital critical vocabulary for narrating their complex histories. At first glance, that would make the two fields seem like natural allies, or at least easy interlocutors, at this moment in time and in the profession's history. But to the contrary, and somewhat paradoxically, there has been a vexed relationship between world historians and historians of masculinity (and of gender and sexuality more broadly). They have largely remained segregated in their own institutional and intellectual spaces, conferences, and journals. From there they have eyed one another with some degree of skepticism and occasionally outright suspicion. Even when their thematics do overlap, historians of gender and sexuality rarely see themselves writing world history, and vice versa.[3] What's the problem? How can it be solved? And what's to be gained?

We contend that the oft vexed issues separating world historians and historians of gender and sexuality relate not only to perceptions and labels (although mistaken attributions do matter),[4] but foremost to diverging intellectual trajectories and partially incommensurate categories. Other trends in each field notwithstanding, at this juncture it is a heavily *materialist* world history, which concerns itself with the conditions of material life and remains affected by Marxist economic ideas, that faces off with a predominantly *culturalist* history of gender and sexuality, which draws heavily on literary and anthropological approaches to explore questions of cultural meaning. Diagnosing such disciplinary unevenness, however, is different from asserting that "never the twain shall meet." In trying to establish intersections between the two fields, we use this chapter to bring a third field into the mix—Latin American Studies, an area of study that has long combined these traditions and hence offers particular insights on the challenges of bringing them together.

Most promising from our point of view is the recent scholarship from Latin American Studies that illuminates how world history and histories of gender and sexuality converge naturally, as it were, around the theme of masculinity. World history commonly centers its analyses on domains of life in which men are the primary actors, be it via patterns of trade and labor exploitation, or empire building and state formation. Histories of gender and sexuality, on the other hand, regularly examine why certain domains or individuals are coded as "masculine," what such codings mean, and how they matter to larger processes. The Latin Americanist literature offers important models for combining these two optics and is suggestive of how world history can usefully be narrated as the story of masculinities. This chapter is *not* intended as a literature review of Latin Americanist histories of gender and sexuality, or even of masculinity.[5] Rather, we invoke Latin American Studies as a research area that often has fluidly blended culturalist and materialist traditions *and* focused on masculinity in ways that are highly relevant to debates within world history today.

Uneven Developments, Unequal Interests:
Gender History and World History

What then troubles the conversation between world historians and scholars of gender and sexuality? Different starting points, for one. Gender history first emerged from and has remained animated by a deep and fruitful commitment to challenging universal claims. For decades, its practitioners have been fine-tuning their critical tools to interrogate narratives that presumed to include all yet elided thorny issues of power, exclusion, and difference. Moving from 1970s social history and Marxist theory to cultural and literary analysis in the wake of the linguistic turn, historians of gender and sexuality have striven to produce ever more nuanced accounts of the dynamics of gender, sexuality, race, and ethnicity at the heart of all historical phenomena.[6] There is no question that this scholarly emphasis has rendered what seemed like familiar stories of, say, state formation, industrialization, or nationalism newly complicated, and in so doing has deepened our understanding of these broader historical processes.[7] But the focus on difference and the distrust of false universalisms has also made historians of gender and sexuality habitually suspicious of meganarratives of any kind. World history is without a doubt a new meganarrative—surely the most ambitious thus far proposed. It raises the specter of a pernicious iteration of universal history, particularly since world historians often rely on 1970s social theory—with its sweeping and purportedly universal narratives of how societies and social life have evolved and continue to evolve—that historians of gender and sexuality spent so much time deconstructing.

Meanwhile, a growing number of scholars of gender and sexuality have in recent years themselves embarked on studies that look across different regions and areas of the world.[8] This has implied abandoning the traditional framework of the nation, which the rich literature on gender and nationalism had already denaturalized from within but simultaneously and ironically also propped up as a privileged unit of analysis. While these scholars do look globally instead of nationally, however, they perform their work not under the sign of "world history" but of "transnational dynamics" (usually concrete instances of global interaction). Focused overwhelmingly on the twentieth century (especially the last half), this scholarship is more immediately attuned to postcolonialism and postmodernism, and from this vantage point is rather wary of the world history paradigm as mired in irredeemable Eurocentrism. Fears that world history is little more than a ruse to reassert the West's myths about itself as the sole bearer of civilization and economic freedom loom large here, if sometimes in exaggerated and unfounded forms.

Indeed, much of the new scholarship in world history has radically upended these very teleologies and challenged historians of gender and sexuality to rethink assumptions about empire and economic development.[9] This newer literature on world or global history, which partially grew out of but mainly superseded the earlier comparative civilizational studies and Eurocentric accounts of the West against the rest, has put to rest a number of scholarly commonplaces about globalization. It has highlighted the fact that the contemporary moment of the late twentieth and early twenty-first centuries, so often hailed as unique for their startling degree of market integration and population flows, is only the most recent, even if particularly intense, instantiation of global connectivity. Furthermore, the new world history has been especially concentrated on the period of European imperial expansion (1500–1900) as another key moment in the evolution of transregional markets and political regimes, but only to undercut the presumed inevitability of European imperial domination and economic hegemony in the modern world.[10]

It is true, however, that in this revisionist world history enterprise questions of the political economy have taken center stage and so has the goal of (re)mapping global connections. Related to this is the prominence of nineteenth- and early twentieth-century social theory in world history discourses (albeit often as an object of critical appraisal) and a traditional, institution-centered view of politics. As world historians themselves have noted, a deep engagement with culturalist theoretical paradigms from anthropology or literary studies remains the exception rather than the rule.[11]

Not surprisingly, then, the cultural production of difference and its political deployment in all spheres of life, issues that are of paramount importance to historians of gender and sexuality, inhabit the analytical periphery of the world historical debate. More frustrating still, while a materialist emphasis does not per se preclude gender analysis—one only needs to recall the many superb feminist labor histories written within national frameworks—much of world history marches along merrily without paying much attention to gender and sexuality at all. Beyond their presumed transparent relation to demography, gender and sexuality remain altogether invisible, not to mention inoperative as categories of historical analysis.

En-Gendering World History within Area Studies: The Case of Latin America

But the materialist and culturalist approaches that often separate world history and gender and sexuality studies are by no means inherently incompatible. For reasons specific to the history of Latin American Studies as a field, Latin American history anticipated the concern of both world history and transnational cultural studies with international dynamics of domination, dependency, and difference.[12] It has long been both comparative and interested in how a particular region fits into a global story. Like world history, the dominant narratives of Latin American history have been those of empire building, global capitalism, and state formation. At the same time,

Latin Americanist feminist scholarship and studies of sexuality have been heavily materialist, even as they incorporated the linguistic turn's emphasis on meaning. Scholars have engaged poststructuralist calls to see gender as a multilayered field of power, and sexuality as constituted through ideology and performance. Yet what they have most produced is an outpouring of social and political history on gender and sexuality—in labor relations, government institutions, social movements, and national modernization. Much of this literature reworks rather than jettisons older notions of political economy and the state, even as Michel Foucault and Jacques Lacan enter more prominently into the framework. It is not that Latin Amercanists "lagged behind" or failed to take *enough* of a cultural turn, but rather that different questions were being asked about Latin America than about Europe and the United States, which compelled different uses of—and investments in—materialism, gender, and sexuality.

As was true of other area studies fields, Latin American Studies emerged in full during the Cold War, with U.S. government funding, for the purpose of assessing the fitness of "developing countries" for capitalist democracy, or at least military compliance with NATO (North Atlantic Treaty Organization). Yet area studies were never mere tools of empire, but hotly contested and productive of a wide range of knowledges. This was especially true of Latin American Studies, whose "area focus" was the first and most enduring region of U.S. imperial design. Indeed, since the mid-nineteenth century, Latin America was a constant site of U.S. military intervention, economic investment, and democracy-building projects, an agenda that received zealous recommitment in the aftermath of the 1959 Cuban Revolution. This ensured that Latin American Studies, from its inception, was intensely polemical terrain, pitting Cold War hawks and reform-minded liberals against a growing leftist critique from inside the United States which denounced U.S. actions in the Caribbean and South America as imperialist and antidemocratic. From *within* Latin America itself, Latin American Studies gave conceptual and financial backing to a host of radical projects at odds with U.S. State Department goals, from dependency theory's indictment of Latin America's systematic underdevelopment by the industrialized world, to Latin America's identification with Pan-Third Worldism and the Non-Aligned Movement.[13] The discipline of history, together with the historically minded social sciences, often served as a vital "proving ground" for arguments about the origins of Latin America's political violence, unequal development, and utopian revolutions. Often mobilized in unabashedly partisan ways, Latin American Studies, even in its most nuanced forms, became a field disproportionately critical of U.S. intervention and the legacies of European colonialism.

Materialist frameworks have been central to most questions motivating Latin American Studies, from debates over economic development and persistent poverty to arguments about imperialism and the supposed legacies of Hispanic authoritarianism. Marxism has enjoyed a particularly lasting privilege, and in various incarnations: economic histories of commodities, labor histories of class formation and resistance, a voluminous Gramsci-inspired scholarship on the state and hegemony.[14] Marxism's endurance sprang from its conceptual affinity with questions about inequality and exploitation as well as from the fact that Marxism continued to have great currency *inside* Latin America into the twenty-first century. In the United States and Western Europe, academic Marxism and leftist politics were in decline by the 1980s. Many feminists working on these areas began pursuing agendas that increasingly questioned the coherence of universal categories such as "class" and "woman."[15] By contrast, in Latin America the 1980s and the election of Ronald Reagan signaled not the eclipse of leftist radicalism but the hyperpolarization of Cold War dichotomies. The U.S. government massively funded bloody "counterinsurgency" wars in El Salvador, Guatemala, and Nicaragua, and proclaimed military despots, such as Augusto Pinochet, key allies in the fight against communism. In Latin American Studies, this recharged older debates about dependency and imperialism which had been central to Latin American intellectual radicalism since the 1950s, but engaged new paradigms provided by social history for thinking about political agency and resistance within the nation. Many Latin American feminists sharply criticized Marxism on much the same grounds that did U.S. and European feminists, and Marxism itself underwent innumerable rearticulations. Nonetheless, ideas about class and class-based struggles over the state and economy were reinvigorated as sites of study and activism, including among feminists, precisely because Marxism was tied to debates over national liberation and democracy in ways that it never had been in the United States or even much of Western Europe.

In addition to the long shadow of Marxism, the investment of Latin American Studies in materialist frameworks stems from Latin America's different relationships to the nation and the questions raised by poststructuralism. In the U.S. academy, for example, the cultural turn of the 1980s and 1990s meant not only that historians of gender and sexuality shifted from studying "causation" to studying "meaning," but also shifted from privileging national history to developing historical critiques *of* the nation and of modernity more broadly. For scholars in and of Latin America, by contrast, national and even nationalist narratives about modernization operated as critical tools for challenging authoritarianism at home and accusations of underdevelopment from abroad. Essentialist renderings of "women" or "workers," and the pitfalls of economic determinism, are no less problematic for Latin American scholars than they are for any U.S. and European historians. But given past and present histories of empire, what has been at stake in jettisoning frameworks that probe questions of national sovereignty and universal inclusion are different across the region.

To be sure, Latin American Studies' materialist commitments built upon and elaborated a number of problematic binaries that also haunt world history: developed versus undeveloped, first world versus third world, imperialists versus nationalists, democracy versus tyranny. Such dichotomies were first produced in U.S. political and academic culture in relationship to Latin America, and later became integral to other "non-Western" area studies (Africa and Asia, for example) sponsored by the United States. In our contemporary moment, this taxonomy intimately informs discussions and policy toward the Middle East, arguably constituting a legacy as great as (or greater than) older discourses of Orientalism.[16]

And yet, like world history, much of the most innovative work in Latin American Studies has actively sought to upend Eurocentricism, even while emphasizing global dynamics of difference and domination. Arguments that Latin America's very birth was an extension of sixteenth-century European kingdoms, and that in the nineteenth century Latin America consolidated far more independent republican nation-states than did Europe, have challenged cherished notions about the cohesive origins and spread of modernity.[17] The voluminous historiography on colonialism and imperialism has stressed Latin American agency, and the ways such agency mattered to very different outcomes (sometimes "more enlightened" outcomes) than elsewhere.[18] Political histories of the twentieth century have emphasized that, despite being an object of overt outside intervention and violence, Latin America also produced numerous inspirational models for the rest of the world.[19] More deprovincializing still has been the simple insistence that Latin America has always been part of "the West."

Masculine Conquest, Family Men, and Male Laborers

Histories of gender and sexuality have been an integral part of Latin American Studies for a good twenty-five years, and have been especially important to challenging essentialist notions of Latin American difference (that is, backwardness) and narratives of unidirectional change. Interestingly, questions about masculinity were present from the very beginning, thanks partly to the way women's history and gender history entered Latin American

Studies almost simultaneously, rather than consecutively. This sprang from the relatively "later timing" of gender analysis in Latin American history, itself the result of a certain hostility from Marxism. Yet while discussions of gender and sexuality have radically reworked materialist paradigms (Marxism in particular), they have maintained a central engagement with narratives of political economy.[20] Within this, they have made the masculine nature of men, and its making, a key subject of study. For this reason, they provide inspiration for integrating a central world historical concern, the changing face of the political economy, with a critical aspect of gender history, namely, the shifting nature of masculinity. The lessons that stand out are of three genres.

First, one of the most long-lived traditions for considering masculinity within Latin American history are studies of Spanish and Portuguese conquest and colonialism in the Americas. This is a literature, beginning in the 1980s and including more recent innovations, that has stressed the importance of sexuality to the religious and political authority of Inca and Aztec warriors, from ritual celibacy, to penal bloodletting, and cross-dressing. Historians have also considered how pre-Columbian empires were maintained through royal "taxes" in female virgins and young males. For Iberian empires, scholars have examined the Spanish conquistador and priest, as different kinds of masculine subjects, and the key role of sexual violence and forced Christian marriage.[21]

Joining the literature on sex and conquest has been a vibrant scholarship about sexual honor: In particular, the early idea that male sexual honor (via the enforcement of female chastity) was key to acquiring political office and economic power in the colonial world.[22] What has counted as "masculinity" in these studies has ranged widely, and undergone an evolution away from conflating masculinity with patriarchy to the idea of masculinity as a contested constellation of various empowerments and disempowerments, which apply to elites as well as subaltern men (that is, those men in inferior social, political, and economic positions whose voices were often silenced).[23] Most recently, scholarship on sexual symbolism has upended heterosexual binaries entirely by showing how many forms of power in the pre-Columbian and Iberian worlds were understood in terms of same-sex or transsexual gendered formations.[24]

Collectively, what such studies of Latin American history offer world history is a long tradition of seeing masculinity as key to understanding the world historical moment of encounter and conquest between Europe and the Americas. This is a literature that has focused heavily on high politics of statecraft and empire building. It links kinship to governance and economy, but it does not locate the "origin" or "function" of masculinity in the family. Importantly, it is a literature especially indebted to anthropology, a discipline whose insights world historians have barely begun to absorb. Indeed, while the cross-pollination of history and anthropology happened in multiple fields, it was especially strong in Latin American Studies. This was a fusion born of anthropology's long focus on ethnic Otherness (Indians) and symbolic systems (religion), together with Latin America's special place in the U.S.-American imagination as a "fieldwork site" for studying alterity. A majority of the first wave of women's studies on Latin America were by anthropologists as were the first gendered histories of Iberian conquest in the Americas.[25] Anthropology's most valuable gift to Latin American history, and most promising possibility for world history, has been to model ways for thinking about the cultural production of difference (gendered, sexual, racial, religious), while allowing scholars to hold fast to narratives about political domination and economic transformation.

A second genre of masculinity studies within Latin American history with important implications for world history is the rich literature on gender and modernization. This encompasses a series of debates about the relationship between nation building and the promotion of male-headed families and civic domesticity. As the story goes, from the late nineteenth century on, an array of constituencies—industrial leaders, liberal professionals, feminists, the labor movement, and the Left—all pushed varying ideals of nuclear family in which men were breadwinners and women dedicated themselves to scientific motherhood. This is the "modernization of patriarchy" thesis, and some version of it plays a central role in historiographies as diverse as that on the Mexican Revolution, Perón's Argentina, Brazilian myths of racial democracy, and Puerto Rican anti-imperialism.[26] It is the linchpin for arguments about the resolution of "the social problem" of nineteenth-century industrialization, the birth of the welfare state, the failures of socialism, and the emergence of the modern "homosexual" as a deviant and criminal.[27] As historians would have it, for a good hundred and twenty years, there was a concerted effort to get even very poor men to settle down and marry, and to commit to becoming producers for the nation and providers for families. This is a productive, domesticated, heteronormative, and nationalist masculinity that is promoted with astonishing breadth by a range of very different kinds of political projects. It is the hegemonic masculinity of the Family Man.

Obviously, this line of argument has its counterparts in the vast literature on the U.S. and Europe on domesticity and citizenship (as well as homosexuality), which locate its origins quite a bit earlier.[28] But the Latin Americanist scholarship is especially noteworthy for two reasons in particular. First, because, for better or worse, there has been an overarching emphasis on the role of the state in promoting the male-headed family, or the state as a site of contestation over what kind of masculine citizenship was desirable. Debates over hegemony have especially underscored the crucial role of gender and family in everyday forms of governance. Second, the Latin Americanist literature has paid much attention to the ways in which the ideal of the modern family was in constant dialogue with debates from elsewhere in the world, especially the U.S. and Europe. The aspiration for modernity—and anxiety that Latin America was not modern enough—was a constant theme for historical actors. So, Latin Americanist historians have paid attention to the circulation of ideas from abroad: looking at pan-American conferences on eugenics, or the export of gender models through international development schemes like the United States Agency for International Development (USAID), the United Nations Children's Fund (UNICEF), and Protestant missionaries.[29] Latin Americanists also have paid conscious attention to the ways in which such internationally produced ideologies as socialism, Catholic social doctrine, liberalism, and fascism become global languages, spoken with different accents.

Different versions of the Family Man as the basis for national belonging are obviously present in scholarship on twentieth-century Asia and Africa. And there too, the ideal worked in hegemonic ways: ideologically powerful in state policy, if never a reality for most people. One interesting challenge for world history is to make connections, or speak to the differences, between these different Family Man fantasies that occurred globally, and that are often promoted by similar international actors (missionaries, development agencies) or ideologies (liberalism, socialism). But it is also worth recognizing the tension between tracing different histories of masculinity versus using masculinity as an analytical category. There is a certain danger that in looking for the place of masculinity in different projects (colonial empires, or modernizing nation-states) we come up with strikingly similar stories across vastly different societies and temporal moments. Certain kinds of masculinity are extremely modern and very specific to certain places, but that doesn't mean that masculinity as an analytic concept is useless for asking questions about other periods.

One last genre of the lessons from Latin American history which deserves mention is labor history. This literature has explored not only how labor's gender divisions are fundamental to the economy but, in particular, the importance of international dynamics in their creation. Studies of masculinity and chattel slavery speak to obvious trans-Atlantic ties between gender, commerce, and violence. Likewise, there is an important scholarship on the masses of itinerant and roving migrant men who throughout the nineteenth and early twentieth centuries made up the bulk of workers in mines and haciendas: mestizo copper miners in Chile, Chinese guano workers in Peru, Almayra tin miners in Bolivia, Maya banana workers in Guatemala, indentured South Asian laborers in Trinidad.[30] These are the worlds of men created by export economies and coercive liberal republics, in which employers and companies were often "foreigners" (British, U.S.-American). In the mid-twentieth century, many of these men underwent domestication as both U.S. companies (modeling Henry Ford's philosophy of welfare capitalism) and Latin American welfare states (with their eyes on European state models) actively promoted marriage and family as the basis for social peace and labor control. As scholars point out, a great deal of the labor militancy for which Latin America became famous sprang from men's reconstituted masculinity as "family men" who demanded "rights," to a just standard of living for wives and children.[31]

What such engendered labor history offers world history is a model for making masculinity a central object of study in stories where "there are no women," and where the preferred storyline is focused on the global flows of commodities, including human bodies. Obviously, world history needs to pay just as much attention to femininity and the production of goods (the women usually *are* "there"). Not all world history *needs to* privilege economy and trade. But given existing tendencies within the field, Latin American labor history offers some instructive lessons. By looking at the construction and forms of masculinity in labor systems (as distinct from merely recognizing that all the workers were men) the overall picture of "the economy" changes, bringing new things into view. The everyday forms of coercion that underlay sugar plantations or nitrate mines involved ritual violence, containment, or contests between different men, that is, different deployments of masculinity. Men with families were by no means a natural or obvious way to organize production; on the contrary, domestic masculinity had to be consciously promoted or imposed by states, employers, and religion, and was often resisted. In other words, world history needs to take up the ways in which masculinity constitutes a terrain of power through which the world's workers, bosses, and products get produced.

Narrating World History through Masculinity

In offering these examples from Latin American history, we do not propose that Latin American Studies is somehow *better* positioned than other area studies to be a model for world history on issues of gender and sexuality. All area fields—Europe, Asia, Africa, U.S.-America, and so on—have engaged feminism and studies of sexuality. All are being transformed by discussions of the global and transnational, and some have produced outstanding work on the history of masculinity in an imperial context. But it is worthwhile that we not flatten these into a generic, singular "area studies." Each areas studies field emerged out of different concerns and political contexts, even though they may share Cold War roots. Our exploration of Latin American Studies is meant as an invitation to think about the trajectories taken by other area fields and field-specific ways of narrating masculinity as a global history.

In European gender history, for example, scholarship on masculinity arrived on the historiographical scene when the "linguistic turn," which emphasized the centrality of language to the production of cultural meaning and advocated the analysis of representations and discourses, was well on its way. The split was already deep between those engaged in materialist social-historical work under the banner of "experience" and those committed to a deconstructive cultural-historical project focused on "representation."[32] Historians of European masculinity were bound to land in one camp or the other. Thus the field is still struggling to integrate the methodologies of cultural and social history into a more comprehensive approach.[33]

Add to this the predominance of studies on British masculinities (especially in English-language publications) in the European literature, and it becomes clear why meaningful comparisons of different masculinities across times as well as regions remain high on the wish list of scholars.[34] At the same time, however, British scholarship includes several superb works on masculinity in an imperial context. These studies address the function of masculinity in empire building, and in so doing provide suggestive models for telling the story of European masculinities, and not just British masculinity, as a global story.[35]

It is important to emphasize at this juncture that world history should not be conceived of merely as a matter of "mix and stir," or as a comparative show and tell of case studies of area "civilizations." In fact, one of the most exciting and radical things about world history is the way conventional "areas" such as "Latin America," "Asia," "U.S.-America" or "Europe" begin to look very different when stories are told that consciously breach those gulfs: when we think of Haiti as producer of Enlightenment thought; early modern China as foundational to the making of the Latin American economy; the Philippines as a part of the Americas, rather than Asia; the Ottoman empire as integral to the formation of European self-understandings, rather than Europe's Other. The promise of world history lies precisely in its capacity to reframe how we think of "area" and to ask new questions about points of dialogue, conflict, and interaction taking place across world regions.[36]

One of the effects of the new global history is the emergence of European Studies as a new form of area studies in campus curricula. No longer part of the unquestioned center called "the West," "Europe" is now being examined as a historical rather than a fixed geographical entity. It is viewed as much as an idea as a place, and as deeply embedded in a transnational matrix. This perspective highlights the intense cross-pollination of peoples, ideas, and institutions between different regions of Europe that dates back well before the emergence of nation-states but lasts into the present (with the European Union as one of its more recent instantiations). It further highlights the fact that cross-border existence and migrations of different religious, ethnic, and political groups have been constants in European history both before and after colonial expansion overseas, shaping how Europe's different peoples understood themselves vis-a-vis one another, as well as their role as a collective force on the global stage. In other words, to think of Europe from this perspective has made it possible to ask new questions about Europe's political and cultural diversity and its historical legacies up to the present time.

Placing different histories of masculinity in dialogue with each other sheds light on the very processes that construct regional areas to begin with. Let us conclude with two examples to drive home this point, one from modern and one from early modern history. Taken together, they illustrate the fact that masculinity, like globalization, is best explored in terms of the longue duree to avoid facile conclusions about its "essential features." Our examples stem from the world history classroom where much of the hard conceptual work is taking place at this point as more and more college campuses in the U.S. offer world history courses and an increasing number of historians of gender and sexuality participate in teaching them.[37]

For example, in a survey course Heidi Tinsman has taught on Modern World History, the *de rigeur* topic of nineteenth-century imperialism and nationalism juxtaposes the life stories and political contexts of Theodore Roosevelt (U.S.), Cecil Rhodes (Britain), and Domingo Sarmiento (Argentina). Assigned readings include Roosevelt's, "The Strenuous Life" (1897), on the importance of manly vigor achieved through military escapades and the need for the U.S. occupation of the Philippines; Cecil Rhodes, "Confessions of Faith" (1899), on the link between British character and men's rugged adventure and enterprise in Africa; Sarmiento's "Barbarism and Civilization" (1854), justifying the extermination of native peoples of the pampa and Patagonia so Argentina could realize its manifest destiny and racial homogenization.

One important point in this lesson (and a surprise to many students), is that Latin American statesmen, like their U.S. and British counterparts, tied notions of modern masculinity to deeply racist projects of territorial expansion: Latin America is both a site of imperialist intervention and a military aggressor in its own right. Theodore Roosevelt made his name leading a brigade of "Rough Riders" in the 1898 Spanish-American War that placed Cuba under U.S. control; nineteenth-century Argentina is hugely dependent on British capital. At the same time, Mexico and Brazil have "Indian Wars" similar to Argentina's. Chile militarily seizes huge swaths of Bolivia and Peru, with British backing. In this context Latin America appears more complex than a passive object of foreign domination.

Yet one must also note the differences between Roosevelt's, Rhodes's, and Sarmiento's masculine ideals, and the ways in which these differences are about a set of connected world inequalities. For Roosevelt and Rhodes, achieving vigorous masculinity is linked to military adventure and achievements in Nature or in lands inhabited by "primitives." Both men are deeply anxious about the dangers posed by overly urban, industrial life in New York or London, and both see active participation in military ventures, hunting parties, and exploration missions as important counters to effeminate urbanity. For a Latin American statesman such as Sarmiento, the concern and antidote are exactly the inverse: the City (especially Buenos Aires) is the source of masculine civilization. More high culture in literature, theater, and music (via schools) is his answer, not rough-riding or military adventures. If the Indians are to be exterminated, it will not be Sarmiento who leads the actual charge. Argentina's iconic gauchos (cowboys) are, for Sarmiento, effeminate and weak, racially inbred. Whereas Cecil Rhodes points to the heavy presence of German immigrants in the United States as evidence of U.S. racial degeneration, Sarmiento praises German immigrants in Argentina as models of orderly civilization. Whereas Roosevelt disparages Europe as a place full of dandies, Sarmiento sees cosmopolitan citizens. Where Roosevelt and Rhodes see Latin America and Africa as "not yet fit" for self-government, Sarmiento defends the Argentine capacity for Progress.

These different masculinities speak directly to the global relationship between the United States, Britain, and Argentina in the nineteenth and early twentieth centuries. At this moment, the U.S. was emerging as a serious challenge to British hegemony while, with the collapse of the Spanish empire, Latin America had been transformed into the inferior stepsister of North America. Anxiety about modernity and masculinity cut multiple ways, and are intimately connected: Rhodes's sense of a vulnerable British empire; Roosevelt's desire to establish American exceptionalism and hemispheric leadership; Sarmiento's fears that Argentina is not modern or white enough. What we get by putting these tales in dialogue with each other is a world story where the portraits of these men are similar and related, but not at all the same.

We want to stress here that we view this type of focus on masculinities as a starting point rather than a final destination of feminist world historical work. Studies of masculinity have not proven themselves to be immune from erasing men's power over women and thereby underwriting the traditional invisibility of women in history. Far from it, this has been a disconcerting feature of a significant segment of recent Men's History and Men's Studies.[38] If our examination of masculinities in world history dead-ended in a recentering of powerful men in the dominant storylines, little would have been gained. Of course, world history needs to pay more attention to women. We need more scholarship on femininities and women as actors in world history. We need many more world history textbooks and source collections that synthesize this scholarship for classrooms and aid feminist teachers in designing courses and crafting lecture narratives.[39]

In the meantime, however, there remains the immediate need for feminist scholars to make meaningful interventions in a rapidly growing literature whose plot lines have cast men as world history's protagonists in a manner no longer acceptable in most national historiographies. Problematizing masculinity, we contend, is one effective means of problematizing these narrative choices and paving the way for the analysis of women within world history. No serious exploration of masculinity is complete without an exploration of men's power over women. Our second teaching example illuminates the intimate connection between masculinity and male control over women, while further illustrating how a focus on masculinity can recast conventional areas of study.

Questions of European empire building are also important questions of early modern world history. Yet it is challenging to narrate the importance of European expansion to global developments without falling into the trap of thinking that "all history starts in Europe." One way to avoid this danger is to fold European expansion into a more global story of masculine state formation and empire building. We made this attempt in the context of a course on Early World History which we began not in Europe but in the Americas and with the case of the Inca empire. For the Inca, control of women was constitutive of masculinity and empire at the same time. Tribute in women—some of whom were sacrificed, while others were married to the king or his noblemen, or given to high priests and secluded in temples—was critical to the growth of Inca bureaucracy and control over conquered territories. The compliance of "conquered men" was secured by enabling local elites to determine the allocation of women in marriage. Penultimate control over the distribution of all women marked the king as the most powerful of all men.

This makes for rich comparison and contrast with Christian European developments. During the sixteenth and seventeenth centuries states in Europe sought to further the process of political centralization through the regulation of gender and the empowerment of some men. This was equally true of the Protestant and Catholic parts of Germany as it was of uniformly Catholic countries like Spain. Rulers resorted to metaphors of fatherhood and patriarchal household governance to justify the extension of their powers into realms previously claimed by family members and local networks. They saw it as their divinely ordained task to strengthen paternal authority in society and subject women to male control within marriage or (in Catholic contexts) convents. Through legal changes, state authorities built alliances with male heads of households around shared patriarchal interests, turning them into quasi-bureaucratic agents who had to represent the family vis-à-vis the state but were also empowered to control it internally.

With the Spanish conquest of Mexico and Peru, these European patterns of gendered rulership traveled back to the Americas. One can usefully narrate the colonial encounter as an encounter between distinct conceptions of gender, power, and sexuality, including partially compatible, partially conflicting forms of masculinity. The honor-coded, fiercely violent masculinity of the conquistador was key to the initial phase of military conquest. The permanent establishment of empire, however, required modulating and directing male affect toward the building of Christian communities on the bedrock of monogamous marriages. Spanish-Catholic marriage practices shaped political, class, and racial hierarchies in the newly emerging colonial urban centers. Priests in the Americas were particularly concerned with enforcing monogamy, cracking down on sexual irregularities, and prosecuting witchcraft, which in the former Inca empire was often associated with female goddess cults.

Juxtaposing these stories of masculinity and empire means remapping global connections. When historians tell the story of "European expansion" during this period, they often look first to Spain (or Portugal), less often to the Inca or Aztec empires (other than as obstacles to European empire building), and virtually never to the Holy Roman Empire of the German nation. A focus on gender and sexuality makes visible "colonial" Spain's enmeshment in a much broader early modern European culture of sexual regulation. It shows that in spite of its lack of colonies the German empire could still cofashion technologies of rule that were transferable to colonial contexts.

And it highlights that patriarchal empire building in the Americas preceded the arrival of European Christianity with its singular male God, and included the Andean world of goddess religions.

At the same time, while masculinity and male power are key to all three political projects—Incan empire, European state formation, and Spanish colonialism—the projects only partially overlap and they each produce their irreducible differences with one another. The same can be said of the distinct yet related modern imperial enterprises embodied by Roosevelt, Rhodes, and Sarmiento. Tracking such differences in the meaning and deployment of masculinity in imperial contexts is one way to shed light on the complicated mechanisms of empire; as such, our teaching ventures raise new questions and exciting possibilities for research as well.

Although somewhat surprising for a literature dedicated to the exploration of macrophenomena, within world history comparative imperial history is a woefully underdeveloped form of global political analysis even as imperial studies have taken off in individual fields. The world historian Patrick Manning bemoans this lacuna in his comprehensive account of the state of world history writing in the early twenty-first century, a moment in time when new forms of imperialism, together with new forms of globalization, are profoundly marking our experience of the transnational," but apparently not yet transforming the field of world history. "To a remarkable degree," Manning notes, "the study of individual empires has superceded any broad effort to explore the role of empires in world history, to explore the changing institutions of empires, or to investigate the patterns of relationship between empires and other political units."[40]

We argue that the historical study of masculinity can serve as a lens for bringing all these dimensions of empire into focus: from the large global dynamics that shape and sustain imperial practice to the inner institutional workings of empire and the manifestations of imperial projects in the smallest political institutions like the family. Further still, the study of masculinity directs attention to the individual person as a gendered being, male and female, and the embodied, psychosocial experiences of world historical processes—be they empire building or capitalist expansion in the premodern, modern, or postmodern world.

NOTES

1. Earlier versions of this chapter appeared in *Historische Anthropologie* 16, 2 (2008): 271–90, as "Männerdomänen? *World History* trifft Männergeschichte—das Beispiel der Lateinamerikastudien." That version was then translated into English and published in the *Journal of World History* 21, 1 (March 2010): 75–96. We thank both *Historische*

Anthropologie and the *Journal of World History* for permitting us to print a revised and expanded version here.

    This chapter builds on conversations generated by a double-session round table we organized at the 2007 meeting of the American Historical Association in Washington, D.C., entitled "Narratives of Difference and Domination: World Histories and Studies of Masculinity." Featured as a Presidential Session and including scholars working on various world "areas," the panels drew a large audience and lively debate. Round-table participants included Kathryn Babayan, Kenneth Pomeranz, Wendy Urban-Mead, Indrani Chatterjee, Temma Kaplan, Merry E. Wiesner-Hanks, Clare Lyons, Adam McKeown, Heidi Tinsman, and Ulrike Strasser. The session also generated interest in Europe, where conversations about world history are beginning to gather steam. We were invited by the German-language journal *Historische Anthropologie* to publish an article on our reflections under the title, "Männerdomänen? World History trifft Männergeschichte-das Beispiel der Lateinamerikastudien," in 16, 2 (November 2008): 271–90. Because the relationship between gender, sexuality, and world history is of more long-standing concern within the U.S. academy, we were eager to have our chapter made available in English.

2. To name just a few examples, the 2008 meeting of the American Historical Meeting took "Uneven Developments" as its central theme, and purposely invited scholars to contemplate global relationships. The 2005 meeting of the American Studies Association and 2006 meeting of the Latin American Studies Association were each organized around the theme of area studies and globalization.

3. There are notable exceptions: Bonnie Smith, ed., *Women's History in Global Perspective*, vols. 1–3 (Urbana: University of Illinois Press, 2004–05); Mary Jo Maynes and Anne B. Waltner, "Women's Life Cycle Transitions in a World-Historical Perspective: Comparing Marriage in China and Europe," *Journal of Women's History* 12, 4 (2001): 11–21; Teresa A. Meade and Merry E. Wiesner-Hanks, eds., *A Companion to Gender History* (Oxford: Blackwell, 2004). On the world history side of things, see Kenneth Pomeranz, "Under Construction: Gendered World Histories and Global Studies of Masculinity," paper delivered at the Annual Meeting of the American Historical Association, Washington, D.C., January 2008.

4. Wiesner identifies a central problem in the outdated views each field holds of the other, but she also notes conceptual differences. See Merry E. Wiesner, "World History and the History of Women, Gender, and Sexuality," *Journal of World History* 18 (March 2007): 53–68.

5. Heidi Tinsman recently published an essay more thoroughly devoted to surveying histories of gender and sexuality in Latin America as related to Joan Scott's impact on the field. See Heidi Tinsman, "A Paradigm of Our Own: Joan Scott in Latin American History," *American Historical Review* 113 (December 2008): 1357–74. Also see Sueann Caulfield, "The History of Gender in the Historiography of Latin America," *Hispanic American Historical Review* 81 (2001): 3–4; William E. French and Katherine Elaine Bliss, "Introduction: Gender, Sexuality and Power in Latin America since Independence," in William E. French and Katherine Elaine Bliss, eds., *Gender, Sexuality, and Power in Latin America since Independence* (New York: Rowman & Littlefield, 2007), 1–30; Elizabeth Quay Hutchison, "Add Gender and Stir? Cooking Up Gendered Histories of Modern Latin America," *Latin American Research Review* 38, 1: 267–87.

6. See, for example, Joan W. Scott, *Gender and the Politics of History* (New York: Columbia University Press, 1988); Laura Lee Downs, *Writing Gender History* (Oxford: Oxford University Press, 2005); Judith Bennett, *History Matters: Patriarchy and the Challenge of Feminism* (Philadelphia: University of Pennsylvania Press, 2006).

7. See, e.g., Isabel Hull, *Sexuality, State and Civil Society in Germany, 1700–1815* (Ithaca: Cornell University Press, 1996); Ulrike Strasser, *State of Virginity: Gender, Religion and Politics in an Early Modern Catholic State* (Ann Arbor: University of Michigan Press, 2004; paperback 2007); Ida Blom, Karen Hagemann, and Catherine Hall, eds., *Gendered Nations: Nationalisms and Gender Order in the Long Nineteenth Century* (Oxford: Oxford International Publishers, 2000); Louise A. Tilly and Joan Scott, eds., *Women, Work and Family* (London: Routledge, 1987); Kathleen Canning, *Languages of Labor and Gender. Female Factory Work in Germany 1850–1914* (Ann Arbor: University of Michigan Press, 1996).
8. Examples include Nina Glick Schiller, Linda Basch, and Cristina Szanton Blanc, *Nations Unbound: Transnational Projects, Postcolonial Predicaments, and Deterritorialized Nation-States* (New York: Gordon and Breach, 1994); Ann McClintock, *Imperial Leather: Race, Gender, and Sexuality in the Colonial Contest* (New York: Routledge, 1995); Anne McClintock, Aamir Mufti, and Ella Shohat, eds., *Dangerous Liaisons: Gender, Nation, and Postcolonial Perspectives* (Minneapolis: University of Minnesota Press, 1997); Jacqui Alexander and Chandra Mohanty, eds., *Feminist Genealogies, Colonial Legacies, Democratic Futures* (New York: Routledge, 1997); Ann Laura Stoler, *Carnal Knowledge: Race and the Intimate in Colonial Rule* (Berkeley: University of California Press, 2002); Inderpal Grewal and Caren Kaplan, eds., *Scattered Hegemonies: Postmodernity and Transnational Feminist Practices* (Minneapolis: University of Minnesota Press, 1994).
9. Eric R. Wolf, *Europe and the People Without History* (Berkeley: University of California Press, 1982); Fernand Braudel, *The Wheels of Commerce* (New York: Harper & Row, 1982); Immanuel Wallerstein, *The Modern World System* (New York: Academic Press, 1974); *The Capitalist World Economy* (Cambridge: Cambridge University Press, 1979); Kenneth Pomeranz, *The Great Divergence: Europe, China, and the Making of the Modern World Economy* (Princeton: Princeton University Press, 2000); Dipesh Chakrabarty, *Provincializing Europe: Postcolonial Thought and Historical Difference* (Princeton: Princeton University Press, 2000); Frederick Cooper et al., *Confronting Historical Paradigms: Peasants, Labor, and the Capitalist World System in Africa and Latin America* (Madison: University of Wisconsin Press, 1993); Roy Bin Wong, *China Transformed: Historical Change and the Limits of European Experience* (Ithaca: Cornell University Press, 1997); Prasenjit Duara, "Transnationalism and the Challenge to National Histories," in Thomas Bender, ed., *Rethinking American History in a Global Age* (Berkeley: University of California Press, 2002).
10. See especially Pomeranz, *The Great Divergence*.
11. For an extremely useful overview of the field, see Patrick Manning, *Navigating World History: Historians Create a Global Past* (New York: Palgrave Macmillan, 2003).
12. For a discussion of the promise of bridging area studies and transnationalist optics, see Heidi Tinsman and Sandhya Shukla, "Talking Across the Americas," in Sandhya Shukla and Heidi Tinsman, eds., *Imagining Our Americas: Towards a Transnational Paradigm* (Durham: Duke University Press, 2007), 1–30. For a critique of area studies, see Masao Miyoshi and H. D. Harootunian, eds., *Learning Places: The Afterlives of Area Studies* (Durham: Duke University Press, 2002); David L. Szanton, ed., *The Politics of Knowledge: Area Studies and the Disciplines* (Berkeley: University of California Press, 2004).
13. Fernando Henrique Cardoso, *Dependencia y Desarrollo en América Latina: Ensayo de Interpretación Sociológica* (Mexico City: Siglo XXI, 1969); André Gunder Frank, *Capitalism and Underdevelopment in Latin America* (New York: Monthly Review Press, 1967).
14. Important early examples in Marxist histories of Latin America include Stanley Stein, *Vassouras, A Brazilian Coffee County, 1850–1900: The Role of Planter and Slave in a Changing*

Plantation Society (Cambridge: Harvard University Press, 1957); John Womack, *Zapata and the Mexican Revolution* (New York: Alfred Knopf, 1968); and Walter LaFeber, *Inevitable Revolutions: The United States in Central America* (New York: W. W. Norton, 1984).

In the more recent labor historiography, see Florencia Mallon, *Defense of Community in Peru's Central Highlands: Peasant Struggle and Capitalist Transition, 1860–1940* (Princeton: Princeton University Press, 1983); Peter Winn, *Weavers of Revolution: The Yarur Workers and Chile's Road to Socialism* (New York: Oxford University Press, 1986); Daniel James, *Resistance and Integration: Peronism and the Argentine Working Class, 1946–1976* (New York: Cambridge University Press, 1988); John D. French, *The Brazilian Workers' ABC: Class Conflict and Alliances in Modern Sao Paulo* (Chapel Hill: University of North Carolina Press, 1992).

On hegemony, see Florencia Mallon, *Peasant and Nation: The Making of Post-Colonial Mexico and Peru* (Berkeley: University of California Press, 1995); Gilbert M. Joseph and Daniel Nugent, *Everyday Forms of State-Formation: Revolution and the Negotiation of Rule in Modern Mexico* (Durham: Duke University Press, 1994); William Roseberry, *Anthropologies and Histories: Essays in Culture, History, and Political Economy* (New Brunswick: Rutgers University Press, 1989); James, *Resistance and Integration*.

15. Scott, "Women in *The Making of the English Working Class*," *Gender and the Politics of History*, 68–92.
16. This argument has been made in an explicit form by Greg Gandin, *Empire's Workshop: Latin America, the United States, and the Rise of the New Imperialism* (New York: Metropolitan Books, 2006).
17. Walter Mignolo has argued that Iberia saw the Americas as a place of self-realization rather than as a radical Other. Mignolo, *Local Histories/Global Designs: Coloniality, Subaltern Knowledges, and Border Thinking* (Princeton: Princeton University Press, 2000). Benedict Andersen drew early attention to the ways in which the Americas, including Latin America, rather than Europe, created the first bonafide nation-states. Benedict Anderson, *Imagined Communities: Reflections on the Origin and Spread of Nationalism* (London: Verso, 1983). On the fundamentally European essence of Latin American republicanism, see Jaime Rodriguez O., *The Independence of Spanish America* (Cambridge: Cambridge University Press, 1998).
18. Examples include Gilbert Joseph, Catherine LeGrand, and Ricardo Salvatore, eds., *Close Encounters of Empire: Writing the Cultural History of U.S.-Latin American Relations* (Durham: Duke University Press, 1998); Ana María Alonso, *Thread of Blood: Colonialism, Revolution, and Gender on Mexico's Northern Frontier* (Tucson: University of Arizona Press, 1995); Emilia Viotti da Costa, *Crowns of Glory, Tears of Blood: The Demerara Slave Rebellion of 1823* (New York: Oxford University Press, 1994); Patricia Seed, *To Love, Honor, and Obey in Colonial Mexico: Conflicts over Marriage Choice, 1574–1821* (Stanford: Stanford University Press, 1988), and *Ceremonies of Possession in Europe's Conquest of the New World* (Cambridge: Cambridge University Press, 1995); Steven C. Topik and Allen Wells, eds., *The Second Conquest of Latin America: Coffee, Henequen, and Oil during the Export Boom, 1850–1930* (Austin: University of Texas Press, 1998).
19. See contributions in Gilbert M. Joseph, ed., *Reclaiming the Political in Latin American History: Essays from the North* (Durham: Duke University Press, 2001).
20. For a discussion of the different timings and focus of Latin Americanist feminist scholarship, see Tinsman, "A Paradigm of Our Own."

21. Richard C. Trexler, *Sex and Conquest: Gendered Power, Political Order, and European Conquest of the Americas* (Ithaca: Cornell University Press, 1995); Inga Clendinnen, *Aztecs: An Interpretation* (Cambridge: Cambridge University Press, 1993), and *Ambivalent Conquests: Maya and Spanish in Yucatán, 1517–1570* (Cambridge: Cambridge University Press, 1987); Irene Silverblatt, *Moon, Sun, and Witches: Gender, Ideologies and Class in Inca and Spanish Peru* (Princeton: Princeton University Press, 1987); Tzvetan Todorov, *The Conquest of America: The Question of the Other* (New York: Harper Perennial, 1984).

22. Early studies of honor included Verena Stolke, *Marriage, Class and Colour in Nineteenth Century Cuba: A Study of Racial Attitudes and Sexual Values in a Slave Society* (New York: Cambridge University Press, 1974); Asunción Lavrin, ed., *Sexuality and Marriage in Colonial Latin America* (Lincoln: University of Nebraska Press, 1989); Sandra Lauderdale Graham, *House and Street: The Domestic World of Servants and Masters in 19th Century Rio de Janeiro* (New York: Cambridge University Press, 1988); Seed, *To Love, Honor and Obey*.

23. Important recent work on honor includes María Martínez-Lopez, *Genealogical Fictions: Limpieza de Sangre, Religion, and Gender in Colonial Mexico* (Stanford: Stanford University Press, 2008); Susan M. Socolow, *The Women of Colonial Latin America* (Cambridge: Cambridge University Press, 2000); Ann Twinam, *Public Lives, Private Secrets: Gender, Honor, Sexuality, and Illegitimacy in Colonial Spanish America* (Stanford: Stanford University Press, 1999); Kathryn Burns, *Colonial Habits: Convents and the Spiritual Economy of Cuzco, Peru* (Durham: Duke University Press, 1999); Steve J. Stern, *The Secret History of Gender: Women, Men, and Power in Late Colonial Mexico* (Chapel Hill: University of North Carolina Press, 1995); Sarah C. Chambers, *From Subjects to Citizens: Honor, Gender, and Politics in Arequipa, Peru, 1780–1854* (University Park: Penn State University Press, 1999); Lyman L. Johnson and Sonya Lipsett-Rivera, eds., *The Faces of Honor: Sex, Shame, and Violence in Colonial Latin America* (Albuquerque: University of New Mexico Press, 1998).

For masculinity and honor in the modern period, see Sueann Caulfield, *In Defense of Honor: Sexual Morality, Modernity, and Nation in Early Twentieth Century Brazil* (Durham: Duke University Press, 2000); Suenn Caulfield, Sarah Chambers, and Lara Putnam, eds., *Honor, Status, and Law in Modern Latin America* (Durham: Duke University Press, 2005); Lara Putnam, *The Company They Kept: Migrants and the Politics of Gender in Caribbean Costa Rica, 1870–1960* (Chapel Hill: University of North Carolina Press, 2002).

24. The Latin American literature on homosexuality and transgender is especially noteworthy for making empire and trans-Atlantic religious and cultural conflict central to arguments about sexual deviance and homosexuality. On the colonial period, see Peter Sigal, *From Moon Goddesses to Virgins: The Colonization of Yucatecan Maya Sexual Desire* (Austin: University of Texas Press, 2000), and contributions to Peter Sigal, ed., *Infamous Desire: Male Homosexuality in Colonial Latin America* (Chicago: University of Chicago Press, 2003).

For the modern period, see James Naylor Green, *Beyond Carnival: Male Homosexuality in 20th Century Brazil* (Chicago: University of Chicago, 1999); Peter M. Beattie, *The Tribute of Blood: Army, Honor, Race, and Nation in Brazil, 1864–1945* (Durham: Duke University Press, 2001); Robert Buffington, *Criminal and Citizen in Modern Mexico* (Lincoln: University of Nebraska Press, 2000); Robert McKee Irwin, *Mexican Masculinities* (Minneapolis: University of Minnesota Press, 2003); Robert McKee Irwin, Edward J. McCaughan, and Michelle Rocio Nasser, eds., *The Famous 41: Sexuality and Social Control in Mexico, c. 1901* (New York: Palgrave Macmillan, 2003); Roger

Lancaster, *Life Is Hard: Machismo, Danger, and the Intimacy of Power in Nicaragua* (Berkeley: University of California Press, 1992).

25. A great deal of early work in Latin American women's studies emphasized questions of women's work and issues of gender and development. See contributions in June Nash and Helen Safa, eds., *Sex and Class in Latin America* (New York: Praeger, 1976); June Nash and María Patricia Fernández-Kelley, eds., *Women, Men, and the International Division of Labor* (Albany: SUNY Press, 1983); María Patricia Fernández-Kelly, *For We Are Sold, I and My People* (Albany: SUNY Press, 1985); Eleanor Leacock and Helen Safa, eds., *Women's Work: Development and the Division of Labor by Gender* (South Hadley: Bergin and Garvey, 1986).

    One of the first histories of the conquest to focus on gender was Tzvetan Todorov's *The Conquest of America* (1984). Although not formally "an anthropologist," Todorov drew heavily on debates in anthropology, in combination with literary analysis. Other conquest histories by anthropologists included Inga Clendinnen, *Ambivalent Conquests*, and Irene Silverblatt, *Moon, Sun, and Witches*.

26. This is a truly vast literature. Representative examples include Susan K. Besse, *Restructuring Patriarchy: The Modernization of Gender Inequality in Brazil, 1914–1940* (Chapel Hill: University of North Carolina Press, 1996); Barbara Weinstein, *Social Peace in Brazil: Industrialists and the Remaking of the Working Class in Brazil, 1920–1964* (Chapel Hill: University of North Carolina Press, 1996); Mary Kay Vaughan, *Cultural Politics in Revolution: Teachers, Peasants, and Schools in Mexico, 1930–1940* (Tuscon: University of Arizona Press, 1997); Katherine Bliss, *Compromised Positions: Prostitution, Public Health, and Gender Politics in Revolutionary Mexico City* (University Park: Penn State University Press, 2001); Eileen Findlay, *Imposing Decency: The Politics of Sexuality and Race in Puerto Rico, 1870–1920* (Durham: Duke University Press, 1999); Elizabeth Quay Hutchison, *Labors Appropriate to Their Sex: Gender, Work, and Politics in Urban Chile, 1900–1930* (Durham: Duke University Press, 2001); Heidi Tinsman, *Partners in Conflict: The Politics of Sexuality, Gender, and Labor in Chilean Agrarian Reform, 1950–1973* (Durham: Duke University Press, 2002); Elizabeth Dore, *Myths of Modernity: Peonage and Patriarchy in Nicaragua* (Durham: Duke Univesity Press, 2006); Karin Alejandra Rosemblatt, *Gendered Compromises: Political Cultures and the State in Chile, 1920–1950* (Chapel Hill: University of North Carolina Press, 2000); Elizabeth Dore and Maxine Molyneux, eds., *Hidden Histories of Gender and the State in Latin America* (Durham: Duke University Press, 2000).

27. See especially Green, *Beyond Carnival*; Beattie, *The Tribute of Blood*; Buffington, *Criminal and Citizen*; Irwin, *Mexican Masculinities*. Also see contributions in French and Bliss, eds., *Gender, Sexuality and Power in Latin America since Independence*.

28. Classical examples include Lynn Hunt, *The Family Romance of the French Revolution* (Berkeley: University of California Press, 1992); Joan Landes, *Women in the Public Sphere in the Age of the French Revolution* (Ithaca: Cornell University Press, 1988); Linda Kerber, *Women of the Republic: Intellect and Ideology in Revolutionary America* (Chapel Hill: University of North Carolina Press, 1980); Mary Beth Norton, *Liberty's Daughters: The Revolutionary Experience of American Women, 1750–1800* (Cornell: Cornell University Press, 1996).

29. See especially Donna Guy, *Sex and Danger in Buenos Aires: Prostitution, Family, and Nation in Argentina* (Lincoln: University of Nebraska Press, 1991), and *White Slavery and Mothers Alive and Dead: The Troubled Meeting of Sex, Gender, Public Health, and Progress in Latin America* (Lincoln: University of Nebraska Press, 2000); Mrinalini Sinha, Donna Guy, and Anglea Woollacott, eds., *Feminisms and Internationalism* (Oxford: Blackwell, 1999). For a discussion of the transnational influences on sexuality and gender in the Mexican

revolution, see Jocelyn Olcott, *Revolutionary Women in Post Revolutionary Mexico* (Durham: Duke University Press, 2007); Jocelyn Olcott, Mary Kay Vaughan, and Gabriela Cano, eds., *Sex and Revolution: Gender, Politics and Power in Modern Mexico* (Durham: Duke University Press, 2007).

30. Thomas Miller Klubock, *Contested Communities: Class, Gender and Politics in Chile's El Teniente Copper Mine, 1904–1951* (Durham: Duke University Press, 1998); June Nash, *We Eat the Mines and the Mines Eat Us: Dependency and Exploitation in Bolivian Tin Mines* (New York: Columbia University Press, 1979); Michael Taussig, *The Devil and Commodity Fetishism in South America* (Chapel Hill: University of North Carolina Press, 1980); Aviva Chomsky, *West Indian Workers and the United Fruit Company, 1870–1940* (Baton Rouge: Louisiana State University Press, 1996); Alonso, *Thread of Blood*.

31. Other important studies stressing connections between masculinity, sexuality, and working-class politics include Anne Farnsworth-Alvear, *Dulcinea in the Factory: Myths, Morals, Men and Women in Colombia's Industrial Experiment, 1905–1960* (Durham: Duke University Press, 2000); Matthew C. Gutmann, *The Meaning of Macho: Being a Man in Mexico City* (Berkeley: University of California Press, 1996); Weinstein, *For Social Peace in Brazil*; Hutchison, *Labors According to Their Sex*; Rosemblatt, *Gendered Compromises*; Findlay, *Imposing Decency*; Tinsman, *Partners in Conflict*; Daniel James and John D. French, eds., *The Gendered Worlds of Latin American Women Workers* (Durham: Duke University Press, 1997); Peter Winn, ed., *Victims of the Miracle: Workers and Neoliberalism in Pinochet's Chile, 1973–2002* (Durham: Duke University Press, 2004).

32. European labor history was the place of origin for this divide, after all. See the now classic contributions by Joan W. Scott, "Gender: A Useful Category of Historical Analysis," *American Historical Review* 91 (1986): 1053–75; Laura Lee Downs, "If 'Woman' Is Just an Empty Category, Then Why Am I Afraid to Walk Alone at Night? Identity Politics Meets the Postmodern Subject," *Comparative Studies in Society and History* 35 (1993): 414–37; Joan W. Scott, "The Tip of the Volcano," *Comparative Studies in Society and History* 35 (1993): 438–43; Laura Lee Downs, "Reply to Joan Scott," *Comparative Studies in Society and History* 35 (1993): 444–51. For a thoughtful attempt to mediate between these polar positions, see Kathleen Canning, "Feminist History after the Linguistic Turn: Historicizing Discourse and Experience," *Signs* 19 (1994): 368–404.

33. Karen Harvey, "The History of Masculinity, circa 1650–1800," *Journal of British Studies* 44, 2 (April 2005): 296–311. Karen Harvey and Alexandra Shepard, "What Have Historians Done with Masculinity? Reflections on Five Centuries of British History, circa 1500–1950," *Journal of British Studies* 44, 2 (April 2005): 274–80.

34. For an attempt to connect literatures across time within Britain, see Alexandra Shepard, "From Anxious Patriarchs to Refined Gentlemen: Manhood in Britain, ca. 1500–1700," *Journal of British Studies* 44, 2 (April 2005): 281–95. For a collection that tries to integrate scholarship about different European countries from the Middle Ages to the nineteenth century, see Susan Broomhall and Jacqueline Van Gent, ed., *Governing Masculinities in the Early Modern Period: Regulating Selves and Others in the Early Modern Period* (Farnham: Ashgate Publishing, 2011).

35. See Mrinalini Sinha, *Colonial Masculinity: The "Manly Englishman" and the "Effeminate Bengali" in the Late Nineteenth Century* (Manchester: Manchester University Press, 1995); John Tosh, *Manliness and Masculinities in Nineteenth-Century Britain: Essays on Gender, Family and Empire* (Harlow: Pearson Longman, 2005). Less explicitly situated within the history of masculinities than in world history discussion but no less important in this context, is

Alison Games, *The Web of Empire: English Cosmopolitans in an Age of Expansion 1560–1660* (Oxford: Oxford University Press, 2008).

36. Tinsman and Shukla, "Thinking Across the Americas."
37. Judith P. Zinsser, "And Now for Something Completely Different: Gendering the World History Survey," in Ross E. Dunn, *The New World History: A Teacher's Companion* (Boston: Bedford, 1999), 476–78, and "Women's History, World History, and the Construction of New Narratives," *Journal of Women's History* 12, 3 (2000): 196–206; Bonnie Smith, "Introduction," *Women's History in Global Perspective*, vol. 1 (Urbana: University of Illinois Press, 2004), 1–8; Merry Wiesner-Hanks, "Women's History and World History Courses," *Radical History Review* 91 (Winter 2005): 133–50. Ulrike Strasser and Heidi Tinsman, "Engendering World History," *Radical History Review* 91 (Winter 2005): 151–65, and "Engendering World History: A Team-Taught Survey at the University of California, Irvine," in *World History Connected* 4, 3 (June 2007): worldhistoryconnected.press.uiuc.edu.
38. For a poignant critique of the founding analytical principles of men's history and men's studies, see Toby L. Ditz, "The New Men's History and the Peculiar Absence of Gendered Power: Some Remedies from Early America," *Gender & History* 16, 1 (April 2004): 1–35.
39. For an excellent online resource for the world history classroom, see "Women in World History," Roy Rosenzweig Center for History and New Media, George Mason University, http://chnm.gmu.edu/wwh/.
40. Manning, *Navigating World History*, 189–91. Quote on 190.

9

Connecting Histories of Gender, Health, and U.S.-China Relations

CRISTINA ZACCARINI

Introduction

Like other historical fields, especially those deeply engaged with politics, the study of U.S. foreign relations came late to incorporate a gendered perspective. Eventually, new scholarship on women's and gender history affected its historiography, as scholars repositioned a field traditionally concerned with masculine narratives of nationalism, military interventions, and diplomacy toward "intercultural scholarship,"[1] and as they recognized gender as yet another factor intimately engaged in shaping international affairs.

This is no less true of the historical study of Sino-American relations. Recognizing the links made by male Chinese elites at the turn of the century, who argued that China's victimization by imperialist powers was entwined with the need to improve China's health care system and the status of women, historians in the fields of women, gender, and medicine influenced the field's historiography. Drawing from reformers' assertion that for the Chinese nation to survive and thrive, the conditions and roles of women, like China's health care system, must be modernized, these historians have explored the resultant cross-cultural exchanges between the U.S. and China. They have linked women's changing roles and representations in the developing nation-state to China's interaction with the U.S. They have also explored women's roles in interpreting both Western and traditional Han understandings of healing.[2]

Historians have shown that when male Chinese elites crafted the prescription for survival of the Chinese nation-state, they looked to the westernized nations and to Japan for models. Most male reformers thus came to view Western medicine as superior to the healing traditions of Han China, and concluded that women's status as oppressed and backward was because of China's past.[3]

Utilizing Chinese language and U.S. sources, scholars of Chinese women's history have uncovered hitherto silent female voices. They reveal that

>> 211

Chinese women's perceptions of Western and Han cultures differed from those of elite male Chinese. Chinese women interpreted these cultures to enable women to exercise both autonomy and power as individuals.

This new scholarship on women, gender, and medicine in China has compelled historians of Sino-American relations to ask, as Heidi Tinsman and Ulrike Strasser do elsewhere in this volume, "new questions about points of dialogue, conflict, and interaction" that shaped China-U.S. relations in the past.[4] Some examples of the relevance of this new scholarship can be viewed through studies of women missionaries, and of contacts among women in China and the U.S.

Scholarly attention to early-twentieth-century women's foreign missionary societies in China sheds new light on "cross-cultural exchange in the mission field."[5] Scholars have shown that this cultural exchange, which Jane Hunter called "imperial evangelism,"[6] between female missionaries and the Chinese women they sought to convert to Christianity, allowed Chinese women to exert power as they chose from Chinese and Western models. Carol Chin characterized American women missionaries, admired by Chinese elites, as "beneficent imperialists,"[7] but she would also show that, while male Chinese elites believed that women should embrace Western ideas to serve the nation-state, Chinese feminists deliberately rejected an "American-type modernity."[8] Rather, when Chinese women negotiated the imperial evangelism of American Christian missionaries, they joined in the project of imagining the Chinese nation-state, defining it in their own terms.

Chinese women's interpretations of Western ideas expose their awareness of the contradictions between Western concepts of rights, touted as universal, and the reality of gender inequality. Dorothy Ko concludes that the critical Western notion of "natural rights," which had fueled the Enlightenment and which would pave the way for Western modernization, was appropriated more completely by elite male Chinese nationalists. She explains that "the nation imagined here was modeled after Western nation states that were based on rigid gender divisions of labour"; however, the "inherent contradictions in the West between a gender-neutral concept of 'natural rights' and a gender-specific practice of nation state went unnoticed by most Chinese reformers."[9] When Chinese women contested "the boundaries and meanings of 'women's rights' in China," it was, as Ko puts it, a consequence of the "contradiction inherent in the Anglophone formulation."[10] This demonstrates the different ways that Western notions of "rights" were contested in China.

Likewise, historians have shown that, when male Chinese elites argued that traditional Chinese ways of healing were inferior to those of the West, women too engaged in this discourse, sometimes challenging masculinist interpretations. Since the Chinese nation-state's success hinged upon the necessity of both uplifting women and improving health care, women were intimately connected to its success, as citizens, patients, and healers. Historians have shown Chinese women appropriating Western medical professions to give women autonomy and to strengthen the nation-state. But women, at times, also upheld Chinese healing traditions, thus thwarting U.S. cultural imperialism as well as the elite male reformers.

Like Chinese women, American women too interpreted culture in ways that brought women power. American women supported the exportation of Western ideas to China through missionaries, promoting education and the professions for Chinese women at a time when women in the U.S. were largely restricted from these professions. Additionally, when American women preferred a Chinese healer over a modern physician, they likewise shifted power away from the male-dominated American medical profession.

This chapter examines two approaches which seem historiographically distinct, carving a swathe through the rich works produced within this broad tent of transnational explorations of the connections between women in China and the U.S. The works of historians discussed here illustrate how modernity, a "cultural consciousness or mind-set," was conceptualized and contested by Chinese women and by American women, as historical actors, feminists, patients, healers, and representatives of their respective nation-states.[11] These historiographies reveal how women's conceptions of culture and their actions contributed to redefining understandings of power in the Sino-American relationship.

China, the Nation-State, and the West

The present-day boundaries of the People's Republic of China are based largely upon the territory controlled by the last Chinese dynasty, the multiethnic Manchu, or Qing dynasty.[12] The end of Qing rule in 1911 brought to a close the two-millennial dynastic history of one of the world's oldest and most powerful empires. Replete with stunning achievements in science, culture, and navigation, the Chinese had understood the greatness of their civilization, and believed that they could transform other nations considered barbarian, maintaining a central position as the Middle Kingdom, by virtue of their superior high culture and morality. However, nineteenth-century Western incursions, the Sino-Japanese War of 1895, and natural calamities of disastrous proportions shook China and shaped, in crucial ways, its future identity as a nation-state.[13] As noted by George Wei and Xiaoyuan Liu, the Chinese visualized "a mental map of the modern world order," and "sadly found that China was not the Middle Kingdom anymore; it had fallen into a peripheral and even semicolonial status. Rather, the West now was the center."[14]

In the nineteenth century China and the West had multifaceted exchanges. Britain and other Western powers were determined to open new markets, and, through military engagements, aggressively stripped the Qing dynasty of power. Protestant missionaries from Britain and the United States formed the cultural arm of this aggressive imperialism. Their Protestantism admitted little compromise with Chinese ways and ignited several "international incidents," even as they built schools, hospitals, and orphanages. As these missionaries promoted education and provided health care for women, they put in place mechanisms that transformed Chinese notions of gender roles.[15]

Chinese thinkers and literati, tied to the Manchu leaders and disillusioned by military defeat by Japan in 1895, gradually abandoned a worldview that was traditionally Sinocentric and set out to assimilate the "new learning," *xinxue*, of the West. During the late Qing modernization drive, this new learning bore fruit, leading to the collapse of the dynasty in 1911 and the birth of the Chinese nation-state.[16] This entailed a radical redefinition of the place of women in Chinese society. It was in the midst of this grappling with the issues of modernization, including the modernization of gender roles and exposure to Western medicine, that China was invented as a nation.

As the Chinese nation-state developed, intellectuals looked toward Western ideas, often transmitted through interactions with missionaries. Westerners' claims of superiority hinged upon arguments about the need to uplift China's inferior civilization, and missionaries, many of whom (sometimes even a majority of whom) were female, were central to the transfer of knowledge promoting a superior West and inferior China.[17]

Scholars have shown how male Chinese reformers incorporated missionary notions of Chinese deficiency and advocated Western models. Qing dynasty-era reformer Liang Qichao was profoundly influenced by American ideas and often pointed to the "high value Americans apparently place on women and their education."[18] Liang discussed the survival of China in the context of the status of women, viewing the inferior status of Chinese women as reflective of problems endemic to China, heralding the ideal woman as one who was a product of missionary education.

Liang Qichao admired the missionary model and sought to impose it on Chinese women while eschewing traditional culture as represented by Chinese women poets, the *cainü*. For example, as noted by literary scholar Hu Ying, "The burial of the *cainü* heralds the birth of the new woman . . . first introduced by Liang Qichao himself." The new woman admired by Liang was a missionary-educated Western doctor. Hu explains: "She is Dr. Kang Aide, the first new woman knowledgeable in Western medicine—the modern *cai* par excellence."[19]

Liang's attitude toward traditional Chinese culture and espousal of the Western model did not preclude him from being a critic of imperialism. Lydia Liu has explained that Chinese thinkers who were the "foremost critics of Western imperialism of their time" subscribed to the very "discourse that European nations first used to stake their claim to racial superiority."[20] Scholars have shown, however, that some women who were critics of imperialism viewed Chinese culture differently.

Scholar Nanxiu Qian's work revealed that during the 1898 Reform Movement, women reformers approached national strengthening by drawing from Chinese traditions of learning that went back to the seventeenth- and eighteenth-century Yangzi Delta community. These women espoused Western knowledge; however, unlike the male reformers, most of whom saw the traditional roles of Chinese women as a hindrance to national progress, they found in them the impetus to organize and champion reform.[21]

Early historians of Sino-American relations examined missionaries' views of China, including representations of oppressed women, without the benefit of later understandings of scholarship such as that of Nanxiu Qian, thus strengthening the belief that the Chinese accepted the superiority of Western culture.[22] As Jessie Lutz has noted, "Western missionary writings, which were the West's major source of information about China until well into the twentieth century, highlighted female infanticide, bound feet, seclusion, the preferential treatment of sons, and the absolute authority of the husband over his wife."[23] Indeed, missionaries' views of Chinese women and these traditional histories of the nation-state, which favored a "linear history of the nation," masked the far more nuanced history of Chinese women.[24]

Beginning as early as the 1970s, historians writing about the roles of Chinese women noticed their heretofore hidden agency.[25] For example, in her 1994 book about upper-class women in the lower Yangzi Delta region from 1570 to 1720, Dorothy Ko,[26] using sources *by* Chinese women rather than *about* them, uncovered a group of literate, elite women who transmitted knowledge to each other and were active participants in elite male culture.[27] These highly educated upper-class women profited from the economy's new commercialization and their connections to powerful men. They had thus moved beyond women's roles fixed in Chinese culture within the frame of "Thrice Following," the schema that dictated a woman's subordination to her father when young, her husband when an adult, and her son in her old age. Ko's work also uncovered the importance of the "inner" sphere composed of women and the imperial state's recognition of the family—which Western scholarship denotes as a private or domestic sphere, and hence peripheral in terms of power—as a foundational source of social and legal power.[28] This nuanced reading of Chinese women's history also offered new perspectives on the custom of footbinding, showing it to be far more complex than the consensus missionary view of it as another example of female victimization.

If the missionaries could only understand Chinese women through the prism of "victimization and uplift," the schools they created helped challenge traditional paradigms for Chinese girls and women by providing avenues for women's movement outside the "inner sphere." These schools were especially significant when we consider the links between Chinese women's roles and the evolution of Chinese modernity.

Tani Barlow has observed that, prior to the invention of the Chinese nation-state, there was no single Chinese word for woman; rather the category "woman" could only be expressed relationally through the words for wife, mother, daughter, and mother-in-law.[29] Indeed, Chinese culture has always assumed that "man and woman" are socially constructed categories. According to Charlotte Furth, the identities of women as "daughter, wife or mother were among the most significant social markers for women in Confucian society." Thus, the identification of "wife as an 'inner person,' *nei ren*, constructed her femininity via bodily location rather than biology."[30] This is important when we consider that women's changing roles occupied "center stage in the [Chinese] conceptualization of modernity."[31]

Paradoxically, during the late nineteenth and early twentieth centuries, when women's occupations outside the home were predominantly frowned upon, missionary education, provided by American women, exposed Chinese women to Western liberal arts and professional education. Consequently, missionary schools became significant locations where young women engaged in social activism. It is true that male reformers saw women as serving the nation-state for its own sake, rather than for themselves, and that the missionary agenda was likewise not one that scholars would consider feminist; however, in the end, when some Chinese women interpreted modernity and utilized Western ideas, they did so in a way that was uniquely Chinese, thereby thwarting both Western cultural domination and patriarchal dominance.

Missionary periodicals equated democracy for China with modernization and such modernization required a place in the new social order for Chinese women. As Rebecca Karl has noted, as a new "political topos" women were "interpellated" as political beings, so that by the May 4th period (1915–19), some mission schoolgirls and teachers engaged in public protests alongside male students and workers.[32]

In letters home, and in newspapers and other publications, images and symbols of Chinese women, Chinese nationalism, and American womanhood flew back and forth. This knowledge exchange influenced the public mood toward China in the United States and Chinese perceptions of Americans, not only early in the twentieth century but also during the critical decade of the 1930s—when Japan attacked China (1937)—during World War II, and during the Chinese Civil War (1946–49). Through contact with the West during these turbulent times, ideas of women serving the nation-state were promoted; however, women moved beyond this role, as it was at this time that feminism emerged in China. Indeed, as Dorothy Ko has noted, "from around 1895. . . feminism has been entangled in China's political, cultural and social transformations," and women have been "political and social actors in the drama of envisioning and constructing modernity."[33]

Chinese Feminists Dialogue with the West

Joan Judge has observed: "Unlike Western societies, where women's rights were not fully addressed until almost a century after modern conceptions of the nation were put forward, in early twentieth-century China 'the national question' and 'the women's question' were confronted simultaneously."[34] New ideas about Chinese womanhood advocating the "independent" politically informed woman as a positive good were explicitly linked to the project of Chinese nation building. In the waning days of the Qing dynasty, as Louise Edwards and others have shown, feminist struggles promoting women's education and women's political activism were inextricably woven with the nationalist struggle. The Chinese woman suffrage movement was linked to anti-Qing, early Republican ideology, and later to Nationalist and Marxist ideology. Even though this movement engaged only a small number of women through student protests and patriotic activism, it revealed how integral revisioned gender roles were to the project of building the nation.[35] Louise Edwards considered the women activists of the 1911 to 1913 period part of the "first wave of woman's suffrage activism."[36]

Dorothy Ko has observed that these early Chinese feminists, seldom numbering more than one hundred, became "important agents in imagining China as a nation and reconfiguring the place of women in it." They espoused Western ideas of equality and "denounced the oppression of women over thousands of years of Chinese history, calling for a revolution in beliefs and practice."[37] China's first suffragists were "few in number," often educated in

Japan, and from elite, gentry families. Rejecting the Qing dynasty and believing that only a democratic republic could ensure women's political participation, they joined the Revolutionary Alliance which subscribed to equality between men and women. These women made bombs and formed "assassination squads," anticipating that they would hold "equal rights within the future republic."[38] When the Republic of China was established in 1911 and they were denied the right to vote and have access to political power, they continued their struggle.

When this first wave of suffrage activism largely ended in 1913, a broader cross-section of moderate women emerged during what Louise Edwards terms a "second-wave of suffrage activism."[39] These activists were influenced by contacts with the West: meetings with U.S. suffrage leader Carrie Chapman Catt and contacts with the American Woman's Christian Temperance Union, and this group spent time in America rather than in Japan.[40] Scholars have shown how, influenced by Western models, this second wave of suffrage activism achieved successes for women during a chaotic time in Chinese history, when power was decentralized and China was ruled by provincial warlords. The rich and unique work of Chinese historian Tan Sheying has shown that this group of women achieved the passing of constitutions guaranteeing gender equality in the provinces of Hunan, Guangdong, Zhejiang, and Sichuan.[41]

Ardent advocates of education for women, these elite woman suffrage advocates may have espoused Western ideas while remaining true to Han Chinese principles, but they refused merely to serve the nation as dictated by elite Chinese males. Theirs was a Han Chinese interpretation of Western equality, as they did not employ class distinctions as did Western suffragists. According to Louise Edwards, they instead insisted that girls, no matter their social class, have equal access "to the same schools and tertiary institutions as boys." Thus, while these women utilized Western ideas, they challenged the notion that only boys should be educated by applying the Chinese tradition of "clan welfare," which permitted boys from poor families to be "educated in clan schools." These women equated, for girls of all social classes, Confucian morality and "education with the right to exercise political power."[42]

Thus, scholars of women's history showed that while male Chinese advocates of "women's rights" aspired merely to strengthen the nation-state, women drew freely from both Western and Han Chinese principles in order to achieve autonomy and power for women. Some Chinese women, drawing upon both Western and Chinese cultural contexts, strove to attain female agency and power by demanding and achieving a degree of political power for women as suffragists and feminists. Importantly, historians of the

U.S.-China relationship have utilized the aforementioned work of women's historians to explain how the image of the educated and modern Chinese woman, a product of the ideas of the West and Han China, would increasingly become synonymous with the Chinese nation-state.

Sino-American Relations and the Turn to Gender

Historians of U.S. foreign relations, traditionally concerned with military and diplomatic affairs, initially examined the interactions of nations by analyzing the exchanges among nation-state official representatives. In the early 1990s, the distinguished scholar Robert L. Beisner, observing the dominance of "nationalistic monographs," intimated the field's reliance on masculine narratives. However, already scholars were turning in new directions, seeking to "advance intercultural scholarship." Akira Iriye pioneered this new course by looking at the influence of culture on U.S.-Japanese relations.[43] Subsequently, feminist scholars, relying upon the theories of Michel Foucault and Joan Scott, began examining women's roles and representations in the domestic, national, and international spheres.

Drawing upon this rich scholarly context, Sino-American scholar Hong Zhang illustrates how the Chinese linked concepts of the nation-state to concerns for the morality and status of women and how that impacted Chinese attitudes toward the U. S. during the Chinese Civil War (1945-49). Hong Zhang wrote of Chinese outrage over the 1946 rape of a young female student, Shen Chong, by an American soldier. The rape made headlines, became "known all over China," and sparked student protests. Outraged students called her "*mingmen guixiu*," or a "well-educated" elegant lady from a prestigious Chinese family. Her assailant, an American GI, was described as a lowly drunk and a "sex wolf."

Hong Zhang explains how the rape came to represent a "national humiliation." The image of Shen as "a chaste and well-brought-up upper-class modern girl," a representative of the new Chinese woman who stood for the emerging nation, violated by a lowly American soldier, signified the rape of the nation-state by a foreign intruder.[44] Although scholars of U.S.-China relations had studied the episode before, noting its significance as a reflection of China's national hopes, Zhang demonstrated that it represented a valorization of new notions of Chinese womanhood. This contrasted with what Prasenjit Duara has referred to as the so-called "timeless feminine behaviors which historically had deprived Chinese women of direct political agency."[45] Shen's valuable characteristics included her high class and allegiance to "old moral codes such as chastity, virtue, and modesty." While she was valued for the way she represented what was traditionally Han Chinese, students also emphasized her modernity by noting her education and the fact that she had "gone to see a movie *Supremacy of Nationalism* (*minzu zhishang*) on that eventful night."[46] Shen embodied what was Han Chinese; yet her awareness and concern for the fate of the Chinese nation-state made her modern. These became important elements for projecting China's national humiliation, as well as a gendered and class-specific version of nationalism.

Zhang built upon the work of scholars Louise Edwards and Lydia Liu, who had previously explored connections between gender and nationalism, to demonstrate how students heralded the assaulted Shen as symbolic of the Chinese nation-state, victimized by foreign imperialism. Louise Edwards asserted that gender played a "prominent role in class-based nationalist discourse in Republican China," as reform-minded intellectuals became concerned with the "moral attributes of women."[47] Lydia Liu's earlier work drew a parallel between women's physical bodies and the victimization of the Chinese nation-state by Japan during World War II.[48] Zhang explained Shen's rape within the context of American violation of China's culture of morality. Zhang also enhanced Sino-American relations scholars' understanding of China's response to U.S. efforts to establish a foothold in China after the war and the subsequent appeal of the anti-imperialist Chinese Communists.

Historians of women and gender have helped scholars of Sino-American relations understand not only sources of conflict in the Sino-American relationship, but also the ways in which some women functioned as informal diplomats by drawing from both cultures. T. Christopher Jespersen and Thomas A. Delong focused on American perceptions of Nationalist Chiang Kai-shek's wife, May-ling Soong Chiang, offering examples of how she did this by playing the role of cross-cultural communicator.

Delong demonstrated that Madame Chiang's "intensified commitment to the advancement of women, her efforts to aid the plight of orphans and widows, and support of the air force that she built with American help endeared her to the West."[49] Utilizing the work of Joan Scott, Jesperson explained that part of Madame Chiang's appeal stemmed from what could be called the prevailing "cultural constructions of gender," while the studies of Susan Hartmann and Elaine Tyler May allowed Jesperson to see that women's emergence in the public sphere masked the continued "centrality of women's domestic lives and their relationship with men."[50] Thus, Jesperson understood Madame Chiang Kai-shek as simultaneously representative of "women's ability to hold a position of power and authority" and as carefully positioned within traditional domestic roles as her husband's helpmate. Pleading for American aid in 1943 as women's roles in the U.S. shifted to enable them to dive into the workforce to meet wartime needs, Madame Chiang benefited by the dual images she represented in the minds of Americans.

Jesperson and Delong both demonstrated that Madame Chiang's agency stemmed from her Christian upbringing and Western education. According to Delong, "an American education remained a priority" for Madame Chiang's entire family, and consequently she had attended Wesleyan College. Delong added that, like her sisters, Chiang was "part of the new emerging China that pushed aside the centuries-old practice of bound feet to restrain movement as well as attract the opposite sex."[51] However, Madame Chiang utilized Western ideas to her own and her nation's advantage.

Sino-American scholar Catherine Forslund's study of Anna Chennault as an informal diplomat shows that, like Madame Chiang, Chennault also used culture to acquire power for China. A powerful international player and a conventional wife, Anna Chennault married a man of international influence. This marriage to Claire Chennault, retired U.S. Army Air Corps Officer and Commander of the Flying Tigers American Volunteer Group in China, gained her entrance into the elite male political culture of the Republican Party. There she would move easily among U.S. policymakers, influencing the political opinions of twentieth-century Chinese and Americans during critical times in the Sino-American relationship. She promoted American support for Chinese Nationalist Chiang Kai-shek beginning in the 1930s, and from the 1970s, when Nixon initiated détente, for a strengthening of ties between the United States and the People's Republic of China.[52] These achievements were fueled by a confidence that stemmed not only from an understanding of Western culture and values, but also from an awareness of the history of fluidity and potential in Chinese women's traditional roles. Forslund's study benefited from Dorothy Ko's earlier work which had uncovered the heretofore hidden agency of women in Confucian culture and the ways that late imperial women had moved outside circumscribed roles by drawing upon their connections with male elites.[53]

Chennault recalled that her grandmother embodied not only "traditionalism and piety," but also an "outspoken nature," thus suggesting that Anna Chennault perceived her grandmother's time, when "old Confucian traditions held sway" as representing the possibility of agency for Chinese women.[54] While Madame Chiang's family had seen the path to power as rooted in Western values, Chennault's father "believed that his own education and maturation experiences" outside China were disadvantageous. Consequently, he "stressed Chinese traditions in their household" and emphasized an education in Asia.[55] Chinese educators and Chinese cultural traditions were critical to Anna Chennault's success as a writer and later a representative of China's national goals. Chinese educators encouraged the development of her natural talent as a writer and pointed to Chinese cosmology, revealing that her birthdate "portended the destiny of a writer."[56] Thus, at a time when China aimed to westernize, Chennault's choice of a career in writing was rooted in the encouragement of Chinese teachers and the influence of predominantly Chinese, rather than Western, ideas.

Women with political connections were not the only ones who used culture to serve power while influencing U.S. relations with China. Historian Rhodri Jeffreys-Jones has argued that some women "outside politics" might "collectively with many others, make up the public opinion that is the inescapable driving force behind many political decisions."[57] Lesser known historical figures, such as missionaries serving lengthy tenures in China, with unique access to women supporters in the American home field through letters, likewise helped influence American public opinion about China and about women. Historian James Reed has argued that missionaries influenced U.S. foreign policy toward China,[58] and, as Priscilla Roberts observes, American public opinion of China was shaped by missionaries because "through their letters home, they also often served as interpreters of their host country to their own."[59]

Scholars have shown how missionaries communicated the ways in which Western ideas traveled from the West to China and were interpreted to supporters, and how these fueled the agency of both Western and Chinese women.[60] This is important when we consider that women, who comprised a large number of mission field supporters, contributed to U.S. relief efforts on China's behalf during the early decades of the twentieth century.[61]

My own work on Dr. Ailie Gale, wife of a Methodist missionary, explored the extensive letters Gale sent to the American home field. These communicated the message that a woman doctor could engage in professional activities in the China mission field that were largely unavailable to women in the U.S. Beginning in the nineteenth century, when medical work was a smaller missionary undertaking than education or evangelism, missionary perception of "the need for female doctors to attend to Chinese women" (because sex segregation precluded male doctors from coming into contact with female patients) drew Western-trained female doctors to China. As Jane Hunter notes, "mission needs inspired the professional education of numbers of women who would probably have remained schoolteachers at home."[62] In the early twentieth century, when women doctors in the U.S. were struggling to enter medical schools and practice medicine, female mission supporters donated money so that Gale could provide health care to the Chinese and even build and maintain several hospitals in China. My work argues that by sustaining professional endeavors for women such as Ailie Gale in the mission field, home field mission activists believed they were aiding women in the professions at a time when professional women had limited options for careers in the U.S.[63]

Through letters from the China mission field to the home field, Christian women also learned that their contributions led to the advancement of Chinese women, exposing them to the Western liberal arts, professional education, and ultimately to leadership roles and careers.[64] This work illustrates the ways that women utilized Western ideas based on Christianity and modernity in a way that enhanced the power of women. Letters by women missionaries helped prompt Americans to compare China to the U.S. and connect the welfare of the two nations. As Christopher Jesperson notes, United China Relief raised monies during World War II with the message that Americans must aid China in order to promote democracy there to insure a "brighter American future."[65]

Health, Women, and the Nation-State

China's future was also linked to the U.S. when, at the end of the nineteenth century, reformers Kang Youwei and Liang Qichao, who had correlated Chinese women's weaknesses to the nation's shortcomings, made a similar connection between the nation's problems and the health of its people.[66] Historians Linda Barnes and Susan Starr Sered explain that, in evaluating national heritage "in an effort to discover the secret of foreign powers' strength and the root of China's weakness," they found "that medicine was a vital element contributing to this strength." Consequently, Chinese medical literature would discuss Western "biomedicine as a standard" against which traditional Chinese healing practices "were being measured."[67] This linkage would continue through the Republican and later Nationalist periods, and in each phase, it would involve women as patients, providers, discursive agents, and representatives of health care modernization.

Charlotte Furth's pathbreaking *A Flourishing Yin* was the first book to view Chinese medical history through the lens of gender.[68] Furth began with an analysis of the normative standard of androgyny which emphasized the complementarity of the female force of yin and the male force of yang and their relationship to Chinese principles of health and cosmology.[69] Drawing from the work of feminist historians Dorothy Ko and Francisca Bray, Furth delineated the evolution of medicine for women, *fuke*, through the Song (960–1276), and Ming dynasties (1368–1644) in the context of the overlapping and fluid inner and outer spheres which fixed the parameters of Chinese women's lives.

While Thomas Laqueur had described a pre-Enlightenment European view as emphasizing a "male body... taken as the ideal human norm" with the female as "variant," the Chinese model began in a way that was "more truly androgynous, balancing yin and yang functions in everyone." The androgynous body saw "yin and yang relationships that are hierarchical and encompassing." However, while the Chinese medical system paid heed to the needs of females, it came to privilege male healers.[70] Medical practitioners theorized that the female body was governed by blood, *xue*, and the male body by *qi*, a form of energy. They concluded that this necessitated different health care prescriptions for men and for women.[71] During the Song dynasty, the domain of the home was recognized as the space in which ritual obstetrics were to be practiced, and female healers dominated, as they were specialists in Daoist rituals and familiar with ideas of pollution, the spirit world, and astrology. Males would act as ritual advisors, thereby negotiating the domestic sites where *fuke* was practiced. By the time of the Ming dynasty, several factors associated with blood and women, and related to issues of pollution, led to increasingly segregated medical care and a "more stratified" system of healing. The "literati physician" took his place "at the top" of the order,[72] and midwifery came to be identified with "lower class and female practitioners."[73]

As noted by Bridie Andrews, it was not only midwifery but "all female occupations outside the home" that "were looked down upon by wealthy Chinese."[74] Thus, while midwives were experts in Daoist ritual, pollution, the spirit world, and astrology, their occupations, associated with manual labor, were not as respected as those of male healers such as herbalists. The women's positions declined even further in status with the introduction of Western "anatomy-based obstetrics" in the nineteenth century. Female healers lost power and took a peripheral role in Chinese society. This led to increasing changes for Chinese women, both as patients and as healers.[75]

Historians in the U. S. and China have explored the transfer of Western medical knowledge to China by utilizing various models. The diffusionist model shows Western knowledge traveling to China through the vehicle of missionaries and other outsiders.[76] A more complex picture emerged when historians began to examine the shaping of Chinese views of Western medicine as an intricate and fluid process of borrowing and adaptation, and as they explored the value of Chinese medical practices. They showed how Chinese healing practices survived but were also displaced by Western medical ideas, and how these shifts impacted women.[77] Scholar Yang Nianqun illustrated that Western ideas about health had a detrimental impact on Chinese midwives and cultural expressions. During the early Republican period, modernization and state control of health care in Beijing caused a decline in the status of midwives and also of funeral specialists, women with knowledge of traditional Chinese rituals and cosmology.[78]

At the same time, changes in health care for women tied to understandings of modernity and the strengthening of the nation-state, created new possibilities for women's empowerment. Bridie Andrews's study of female Chinese revolutionary Qiu Jin (1875–1907) revealed Qiu Jin's view of the nursing profession as both a vehicle to liberate women and to strengthen the nation-state. Andrews notes that "for Qiu Jin and the women who emulated her, nursing as a profession was not an aim in itself, but was seen as a potential means to achieve economic emancipation for women and to contribute to the creation of a modern state in China." In China, there was no such thing as a hospital in the Western sense of the term, but as Western hospitals were founded and proliferated and Chinese women became nurses and doctors, negative ideas regarding women's work outside the home began to change. Indeed, Andrews argues that "nursing was in itself a revolutionary profession for women."[79] Thus, when Qiu Jin absorbed Western ideas, adhering to the agenda of reformers and missionaries, she utilized them to make women more independent.

Historians have revealed numerous examples of this phenomenon as other Chinese women also selectively adopted Western medical ideas to strengthen the nation-state while achieving personal independence. Dr. Ailie Gale's adopted daughter, Mary Gao Chen, initially shunned traditional wifely and motherly duties, and was motivated by the nationalistic reforms of Chiang Kai-shek during the Nanjing Decade (1927–37). As the Nanjing government implemented health care reform, Chen chose a highly paid nursing career. Her vaccination campaigns introduced rural Chinese to the concept of national government, thus expanding its reach. At the same time, her Western profession rendered her independent and financially secure.[80]

The westernization of midwifery during the Nanjing Decade led to the production of a cohort of Western-style Chinese midwives. Historian Tina Johnson has written about government-sponsored midwifery reform programs designed to teach traditional Chinese midwives Westernized techniques.[81] These women contributed to China's nation-state building during the Nanjing Decade (1927–37), visiting rural areas and introducing Western methods of obstetrics and pediatrics to villagers. The midwives, whose work gave them a measure of independence, affected the Chinese women they encountered.

My work highlights the midwifery school of the American missionary Dr. Marion Manly, which complemented the Nationalist government midwifery reform work described by Johnson. Manly's midwifery school falls within my broader study of how the Chinese coopted missionary ideas and institutions to strengthen the nation-state. Manly's Chinese students accepted Western models, yet interpreted them in ways uniquely Chinese. For example, during one graduation ceremony, the students dressed as Goddesses of Mercy, representations of the Buddhist goddesses of fertility.[82]

As patients, Chinese women likewise exercised agency in interpreting modernity. Of course, there remained a shortage of Western doctors in early twentieth-century China, but this does not take away from the autonomy exercised by Chinese women as they chose selectively from a variety of birthing assistants, including the Western doctor and the midwife.[83] As has been argued by Andrew Nathan, Chinese consumers of medicine did not perceive healing choices as dualistically falling within either "Chinese medicine" or "Western medicine." Rather, "Chinese chose freely throughout history—as freely as their social and financial circumstances permitted—among priests, spirit mediums, magicians, itinerant herbalists and acupuncturists, classical physicians and other healers."[84] The survival and thriving of Chinese healing through patients, and the fact that a branch of the Chinese government, the Nationalist Ministry of Health, sought to preserve Chinese medicine, undercut Western power. The flourishing of Chinese healing and its twentieth-century transformations were also tied to notions of gender initially highlighted by Charlotte Furth and deeply embedded in Chinese culture.[85]

Ruth Rogaski's work on the city of Tianjin demonstrated that Chinese health practices—like *qi* regulation, breathing, and divination—were supplanted by foreign ideas of public health and sanitation. However, she also illustrated the retention of basic elements of Chinese health culture, particularly as they relate to women, despite modernization.[86] Chinese intellectuals and reform advocates operated in what historian Lydia Liu has called a "middle zone of hypothetical equivalence." This would become "the very ground for" a change advancing modernity in China in ways "not necessarily un-Chinese," allowing for core elements of Chinese ideas about health and medicine to be sustained while accepting Western medical concepts.[87]

Rogaski offers the example of Dr. William's Pink Pills for Pale People, which were sold in the 1920s "from Shanghai to Singapore," and were touted as effective for strengthening blood. Rogaski argues that "Pink Pills" advertisements represented "a belief that bodies around the world are essentially the same—and that Western medicines do the best job for all bodies"; however, in China, the pills were promoted to reflect traditional Chinese beliefs, promising *bu xue*, or blood nourishment for both women and men.

Traditionally, "Chinese pharmacopoeia abounded with recipes to *bu xue*." The Pink Pills promised gender-specific results, offering "better health for men" by giving them "strong bones and muscles," and promising women the possibility of becoming "vibrant" and "energetically filial."[88] However, as Rogaski notes, the "xue is a yin form of qi, a basic quality of the energy material that ebbs through, collects in, and makes up all human beings, but it is particularly crucial in the health problems of women" because they lose blood due to menstruation. For this reason, Rogaski argues, "women are the predominant target audience" for these advertisements, as the danger is that without these pills they might not "fulfill their filial duties as mother, wife, and caretaker for the family's elderly."[89]

Chinese creative syncretism and shifting understandings of womanhood and modernity are also evidenced in Sherman Cochran's 2006 study of Chinese medicine as portrayed in men's advertisements from the 1880s to the 1950s. Here a complex picture emerges. What was packaged as "new medicine," "displayed nationalistic gendered images and advanced simultaneously nationalism, traditional Chinese culture, and modernity."[90] For example, Chinese businessman Huang Chujiu, born in 1872 near Shanghai and educated in China, advertised completely Chinese-made drugs to Chinese and Southeast Asians, which he packaged to appear Western. He appropriated modern ideas cherished by China's intellectual elites: Western medicine, economic nationalism, and women's liberation. He sold a brain tonic that was wholly Chinese, promoting it through Chinese-language media, and locating it "in a Chinese medical context." However, he used carefully selected Western terms to present the medicine as Western and argued that it would "make up for the deficiencies of Chinese medicine."[91] Huang commissioned painters to produce images of suggestive and sometimes nude portraits of modern women, a strategy that contrasted markedly with other contemporary Chinese artists who clothed women's bodies heavily. Cochran notes that Huang's depictions of the medicine and the portraits of the beautiful women he used in his advertisements

> [s]ubstantially altered the contents of the Chinese formulations, freely substituting familiar Chinese terms (such as body orbs in Chinese medicine) for unfamiliar foreign ones (such as body organs in Western medicine), loosely mixing old notions (such as traditional harmonization of opposites) with seemingly contradictory new ones (such as competitive economic nationalism) and unabashedly depoliticizing images (such as pictures of liberated women whom he portrayed as fashionable beauties rather than as serious campaigners for women's rights).[92]

Huang's appropriation of some Western ideas and images of women to present what was traditionally Chinese in modern dress illustrates the fluid cross-cultural lines connecting the transmission of ideas about Chinese nationalism, gender, and healing. Huang's creative agency mirrors that of the early-twentieth-century Chinese women described by Carol Chin who selectively chose from the West what they perceived to be "modern," disregarding the rest, as these women too had believed that "modernity was not something that the West would impose or bestow on China."[93]

Chinese Healing in the United States

Just as Chinese women utilized both Western and Chinese medicine to support the nationalist project, exercising agency as patients and healers, American women made independent choices, sometimes choosing Chinese medicine, even though Western medicine was more easily available. During the nineteenth and twentieth centuries this represented a contestation of the patriarchal authority of the modernizing medical field and of Western medicine's perceived failure to address women's unique health issues as successfully as Chinese medicine had, with its special attention to female needs and disorders.

Historian Susie Lan Cassel explains the myriad reasons for American women's attraction to Chinese medicine. In the nineteenth century, when separate spheres ideology for men and women marked out aspects of American culture and when medicine became a professionalized male bastion, European-American women who had previously received informal care from unlicensed female healers, increasingly found that their health care providers were male.[94] Lan Cassel reveals that in these years 60 to 70 percent of U.S. Chinese doctors' patients were female European Americans, some surely attracted by the fact that "Chinese medicine has recognized illnesses," such as premenstrual syndrome and other blood-related issues, which were treated by traditional Chinese healers but often "denied or ignored by Western counterparts."[95]

Lan Cassel also argues that Euro-American women were likely attracted to Chinese healing because of its alternatives to the harsh and often expensive chemical drugs of Western medicine, its proclivity to be less authority-based than its Western counterparts, and its "noninvasive, receptive doctor-patient" relationship.[96] She suggests that American women might have opted for the Chinese doctor over the Western one because they believed they would be "more sensitively treated" by the Chinese healer than by the "stern, forbidding, bearded" Western physician.[97]

During the "heyday of Chinese medicine" (1871–1912), a time when it "reached near or equal footing with Western medicine . . . as word of Chinese medicine and Chinese herbal doctors spread, reaching non-Chinese, who in turn sought out the doctors," Hispanic women also joined Euro-American women as its consumers.[98] Thus, as Western medicine was modernized and dominated by male doctors, women of varied ethnicities expressed an affinity for Chinese healing.

For a good portion of the twentieth century, racist attitudes and hygienic concerns legally limited Chinese medicine to isolated Chinatowns in the U.S. But following the diplomatic breakthrough in 1972 which ended two decades of silence between the two nations, Chinese medicine proliferated in the U.S. and since then it has grown in importance, transforming American attitudes toward health care. As Linda Barnes explains, these Chinese healing methods, now available in the U.S., grew out of the traditional Chinese medicine systematized by the People's Republic of China (PRC). Chinese healing practices adopted by Americans include acupuncture, herbs, *taijiquan, qigong,* as well as "relationships with the dead in the form of gods, ghosts, ancestors, medicinal understandings of food."[99] While Americans may not fully understand these practices, they increasingly utilize them.[100] Moreover, Lan Cassel reveals that in the U.S., at a time when Euro-Americans began to dominate the field of Chinese medicine, "female practitioners . . . became more conspicuous than men."[101]

Conclusion

The scholarship on women, gender, and health care discussed in this chapter has extended the historiography of U.S.-China foreign relations in new directions. Uncovering interactions among and representations of Chinese and American women through the prisms of missionary education and health care has expanded the actors in U.S. foreign relations to those who were not state officials and extended the arenas of study to mission schools, clinics, and advertisements. These works also highlight historical female agency—the home field mission women who sponsored female doctors in China when they could not have supported them back at home; the Chinese elite female reformers who joined the nationalist struggle against the Qing dynasty. The histories discussed here have shown how Chinese women appropriated Western ideas as they saw fit and drew from Han Chinese traditions that had been a source of power for women. They redefined modernity for China and for themselves, using understandings of culture to serve power.

This scholarship on gender, women, and health has highlighted the nuances of new points of dialogue, conflict, and interaction in the transnational historiography on U.S.-China foreign relations. The uncovering of voices of Chinese and American women in order to imagine the nation-state and interpret modernity interjects critical new components for understanding the movement of ideas across geographic boundaries. Cultural exchanges are a significant aspect of what leaders today consider a "China-U.S. cooperative partnership based on mutual respect and mutual benefit."[102] By linking the local—women home-field supporters of missionaries, patients choosing Western or Chinese medicine—to greater global forces, the works considered in this chapter shed important light upon new sources of power in the U.S.-China relationship.

ACKNOWLEDGMENTS

I would like to gratefully acknowledge the expert guidance of the editors of this volume, Pamela Nadell and Kate Haulman, and also Joseph Lee of Pace University for his helpful comments.

NOTES

1. For example, Robert L. Beisner's 2003 *Guide to American Foreign Relations since 1700* explains that, since the publication of the 1983 volume, the entries on missionaries and gender, like the entries on race, have "increased in number." Robert L. Beisner, *American Foreign Relations since 1600: A Guide to the Literature*, vol. 1, quote on (ABC-CLIO, 2nd edition, June 10, 2003) 477.
2. While this chapter is about the United States, the term "West" represents the broader British and modern Japanese models for modernization as well. While some scholars believe that China is an "exception to the idea of the invented nation because China already had the features of a nation state such as common language and culture, as well as a single bureaucracy whose members could serve in any part of the state," I concur with Henrietta Harrison's argument that China "as it exists today was invented through the construction of a modern state." See Henrietta Harrison, *China: Inventing the Nation* (New York: Oxford University Press, 2001), quotes on 2 and 3. While there is rich literature about the culture and healing practices of Chinese minorities, here I will focus solely on that of the majority of Han Chinese. Chinese intellectuals used the idea of "national essence" to promote anti-Manchu sentiment among the Han Chinese against the Manchu dynasty. See Yu Ying-shih, "Changing Conceptions of National History in Twentieth-Century China," in Erik Lonnroth, Karl Molin, and Ragnar Bjork, eds., *Conceptions of National History: Proceedings of Nobel Symposium* (Berlin, New York: Walter de Gruyter, 1994), 78.
3. Rey Chow, "'It's You, and Not Me': Domination and 'Othering' in Theorizing the Third World," in Elizabeth Weed, ed., *Coming to Terms: Feminism, Theory, Politics* (London: Routledge, 1989), 152–53.
4. See Ulrike Strasser and Heidi Tinsman, "World History Meets History of Masculinity in Latin American Studies," in this volume.

5. See, for example, Dorothy C. Bass's review of Jane Hunter, *The Gospel of Gentility* in *Journal of Religion* 67, no. 4 (October 1987): 562–63.
6. Jane Hunter, *The Gospel of Gentility: American Women Missionaries in Turn-of-the Century China* (New Haven: Yale University Press, 1989). Hunter examines the feminization of missionary work in China as the cultural arm of imperialism. Hunter discusses "Imperial Evangelism" in chapters 6 and 7.
7. Carol Chin, "Beneficent Imperialists: American Women Missionaries in China at the Turn of the Twentieth Century," *Diplomatic History* 27, no. 3 (2003): 327–52.
8. Joan Judge, "Talent, Virtue, and the Nation: Chinese Nationalisms and Female Subjectivities in the Early Twentieth Century," *American Historical Review* 106, no. 2 (June 2001): 765–803, quote on 765. Carol Chin, "Translating the New Woman: Chinese Feminists View the West, 1905–15," in Dorothy Ko, *Translating Feminisms in China* (Oxford: Blackwell, 2007), quote on 43. See also Rey Chow, *Woman and Chinese Modernity: The Politics of Reading between West and East* (Minneapolis: University of Minnesota Press, 2003).
9. Ko, 2007, 1–4.
10. Ko, 2007, 4.
11. I utilize Carol Chin's definition of modernity. Chin, in Ko, 2007, 36.
12. The People's Republic of China (PRC) believes its claim to Taiwan legitimate because Taiwan was a part of the Qing empire. See Richard C. Kagan, *Taiwan's Statesman, Lee Teng-Hui and Democracy in Asia* (Annapolis: Naval Institute Press, 2007), 8.
13. See J. W. Wong, *Deadly Dreams: Opium and the Arrow War (1856–1860) in China* (Cambridge: Cambridge University Press, 1998); Kathleen L. Lodwick, *Crusaders against Opium: Protestant Missionaries in China, 1874–1917* (Lexington: University Press of Kentucky, 1996).
14. George Wei and Xiaoyuan Liu, *Chinese Nationalism in Perspective: Historical and Recent Cases* (Westport, Conn.: Greenwood, 2001), 103.
15. Patricia Hill, *The World Their Household: The American Woman's Foreign Mission Movement and Cultural Transformation, 1870–1920* (Ann Arbor: University of Michigan Press, 1985); Kowk Pui-lan, *Chinese Women and Christianity 1860–1927* (Atlanta: Scholar's Press, 1992). Helen Schneider, "The Professionalization of Chinese Domesticity: Ava B. Milam and Home Economics at Yenching University," in Daniel Bays and Grant Wacker, eds., *The Foreign Missionary Enterprise at Home: Explorations in North American Cultural History* (Birmingham: University of Alabama Press, 2010), 125–146. Joseph Tse-Hei Lee, "Gospel and Gender: Female Christians in Chaozhou, South China," in Jessie Lutz, ed., *Pioneer Chinese Christian Women* (Bethlehem: Lehigh University Press, 2010).
16. Charlotte Furth, "Intellectual Change: From the Reform Movement to the May Fourth Movement, 1895–1920," in John K. Fairbank, ed., *Republican China 1912–1949* (Cambridge: Cambridge University Press, 1983).
17. According to Mary Keng Mun Chung, in 1889, for example, women made up 54.55 percent of Protestant missionaries to China and during 1920–37, they made up 56 percent. See *Chinese Women in Christian Ministry: An Intercultural Study* (New York: Peter Lang, 2005), 90. The Methodist Episcopal Church, with one of the largest Protestant missions in China, had 371 missionaries in China in 1920, 261 of them women. Methodist Episcopal Church Board of Foreign Missions, *Annual Report 1920*, Methodist Episcopal Church Board of Foreign Missions, 576–78. Patricia Hill states that by 1900, women comprised 60 percent of the missionary force in all foreign lands. According to Barbara Welter, women made up 60 percent of the missionary force in 1893. See "She Hath Done What She Could: Protestant

Women's Missionary Careers in Nineteenth-Century America," *American Quarterly* 30 (1978): 624–38, quote on 632.
18. Hu Ying, *Tales of Translation: Composing the New Woman in China, 1899–1918* (Stanford: Stanford University Press: 2000), quote on 3. Liang's views were echoed by others who had read the works of Western Enlightenment thinkers such as Rousseau. For example, see 133, 135, 188, 189.
19. Hu Ying, "Naming the First 'New Woman,'" in Rebecca E. Karl and Peter Gue Zarrow, eds., *Rethinking the 1898 Reform Period: Political and Cultural Change in Late Qing China* (Cambridge: Harvard University Asia Center, 2002), 186. The *cainü* were virtuous wives and mothers of classically trained male writers, who produced beautiful calligraphy and poetry. Liang, like other critical male reformers of the time, called them "ignorant" and "useless" women who "toyed with ditties lamenting spring and bemoaning separation." Quote on 185. For Liang Qichao and missionaries, see Chi-yin Chen, "Liang Ch'i-ch'ao's 'Missionary Education': A Case Study of Missionary Influence on the Reformers," *Papers on China*, vol. 16 (Cambridge: Harvard University Press, 1962), 66–125.
20. Lydia He Liu, *Translingual Practice: Literature, National Culture and Translated Modernity— China, 1900–1937* (Stanford: Stanford University Press, 1995), quote on 49.
21. Nanxiu Qian, "Revitalizing the Xianyuan (Worthy Ladies) Tradition: Women in the 1898 Reforms," *Modern China* 29, no. 4 (October 2003): 399–454.
22. Harold Isaacs, *Scratches on Our Minds* (New York: John Day, 1958).
23. Jessie G. Lutz, *Pioneer Chinese Christian Women: Gender, Christianity and Social Mobility* (Bethlehem: Lehigh University Press, 2010), quote on 35.
24. Ryan Dunch, "'Mothers to Our Country': Education and Ideology among Chinese Protestant Women, 1870–1930," 324–350, in Lutz, 2010, 329.
25. Joanna F. Handlin, "Lu Kun's New Audience: The Influence of Women's Literacy on Sixteenth-Century Thought," in M. Wolf and R. Witke, *Women in Chinese Society* (Stanford: Stanford University Press, 1975).
26. Ko 1994, quotes on vii and viii.
27. Ko utilized superbly rich secondary sources about women as the basis for her account. See Cahill's work on the Tang (618–907), and Ebrey's work on the Song. Suzanne E. Cahill, *Transcendence and Divine Passion: The Queen Mother of the West in Medieval China* (Stanford: Stanford University Press, 1993); Patricia Buckly Ebrey, *The Inner Quarters: Marriage and the Lives of Chinese Women in the Sung Period* (Berkeley: University of California Press, 1993); and Christina K. Gilmartin, Gail Hershatter, Lisa Rofel, and Tyrene White eds., *Engendering China; Women, Culture and the State* (Cambridge: Harvard University Press, 1994).
28. Ko 1994, 10–11.
29. Angela Zito and Tani E. Barlow, eds., *Body, Subject and Power in China* (Chicago: University of Chicago Press, 1994); Charlotte Furth, "Blood, Body and Gender: Medical Images of the Female Condition in China, 1600–1850," chapter 11, 291–314 in Susan Brownell and Jeffery N. Wasserstrom, eds., *Chinese Femininities, Chinese Masculinities: A Reader*, 120–144 (Berkeley: University of California Press, 2002).
30. Mary Backus Rankin, "The Emergence of Women at the End of the Ching: The Case of Ch'iu Chin," in Wolf and Witke, 1975, Ko, 2003, 356. Ko, 2007, 109; Charlotte Furth, *A Flourishing Yin: Gender in China's Medical History, 960–1665*, (Berkeley: University of California Press, 1999), 6.
31. Harriet Evans, review of Tani E. Barlow, *The Question of Women in Chinese Feminism*, Next Wave: New Directions in Women's Studies, *American Historical Review* (June 2005): 110, no. 3 (June 2005) 775.76; Furth, 1999, quote on 7.

32. Karl, 221.
33. Ko, 2007, quotes on 2 and 7.
34. Joan Judge's discussion of the emergence of "the national question" and "the woman question" in "Talent, Virtue and the Nation: Chinese Nationalism and Female Subjectivities in the Early Twentieth Century," *American Historical Review* 106, no. 3 (2001): 765–803.
35. Louise Edwards and Mina Roce, eds., *Women's Suffrage in Asia: Gender, Nationalism and Democracy* (New York: Routledge, 2004); Elisabeth Croll, *Feminism and Socialism in China* (New York: Schocken Books, 1980); Tiesheng Rong, "The Woman's Movement in China before and after the 1911 Revolution," *Chinese Studies in History* 16 (1983): 159–200; Yu-ning Li, "Sun Yat-sen and Women's Transformation," *Chinese Studies in History* 21 (1988): 58–78; Kazuko Ono, *Chinese Women in a Century of Revolution, 1850–1950* (Stanford: Stanford University Press, 1989).
36. Edwards, 2004, quote on 63. Edwards notes that the first phase of the suffrage movement in China was between 1911 and 1913, the time when "China's elite dabbled unsuccessfully with democracy in the aftermath of the collapse of the Qing Dynasty," while the "Second period is that between 1919 and 1927 when the iconoclastic New Culture Movement stirred up a nationalist, anti-Confucian fervor." Edwards, 2004, 59–60.
37. Ko, 2005, *Cinderella's Sisters*, quote on 12.
38. Edwards, 2004, quotes on 60. Yu-ning Li, 1989.
39. Edwards, 2004, 63.
40. Edwards, 2004, 67.
41. Tan, 1990.
42. Edwards, 2004, quotes on 67, 68.
43. Robert L. Beisner, "Sino-American Historians and Sino-American Realities," *Reviews in American History* 19, no. 1 (March 1991): 116–121; Akira Iriye, *Power and Culture: The Japanese-American War, 1941–1945* (Cambridge: Harvard University Press, 1981); Michael H. Hunt, *The Making of a Special Relationship: The United States and China to 1914* (New York: Columbia University Press, 1983).
44. Hong Zhang, *America Perceived: The Making of Urban Chinese Images of the United States, 1945–1953* (Westport, Conn.: Greenwood Press, 2002), quotes on 83–88.
45. Prasenjit Duara, "The Regime of Authenticity: Timelessness, Gender and National History in Modern China," *History and Theory* 37, 3 (1998): 287–309. For previous interpretations of the importance of the episode, see Joseph K. W. Yick, *Making Urban Revolution in China: The CCP-GMD Struggle for Beiping-Tianjin, 1945–1949* (New York: M. E. Sharpe, 1995). Yick states that "the incident . . . became a symbol of crumbling hopes for a sovereign and respected China devoid of foreign imperialism," 100.
46. Zhang, 2002, 87.
47. Louise Edwards, "Policing the Modern Woman in Republican China," *Modern China* 26 (April 2000): 115–47. Zhang, 2002, 87.
48. Lydia H. Liu, "The Female Body and Nationalist Discourse," in Zito and Barlow, 1994.
49. Thomas A. DeLong, *Madame Chiang Kai'shek and Miss Emma Mills: China's First Lady and Her American Friend* (Jefferson, N.C.: McFarland, 2007), quote on 152.
50. Christopher Jesperson, *American Images of China, 1931–1949* (Stanford: Stanford University Press, 1999), quotes on 83 and 97. Susan Hartmann, *The Homefront and Beyond* (New York: Twayne Publishers, 1982); and Elaine Tyler May, *Homeward Bound: American Families in the Cold War Era* (New York: Basic Books, 1988). Elaine Tyler May has argued that domestic images of women during the war remained largely constrained by a "home and hearth" ideology, despite the celebration of Rosie the Riveter; quotes on 87–88.

51. Delong, 2007, quotes on 8 and 9.
52. Catherine Forslund, *Anna Chennault: Informal Diplomacy and Asian Relations* (Wilmington, Del.: SR Books, 2002),
53. Ko, 1994.
54. Delong, 2007, quotes on 5; Forslund, 2002, quotes on 9.
55. Forslund, 2002, 9.
56. Forslund, 2002, 6, 7, 165.
57. Rhodri Jeffreys-Jones, *Changing Differences: Women and the Shaping of American Foreign Policy, 1917-1994* (New Brunswick: Rutgers University Press, 1995), quote on 172.
58. James Reed, *The Missionary Mind and American East-Asian Policy 1911-1915* (Cambridge: Harvard University Press, 1983).
59. Pricilla Roberts and He Pequin, eds., *Bonds across Borders: Women, China, and International Relations in the Modern World* (Newcastle: Cambridge Scholars Publishers, 2007), 7; Robert Gardella, *Missions to China's Heartland: The Letters of Hazel Todd of the China Inland Mission, 1920-1941* (Portland, Maine: Merwin Asia, 2009); Joseph K. S. Yick, "Methodist-Chinese Friendship: Mr. & Mrs. John A. Pilley in Pre-1949 China," *Methodist History*, 45, no. 3 (April 2007); Cindy Yik-yi Chu, *The Maryknoll Sisters in Hong Kong, 1921-1969: In Love with the Chinese* (New York: Palgrave Macmillan, 2004); Zaccarini, 2001; Kathleen Lodwick, *Educating the Women of Hainan: The Career of Margaret Moninger in China, 1915-1942* (Lexington: University Press of Kentucky, 1995).
60. Paul A. Varg, *Missionaries, Chinese and Diplomats: The American Protestant Missionary Movement in China, 1890-1952* (Princeton: Princeton University Press, 1958); Wayne Flynt and Gerald W. Berkley, *Taking Christianity to China: Alabama Missionaries in the Middle Kingdom, 1850-1950* (Tuscaloosa: University of Alabama Press, 1997); Lian Xi, *The Conversion of Missionaries: The Liberalism in American Protestant Missions in China, 1907-1932* (University Park: Penn State University Press, 1996).
61. Shirley S. Garrett, "Sister's All: Feminism and the American Women's Missionary Movement," in Torben Christensen and William R. Hutchison, eds., *Missionary Ideologies in the Imperialist Era: 1880-1920* (Denmark: Christensen Boytrykkeri, Bogtrykkergarden a-s, Struer, 1982), 222-23.
62. Hunter, 1985, 15.
63. Zaccarini, 2001. Regina Markell Morantz-Sanchez, *Sympathy and Science: Women Physicians in American Medicine* (New York: Oxford University Press, 1985). Mary Roth Walsh, *Doctors Wanted: No Women Need Apply: Sexual Barriers in the Medical Profession 1835-1975* (New Haven: Yale University Press: 1979). Carol Marie Desmither, "From Calling to Career: Work and Professional Identity among American Women Missionaries to China, 1900-1950," Ph.D. dissertation (University of Oregon, 1987).
64. Zaccarini, 2001; John R. Stanley Dunch, "Establishing a Female Medical Elite: The Early History of the Nursing Profession in China," 274-91, and Connie Shemo, "'To Develop Native Powers': Shi Meiyu and Danforth Memorial Hospital Nursing School, 1903-1920," in Lutz, 2010.
65. Jesperson, 1999, 55-56.
66. Xiaoqun Xu, *Chinese Professionals and the Republican State: The Rise of Professional Associations in Shanghai, 1912-1937* (New York: Cambridge University Press, 2001), 130-31.
67. Linda L. Barnes and Susan Starr Sered, *Religion and Healing in America* (New York: Oxford University Press, 2005), 321.
68. Furth, 1999.

69. See also Livia Kohn and Catherine Despeux, *Women in Daoism* (Cambridge: Mass.: Three Pines Press, 2005).
70. Furth, 1999, quotes on 46. Thomas Laqueur, *Making Sex: Body and Gender from the Greeks to Freud* (Cambridge: Harvard University Press, 1992).
71. According to David Palmer, *Qi* is a vital force that reverberates in nature. It is seen as cyclical, which "means that it moves in specific cycles, such as day and night, summer and winter, youth and old age." *Qi* is "commonly described as consisting of two major aspects, yin and yang, which alternate in continuous movement and never-ending action." David Palmer, *Qigong Fever: Body, Science, and Utopia in China* (New York: Columbia University Press, 2006), 32. Furth explains that "adjustment of a prescription to accommodate a female condition could apply to some but not all illnesses, or to some but not all individual females. It is easiest to see when medical texts identify an illness as gynecological." Furth, 1999, 51.
72. Furth, 1999, 35.
73. Furth, 1999, 51, 85.
74. Bridie Andrews, "From Bedpan to Revolution." In Ann Hardy and Lawrence A. Conrad, eds., *Women in Modern Medicine* (New York: Rodopi, 2001), 53–70. Quote on 55.
75. Yi-Li Wu, "God's Uterus: Benjamin Hobson and Missionary "Midwifery" in Nineteenth-Century China," presented at the Disunity of Chinese Science conference, University of Chicago, May 10–11, 2002. Barnes, 2005, 321.
76. K. Chimin Wong and Wu Lien examined the beginnings of "the victorious entry of modern medicine" in their work, *History of Chinese Medicine* (Shanghai, second edition, 1937), 257.
77. Bridie Andrews, "The Making of Modern Chinese Medicine, 1895–1937," (Ph.D. dissertation, Cambridge University, 1996).
78. Yang Nianqun, "The Establishment of 'Urban Health Demonstration Districts' and the Supervision of Life and Death in Early Republican Beijing," *East Asian Science, Technology and Medicine* (2004): 22, 68–95. Translated by Larissa Heinrich.
79. Andrews, 2001, quote on 55.
80. Cristina Zaccarini, "Chinese Nationalism and Christian Womanhood in Early Twentieth-Century China: The Story of Mary Gao (Gao Meiyu)," in Lutz, 2010, 351–70.
81. T. Phillips Johnson, "Childbirth Reform in Early Twentieth-Century China: Marion Yang and the First National Midwifery School," paper presented at the Medicine and Culture, Chinese–Western Medical Exchange (1644–c.1950) conference, Ricci Institute for Chinese–Western Cultural History, San Francisco University Center for the Pacific Rim, 2007.
82. Phillips-Johnson; M. Cristina Zaccarini, "Modern Medicine in Twentieth-Century Jiangxi, Anhui, Fujian and Sichuan: Competition, Negotiation and Cooperation," *Social History of Medicine* 23, no. 2 (2009): 338–55.
83. There were roughly 1,500 modern doctors in China, of whom 600 were either missionaries or foreigners, or "one modern doctor per 300,000 people." The Nationalist Ministry of Health sought to preserve Chinese medicine, according to Yip Ka-che. *Health and National Reconstruction in Nationalist China: The Development of Modern Health Services, 1928–1937* (Ann Arbor: University of Michigan Press, 1995), 13.
84. Nathan Sivin, *Traditional Medicine in Contemporary China* (Ann Arbor: Center for Chinese Studies, University of Michigan Press, 1987), 195.
85. Yip, 1995, 14–15; Bridie Andrews has illustrated the ways in which traditional medicine in China became "biomedicalized," as Chinese physicians during the 1920s and 1930s worked to make Chinese medicine more scientific. Bridie Andrews, *The Making of Modern Chinese Medicine* (New York: Cambridge University Press, 2004).

86. Ruth Rogaski, *Hygienic Modernity: Meanings of Health and Disease in Treaty Port China* (Berkeley: University of California Press, 2004). While Western medicine was traditionally concerned with "plethora and overabundance within the body, Chinese medicine emphasized lack as the primary cause of imbalance," 229.
87. Rogaski, 2004, 105. Lydia Liu, *Translingual Practice: Literature, National Culture and Translated Modernity, China, 1900–1937* (Stanford: Stanford University Press, 1995), 70.
88. Rogaski, 2004, 227–228.
89. Rogaski, 2004, 228.
90. Sherman Cochran, *Chinese Medicine Men: Consumer Culture in China and Southeast Asia* (Cambridge: Harvard University Press, 2006).
91. Cochran, 2006, 40.
92. Cochran, 2006, 62.
93. Chin, 2007, 41, 43.
94. Morantz-Sanchez, 1985.
95. Cassel, 2002, 181.
96. Susie Lan Cassel, *The Chinese in America: A History from Gold Mountain to the New Millennium* (Lanham, Md.: AltaMira Press, 2002), 181.
97. Cassel, 2002, 181.
98. Cassel, 2002, 175.
99. Barnes, 2005, 307.
100. Barnes, 2005. The results of a 1993 survey showed that 33.8 percent of Americans used complementary and alternative medicine and paid out of pocket, 323.
101. Cassel 2002, 175.
102. The Xinhua news agency, official voice of the PRC, reiterated the early 2010 agreement of President Hu Jintao and Barack Obama, emphasizing the importance of understanding cultural exchanges. January. http://news.xinhuanet.com/english2010/indepth/2011-04/13/c_13826749.htm, accessed July 15, 2011.

10

A Happier Marriage?

Feminist History Takes the Transnational Turn

JOCELYN OLCOTT

Three decades ago, the feminist economist Heidi Hartmann quipped that the marriage of Marxism and feminism had been "like the marriage of husband and wife depicted in English common law: Marxism and feminism are one, and that one is Marxism."[1] Hartmann called for a "more progressive union" that recognized capitalist structures and patriarchal inequalities. Since then, Marxist and feminist studies have both changed immensely: a new intellectual generation has come of age and issued its own progeny; bitter divorces have given way to mellower second marriages. Among these has been the recent union of transnational and feminist history. Perhaps this late-model marriage seems to work better because the two have much in common—they went to the same schools and run in the same circles of friends. Or perhaps it benefits from a prenuptial understanding that both parties will retain some autonomy within the union, even allowing for the occasional extramarital dalliance. Or perhaps the marriage is simply still in its honeymoon period, and the real challenges of long-term partnership lie ahead.

For now, this happy and fruitful marriage has generated a field not subsumed under a single patronym but rather the scholarly equivalent of a hyphenated surname: transnational feminist history. These two historiographic turns share core values, most notably in that they both trouble conventional narratives by decentering those actors and processes that have often dominated historical studies—provincializing the hegemons, jostling structures, and focusing on less powerful figures.[2] The literature has developed amid a heightened sensitivity to how we produce knowledge—to the limitations and possibilities of sources and methods—and has benefited tremendously from Women's Studies' interdisciplinary orientation, borrowing judiciously from anthropology, sociology, and political science and somewhat more sparingly from literary and psychoanalytic approaches. Since its genealogy passes through postcolonial studies and other fields that resist totalizing approaches, it would be inappropriate to say that this scholarship offers a paradigm shift. It has, however, offered new perspectives on some of historians' core analytical categories and insights that should inform even more closely described local and national studies.[3] This chapter concentrates on four areas of inquiry important in both fields—periodization, place, identification, and infrastructures—that highlight the cross-fertilization between them.

Before getting into some of the payoffs of transnational feminist history, we should describe the contours of these two fields separately. Transnational history explores those phenomena that transcend the boundaries of nations and regions by means other than state-to-state (or international) interactions.[4] Transnational history also stands apart from comparative history, which has yielded important insights but centers on lining up different historical contexts alongside one another rather than examining the connective tissue between them.[5] While many textbooks and edited volumes have taken up a global or comparative approach—developing a global history by aggregating a representative sampling of smaller histories—a much smaller body of scholarship has addressed transnational feminism.[6] This latter field sets in relief the connections and commonalities following what cultural geographer Cindi Katz describes as "contour lines" that follow elevations of experience and networks and disregard political borders.[7] Certainly migration chains follow such contour lines, or communities centered on the production of a particular commodity such as sugar or petroleum, or (more to the point here) feminist networks whose members might experience closer affinities with fellow network members than they do with compatriots, neighbors, or even family members.

The term feminism has, of course, sparked countless debates about its provenance, contents, and implications, and even historians of a single village would struggle to agree upon a complete and exclusive definition. Developments within feminist theory and historiography of the 1990s contested the border-patrol practices that had developed when feminist groups fended off their antifeminist detractors.[8] While desires for feminist solidarity have remained, feminism's outlines have become blurred. The historian Bonnie Smith advocates using the plural *feminisms* to accommodate this diversity, but such a designation still implies discrete, clearly bounded entities or schools of thought.[9] In her pathbreaking work on Latin American feminism, the historian Asunción Lavrin argues instead that feminism's elasticity may be its defining characteristic, making it "capable of evolution and of adapting to changing political realities rather than being a fixed set of ideas."[10] Historical sociologists Myra Marx Ferree and Carol McClurg Mueller also have called for such a flexible conception of feminism that encompasses many different kinds of women's organizations that in practice—regardless of their principal objectives—challenge women's subordination and cultivate a feminist consciousness. Restricting feminism to those ideas and movements that center on sex roles and gender hierarchies, they argue, results in policing the boundaries of "legitimate" feminism to exclude movements that have proliferated in many parts of the world—movements that focus more squarely on, for example, human rights or economic justice but that incubate feminist ideas and practices.[11] Such an understanding underscores a principal insight of both feminist theorizing and the historiography of transnational feminism: that feminism's strength and resilience depend upon its remaining an arena of critique and contestation rather than hardening into a bounded set of convictions.[12]

Period Cramps: Marking Time in Transnational Feminist History

If one of feminist history's objectives is to shake things up and dislodge received wisdoms, among its critical strategies has been to interrogate practices of periodization.[13] Just as transnational historians questioned the primacy of national boundaries, feminist historians—initially under the guise of social history—challenged the demarcation of historical time by wars or presidencies or phenomena (such as the Renaissance or the Industrial Revolution) that put men's experiences at the center.[14] As the U.S. historian Alice Kessler-Harris has argued, the turn to gender history invited transnational historians to explore ways that gender ideologies and practices developed apart from national histories.[15] In modern Mexico, motorized corn mills had a far greater impact on women's quotidian experience than the land reform measures that became the hallmark of the Mexican Revolution. Before the introduction of corn mills, women and girls spent hours on their knees every day grinding corn into meal for tortillas; installing a single motorized corn mill in a community freed its girls to attend school and its women to learn to read or to engage in petty commerce.[16]

If feminist history questioned conventional periodizations (around land reform instead of corn mills, for instance) then transnational feminist history, in the ethos of persistent critique, in turn has challenged feminist periodizations—especially the periodization around "waves" of feminism that labels the suffrage movement of the late nineteenth and early twentieth centuries as the first wave and the feminist revival of the 1960s and 1970s as the second. Bonnie Anderson's study of mid-nineteenth-century women's activism, for example, renders visible transnational feminist networks that predated what we generally dub feminism's first wave.[17] The gender studies scholar Clare Hemmings further argues that the wave model undergirds a distorted, linear account of developments in feminist thought and "stories that claim gender equality as a uniquely Western export."[18]

Studies of regional networks highlight the wave model's limitations. Francesca Miller and Asunción Lavrin have demonstrated that local mobilizations and transnational outreach often escalated in Latin American feminism just as U.S.- and European-based networks quieted.[19] Latin American feminists' decades-long experience with pan-Americanism equipped them to play leading roles in putting women's rights into the 1945 United Nations Charter.[20] As U.S. feminist activism floundered in the 1980s, Latin American women's organizations—galvanized by human rights concerns, democratization efforts, and challenges to neoliberalism—burgeoned and capitalized on newly created transnational nongovernmental organization (NGO) networks that flourished after the 1975 United Nations International Women's Year (IWY) Conference in Mexico City.

Transnational feminist histories have also shown these networks and movements to be chronologically out of phase with the global ebbs and flows of nationalism. While Benedict Anderson has argued that print culture incubated nineteenth-century nationalism, both Bonnie Anderson and Margaret McFadden have stressed that print culture facilitated the creation of transnational networks of women activists that willfully rejected nationalist identifications.[21] Leila Rupp's landmark study of three prominent transnational women's organizations shows that her subjects' intensity and commitment to transnational solidarity deepened as nationalism mounted during World War I and the build up to World War II, and Karen Garner has shown that the same Cold War vitriol that fueled suspicions also galvanized transnational feminists to redouble their efforts to counter nationalist rivalries.[22]

To be sure, transnational feminism's periodization has not remained entirely out of sync with global developments. As indicated by the impact of print media, technological changes, especially those affecting transportation and communication, influenced transnational feminist organizations and networks. Geopolitical developments—most notably the nineteenth-century expansion of European imperialism, the far-reaching impact of the Cold War, and the hegemony of neoliberalism—all informed dynamics both within and among women's organizations. Thus transnational history requires its practitioners to situate their studies within larger metanarratives—even what Ulrike Strasser and Heidi Tinsman have dubbed "meganarratives"—in addition to pointing to the ways that feminist history may trouble them.[23] As Rupp has shown for the early twentieth century and Garner has documented for the latter half, even dedicated internationalists fell into the ideological suspicions that divided liberals from socialists, and activists frequently argued about where the dividing line lay—or if one existed—between "politics" and "women's issues." These suspicions, Francisca de Haan has pointed out, have also intruded upon the historiography itself. Historians of transnational feminism have paid minimal attention to the immensely important (but openly socialist) Women's International Democratic Federation (WIDF), which drew constant attacks from Cold War liberals.[24]

Indeed, the four UN world conferences on women—in Mexico City in 1975, followed by Copenhagen in 1980, Nairobi in 1985, and Beijing in 1995—provide another periodization of transnational feminism but they also reflected the ways that geopolitics and transnational feminism shaped one another. The first UN world conference occurred amid the radical promise of the nonaligned movement and the apparent ascendance of the New International Economic Order, a moment when Third World nations seemed poised to wrest economic and political power from the imperial powers. Longtime transnational feminist activists challenged the new nations to bring their policies regarding women—on political and educational rights, for example—in line with the more established member states, while a growing cadre of new arrivals questioned those priorities. The inclusion of ever-growing parallel NGO conferences challenged conventional politics from another angle. By 1995, NGO activists from what by then was called the "global south" had taken center stage. Over the course of the two decades between Mexico City and Beijing, the Berlin Wall had fallen, the market-oriented policies of neoliberalism had swept the world and begun to face sharp challenges, and NGOs had emerged as the new face of democratization that particularly represented women's interests.

Debates over the dividing line between politics and women's issues points to a final aspect of periodization that merits consideration: striking continuities in the issues linked to sexuality, labor, citizenship rights, and violence (and its corollary of peace). The pervasively liberal orientation of such concerns doubtless results from feminism's roots in the Enlightenment and of the revolutionary upheavals of the late-eighteenth and early-nineteenth centuries as the French Revolution and the independence movements in the United States, Haiti, and throughout the Americas raised questions about who would stand as recognized citizen-subjects of these new republics. The contents and implications of these issues, however, have themselves served as arenas of contestation, as the grounds both for solidarity and for dispute. "Almost nothing happened without conflict," Rupp observes of early-twentieth-century movements. "Debating everything from where they should hold conferences and what languages they should speak, to what constituted a national section and how much autonomy a section should have, to who was a feminist and what should be done about special labor legislation, internationally minded women formed a community as much through struggle as through agreement."[25] But the durability of these focal points, Ferree and Mueller argue, have provided threads of continuity that allow us to consider a history of transnational feminism with a certain degree of coherence, even as the contents and implications of these issues changed over time.[26]

Situated Cosmopolitans and the Politics of Place

If feminist scholarship bequeathed the challenge to periodization, questions about the politics of place come from the transnational side of the family tree as transnational feminists have struggled with tensions between the situated practice of activism and the aspiration to elevate themselves above the muck of place. "In this form," the political scientist Breny Mendoza explains of this imagined placelessness, "politics becomes evanescent, dense and often a virtual activity. . . . Consequently, it is not place per se, but the non-place of networks, flows, circuits—the transcendence of geographical, social, economic, cultural and political locations—that builds transnational politics and history."[27] But such placelessness has proven elusive in practice. Ultimately, as Edward Said reminds us, "Every idea or system of ideas exists *somewhere*, is mixed in with historical circumstances, is part of what one may simply call 'reality.'"[28]

Transnational feminism, however, emerged out of a universalist aspiration to overcome these particularities. "Feminism was born wrapped in one great hope," Lavrin explains,

> that it would be good for all womankind, and able to embrace all women, to dispel all national, racial and cultural barriers. Because it was developed concurrently in many parts of the world—sometimes as a groping desire not well articulated, sometimes as a clear elaboration of much meditation—it had an apparent promise of universality that led many women and men to believe that some day it would be a global canon for all humankind.[29]

Feminists have long struggled with this paradox of simultaneously critiquing and embracing universalism—desiring a shared understanding of womanhood and rejecting its very possibility—and this tension became particularly fraught amid transnational campaigns and organizations that extended the question of difference to an ever greater range of diversity.[30] If nineteenth- and early twentieth-century activists struggled to overcome differences between Dutch and German women of similar class backgrounds, the post-World War II extension of feminist networks to include former colonial subjects, non-Judeo-Christians, and working-class and peasant women posed unprecedented challenges and opportunities that set in relief the specificities of place.

Transnational feminists came from particular backgrounds, established their headquarters in particular cities, and congregated in specific locales. For the transnational feminists who populate Anderson's mid-nineteenth-century history, much like the very local feminists in Anne Enke's late-twentieth-century study, "finding the movement" in a quite literal sense was a critical first step.[31] The location of headquarters and congresses was often a fraught issue for members of transnational organizations, as leaders sought to strike a balance between reaching out to new constituencies and accommodating their dedicated members.[32] When the left-leaning WIDF proposed dubbing 1975 as the UN International Women's Year and began organizing a conference in East Berlin, the U.S. representative to the UN's Commission of the Status of Women hustled to secure a commitment from the Colombian government to host a conference. The U.S. State Department could not tolerate holding the headliner IWY event behind the Iron Curtain and secured the support of Third World members of the Commission by proposing to hold the conference in Bogotá.[33] After the IWY Conference was relocated to Mexico City (due to political and budgetary concerns in Colombia), tensions often surfaced between Geneva- and New York-based activists who eyed each other with suspicion. Noting the WIDF's strong influence on the Geneva committee, former International Council of Women president Mary Craig Schuller-McGeachy insisted that the New York committee assume its "proper place and authority" to ensure that the conference was "truly representative" and had the "essential balance."[34]

Conferences themselves served as important locales, what Ferree and Mueller describe as a "specific type of movement activity [that] offer[s] a particularly useful melding of advocacy network and lifestyle politics" and plays an indispensable role in forging transnational connections. Conferences serve as what Mary Louise Pratt would call contact zones, "social spaces where disparate cultures meet, clash, and grapple with each other, in highly asymmetrical relations of domination and subordination."[35] For this reason, conferences themselves merit attention as spaces distinct from those of the organizations and movements that participate in them.[36] While individual activists arrived to conferences shaped by their own histories and experiences, at international conferences they entered into an entirely synthetic context in which diverse understandings and objectives bumped up against one another in generative—and sometimes explosive—ways, offering critical sites for developing solidarity through struggle.

The politics of place highlighted the constant tug between nationalism and internationalism and the challenges of forging bonds of intellectual and political solidarity across the divide between, on the one hand, those areas dubbed Western, Northern, developed, industrialized, or First World and, on the other, those areas dubbed non-Western, Southern, developing (or even, in some iterations, *under*developed), or Third World.[37] These geopolitical designations vary by context, ideological orientation, and scholarly conversation and do not map unproblematically onto one another. Indeed, the question of *how* to map them without either reifying or eliding meaningful differences of power and resources remains an unresolved question for students of transnational feminism.

Enduring suspicions held by feminists in impoverished regions toward those in wealthy regions only mounted as national liberation and decolonization movements broke from a simmer into a rolling boil in the 1950s and 1960s. The very term *transnational* first entered the lexicon of most Latin American countries, for example, as a designation for sprawling corporations and freeflowing capital rather than grassroots social movements. Like earlier European revolutionary movements, national liberation movements frequently dismissed feminism as a bourgeois import designed to distract women's allegiances from radical nationalist causes.[38] Domitila Barrios de Chungara, the Bolivian tin miner's wife who gained international notoriety after speaking out at the 1975 UN conference in Mexico City, underscored in her memoir that Betty Friedan and her ilk "made mostly feminist points" that "didn't touch on issues that were basic for Latin American women."[39] In a subsequent pamphlet, she described feminism as created by capitalists to undermine class solidarity and illustrated the point with a cartoon of Uncle Sam holding men and women apart.[40]

The tendency to see transnational feminism as emanating from cosmopolitan centers in Europe and the United States generated charges of feminist orientalism, in which feminism remains inextricable from Anglo-European liberalism and its advocates teach (and rescue) women in supposedly antimodern societies.[41] Barrios de Chungara, for example, highlighted the hypocrisy of those at the 1975 IWY Conference in Mexico City who advocated population control among poor populations rather than consumption control among rich ones.[42] Saba Mahmood opens her ethnography of the Egyptian women's mosque movement with a critique of liberal feminists who see Muslim women as "pawns in a grand patriarchal plan, who, if freed from their bondage would naturally express their instinctual abhorrence of the traditional Islamic mores used to enchain them."[43]

Empirical studies of how feminist practices and knowledge production circulate transnationally have revealed far more complex dynamics than simple Western imperialism, however. Kathy Davis has shown, for example, that a quintessentially U.S. feminist text—*Our Bodies, Ourselves*—was redefined as it was translated into different languages and cultural contexts.[44] Similarly, the anthropologist Millie Thayer has argued that feminist theories and practices made their way into the Brazilian hinterlands through NGOs and development projects not as a straightforward example of cultural hegemony but rather through an appropriation and resignification at every point of transfer. "In this process," she explains of the *campesinas*' appropriation of feminist ideas, "the rural women draw on resources of their own, based on the very local-ness whose demise is bemoaned by globalization theorists."[45]

Furthermore, the vectors of influence have not simply gone from metropolitan centers to peripheries for appropriation; ideas and practices have also flowed in the other direction. Margaret Snyder and Mary Tadesse trace the ways in which grassroots African women's organizations connected with the UN's Economic Commission on Africa (ECA) and managed to inform development policies from the ground up.[46] Lavrin demonstrates that the maternalism that has played an enduring role in Latin American feminist movements offers a model for incorporating women's social roles and challenging the neoliberal rush to commodify everything.[47] Although liberal feminists often dismissed maternalism as essentializing women or narrowing their opportunities, in the context of Latin American campaigns against military rule and structural-adjustment policies, maternalism hinged on the idea that motherhood did not render women atomized, particularized subjects unsuited for the elevated status of citizen-subject but rather gave them opportunities to scrutinize the social impacts of public policies. Prominent campaigns, such as the daily demonstrations by the Argentine group the Mothers of the Plaza de Mayo against their government's widespread atrocities, drew international attention and revitalized maternalism as a feminist human rights strategy.

Regardless of the directions in which ideas and practices flowed, they generally funneled through individual cosmopolitan women who participated in international networks and conferences linking like-minded activists most often from urban backgrounds. These cosmopolitans, with the freedom and resources to attend conferences and planning sessions, played powerful roles in shaping the dominant strains of transnational feminism. The maintenance of cosmopolitan networks has required access to technology—be it steamship or telegraph or email—creating another resource barrier for women in more modest circumstances. While the postwar rise of postcolonial cosmopolitan feminism marked a radical expansion of the demographic range of women involved in transnational networks, it retained a strong winnowing effect on the issues and perspectives legitimated within those networks.

For methodological reasons, these (mostly elite) women loom particularly large in the historiography: they tend to leave their papers to well-catalogued college archives, and personal names offer researchers leads to follow in databases and search engines. The emphasis on cosmopolitan individuals allows historians to consider human perspectives as well as structural explanations for transnational feminism's successes and failures, but it also results in conspicuous exclusions and elisions in the historical narrative. The historical action in most accounts occurs wherever these women happen to go, creating a circular logic in which the most important events appear to be the ones involving them (and about which they leave documentation). Oral histories and mass media coverage of more recent transnational feminist activities—those dating since their significant expansion in the 1970s—have drawn attention to less privileged actors and more grassroots activities. Even in studies based on these sources, however, individual cosmopolitans generally remain the actors with the financial, political, and cultural capital to most strongly shape transnational feminist agendas.

These women often lived (or imagined themselves to live) the ideal of placelessness. As Virginia Woolf famously explained in *Three Guineas*, "As a woman I want no country. As a woman my country is the whole world."[48] In a full-throated endorsement of cosmopolitan feminism as a "commitment to critically reinterpreted universal human rights in the context of democratically grounded, emancipatory political projects," the political theorist Niamh Reilly defines it as a "process-oriented framework wherein the direction and content of feminist practice is determined in cross-boundaries dialogue within and across women's movements."[49] While such a definition sidesteps the issue of the power relationships that inform such a dialogue—such as the differential control over resources, access to decision makers, and mastery of cultural and rhetorical tools—it does recognize that organizations, campaigns, and ideas travel principally in the bodies and minds of individual, particularly mobile women.

The growth and diversification of transnational feminist networks over the course of the twentieth century brought what Antoinette Burton has dubbed "postcolonial cosmopolitanism" by which circulations flow in multiple directions and appropriations occur as often in Los Angeles or Berlin as in Lagos and São Paulo.[50] In my own research on the 1975 IWY Conference, I have been struck that the overwhelming number of participants even in the NGO tribune—often dubbed the "people's forum"—who may have been born in Delhi or Kinshasa or Havana but at some point had worked or attended school in London or Paris or Miami. For example, Victoria Mojekwu, who participated in the tribune panel on health matters, attended nursing school in Ibadan, Nigeria, before working as a nurse in London, returning to Ibadan, and then attending graduate school at Boston University and Harvard University before returning to Nigeria to serve as the Chief Nursing Officer. At the IWY Conference, Mojekwu was among those who made common cause with Betty Friedan in opposition to a more politically radical group of women from Third World countries.[51] As political scientist Breny Mendoza has observed, the urban nature of these networks has often made the cosmopolitan linkages tighter than activists' connections with rural women in their own countries.[52]

International conferences also created postcolonial cosmopolitans. Domitila Barrios de Chungara, for example, had been unknown outside Bolivia before the IWY conference but went on to coauthor a widely translated and circulated memoir and played a prominent role in subsequent UN women's conferences. Many IWY tribune participants entered transnational networks as the Ghanaian supreme court justice Annie Jiagge did, through the decidedly liberal YWCA, while others such as the South African domestic worker Florence Mophosho, came in through the left-leaning WIDF, the YWCA's ideological rival. Much as the social and educational backgrounds had informed the perspectives of early-twentieth-century cosmopolitans, women like Jiagge and Mophosho adopted positions at the NGO tribune that reflected their own backgrounds and institutional affiliations but also transformative experiences at the conference itself. Further, while Virginia Woolf could safely disavow national allegiances, for women from postcolonial nations or in countries under the political and economic domination of neoimperialism, transnational loyalties have been, as the political scientists Margaret Keck and Kathryn Sikkink have observed, a "much trickier business," as they appear to adulterate dedication to nationalist causes.[53]

Passionate Feminists and Transnational Identifications

This dramatic diversification of participants in transnational feminist networks, particularly in the wake of the 1975 IWY Conference, exposed the "tricky business" of identification and subjectivity.[54] While some identifications, such as those with generation or with motherhood, appeared amid the first episodes of transnational feminism, others around class, race, ethnicity, and religion intensified as transnational networks incorporated more members from a broader range of backgrounds. In this way, they resembled other transnational phenomena. Studies of transnational *feminism* offer distinct lessons, however, in their emphasis on affect, passion, bodies, and sexuality. As Bonnie Anderson and Rupp both discovered, the personal correspondences of transnational feminists openly expressed passion not only about ideas but also about one another. These passions were sometimes enduring and at other times ephemeral, but they animated transnational feminism either way.

Through these passions and desires, transnational feminists have recognized that not only is the personal political but the political is also intensely personal. The success or failure of a wide range of endeavors often hinged upon personal affinities and animosities, including the extent to which feminists identified with individual leaders. The personal—and often intimate—correspondences of these women not only provide the documentary record for historians but also served as a critical mode of knowledge production and circulation for activists living far from one another. These intense relationships, which really have defined the contents of transnational feminist movements as much as any other factor, frequently transgress the categories of identification that historians adopt. As Temma Kaplan has shown in her study of grassroots women's movements that at moments linked rural North Carolina to urban South Africa, the cultivation of a "female consciousness" grew out of the solidarities of embattled campaigns and struggles for recognition, producing alliances that followed lines of friendship and devotion rather than race, class, or ideology.[55]

Indeed, one of the significant contributions of transnational feminist history has been to insist upon passions—both personal and political—as crucial animators of historical change. As feminist historian Joan Scott provocatively queries, "What if we rewrote Feminism's History as a story of circulating critical passion, slipping metonymically along a chain of contiguous objects, alighting for a while in an unexpected place, accomplishing a task, and then moving on?" Reminding us of feminism's roots as a "restless critical operation, as a movement of desire," Scott insists upon seeing these desires as historically contingent, as a "mutating historical phenomenon, defined as and through its displacements."[56] This disruption of conventional notions of identification has galvanized feminist scholars to rethink the very terms of the debates over universalism and difference.[57]

Such an approach, much like transnational studies more generally, destabilizes fixed conceptions of identification and instead recognizes that all identifications are unpredictable and malleable. Chicanas arriving at the NGO tribune of the 1975 IWY conference, for example, expected to "share a common sisterhood" with Mexican feminists. "We thought, oh, yeah, we're

Mexican Americans," recalled Sandra Serrano Sewell, "we're going to find all this natural connections, you know, and sort of like a romantic view that was quickly dispelled."[58] The well-heeled Mexican women who attended the tribune were more likely to make common cause with Betty Friedan than with the Chicanas who reminded them of their own domestic employees.

Without question, many U.S.-based scholars took up these questions through engagements with postmodernist debates, which themselves grew out of the intellectual ferment of decolonization and postcoloniality that made visible a previously unimaginable array of performances of womanhood and feminism.[59] Some groups, such as the 1961 Afro-Asian Women's Symposium, mirrored the nonaligned conferences that had begun at Bandung in 1955 to forge solidarities among women within the Third World.[60] More established organizations, such as the YWCA and the International Federation of Business and Professional Women, tried to reach out to Third World women to expand what had been largely Euro-American memberships, with a smattering of women from Australia, New Zealand, and Japan. Decolonization meant that antiracist and anti-imperialist politics braided together with ongoing campaigns for peace and for political subjecthood.

Efforts to describe feminist subjects combined with a more widespread practice of policing and protecting women's bodies to generate particular interest in corporeal issues, ranging from headscarves to genital cutting to footbinding.[61] Such campaigns have yielded some of the most fraught exchanges within transnational feminist circles. On the one hand, they exemplify feminists' long-standing resistance against concealing women's issues under the cloak of privacy.[62] On the other, they often reiterated a feminist orientalism that coded particular practices as backward and barbaric.[63] To be sure, prominent activists tried to insist that violence against women—including battery, homicides, and spousal rape—remained as much of an epidemic in whiter, wealthier, predominantly Judeo-Christian spaces as they did in darker, poorer, non-Judeo-Christian ones.[64] Ironically, corporeal and sartorial differences displayed at transnational women's congresses are frequently celebrated as visual evidence of feminist unity and solidarity. Nonetheless, campaigns against gendered violence and corporeal policing, from nineteenth-century missionaries to twenty-first-century bloggers, have persistently reinscribed non-Western bodies with the marks of subjugation.

Structures of Transnational Feminism

The progressive diversification of transnational feminism, which took a particularly dramatic turn during the UN Decade for Women, took place not only on the intimate scale of bodies and personal passions but also on the broader scale of infrastructures and social movements. The relationship between social movements and the institutions and bureaucracies that simultaneously facilitate and contain them has always entailed tensions and negotiations. As scholars of transnational feminism have noted, broadening membership has led to the fragmentation of organizations and, in turn, required increased institutionalization to maintain core agendas and political identifications.[65] Since the 1970s, as governments around the world have progressively curtailed funding for social programs, these networks have also increasingly relied upon private funding through NGOs.[66] While many studies of social movements stress the recent decentering of states, however, scholars of transnational feminism point out that these movements decentered the state from the outset, not least because women in general—and feminists in particular—have had such limited access to official decision making.[67] As Australian historian Marilyn Lake has reminded us, feminist history particularly lends itself to transnational analyses, since feminists, finding themselves marginalized or excluded from decision making within national and local polities, gained more traction waging campaigns through transnational organizations ranging from Christian missionary networks to Communist internationals.[68]

Social movements, including transnational feminist movements, both generate and rely on infrastructures rooted in organizations such as churches, political parties, and labor unions. "Because gender segregation leaves an alternative geography of opportunity open to women more than men," sociologists Ferree and Mueller explain, "women's political openings and allies are more to be found in the institutional domains defined as 'apolitical': communities, grass-roots civic organizations, social work, and social services."[69] Understanding the dynamics of transnational women's movements, they assert, sheds light on the gendered nature of social movements more generally. The boom of Euro-American imperialism yielded anti-imperialist movements and missionary expeditions that served as unwitting incubators of transnational feminism. Indeed, the first transnational women's NGO, the World Women's Christian Temperance Union (founded in 1883) emerged from a network of Christian missionaries.[70] Religious organizations of all varieties have created spaces in which women have developed a feminist consciousness.[71] As Bonnie Anderson shows for early-nineteenth-century Europe and I have found for early-twentieth-century Mexico, socialist and communist parties have fostered women's movements that would certainly conform to Ferree and Mueller's more elastic definition of feminist.[72] Even as iconic a figure as Betty Friedan first developed her feminist perspective through a labor union.⁷³ Such entities have often provided the training and resources that served as the foundations for feminist organizations.

Transnational feminists have both taken advantage of these extant organizations and constructed new ones. Supranational entities, such as the League of Nations and the United Nations as well as their affiliated agencies such as the International Labor Organization and the World Health Organization (not to mention the Commission on the Status of Women), created spaces for women to meet and cultivated the expectation that women could make moral and political claims against states and organizations. As political scientist Elisabeth Jay Friedman has shown, feminist organizations have, in turn, shaped the agendas of these supranational institutions, both because they have consistently pressed for greater input from NGOs and because women's rights advocates were often the "most organized sector at [UN] conferences that were not focused specifically on their own issues, and they mainstreamed their issues in such a way as to influence the overall framing of other conference topics by 'gendering' other agendas."⁷⁴ Most strikingly, transnational feminism has served as a driving force behind the growth of transnational NGOs more generally.⁷⁵ More established NGOs that enjoy consultative status with the UN's Economic and Social Council, such as the World YWCA and International Planned Parenthood Federation, along with internationally minded benefactors such as the Ford and Rockefeller foundations, provided critical resources for transnational feminists, giving them an institutional winnowing effect similar to that of cosmopolitan feminists.⁷⁶

The explosion of transnational NGOs in the 1970s resulted from resistance to such organizations' dominance as well as mounting distrust of states. From the Watergate scandal and antiwar protests in the United States to growing frustration with corrupt politicians in new nations and tyranny in Latin America, midcentury confidence in state apparatuses gave way to a sense that ordinary people—people not corrupted by the power and riches of governing and not beholden to the pressures of elections and interest groups—could form a shadow polity in which NGOs would effectively control governance and resources within their own corners of interest. At the 1975 IWY conference, Third World women attending the NGO tribune insisted that any foreign aid intended to help women should come via NGOs rather than governments, which often diverted the funds.⁷⁷ Indeed, one of the defining differences between old- and new-model NGOs was their degree of willingness to work with and through state apparatuses and more established institutions.

The scholarship on this more recent efflorescence of civil society has sounded a cautionary note about romanticizing its effects.⁷⁸ To be sure, the dramatic diversification of NGOs occurred within the same (or perhaps even greater) unequal distribution of power and resources than had characterized earlier instantiations of transnational feminism. The literary critic Gayatri Spivak has warned against being taken in by the "global radical aura" at settings such as the NGO tribune at the 1995 Beijing UN Women's Conference, in which the inclusion of NGOs from the global south elides the alarming inequalities that persist within as well as between polities and regions. The performative politics of such settings exclude "the poorest women of the South as self-conscious critical agents, who might be able to speak through those very nongovernmental organizations of the South that are not favoured by these object-constitution policies."[79] These new NGOs, in other words, enable a substantially different mode of transnational feminist activism, but they remain embedded within the power structures that produce them.

Object Lessons

Thus, like every union, transnational feminist history faces stresses and strains and miscommunications; the marriage is never as romantic as the courtship. Nonetheless, this partnership proffers some important lessons. If feminist history taught us to question conventional periodizations, transnational feminist history has challenged feminism's own conventions by showing the limitations of the wave model. If transnational history exposed the limitations of national metanarratives, transnational feminist history reminds us of the particularities of place and the impossibility of placelessness. Feminist studies have explored intersectionality—of the many ways that women self-identify—and the power of identification to undergird social movements with solidarity. Transnational feminist studies have revealed the unpredictability of those identifications, the extent to which race and ethnicity, for example, offer a soft foundation for solidarity once they are deracinated from their meaning-making historical contexts. Finally, transnational feminist history developed amid the explosion of NGOs and has highlighted the importance of non-state actors–and women's NGOs in particular—in shaping supranational policy and governance. However the marriage plays out—whether it yields connubial bliss, angry accusations, or quiet disappointments —these insights have repaid the arduous scholarly work that has gone into it.

Transnational feminist history is, arguably, a marriage of necessity precipitated by the need to understand the rapid intensification of transnational feminism itself. Over the past several decades, women's NGOs have spread like kudzu, and historians have responded to the popular and scholarly fascination with these organizations by exploring their genesis and development. In the process, we have discovered that transnational feminism requires its own field of inquiry to understand these peculiarly recontextualized actors and phenomena. Activists who encounter one another at global conferences, for example, confront a radically more diverse array of political and cultural gestures than those attending national congresses. Those whose networks follow the contour lines of transnational feminism find that those networks pass through a wide array of economic and material structures that alter the functioning of those networks. Much as comparative history reveals the distinctions among national and local histories, transnational feminist history applies a different frame to central analytics such as time, space, subjectivity, and structure. Observations made visible by blowing the image up to the scale of the transnational serve as well as we reduce the scale back to the local or national, where variations in periodization or identification may be harder to spot.

NOTES

1. Heidi Hartmann, "The Unhappy Marriage of Marxism and Feminism: Towards a More Progressive Union," in *Women and Revolution: A Discussion of the Unhappy Marriage of Marxism and Feminism*, ed. Lydia Sargent (Boston: South End Press, 1981), 2.
2. On the subversive intent of feminist histories, see Joan Wallach Scott, "Feminism's History," *Journal of Women's History* 16, no. 2 (2004).
3. For excellent reviews of the historiography of transnational feminism, see Francesca Miller, "Feminisms and Transnationalism," in *Feminisms and Internationalism*, eds. Mrinalini Sinha, Donna J. Guy, and Angela Woollacott (Oxford: Blackwell Publishers, 1999); Ulrike Strasser and Heidi Tinsman, "It's a Man's World? World History Meets the History of Masculinity, in Latin American Studies, for Instance," *Journal of World History* 21, no. 1 (2010); Ulrike Strasser and Heidi Tinsman, "Engendering World History," *Radical History Review* 2005, no. 91 (2005); Mary Louise Roberts, "The Transnationalization of Gender History," *History and Theory* 44, no. 3 (2005); Judith P. Zinsser, "Women's History, World History, and the Construction of New Narratives," *Journal of Women's History* 12, no. 3 (2000): 197, and a special issue of *Journal of Women's History* 19, no. 1 (2007).
4. For a useful introduction to the debate over transnational history, see C. A. Bayly et al., "AHR Conversation: On Transnational History," *American Historical Review* 111, no. 5 (2006); John D. French, "Another World History Is Possible: Reflections on the Translocal, Transnational, and Global," in *Workers Across the Americas: The Transnational Turn in Labor History*, ed. Leon Fink (New York: Oxford University Press, 2011).
5. For a helpful discussion of this distinction, see Micol Seigel, "Beyond Compare: Historical Method after the Transnational Turn," *Radical History Review* 91 (2005).
6. For comparative anthologies, see, for example, Bonnie G. Smith, *Global Feminisms since 1945: A Survey of Issues and Controversies* (London, New York: Routledge, 2000); Mrinalini Sinha, Donna J. Guy, and Angela Woollacott, *Feminisms and Internationalism* (Oxford: Blackwell Publishers, 1999).

7. Cindi Katz, "Lost and Found: The Imagined Geographies of American Studies," *Prospects* 30 (2006): 7–8.
8. Judith Butler, "Contingent Foundations: Feminism and the Question of the 'Postmodern,'" in *Feminists Theorize the Political*, eds. Judith Butler and Joan Scott (New York: Routledge, 1992).
9. Smith, *Global Feminisms since 1945*.
10. Asunción Lavrin, *Women, Feminism, and Social Change in Argentina, Chile, and Uruguay, 1890–1940* (Lincoln: University of Nebraska Press, 1995), 352.
11. Myra Marx Ferree and Carol McClurg Mueller, "Feminism and the Women's Movement: A Global Perspective," in *The Blackwell Companion to Social Movements*, eds. David A. Snow, Sarah A. Soule, and Hanspeter Kriesi (Oxford: Blackwell Publishing, 2004): 577–78.
12. See, for example, Scott, "Feminism's History"; Leila J. Rupp, *Worlds of Women: The Making of an International Women's Movement* (Princeton: Princeton University Press, 1997).
13. For the classic feminist interrogation of periodization, see Joan Kelly-Gadol, "The Social Relation of the Sexes: Methodological Implications of Women's History," *Signs* 1, no. 4 (1976).
14. On feminist historians' dispositive role in shaping social and then cultural history, see William H. Sewell Jr., *Logics of History: Social Theory and Social Transformation* (Chicago: University of Chicago Press, 2005), chapter 2.
15. Alice Kessler-Harris, "A Rich and Adventurous Journey: The Transnational Journey of Gender History in the United States," *Journal of Women's History* 19, no. 1 (2007).
16. Jocelyn Olcott, *Revolutionary Women in Postrevolutionary Mexico* (Durham: Duke University Press, 2005), especially chapter 4.
17. Bonnie S. Anderson, *Joyous Greetings: The First International Women's Movement, 1830–1860* (New York: Oxford University Press, 2000).
18. Clare Hemmings, *Why Stories Matter: The Political Grammar of Feminist Theory* (Durham: Duke University Press, 2011), 1.
19. Francesca Miller, *Latin American Women and the Search for Social Justice*, (Hanover, N.H.: University Press of New England, 1991); Lavrin, *Women, Feminism, and Social Change*.
20. Miller, *Latin American Women*.
21. Benedict Anderson, *Imagined Communities: Reflections on the Origin and Spread of Nationalism* (London: Verso, 1983); Anderson, *Joyous Greetings*; Margaret H. McFadden, *Golden Cables of Sympathy: The Transatlantic Sources of Nineteenth-Century Feminism* (Lexington: University of Kentucky Press, 1999).
22. Rupp, *Worlds of Women*; Karen Garner, *Shaping a Global Women's Agenda: Women's NGOs and Global Governance, 1925–85* (Manchester: Manchester University Press, 2010).
23. Strasser and Tinsman, "Engendering World History," 152.
24. Francisca de Haan, "Continuing Cold War Paradigms in Western Historiography of Transnational Women's Organisations: The Case of the Women's International Democratic Federation (WIDF)," *Women's History Review* 19, no. 4 (2010).
25. Rupp, *Worlds of Women*, 208.
26. Ferree and Mueller, "Feminism and the Women's Movement," 585.
27. Breny Mendoza, "Transnational Feminisms in Question," *Feminist Theory* 3, no. 3 (2002): 299–300.
28. Edward W. Said, "Zionism from the Standpoint of Its Victims," in *The Edward Said Reader* (New York: Random House, 2000), 115.
29. Asunción Lavrin, "International Feminisms: Latin American Alternatives," in *Feminisms and Internationalism*, eds. Mrinalini Sinha, Donna J. Guy, and Angela Woollacott (Oxford: Blackwell Publishers, 1999), 175.

30. For an explication of this discussion, see Joan Wallach Scott, *Only Paradoxes to Offer: French Feminists and the Rights of Man* (Cambridge: Harvard University Press, 1996), chapter 1.
31. Anne Enke, *Finding the Movement: Sexuality, Contested Space, and Feminist Activism* (Durham: Duke University Press, 2007).
32. Rupp, *Worlds of Women*, 73–74.
33. Virginia R. Allan, Margaret E. Galey, and Mildred E. Persinger, "World Conference of International Women's Year," in *Women, Politics, and the United Nations*, ed. Anne Winslow (Westport, Conn.: Greenwood Press, 1995), 30.
34. Schuller-McGeachy to Rosalind Harris, February 19, 1974, International Women's Tribune Centre Papers, Acc. # 89S-27, Box 1, Sophia Smith Collection, Smith College, Northampton, Mass.
35. Mary Louise Pratt, *Imperial Eyes: Travel Writing and Transculturation* (London: Routledge, 1992), 4.
36. I have explored these questions in my work on the 1975 United Nations International Women's Year Conference in Mexico City (Jocelyn Olcott, "Transnational Feminism: Event, Temporality, and Performance at the 1975 International Women's Year Conference," in Daniel T. Rodgers, ed., *Cultures in Motion* (Princeton: Princeton University Press, forthcoming). See also Matthew Connelly's consideration of the 1974 UN Population Conference (Matthew Connelly, *Fatal Misconception: The Struggle to Control World Population* [Cambridge: Harvard University Press, 2008], chapter 8) as well as Kathryn Kish Sklar's study of women at the historic 1840 World Anti-Slavery Convention that refused to seat women delegates (Kathryn Kish Sklar, "'Women Who Speak for an Entire Nation': American and British Women Compared at the World Anti-Slavery Convention, London, 1840," *Pacific Historical Review* 59, no. 4 [1990]).
37. For useful reviews of these concerns, see Sinha, Guy, and Woollacott, *Feminisms and Internationalism*; Mendoza, "Transnational Feminisms in Question"; Myra Marx Ferree and Aili Mari Tripp, *Global Feminism: Transnational Women's Activism, Organizing, and Human Rights* (New York: NYU Press, 2006).
38. On the European dismissal of bourgeois feminism, see Marilyn J. Boxer, "Rethinking the Socialist Construction and International Career of the Concept 'Bourgeois Feminism,'" *American Historical Review* 112, no. 1 (2007).
39. Domitila Barrios de Chungara and Moema Viezzer, *Let Me Speak! Testimony of Domitila, a Woman of the Bolivian Mines*, trans. Victoria Ortiz (New York: Monthly Review Press, 1978), 201.
40. Domitila Barrios de Chungara, *La mujer y la organización* (La Paz, Bolivia: UNITAS, CIDOP, CIPCA, 1980), 25.
41. The critique of feminist orientalism clearly owes a debt to Edward Said (Edward W. Said, *Orientalism* [New York: Pantheon Books, 1978]) and has focused most squarely on Western involvements in and scholarship about the Muslim world and South Asia. See, for examples, Lila Abu-Lughod, "'Orientalism' and Middle East Feminist Studies," *Feminist Studies* 27, no. 1 (2001); Antoinette M. Burton, *Burdens of History: British Feminists, Indian Women, and Imperial Culture, 1865–1915* (Chapel Hill: University of North Carolina Press, 1994); Reza Hammami and Martina Rieker, "Feminist Orientalism and Orientalist Marxism," *New Left Review* 170 (1988); Saba Mahmood, *Politics of Piety: The Islamic Revival and the Feminist Subject* (Princeton: Princeton University Press, 2004); Chandra Talpade Mohanty, "Under Western Eyes: Feminist Scholarship and Colonial Discourses," *Feminist Review*, no. 30 (1988); Charlotte Weber, "Unveiling Scheherazade: Feminist Orientalism in the

International Alliance of Women, 1911–1950," *Feminist Studies* 27, no. 1 (2001). Scholars of transnational feminism, however, have also extended the analysis to other regions as well as the demeanor of urban, European-oriented feminists in the non-Western countries toward local indigenous or nonwhite populations. (See, for examples, Christine Ehrick, "Madrinas and Missionaries: Uruguay and the Pan-American Women's Movement," *Gender and History* 10, no. 3 [1998]; Lavrin, "International Feminisms"; Mendoza, "Transnational Feminisms in Question.")

42. Domitila Barrios de Chungara and David Acebey, *Aquí también, Domitila! testimonios* (México, D.F.: Siglo Veintiuno Editores, 1985), 199.
43. Mahmood, *Politics of Piety*, 1–2.
44. Kathy Davis, *The Making of Our Bodies, Ourselves: How Feminism Travels across Borders* (Durham: Duke University Press, 2007).
45. Millie Thayer, "Transnational Feminism: Reading Joan Scott in the Brazilian *sertão*," *Ethnography* 2, no. 2 (2001): 243.
46. Margaret C. Snyder and Mary Tadesse, *African Women and Development: A History* (Johannesburg: Witwatersrand University Press, 1995).
47. Lavrin, "International Feminisms."
48. Virginia Woolf, *Three Guineas*, annotated ed. (Orlando: Harcourt, 2006 [1938]), 129.
49. Niamh Reilly, "Cosmopolitan Feminism and Human Rights," *Hypatia* 22, no. 4 (2007): 181–82.
50. Antoinette M. Burton, *The Postcolonial Careers of Santha Rama Rau* (Durham: Duke University Press, 2007). The postcolonial cosmopolitan might be usefully contrasted with a more conventional counterpart: Mary Kinnear, *Woman of the World: Mary McGeachy and International Cooperation* (Toronto: University of Toronto Press, 2004).
51. Schlesinger Library, Betty Friedan Papers, Carton 107, file 1264.
52. Mendoza, "Transnational Feminisms in Question," 309.
53. Margaret E. Keck and Kathryn Sikkink, *Activists beyond Borders: Advocacy Networks in International Politics* (Ithaca: Cornell University Press, 1998), 16.
54. My understanding of identification here draws on Rogers Brubaker's and Frederick Cooper's historically grounded conceptualization: "If one wants to trace the process through which persons sharing some categorical attribute come to share definitions of their predicament, understandings of their interest, and a readiness to undertake collective action, it is best to do so in a manner that highlights the contingent and variable relationship between mere categories and bounded, solidary groups." (Rogers Brubaker and Frederick Cooper, "Beyond 'Identity,'" *Theory and Society* 29[2000]: 9.)
55. Temma Kaplan, *Crazy for Democracy: Women in Grassroots Movements* (New York: Routledge, 1997).
56. Scott, "Feminism's History," 18–19.
57. For examples, see Inderpal Grewal and Caren Kaplan, *Scattered Hegemonies: Postmodernity and Transnational Feminist Practices* (Minneapolis: University of Minnesota Press, 1994); Jacqui Alexander and Chandra Talpade Mohanty, *Feminist Genealogies, Colonial Legacies, Democratic Futures* (New York: Routledge, 1997). For excellent summaries of these conversations, see Inderpal Grewal and Caren Kaplan, *An Introduction to Women's Studies: Gender in a Transnational World*, 2nd ed. (Boston: McGraw-Hill Higher Education, 2006); David Mills and Richard Ssewakiryanga, "'That Beijing Thing': Challenging Transnational Feminisms in Kampala," *Gender, Place and Culture* 9, no. 4 (2002): 385–88.
58. Marisela R. Chávez, "Pilgrimage to the Homeland: California Chicanas and International Women's Year, Mexico City, 1975," in *Memories and Migrations: Mapping Boricua and*

Chicana Histories, eds. Vicki Ruíz and John R. Chávez (Urbana: University of Illinois Press, 2008), 176.
59. See, in particular, many of Gayatri Spivak's early essays and interviews.
60. Vijay Prashad, *The Darker Nations: A People's History of the Third World*, (New York: New Press, 2007), chapter 4.
61. This literature has been particularly enriched by studies of empire and postcoloniality. See, for example, Tony Ballantyne and Antoinette M. Burton, eds., *Bodies in Contact: Rethinking Colonial Encounters in World History* (Durham: Duke University Press, 2005); Tony Ballantyne and Antoinette M. Burton, eds., *Moving Subjects: Gender, Mobility, and Intimacy in an Age of Global Empire* (Urbana: University of Illinois Press, 2009); Ann Laura Stoler, *Race and the Education of Desire: Foucault's History of Sexuality and the Colonial Order of Things* (Durham: Duke University Press, 1995).
62. Charlotte Bunch, "Transforming Human Rights from a Feminist Perspective," in *Women's Rights, Human Rights: International Feminist Perspectives*, eds. Julie Peters and Andrea Wolper (New York: Routledge, 1995); Charlotte Bunch, *Passionate Politics: Feminist Theory in Action* (New York: St. Martin's Press, 1987).
63. Abu-Lughod, "'Orientalism' and Middle East Feminist Studies"; Mahmood, *Politics of Piety*; L. Amede Obiora, "Bridges and Barricades: Rethinking Polemics and Intransigence in the Campaign against Female Circumcision," *Case Western Reserve Law Review* 47 (1996); Joan Wallach Scott, *The Politics of the Veil* (Princeton: Princeton University Press, 2007); Leti Volpp, "Feminism versus Multiculturalism," *Columbia Law Review* 101, no. 5 (2001).
64. Charlotte Bunch, "Women's Rights as Human Rights: Toward a Re-Vision of Human Rights," *Human Rights Quarterly* 12, no. 4 (1990).
65. Ferree and Tripp, *Global Feminism*; Keck and Sikkink, *Activists beyond Borders*.
66. Sonia E. Alvarez, "Latin American Feminisms 'Go Global': Trends of the 1990s and Challenges for the New Millennium," in *Cultures of Politics/Politics of Cultures: Re-Visioning Latin American Social Movements*, eds. Sonia E. Alvarez, Evelina Dagnino, and Arturo Escobar (Boulder, Colo.: Westview Press, 1998). For a revision of this analysis, see Sonia E. Alvarez, "Beyond NGO-ization? Reflections from Latin America," *Development* 52, no. 2 (2009).
67. For an overview on the growth of transnational civil society, see John Boli and George M. Thomas, *Constructing World Culture: International Nongovernmental Organizations since 1875* (Stanford: Stanford University Press, 1999); Akira Iriye, *Global Community: The Role of International Organizations in the Making of the Contemporary World* (Berkeley: University of California Press, 2002); Peter Willetts, *"The Conscience of the World": The Influence of Non-Governmental Organisations in the UN System* (Washington, D.C.: Brookings Institution, 1996).
68. Marilyn Lake, "Nationalist Historiography, Feminist Scholarship, and the Promise and Problems of New Transnational Histories: The Australian Case," *Journal of Women's History* 19, no. 1 (2007): 182–83.
69. Ferree and Mueller, "Feminism and the Women's Movement," 590.
70. Ian R. Tyrrell, *Woman's World/Woman's Empire: The Woman's Christian Temperance Union in International Perspective, 1800–1930* (Chapel Hill: University of North Carolina Press, 1991).
71. See, for examples, Mary Fainsod Katzenstein, "Discursive Politics and Feminist Activism in the Catholic Church," in *Feminist Organizations: Harvest of the New Women's Movement*, eds. Myra Marx Ferree and Patricia Yancey Martin (Philadelphia: Temple University Press, 1995); Kristina Boylan, "Gendering the Faith and Altering the Nation: Mexican Catholic

Women's Activism, 1917–1940," in *Sex in Revolution: Gender, Politics, and Power in Modern Mexico*, eds. Jocelyn Olcott, Mary Kay Vaughan, and Gabriela Cano (Durham: Duke University Press, 2006); Mahmood, *Politics of Piety*.

72. Anderson, *Joyous Greetings*; Olcott, *Revolutionary Women in Postrevolutionary Mexico*.
73. On Friedan, see Daniel Horowitz, *Betty Friedan and the Making of The Feminine Mystique: The American Left, the Cold War, and Modern Feminism* (Amherst: University of Massachusetts Press, 1998). On labor feminism, see also Dorothy Sue Cobble, *The Other Women's Movement: Workplace Justice and Social Rights in Modern America* (Princeton: Princeton University Press, 2004).
74. Elisabeth Jay Friedman, "Gendering the Agenda: The Impact of the Transnational Women's Rights Movement at the UN Conferences of the 1990s," *Women's Studies International Forum* 26, no. 4 (2003): 317.
75. Sonia E. Alvarez, Nalu Faria, and Miriam Nobre, "Another (also Feminist) World Is Possible: Constructing Transnational Spaces and Global Alternatives from the Movements," in *The World Social Forum: Challenging Empires*, ed. Jai Sen et al. (New Delhi: Viveka Foundation, 2004); Amrita Basu, "Globalization of the Local/Localization of the Global Mapping Transnational Women's Movements," *Meridians* 1, no. 1 (2000); Elisabeth J. Friedman, Kathryn Hochstetler, and Ann Marie Clark, *Sovereignty, Democracy, and Global Civil Society: State-Society Relations at UN World Conferences* (Albany: SUNY Press, 2005); Junhui Joo, "Women's International Non-Governmental Organizations and an International Conference, 1975" (Albany: State University of New York, 1984); Valentine M. Moghadam, *Globalizing Women: Transnational Feminist Networks* (Baltimore: Johns Hopkins University Press, 2005); Sandra Whitworth, *Feminism and International Relations: Towards a Political Economy of Gender in Interstate and Non-Governmental Institutions* (New York: St. Martin's Press, 1994).
76. On the YWCA, see Garner, *Shaping a Global Women's Agenda*. On the IPPF, see Connelly, *Fatal Misconception*. On the Ford Foundation, see Susan M. Hartmann, *The Other Feminists: Activists in the Liberal Establishment* (New Haven: Yale University Press, 1998).
77. "Los Gobiernos del Tercer Mundo Obstaculizan la Ayuda a los Pueblos," *El Universal* (Mexico City), 24 June 1975, 1.
78. See, for example, Arturo Escobar and Sonia E. Alvarez, eds., *The Making of Social Movements in Latin America: Identity, Strategy, and Democracy* (Boulder, Colo.: Westview Press, 1992).
79. Gayatri Chakravorty Spivak, "'Woman' as Theatre: United Nations Conference on Women, Beijing 1995," *Radical Philosophy* (1996). Spivak indicates clearly that *all* politics are performative, but the politics of transnational NGO congresses often implies more radically democratic representation than has thus far been feasible.

ABOUT THE CONTRIBUTORS

Arianne Chernock is Assistant Professor in the Department of History at Boston University, where she specializes in modern British and gender history. Her first book, *Men and the Making of Modern British Feminism*, was published by Stanford University Press in 2010. Related essays have appeared in the *Journal of British Studies*, *Enlightenment and Dissent*, and the edited collection *Women, Gender and Enlightenment*. She is currently researching the politics of queenship in Victorian Britain.

Anna Clark is Professor of History at the University of Minnesota. She is the author of *Desire: A History of Sexuality in Europe* (2008); *Scandal: The Sexual Politics of the British Constitution* (2004); *The Struggle for the Breeches: Gender and the Making of the British Working Class* (1995); and *Women's Silence, Men's Violence: Sexual Assault in Britain, 1780–1845* (1987), as well as numerous articles, including "Twilight Moments" and "Anne Lister's Construction of Lesbian Identity," both in the *Journal of the History of Sexuality*. She is now working on a project entitled "Secret Selves and Victorian Individuality."

Barbara Engel is Distinguished Professor at the University of Colorado, Boulder. A recipient of support from the National Endowment for the Humanities and the John Simon Guggenheim Foundation, among others, she is the author of *Mothers and Daughters: Women of the Intelligentsia in Nineteenth Century Russia* (1983); *Between the Fields and the City: Women, Work and Family in Russia, 1861–1914* (1994), *Women in Russia: 1700–2000* (2004), and most recently, *Breaking the Ties That Bound: The Politics of Marital Strife in Late Imperial Russia* (2011), as well as numerous articles.

Kate Haulman is Assistant Professor of History at American University, where she focuses on early American, women's and gender, and cultural history. She is the author of *The Politics of Fashion in Eighteenth-Century America* (2011), which won the Berkshire Conference of Women Historians Prize for best book focusing on the history of women, gender, and/or sexuality. Other work has appeared in the *William and Mary Quarterly*, the *Journal of Women's History*, and *Major Problems in American Women's History*.

Pamela S. Nadell holds the Patrick Clendenen Chair in Women's and Gender History at American University, where she is also Chair of the Department of History. Her books include *Women Who Would Be Rabbis: A History of Women's Ordination, 1889–1985*, which was a finalist for a National Jewish Book Award, and the edited collection *American Jewish Women's History*. A specialist in American Jewish history, she is also Consulting Historian for Media and a member of the Historians Team of the National Museum of American Jewish History in Philadelphia.

Jocelyn Olcott, Associate Professor of History and Women's Studies at Duke University, is the author of *Revolutionary Women in Postrevolutionary Mexico* (2005) and coeditor of *Sex in Revolution: Gender, Politics, and Power in Modern Mexico* (2006; in translation with Fondo de Cultura Económica, 2009). She is currently working on two book projects: "The Greatest Consciousness-Raising Event in History: International Women's Year and the Challenge of Transnational Feminism" (under contract with Oxford University Press) and "Sing What the People Sing: Concha Michel and the Cultural Politics of Mexican Maternalism." She has published articles in the *Journal of Women's History*, the *Hispanic American Historical Review*, *Gender & History*, and *International Labor and Working-Class History* as well as numerous chapters in edited collections.

Kathy Peiss is the Roy F. and Jeannette P. Nichols Professor of American History at the University of Pennsylvania, where she teaches modern American cultural history and the history of American sexuality, women, and gender. Her research has examined the history of working women; working-class and interracial sexuality; leisure, style, and popular culture; the beauty industry in the U.S. and abroad; and print culture and cultural policy during World War II. She is the author of *Cheap Amusements: Working Women and Leisure in Turn-of-the-Century New York* (1986); *Hope in a Jar: The Making of America's Beauty Culture* (1998), and *Zoot Suit: The Enigmatic Career of an Extreme Style* (2011), among other works.

Lisa Pollard is Associate Professor in the Department of History at the University of North Carolina, Wilmington, where she specializes in modern Middle Eastern and gender history. Her first book, *Nurturing the Nation: The Family*

Politics of Modernizing, Colonizing and Liberating Egypt (1805–1923) was published by the University of California Press (2005). Related essays have been published in *Arab Studies Journal, Social Politics*, the *International Journal of Middle East Studies*, and *Gender and History*. Her current work considers British constructions of race in late nineteenth-century Egypt and the Sudan.

Claire Robertson is Professor of History and Women's, Gender, and Sexuality Studies at The Ohio State University, where she has taught since 1984. She received her M.A. from the University of Chicago and her Ph.D. from the University of Wisconsin-Madison in African History. She has published over fifty articles and six books on the subjects of women and slavery, African women and trade, education, socioeconomic structure, genital cutting, and life histories, with particular reference to Ghana and Kenya. Her present research focuses on Saint Lucia: its African connections, history from the late eighteenth century to the present, and life histories of the elderly. Her interests include ethnobotanical history, feminist theory, political economy, family history, comparative slavery, and local history.

Mytheli Sreenivas is Associate Professor of History and Women's, Gender, and Sexuality Studies at The Ohio State University. Her book, *Wives, Widows, and Concubines: The Conjugal Family Ideal in Colonial India* (2008), was awarded the Joseph Elder Prize in the Indian Social Sciences from the American Institute of Indian Studies. Related essays have appeared in the *Journal of Women's History*, the *Journal of Asian Studies*, and *Feminist Studies*. Her current research focuses on the cultural and political economy of reproduction in modern South Asia.

Ulrike Strasser is Associate Professor of History and Director of European Studies at the University of California, Irvine. Her monograph *State of Virginity: Politics, Religion, and Gender in a German Catholic Polity* won the award for "Best Book Published in 2004" from the Society for the Study of Early Modern Women, and was honored as finalist for "Das Historische Buch, 2004" in Germany. Strasser is also a coeditor, with M. J. Maynes, Ann Waltner, and Birgitte Soland, of *Gender, Kinship, Power: A Comparative and Interdisciplinary History* (1996). She is currently writing a transnational history on the role of early modern German Jesuits in shaping European images of the Pacific.

Heidi Tinsman is Associate Professor of History at the University of California, Irvine and author of *Partners in Conflict: The Politics of Gender,*

Sexuality, and Labor in the Chilean Agrarian Reform, 1950–1973 (2002) and coeditor with Sandhya Shukla of *Imaging Our Americas: Toward a Transnational Frame* (2007). She is currently finishing a book on grapes and consumer culture in Cold War Chile and the United States.

Cristina Zaccarini is Associate Professor of History and Co-Director of the Asian Studies Program at Adelphi University in New York. She is the author of several publications, including *The Sino-American Friendship as Tradition and Challenge: Dr. Ailie Gale in China, 1908–1950* (2001), and "Chinese Nationalism and Christian Womanhood in Early Twentieth-Century China: The Story of Mary Kao (Kao Meiyu)," in *Pioneer Chinese Christian Women: Gender, Christianity, and Social Mobility*, ed. Jessie Lutz (2010).

Index

'Abduh, Ibrahim, 137–138
Achebe, Nwando, 68, 84
Acton, William, 100
African American studies, 24
African Feminism (Mikell), 65–66
African history, 62
African National Congress (ANC), 71
African slavery studies, 63
African studies, 63
African studies Association (ASA), 63
African Womanhood in Colonial Kenya 1900-1950 (Kanogo), 71–72
African Women and Politics (Konde), 67
African women's history, 61–90; African slavery studies, 63; African studies, 63; agricultural labor, 83; American feminists and scholars of, courses taken by, 62; colonialism, 66–67, 82; commodity-centered histories, 78; consumption, 73–74, 82; cooperation between African and Africanist scholars, 82–83; development of, 62–64; dress, 74–75; female genital cutting (FGC), 82; feminism, 4; Francophone and Luzophone literature, 65; funding, 64; gender analysis, 68–69; gender history, 62–64; genderbending in Africa, 72; homosexuality, 72–73, 83; Igbo women, 79; Igbo Women's War (1929), 66, 70; international conferences, 64; Islamic women, 80–81; Maasai women, 79; matriarchy, 67; missionaries, 79–80; Muslim/Islamic women, 80–81, 82; oral historians, 82–83, 83–84; patriarchy, 75, 82; political economy, 61, 77–79; politics, 64–66; power, 82; precolonial political participation, 66; problematizing of assumed categories, 81–82; religion, 79–81; researchers, identity of, 84; sexuality, 72–73; slavery, 70; stereotypes about Africa and women, breaking common, 62; street traders, colonial persecution of, 75; textbooks about African history, 63; translation into local languages, 84; violence against women, 76–77, 83–84; visual representation of African women, 74–75; Western vs. African feminism, 65–66; Western women's agenda in studying, 61; women leaders, biographies of precolonial, 67–68; women's bodies, 75–77, 82; women's political activism, 69–75

African women's history about women in: Algeria, 80; Botswana, 64; Cameroon, 67; Dahomey, 67–68, 76; Egypt, 74; Ghana, 64; Great Lakes region, 69; Guinea, 69; Kenya, 62, 64, 67, 68, 75, 79–80; Lesotho, 64, 68–69; Libya, 65; Morocco, 80; Mozambique, 69; Namibia, 73; Niger, 80–81; Nigeria, 62, 64–65, 67, 70, 72, 74; North Africa, 66; Sierra Leone, 70–71; South Africa, 62, 64, 70, 71, 75; Sudan, 80; Swaziland, 75; Tanzania, 62, 79; the Transkei, 71; Uganda, 64; West Africa, 66; Zimbabwe, 68, 70, 73–74, 75, 76

Afro-Asian Women's Symposium, 249
Age of Consent debate (1891), 103–104
agricultural labor, 83, 169–170
AIDS crisis, 105–107
Aikin, Lucy, 126, 128
A'ishatu, Malama, 81

'Alam al-Din (Mubarak), 143
Alexander II, Tsar, 48
Alidou, Ousseina, 81, 84
All-India Muslim/Islamic Ladies' Conference, 166
Allman, Jean, 63, 69–70
Alloula, Malek, 80
Amadiume, Ifi, 72
amateur historians: Egyptian women's history, 138–139, 149–150, 155; "women worthies," 5–6, 7, 126; women's history, 18
American historians: comparative or transregional approaches, 27; gender analysis, 26; gender history, 17; nuclear families, 26; postcolonial studies, influence of, 27; poststructuralism, 31; women's history, 17
American Historical Association, 18–19, 24
Amin, Qasim, 150–153
Amory, Thomas, 119
Anderson, Benedict, 240
Anderson, Bonnie, 239, 240, 243, 248, 250
Andrews, Bridie, 224, 225
Anthony, Susan B., 18
antiessentialism, feminism and, 29
Appeal to the Men of Great Britain in Behalf of Women (Hays), 127
Appropriating Gender (Basu and Jeffery), 176
area studies, 190–193, 198–199
Arnfred, Signe, 73
Arondekar, Anjali, 106
Astell, Mary, 122
Atkins, Keletso, 63
Awal, Malam, 80–81
Awe, Bolanle, 64

Baartman, Sara (the "Hottentot Venue"), 74
"Backward Workers in Skirts?" (Glickman), 42
Ballard, George, 119–121, 128
Banerjee, Nirmala, 169–170
Bannerji, Himani, 103
Bantebya, Grace, 77–78
"Barbarism and Civilization" (Sarmiento), 199
Barlow, Tani, 216

Barnes, Linda, 223, 229
Barrios de Chungara, Domitila, 244, 247
Basel Mission Society, 79–80
Bastian, Misty, 74
Basu, Amrita, 175–176
Bay, Enda, 67–68
Beard, Mary, 18, 19
Becker, Heike, 73
Bederman, Gail, 25
Behn, Aphra, 128
Beisner, Robert L., 219
Benger, Elizabeth, 126
Bennett, Judith, 97, 130
Bentinck, William, 169
Berger, Iris, 62
Berkshire Conference of Women Historians, 18, 39
Berkshire Conference on the History of Women, 21
Bharatiya Janata Party (BJP), 173
Biographium Faemineum (Amory), 119
births out of wedlock in Europe, 94
Boadicea, 123, 125–126, 128
Bonds of Womanhood, The (Cott), 20
Booth, Marilyn, 154
Borthwick, Meredith, 165
bourgeois intellectuals, Egyptian women's history and, 149
Boycotts, Buses and Passes (Brooks), 70
Boyd, William, 126, 128
Boydston, Jeanne, 31–32
Boys-Wives and Female Husbands (Murray and Roscoe), 72–73
Bradford, Helen, 63–64
Bray, Francisca, 223
Brief Account of the Moral and Political Acts of the Kings and Queens, A (Dinmore), 115, 118, 123
Briggs, Laura, 29
Briquet, Fortunée, 117
Bristed, John, 122
British women's history, 115–136; 1970s, 117; history of the nation, 131–132; late eighteenth century authors, 122; middle-and lower-class women's collective experiences, 117; recuperation rather than advocacy, 119; "women worthies" (*see*

"women worthies" in British women's history); women's position, deterioration of, 125; women's rights, 123–124, 127, 129
"Britishness," 121–122
Brown, Kathleen, 27
Buggenhagen, Beth, 81
bureaucrat historians, 139, 141
Burke, Timothy, 73–74
Burton, Antoinette, 103, 179–180, 246
Butler, Judith, 107
Byfield, Judith, 63, 78

"Calidore" (author), 123, 124
capitalism, 91, 93, 94, 96
Carter, Elizabeth, 122
Castéra, Jean-Henri, 140–141
Catt, Carrie Chapman, 218
Chakravarti, Uma, 168
Changing Role of Women in Bengal (Borthwick), 165
Chaplain, Amy, 28
Chatterjee, Indrani, 180
Chatterjee, Partha, 103, 168–169, 171
Chauncey, George, 25
Cheap Amusements (Peiss), 17–18
Chen, Mary Gao, 225
Chennault, Anna, 221–222
Chennault, Claire, 221
Chernock, Arianne, 18, 40
Chiang, Madame (May-ling Soong Chiang), 220–221
Chiang Kai-shek, 221
Chicago, Judy, 18
Chin, Carol, 212, 228
China, hospitals in, 225
China, modernization in, 9
Chinese healing, 226–229
Chinese women's history, 211–236; American missionaries and Chinese women, 27, 212, 214, 215–217, 222–223; Chinese healing, 226–229; Chinese medical history, 223; Chinese women's interpretation of Western ideas, 212, 213; conflict between gender-neutral "natural rights" and gender-specific practices of nation-states, 212; family, imperial recognition of, 216; feminism, 217–219; gender, 220–222, 223; health care, 213, 223–228; man and woman as socially constructed categories, 216; midwives, 224–226; modernity, 213; modernization, 216–217; nation-state, notion of, 213–217; nursing profession, 225; Sino-American relations, 219–223, 229–230; "Thrice Following" custom, 9, 215; woman suffrage movement, 217–219; women's political activism, 215, 217–219; women's rights, 218–219; women's work outside the home, 224, 225; yin and yang relationships, 233–234
Chowdhry, Prem, 169–170
Choy, Catherine, 28
Chronicle of Higher Education (journal), 30, 31
Church of Women, The (Hodgson), 79
Clancy-Smith, Julia, 80
Clark, Anna, 5
class, 21, 23
cleanliness, Egyptian women's history and, 148–149
Clements, Barbara, 40
Clothing and Difference (Bastian), 74
Cochran, Sherman, 227
Cocks, H. G., 106
Cold War: area studies, 198; end of, 23–24, 44–45; masculinity during, 29, 30; Russian and Soviet women's history, 38, 39, 44–45, 55–56; transnational feminist history, 240; women's history, 23–24, 38
Cole, Ernest, 71
Colman, George, 119, 120, 121
Colonial Lexicon of Birth, A (Hunt), 76
Colonial Masculinity (Sinha), 171
colonialism: African women's history, 66–67, 82; Egyptian women's history, 144–147; Indian women's history, 162–163, 168–169, 171–172; Latin American women's history, 191; nationalism, 168–169; "saving brown women from brown men," 10–11; "white men saving brown women from brown men," 163
Communism, collapse of, 23–24
comparative history, 238
Comparison between Women and Men, A (O'Hanlon), 166

Concise History of Ancient and Modern Egypt, A (Hakim), 150
Concubines and Power (Nast), 68
"Confessions of Faith" (Rhodes), 199
Consumers' Imperium (Hoganson), 28
consumption, 25, 44, 73–74, 82
Contagious Diseases Acts, 100, 102, 103
Cook, Matt, 105
Cooper, Barbara, 63, 78–79
Cott, Nancy, 20
Courses for Egyptian Minds in the Joys of Contemporary Manners (manahij al-albab al-misriyya fi mabahij al-adab al- 'asiriyya) (Tahtawi), 143
Creating the New Egyptian Woman (Russell), 74
Criminal Law Amendment Act (1885), 102, 104
Critical Gender Discourse in Africa (Ukhun), 65
Cromer, Evelyn Baring, 1st Earl of, 146–147, 152
Cuban Revolution (1959), 191
cult of domesticity, 47–48
"Customs in a Peasant Economy" (Chowdhry), 169–170
Cutting Down Trees (Moore and Vaughan), 77
Cynthia Nelson Institute for Gender and Women's studies, 138

Daughters of the Goddess (Amadiume), 72
Davis, Kathy, 245
Davis, Natalie Zemon, 21, 117–118, 132n3
Dean, Robert, 29
Deep Histories (Woodward, Hayes and Minkley), 70
Delong, Thomas A., 220–221
D'Emilio, John, 96
demographic revolution in European women's history, 93
Depping, Georges-Bernard, 141, 142
Des Jardins, Julie, 18
Descent into Discourse (Palmer), 23
Development of the Women's Awakening in Egypt, The (Shafiq and 'Abduh), 137–138
Di Capua, Yoav, 144

Dickinson, Edward Ross, 107–108
Dictionnaire historique, littéraire et bibliographique des Françaises (Briquet), 117
Dinmore, Richard, 115, 118, 122, 123, 124, 125
Dinner Party (Chicago), 18
divorce in Russian and Soviet women's history, 51
Dr. William's Pink Pills for Pale People, 226–227
domestic affairs in Egyptian women's history, 142–143, 145, 147–155
Doran, John, 126, 131
Downs, Laura Lee, 30
Dowry Murder (Oldenburg), 176
Dramé, Aly, 81
dress in African women's history, 74–75
Duara, Prasenjit, 219
DuBois, Ellen, 19
Duncombe, John, 119, 120, 121, 122–123
Dwelling in the Archive (Burton), 179–180
Dworkin, Andrea, 100

Eccentric Biography (Boyd), 128
Edgar, Adrienne, 55
Edwards, Louise, 217, 218, 220
Egypt, modernization in, 7
Egyptian National Archives, 158
Egyptian women's history, 137–160; amateur historians, 138–139, 149–150, 155; biographies in women's journals, 153–155; bourgeois intellectuals, 149; British-authored reforms, 139, 146–147; bureaucrat historians, 139, 141; cleanliness, 148–149; colonialism, 144–147; domestic affairs, 142–143, 145, 147–155; Egyptian press, 147–148; family life, reform of, 151–152; harems, 144–147; home economics columns, 148–149; institutional support for, 138; "Lady Egypt," 7, 139–140, 153, 155, 156–157, 158; marginalization within Egyptian universities, 138; modernity, 139, 141, 142–143, 147; modernization, 140–143, 149–151; "show and tell" genre, 142; textbooks, 152; travel literature, 144–147; "woman question," 138–140, 150, 154, 155; "women worthies," 153–155; women's

education, 152, 156; women's political activism, 137, 156; women's work outside the home, 156–157
Egyptian writers, 7
Ejituwu, Nkparom C., 64–65
Elizabeth I, Queen of England, 122, 123, 124, 125, 126
Ellis, Havelock, 105
Elstob, Elizabeth, 120
empire, 52–55, 103, 202–203
Enfield, William, 122
Engaging Modernity (Alidou), 81
Engelstein, Laura, 43
England, Lynndie, 30
England in Egypt (Milner), 146–147
Enke, Anne, 243
Enlightenment, 6, 46, 241
Epistles on Women (Aikin), 128
Epprecht, Marc, 63, 68–69, 72
Essays on Subjects Connected with Civilization (Malkin), 123
essentialism, 31, 33, 96–97
ethnicity, 189
Eulenberg scandal (1908), 105
European studies, 199
European women's history, 91–112; births out of wedlock, 94; demographic revolution, 93; French Revolution, 92–93; industrial revolution, 93; masculinity, 198; revolutions, age of, 92–99; sexual crisis, 91–92, 93, 99–108, 109
Extended Family, The (Minault), 165–166
Ezell, Margaret, 119

Fair, Laura, 64
Fall, Fatima, 74–75
Family, Sex and Marriage, The (Stone), 94
family life, 42, 51, 151–152. See also domestic affairs in Egyptian women's history
Family Man paradigm, 195–196
Family Romance of the French Revolution, The (Hunt), 97–98
Fanon, Frantz, 80
Fashioning Africa (Allman), 4
Female Advocate, The (Scott), 122–123
Female Biography (Hays), 127–128
female genital cutting (FGC), 76, 82

Female King of Colonia Nigeria, The (Achebe), 68
"Female World of Love and Ritual" (Smith-Rosenberg), 19
feminism: 1960s, 3, 17; 1970s, 17; African women's history, 4; antiessentialism, 29; child sexual abuse, 101; Chinese women's history, 217–219; class struggle, 93; diversity within, 238–239; divisions within, 244; Egyptian movement, 150; essentialism, 33; German feminists, 102; "great woman" view of history, moving beyond, 22; identity politics, 24; Indian women's history, 161; Latin American feminists, 192, 245; liberal feminists, 245; Marxism, 41, 237; materialist analysis, 245; postcolonial feminism, 161; prostitution, 101, 102–103; radical approaches, 19; radical vs. "sex positive" feminists, 101; Russian and Soviet women's history, 39; scientific understanding of women's nature, 20; second-wave feminism, 4, 5, 19, 20, 39; "sex wars" among feminists, 101; sexuality, 100–101; socialist feminists, 102; socialist-feminist framework, 21; Swedish feminists, 102; transnational feminism, 238, 248–253; wave model of, 239–240; Western vs. African feminism, 65–66; women's history, 17; working-class unity, fissures in, 95
Feminism and Suffrage (DuBois), 19
feminist historians, 32, 103, 239–242
Feminist History Workshop, 93
Feminist studies (journal), 71
Ferminiad, The (Duncombe), 120, 122–123
Ferree, Myra Marx, 238–239, 242, 243, 250
Filipino nurses in the U.S., 28
Fine Woman's Exhibition of Biographies of Famous Women (Nawfal), 154
Flourishing Yin, A (Furth), 223
Forbes, Geraldine, 165, 166, 167
Ford, Henry, 197
Forslund, Catherine, 221
Foucault, Michel: "bio-power," 75; feminist scholars, influence on, 219; on homosexuality, 104; Latin American women's history, 191; power, 92, 104; Rubin, Gayle, 101;

Foucault, Michel *(continued)*: Russian and Soviet women's history, 50; scholar activists, influence on, 107; sexuality, 99–100; sexuality, study of, 92
Foul Bodies (Brown), 27
France, modernization in, 142–143
French Revolution, 92–93
Friedan, Betty, 244, 247, 249, 250–251
Friedman, Elisabeth Jay, 251
From Patriarchy to Empowerment (Moghadam), 66
Furth, Charlotte, 216, 223, 226

Gage, Matilda Joslyn, 18
Gale, Ailie, 222–223, 225
Garner, Karen, 240–241
Garnett, Thomas, 122
Gaudio, Rudolf, 73
Gay New York (Chauncey), 25
Geiger, Susan, 62, 63, 69–70
"gender" (the term), 21, 31
gender, 49–55; American foreign policy, 28–29; body, history of the, 26; Chinese women's history, 220–222, 223; class, 23; conflict between gender-neutral "natural rights" and gender-specific practices of nation-states, 212; empire, 52–55; explanatory power, 32–33; Indian women's history, 167, 168; instability in systems of, 109; Marxism, 188; modernity, 7–8; nationalism, 220; power, 22; as a representation of perceived biological differences, 22; Russian and Soviet women's history, 49–52; Scott on, Joan, 107; as set of practices, 108–109; sexuality, 92, 101, 179, 189; Sino-American relations, 211; as a social role or relation, 22; Stalinism, 51–52; U.S. foreign relations, 211; women's history, 21; working class, 96
"Gender: A Useful Category of Historical Analysis" (Scott), 22–23
gender analysis, 29–32; African women's history, 68–69; American historians, 26; application of, 31; consumption, 25; essentialism, 31; feminist historians, 32; Latin American women's history, 194, 195; male identity, naturalness, 25; materialist paradigms, 190, 194; national histories, gendering of, 68–69; pervasiveness of, 30; political economy, 31; Russian and Soviet women's history, 53; Scott, Joan, 30, 98; slavery, 69; U.S. history, 24–25, 29–32, 33; women's history, 30
Gender and the Making of a South African Bantustan (Mager), 71
gender historians, claims by, 23
gender history, 20–25, 188–193; African women's history, 62–64; American historians, 17; area studies, 190–193; emergence of, 188–189; Engelstein, Laura, 43; ethnicity, 189; Latin American studies, 188; Marxism, 189; meganarratives, 189; origins, 130; race, 189; Scott, Joan, 43; U.S. history, 4; "women worthies," 130; women's history, 20–25; world history, 188–193
Gender of History, The (Smith), 6
Gender Politics in Sudan (Hale), 80
"gender relations" (the term), 21
"gender role" (the term), 21
"gender turn" (the term), 22
Gender Violence in Africa (Green), 77
Gengenbach, Heidi, 69
geography in women's history, 3
George, Henry, 148
Gilmore, Glenda, 26
Glickman, Rose, 42
globalization and historiography, 2, 187
Goheen, Miriam, 77
Goldman, Wendy, 43
Gordon, Linda, 26
Gorman, Anthony, 139
Graham, Loren, 40
Great Britain, 92, 118–119
Green, December, 77
Green, Mary Anne Everett, 126, 129
Green Place, A (Schoenbrun), 69
Griffith, Marie, 26
Guha, Ranajit, 172
Gynaikeion or Nine Books of Various History Concerning Women (Heywood), 117

Haan, Francisca de, 241
Hakim, Mohammed Diyab 'Abd al-, 150
Hales, Sondra, 80

Hall, Catherine, 93–94
Hall, Mrs. Matthew, 126
Hall, Radclyffe, 104
Hanretta, Sean, 63
Harb, Mohammed Talaat, 152
Hartmann, Heidi, 237
Hartmann, Susan, 220
Hay, Margaret Jean, 62
Hays, Mary, 126, 127–128
health care in Chinese women's history, 213, 223–228
Hemmings, Clare, 239–240
Herbert, Eugenia, 66
"herstory" (the term), 18
"heteronormativity," 107
heterosexuality, reconstruction of, 108
Heywood, Thomas, 117
Hickes, George, 124
Hicks, Philip, 118, 119
Hidden from History (Rowbotham), 18
hijras, 106
Hindu nationalism (Hindutva), 173–174, 175–176
Hirschfeld, Magnus, 105
Historical Memoirs of the Queens of England (Lawrance), 129
historiography, 187–190; 1980s and 1990s, 192; amateur historians (*see* amateur historians); American historians (*see* American historians); bureaucrat historians, 139, 141; comparative history, 238; Eurocentrism, upending of, 193; feminist historians, 32, 103, 239–242; gender historians, claims by, 23; globalization, 2, 187; historical study of masculinity, 187–188; labor history, 196–197; nation-state, relation to, 11; oral historians, 82–83, 83–84; postcolonial history, 180–181; refocusing from "causation" to "meaning," 192; "show and tell" genre, 142; transnational history, 238; transnational turn in, 187; travel literature, 144–147; turn away from social history toward cultural history, 98; women's historians, 24; women's history (*see* women's history); world history, 188–190
History Matters (Bennett), 130

History of Sexuality (Foucault), 100
History of Woman in England (Lawrance), 129
History of Woman's Suffrage (Stanton, Anthony and Gage), 18
History Workshop movement, 93
Hodgson, Dorothy, 79–80
Hoganson, Kristin, 28
Homosexual Africa? (Epprecht), 72
homosexuality, 72–73, 83, 96–97, 104–108
Honest Guide for Training Boys and Girls, An (al-murshid al-amin fi tarbiyyat al-banat wal-banin) (Tahtawi), 143
Hong Zhang, 219–220
Hopkins, Ellice, 101, 102
Houlbrook, Matt, 106
House of Bondage (Cole), 71
Hu Ying, 214–215
Huang Chujiu, 227–228
Hunt, Lynn, 97–98
Hunt, Nancy Rose, 76, 84
Hunter, Jane, 212, 222

identity politics, feminism and, 24
"If 'Woman' Is Just an Empty Category" (Downs), 30
Igbo women, 79
Igbo Women's War (1929), 66, 70
imperialism, 103
Inca, 201–202
"India" (the term), 162
Indian Council of Social Science research, 164
Indian National Congress, 163, 178
Indian nationalism, 162, 170
Indian women's history, 161–184; 1970s, 164; 1980s, 165; Age of Consent debate (1891), 103–104; agricultural labor, 169–170; all-India women's movement, 163–164; in Bengal, 165, 169, 177–178; child marriage, 178; colonialism, 162–163, 168–169, 171–172; documenting women's voices and lives, 165–167; elite *vs.* nonelite subjects, 172; future developments, 176–191; gender, 167, 168; in Haryana, 170; "Hindu" history, 173–176; "home" as a historical site, 180; in Hyderabad, 166;

Indian women's history *(continued)*: Indian nationalism, 162, 170; India's sex ratio, 176; marriage, female consent in, 178; modernity, 167, 168; modernization, 169–170; national liberation movements, 8; nationalism, 8, 163; nation-state as a form, 170–172; ongoing oppression of women, 161–162; patriarchy, 8, 162, 167, 168, 174, 177; postcolonial feminism, 161; postcolonial history, 180–181; power, 167; pre-1947 history, scholarship on, 162; prostitution, 106; in Rajasthan, 174; sati, 169, 174–175; South Asian historiography, as subfield of, 167; South Asian women's history, 165; upper-cast Hindu women, 175; violence against women, 164–165; "woman question," 163–164; women's political activism, 163–164; women's rights, 164
industrial revolution in European women's history, 93
International Federation of Business and Professional Women, 249
International Interdisciplinary Congress for Women (2002), 64
International Labor and Working-Class History (journal), 23
International Labor Organization, 251
International Planned Parenthood Federation, 251
interracial sex, 103
Invention of Women (Oyěwùmí), 61
Iriye, Akira, 219
Islamic/Muslim women, 54, 80–81, 82

Jackson, Lynette, 75
James, Stanlie, 76
Jameson, Anna, 126
Jeffery, Patricia, 176
Jeffreys, Sheila, 96–97, 100, 101–102, 104
Jesperson, T. Christopher, 223, 230–231
Jesse, John Heneage, 126, 131
Jiagge, Annie, 247
John, Mary E., 179
Johnson, Tina, 225–226
Johnson-Odim, Cheryl, 68
Jones, Rhodri Jeffreys, 222

Journal of African History (JAH), 63
Journal of American History, 30
Judge, Joan, 217

Kang Aide, 215
Kang Youwei, 223
Kanogo, Tabitha, 71–72, 75, 83
Kanwar, Roop, 174–175
Kaplan, Flora Edouwaye S., 67
Kaplan, Temma, 248
Karl, Rebecca, 216–217
Katz, Cindi, 238
Katz, Jonathan Ned, 107
Kauffmann, Angelica, 128
Keck, Margaret, 247
Kelly, Joan, 21
Kenyan, George, 30
Kenyan National Archives, 75
Kessler-Harris, Alice, 26, 30, 31, 239
Kewes, Paulina, 118
"Khomo Lia Oela" (Maloka), 63
Kidwai, Saleem, 179
Ko, Dorothy, 212, 215, 217–218, 221, 223
Kollman, Nancy Shields, 46
Kollontai Alexandra, 40–41
Konde, Emmanuel, 67
Krafft-Ebbing, Richard von, 100, 105
Kriger, Colleen, 63
Krylova, Anna, 52

labor history, 196–197
labor militancy, masculinity and, 197
Laboring Women (Morgan), 27
Labouchère Amendment, 106
Lacan, Jacques, 191
Ladies' National Association, 100
"Lady Egypt," 7, 139–140, 153, 155, 156–157, 158
Lake, Marilyn, 250
Lalitha, K., 166
Lan Cassel, Susie, 228, 229
Laqueur, Thomas, 26, 97, 224
Latin America, 192–193
Latin American history, 191
Latin American nationalism, 193
Latin American studies, 188, 190, 191, 193–194, 195

Latin American women's history, 187–210; 1980s, 192; colonialism, 191; empire building, 202–203; Eurocentrism, upending of, 193; Family Man paradigm, 195–196; Foucault, Michel, 191; gender analysis, 194, 195; history and anthropology, cross-pollination of, 195; labor history, 196–197; Marxism, 194; masculinity, 194–195, 197–203; modernization, 192–193, 195; patriarchy, 195, 202–203; sexual honor, 194; social and political history, 191
Latin American women's organizations, 240
Latin Americanist literature, 188
Latin Americanist scholarship, 195–196
Lavrin, Asunción, 238, 240, 242
Lawrance, Hannah, 126, 129
Lawton, Susan, 53
League of Nations, 251
Lerner, Gerda, 1, 5
Levine, Philippa, 103
Liang Qichao, 214–215, 223
liberalism, women's history and, 43
Liberating the Family? (Scully), 70
Liberation of Women (Tahrir al-Mara') (Amin), 150
Lifebouy Men, Lux Women (Burke), 73–74
Lindsay, Lisa, 63, 70
Lister, Anne, 97
Liu, Lydia, 220, 226
Lives of the Queens of England, The (Strickland), 126, 129–130
Lochrie, Karma, 107
London and the Culture of Homosexuality (Cook), 105
London Feminist History group, 93, 95
Luibhéid, Eithne, 28
Lunbeck, Elizabeth, 31
Lutz, Jessie, 215
Lynch, Jessica, 30

Macdonald, Andrew, 123
Machobane, L. B. B. J., 68–69
Mackinnon, Catherine, 100
Mager, Anne Kelk, 71
Mahmood, Saba, 244
Makerere University, 64
Makeri, Wangu wa, 68

Making Sex (Laqueur), 26
Malabari, Benjamin, 103–104
Male Daughters, Female Husbands (Amadiume), 72
Malkin, Benjamin Heath, 122, 123
Maloka, Tshidiso, 63
Malte-Brun, Conrad, 141, 142
Malthus, Thomas, 93
Mani, Lata, 168–169, 174
Manicom, Linzi, 63
"manifest domesticity," 28
Manly, Marion, 225–226
Manning, Patrick, 203
Marcus, Sharon, 97
Marcus, Steven, 94
Margaret, Queen of England, 129
Marrese, Michelle Lamarche, 47
marriage: child marriage, 178; Egypt, 157; Enlightenment, 46; evolutionary thought, 99; female consent in, 178; Indian customs, 103; Russian and Soviet women's history, 46–47, 48–49; unhappiness of, 108
Marriage in Maradi (Cooper), 78–79
Marsot, Afaf, 145
Marxism: 1980s, 192; class struggle, 93; feminism, 41, 237; gender, 188; gender history, 189; "gender relations" and, 21; Latin American feminists, 192; Latin American studies, 192–193; Latin American women's history, 194; Marxist-Leninist ideology, 49; materialist analysis, 93; reworking of, 20; Russian and Soviet women's history, 49; Scott, Joan, 23, 98; sexuality, 5, 188–189; Subaltern studies, 103; women's history, 20, 93; work to, 100
Mary, Queen of Scots (Jesse), 131
masculinity, 194–203; during Cold War, 29, 30; comparisons across time, 198; empire, 203; European women's history, 198; historical study of, 187–188; labor militancy, 197; Latin American women's history, 194–195, 197–203; modernity, 196; power, 201; problematizing of, 201; Rhodes on, Cecil, 200; Roosevelt on, Theodore, 200; Russian and Soviet women's history, 44; Sarmiento on, Domingo, 200; working class, 96; world history, 8, 197–203

Masquelier, Adeline, 80–81
Massell, Gregory, 55
Matemba, Yonah Hisbon, 69
Matembe, Miria, 68
matriarchy in African women's history, 67
Mau Mau's Daughter (Wambu Otieno), 68
Maude, Queen of England, 129
May, Elaine Tyler, 220
Mayo, Katherine, 178–179
Mazumdar, Shudha, 165
Mba, Nina Emma, 68
McFadden, Margaret, 240
McIntosh, Marjorie Keniston, 77–78
meganarratives, 189
Mehmet 'Ali Pasha, 140, 141–142
Meisel-Hess, Grete, 91, 108, 109
Memoirs of Queens (Hays), 128
Memoirs of Several Ladies of Great Britain (Ballard), 119–120, 121
Memoirs of Several Ladies of Great Britain, Interspersed with Literary Reflections (Armory), 119
Men Own the Fields, Women Own the Crops (Goheen), 77
Mendoza, Breny, 242, 247
Merrick, Jeffrey, 96
Mexico, 239
Middle East, 27
midwives in Chinese women's history, 224–226
Mikell, Gwendolyn, 65–66
Millennium Development Goals, 177
Miller, Francesca, 240
Miller, Joseph, 63
Milner, Alfred, 146–147
Minault, Gail, 165–166
missionaries, 214–217; African women's history, 79–80; American missionaries and Chinese women, 27, 212, 214, 215–217, 222–223; American public opinion of China, 222
Mitchell, Rosemary, 129
Modern Egypt (Cromer), 146
Modern History of Egypt, A (Zaydan), 149–150, 157
modernity: Bengali, 178; Chinese women's history, 213; cleanliness, 149; domestic affairs, 142–143; Egyptian women's history, 139, 141, 142–143, 147; Enlightenment, 6; gender, 7–8; Indian women's history, 167, 168, 178; masculinity, 196; Russian and Soviet women's history, 52, 55; Soviet Union, 55; women, 11
modernization: China, 9; Chinese women's history, 216–217; Egypt, 7; Egyptian women's history, 140–143, 149–151; France, 142–143; India, patriarchy in, 8; Indian women's history, 169–170; Latin American women's history, 192–193, 195; patriarchy, 195
Moghadam, Valentine, 66
Mojekwu, Victoria, 247
Moore, Henrietta, 77
Mophosho, Florence, 247
Morgan, Jennifer, 27
Mother India (Mayo), 178–179
motherhood in Russian and Soviet women's history, 48
Mothers of the Plaza de Mayo, 245
Mubarak, 'Ali, 143
Mubarak, Mohammed Husni, 137
Mueller, Carol McClurg, 238–239, 242, 243, 250
Mugo, Micere, 68
Muntemba, Maud, 64
Muridiyya, 81
Musa, Nabawiyya, 156
Musisi, Nakayike, 69–70
Muslim/Islamic women, 54, 80–81, 82
Mutongi, Kenda, 78–79, 84

Nair, Janaki, 171–172, 179
Nameless Offenses (Cocks), 106
"Naming the Past in a 'Scattered' Land" (Gengenbach), 69
Nanxiu Qian, 215
Nasser, Gamal Abdel, 157
Nast, Heidi, 67–68
Nathan, Andrew, 226
National Endowment for the Humanities, 43
national liberation movements in Indian women's history, 8
nationalism: colonialism, 168–169; gender, 220; Hindu nationalism (Hindutva), 173–174, 175–176; Indian nationalism, 162,

170; Indian women's history, 8, 163; in Latin America, 193; "woman question," 10; women's history, 6–7
nation-state: Chinese women's history, 213–217; conflict between gender-neutral "natural rights" and gender-specific practices of nation-states, 212; Egypt as, 7; historiography, 11; imagining of, women's history and, 2; Indian women's history, 170–172
Nawfal, Maryam Nahhas, 154
Ndambuki, Berida, 77
Neptune, Harvey, 29
New International Economic Order, 241
New Perspectives on Islam in Senegal (Diouf and Leichtman), 81
New Woman, The (al-Mara' al-Jadida) (Amin), 150, 151
Newton, Esther, 104
NGOs (non-governmental organizations), 241, 250, 251
Nhongo-Simbanegavi, Mosephine, 76
Nichols, Jeannette P., 19
Nnaemeka, Obioma, 65
Non-Aligned Movement, 191
Norgate, Thomas Starling, 122, 123–124, 125, 129
Northrup, Douglas, 55
Ntabeni, Mary Nombuela, 68–69
nuclear families, 26
nursing profession in Chinese women's history, 225

O'Brien, Karen, 119, 127
Ogbomo, Onaiwu, 67
Ogundipe, Ayodele, 65
O'Hanlon, Rosalind, 166
Okeke, Philomena, 83
Okonjo, Kamene, 64, 66
Oldenburg, Veena Talwar, 176
"On the Rights of Women" (Norgate), 123–124
Oosterhuis, Harry, 105
Organization of American Historians, 19
Orr, Clarissa Campbell, 130–131
Other Victorians, The (Marcus), 94
Our Bodies, Ourselves (Our Bodies Ourselves), 245

Owenites, 95
Oyěwùmí, Oyèrónké, 61, 66, 82

Padmini, 180
Pakington, Dorothy, 120
Pala, Achola, 64
Palmer, Bryan, 23
Pankhurst, Christabel, 102
Pan-Third Worldism, 191
passions, 248–249
patriarchy: African women's history, 75, 82; Indian women's history, 8, 162, 167, 168, 174, 177; Latin American women's history, 195, 202–203; modernization, 195; power, 94; sati, 174–175
Peiss, Kathy, 39
Pembroke, Mary Sydney, Countess of, 120
periodization, feminist historians and, 239–242
Perry, Ruth, 120
Peter the Great, 46
Phillips, Mark, 119
Pleasure and Danger (Vance), 101
Poems by Eminent Ladies (Colman and Thornton), 120
political economy, 31, 61, 77–79
politics: African women's history, 64–66; formal politics, 10; identity politics, 24; institutions of governance, 10; Russian and Soviet women's history, influence on, 40; statist political movements, 11; women's history, 2–3, 4, 6–7, 10–11; women's issues and, dividing line between, 241
Politics of the Womb (Thomas), 75
Pollard, Lisa, 18
postcolonial feminism, 161
postcolonial history, 180–181
poststructuralism: American historians, 31; feminist historians, 32; women's history, 22, 23, 33
power: African women's history, 82; births out of wedlock, 94; discourse about, 98; exercise of, 98; Foucault, Michel, 92, 104; gender, 22; "heteronormativity" as the norm, 107; Indian women's history, 167; masculinity, 201; patriarchy, 94
Pratt, Mary Louise, 243

Précis de la géographie universelle (Malte-Brun), 141
Preiss, Kathy, 116
Priestly, Margaret, 63
prostitution, 101, 102–103, 106
Prostitution in Victorian Society (Walkowitz), 100
Przheval'skii, Nikolai, 53–54
Psychiatric Persuasion, The (Lunbeck), 31
psychology, women's history and, 20
Psychopathia Sexualis (Krafft-Ebbing), 100
Puerto Rico, 29

Queer London (Houlbrook), 106
Queering India (Vanita), 179
queerness as a transgressive desire, 107
Question of Silence?, A (John and Nair), 179
Queens, Queen Mothers, Priestesses, and Power (Kaplan), 67

race, 21, 189
Radcliffe College, 19
Radicalesbians, 19
Ramphele, Mamphela, 68
Ramusack, Barbara, 166
Randolph, John, 46
Ransel, David, 42
Reagan, Ronald, 192
Recasting Women (Sangari and Vaid), 167–168, 170, 172
Redding, Sean, 71
Reed, James, 222
Refinement of Gold in the Summary of Paris, A (takhlis al-ibriz fi talkhis bariz) (Tahtawi), 142
Reich, Wilhelm, 91
Reilly, Niamh, 246
Re-Inventing Africa (Amadiume), 72
religion in African women's history, 79–81
Renda, Mary, 29
Rendall, Jane, 119
Reproducing Empire (Briggs), 29
Research Center for Women's studies at SNDT Women's University in Mumbai, 164
Re-Thinking Sexualities in Africa (Arnfred), 73
Rhodes, Cecil, 199–201

Rich, Adrienne, 96–97
Rise of the Egalitarian Family (Trumbach), 94
Roberts, Priscilla, 222
Rogaski, Ruth, 226–227
romantic love, Enlightenment and, 46
Roosevelt, Theodore, 199–201
Rosander, Eva Evers, 65, 80
Ross, Ellen, 95
Rowbotham, Sheila, 18
Rubin, Gayle, 101, 102
Rupp, Leila, 240–242, 248
Russell, Mona, 74
Russian and Soviet women's history, 38–60; Azeri Bolshevik women, 54; Cold War, 38, 39, 44–45, 55–56; consumption, 44; cult of domesticity, 47–48; culturedness *(kulturnost)*, 51; divorce, 51; domestic sphere, 50–51; educated elites, 49; elite women, 41; empire, 52–55; Engelstein, Laura, 43; equality of the sexes, 50; family life, 42, 51; Foucault, Michel, 50; gender, 49–52; gender analysis, 53; gendered consequences of state policy, 56; industrialization, gendered consequences of, 48; marriage, 46–47, 48–49; Marxism, 49; Marxist-Leninist ideology, 49; masculinity, 44; middle classes, 44; modernity, 52, 55; motherhood, 48; Muslim/Islamic women, 54; native women's status, 53–55; "new socialist family," 51; nineteenth century female radicalism, 38; noblewomen, 47; peasant women, 41–42; politics, influence of, 40; revisionist historians, 42–43; Russian relationship with Western Europe, 45–49; Russian-language scholarship, 45; second-wave feminism, 39; Soviet archives, access to, 39–40, 41; Soviet Union, collapse of, 44; Stalinism, 51–52; violence against women, 54–55; "woman question," 48; women in the labor force, 48–49, 50, 51; "women worthies," 40–41; women's political activism, 4; women's property rights, 47; women's "virtue," 48; working-class women, 42, 43; Zhenotdel (Women's Bureau), 40–41, 54

Russian Labor History Conference (1982), 42
Russian Orthodox Church, 46–47
Ruthchild, Rochelle, 39

Said, Edward, 242
Salmon, Lucy Maynard, 18
Same-Sex Love in India (Vanita and Kidwai), 179
Sangari, Kumkum, 167–168, 174
Sarkar, Tanika, 104, 175, 177–178
Sarmiento, Domingo, 199–201
sati, 169, 174–175
Schlesinger, Arthur, Jr., 30
Schlesinger Library at Radcliffe College, 19, 33
Schmidt, Elizabeth, 69
Schoenbrun, David, 69
Schuller-McGeachy, Mary Craig, 243
Scott, Joan: discourse, emphasis on, 98; feminist history, 248; feminist scholars, influence on, 219; on gender, 107; gender analysis, 30, 98; gender as a representation of perceived biological differences, 22; gender history, 43; Jesperson, T. Christopher, 220; Marxism, 23, 98; Palmer, Bryan, 23; unmarried mothers, 94
Scott, Mary, 122
Scully, Pamela, 70
"sex" (the term), 21
Sered, Susan Starr, 223
Serlin, David, 26
Sewell, Sandra Serrano, 249
"sex role" (the term), 21
sexual crisis in European women's history, 91–92, 93, 99–108, 109
Sexual Dynamics of History (London Feminist History group), 95
sexual honor, 194
Sexual Inversion (Ellis), 105
sexual repression, capitalism and, 94
sexuality, 99–109, 190–194; African women's history, 72–73; AIDS crisis, 105–107; area studies, 190–193; capitalism, 91; equality of the sexes, 50; ethnicity, 189; feminism, 100–101; Foucault, Michel, 92, 99–100; gender, 92, 101, 179, 189; "heteronormativity" as the norm, 107; heterosexuality, reconstruction of, 108; hijras, 106; historians of, 5, 94, 189; historiography of, 5; history of, 108; homosexuality, 72–73, 83, 96–97, 104–108; instability in systems of, 109; interracial sex, 103; late nineteenth and early twentieth centuries, 5; male domination, essential means of, 100; Marxism, 5, 188–189; materialist paradigms, reworking of, 194; meganarratives, 189; one-sex *vs.* two-sex models of, 97; as set of practices, 108–109; sexual antagonism, 96; sexual honor, 194; world history, 188–190
Sha'arawi, Hoda, 156
Shafiq, Doria, 137–138
Sharing the Same Bowl (Robertson), 66
Sheldon, Kathleen, 78
Shen Chong, 219
Shinde, Tarabai, 166
Shorter, Edward, 94
Shulman, Elena, 52
Signs: Journal of Women in Culture and Society, 19
Sikkink, Kathryn, 247
Sinha, Mrinalini, 104, 171, 178
Sino-American relations, 211, 219–223, 229–230
Sirleaf, Ellen Johnson, 68
Sisterhood, Feminism and Power from Africa to the Diaspora (Nnaemeka), 65
Skocpol, Theda, 26
slavery, 63, 69, 70
Smith, Bonnie G., 6, 18, 117, 238
Smith College, 19
Smith-Rosenberg, Carroll, 19, 96–97
Snyder, Margaret, 245
Sophia Smith Collection at Smith College, 19, 33
South Asian history, 161
South Asian women's history, 165
Soviet Sisterhood (Holland), 42
Specters of Mother India (Sinha), 178
Spinster and Her Enemies, The (Jeffreys), 101–102
Spivak, Gayatri, 10, 163, 172–173, 252
Spongberg, Mary, 118, 129
Sreenivasan, Ramya, 180
Stalin, Joseph, 43, 51

Stalinism, 51–52
Stanton, Elizabeth Cady, 18
Steegstra, Mirijke, 79–80
Stepping Forward (Higgs, Moss and Ferguson), 70–71
Stites, Richard, 39
Stoler, Ann, 27, 103
Stone, Lawrence, 94
Strasser, Ulrike, 240
Stree Shakti Sanghatana, 166
"Strenuous Life, The" (Roosevelt), 199
Strickland, Agnes, 126–127, 129–130
Strickland, Elizabeth, 126–127
Strobel, Margaret, 62
Struggle for the Breeches, The (Clark), 95
Subaltern studies, 103, 161, 172
Sudarkasa, Niara, 62
Summers, Martin, 25
Sunseri, Thaddeus, 64
Svanstrom, Yvonne, 102–103
Sweden, prostitution in, 102–103
Sydney, Mary (Countess of Pembroke), 120

Tadesse, Mary, 245
Tahtawi, Rifaʿa Rafiʿ al-, 141–144, 149
Taking Haiti (Renda), 29
Tan Sheying, 218
Taylor, Barbara, 95
Taymur, ʿAisha, 154
Thapar, Romila, 174
Tharu, Susie, 166
Thatcher, Margaret, 105–106
Thayer, Millie, 245
Thomas, Lynn, 64, 75
Thompson, E. P., 93, 96
Thornton, Bonnell, 119, 120, 121
Three Guineas (Woolf), 246
"Thrice Following" custom, 9, 215
Tilly, Louise, 94
Tinsman, Heidi, 32, 199, 240
Tomes, Nancy, 95
Towards Equality: Report of the Committee on the Status of Women in India, 164
"Traffic in Women, The" (Rubin), 101
Transforming Female Identities (Rosander), 65

"transnational" (the term), 244
transnational feminism, 238, 248–253
transnational feminist history, 237–258; Cold War, 240; correspondences among transnational feminists, 248; cosmopolitan centers, 244–247; international conferences, 243–244, 247; lessons of, 252–253; NGOs (non-governmental organizations), 250, 251; passions, importance of, 248–249; periodization of, 241; place, aspiration to rise above, 242–243; politics and women's issues, dividing line between, 241; roots, 242–243; roots of, 237–238; scope of, 9; transnational feminism, 248–253; transnational identifications, 247–249
transnational history, 238
transnational identifications, 247–249
Transnational Sisterhood and Genital Cutting (James and Robertson), 76
transnationalism in historiography, 187
travel literature about Egypt, 144–147
Trinidad, 29
Trouble Showed the Way (Ndambuki and Robertson), 77
Trumbach, Randolph, 94, 96, 97

Ukhun, Christopher E., 65
Ulrich, Hans, 105
UN Economic and Social Council, 251
UN Economic Commission on Africa (ECA), 245
UN End of the Decade for Women conference, 64
UN International Women's Year (IWY), 240, 243, 244, 246–249
UN Millennium Development Goals, 177
United China Relief, 223
U.S. foreign relations, 211
U.S. history, 17–37; gender analysis, 24–25, 29–32, 33; gender history, 4; immigration policies, 28; Latin American history, 191; Latin American studies within, 191; women's history, 22–23, 33
USAID (United States Agency for International Development), 196
Vaid, Sudesh, 167–168, 174
Van Allen, Judith, 66

Vanita, Ruth, 179
Vaughan, Megan, 77
Victoria, Queen of United Kingdom, 126
Vietnam War, 29
"Vindication of Female Political Interference" (Waddington), 125–126
Vindication of the Rights of Women (Wollstonecraft), 115–116
violence against women: African women's history, 76–77, 83–84; Indian women's history, 164–165; Russian and Soviet women's history, 54–55; against working-class women, 95
Voltaire, 140–141

Waddington, Samuel Ferrand, 125–126
Wahrman, Dror, 97
Walkowitz, Judith, 100, 102
Walsh, Judith, 47
Wambu Otieno, Waiyaki, 68
Wanyoike, Mary, 68
Warner, Michael, 107
We Only Come Here to Struggle (Ndambuki and Robertson), 77
"We Were Making History" (Stree Shakti Sanghatana), 166
Weeks, Jeffrey, 104
Wei, George, 213–214
Well of Loneliness, The (Hall), 104
Wells, Julia, 63
Wexler, Laura, 28
"Whatever Happened to the Vedic *Dasi*?" (Chakravarti), 168
When Men and Women Mattered (Ogbomo), 67
Whole Duty of Man, The (anonymous), 120–121
Wilde, Oscar, 104, 106
Wives of the Leopard (Bay), 67–68
Wollstonecraft, Mary, 115–116, 123, 127, 128
"Woman Identified Woman, The" (Radicalesbians), 19
"woman question": Egyptian women's history, 138–140, 150, 154, 155; Indian women's history, 163–164; nationalism, 10; Russian and Soviet women's history, 48
woman suffrage movement in China, 217–219

"Women, Trade and the Yourba Family" (Sudarkasa), 62
Women and Law in Colonial India (Nair), 171–172
Women and Memory Forum, 138, 157–158
Women and ZANLA in Zimbabwe's Liberation War (Nhongo-Simbanegavi), 76
Women in African Colonial Histories (Allman, Geiger and Musisi), 69–70
Women in Borderland (Rosander), 80
Women in Modern India (Forbes), 167
Women in Russia (Atkinson, Dallin and Lapidus), 40
Women in South Africa (Magubane and Lazar), 71
Women in South African History (Gasa), 69
Women of Africa and African Diaspora (WAAD) conference, 65
"women worthies": amateur historians, 5–6, 7; biographies in women's journals, 153–155; in British women's history (*see* "women worthies" in British women's history); Davis on, Natalie Zemon, 117–118, 132n3; Egyptian women's history, 153–155; gender history, 130; as role models, 6; Russian and Soviet women's history, 40–41; Smith on, Bonnie G., 117; women's history, 117–118, 130
"women worthies" in British women's history, 115–132; amateur historians, 126; commercial success of the genre, 126–127; critique, as source of, 124; fear of forgetting women's contribution to the nation, 129; historical attention paid to, 116; lack of nuance about, 117; late eighteenth century authors, 122; legacies, 130–132; male *vs.* female approaches to, 131; national identity, conception of, 124; in nineteenth century, 125–130; as objects of fascination, 119–120; promotion of women's progress using royal women, 128; women's capacities, defense of, 121, 126; women's rights, 123–124, 127, 129
Women Writing in India (Tharu and Lalitha), 166
"women's and gender history" (the term), 32

Women's and Gender studies Program an Makerere University, 64
women's bodies, 43, 75–77, 82
women's education in Egyptian women's history, 152, 156
women's historians, 24
women's history, 1–11, 17–25; 1930s, 19; 1960s, 3, 18; 1980s, 20, 21, 22, 23; 1990s, 23; activist women of color, 21; of African women (*see* African women's history); agency, concern with, 20; amateur historians, 18; American historians, 17; as an integrated, "intersectional" analysis, 21; analytical frameworks and methods, 19–20; of British women (*see* British women's history); characteristics of, 1; of Chinese women (*see* Chinese women's history); class, 21; class hierarchies, maintenance of, 11; Cold War, 23–24, 38; Communism, collapse of, 23–24; conflict between gender-neutral "natural rights" and gender-specific practices of nation-states, 212; of Egyptian women (*see* Egyptian women's history); of eighteenth- and nineteenth-century, 7; emergence of, 17–20; of European women (*see* European women's history); feminism, 17; gender, 21; gender analysis, 30; gender turn, 20–25, 30–31; gendered labor, maintenance of, 11; geography, 3; history of sexuality, 108; inclusion in main currents of historical writing, 33; of Indian women (*see* Indian women's history); of Latin American women (*see* Latin American women's history); liberalism, 43; Marxism, 20, 93; materialist analysis, 91; nationalism, 6–7; origins, 18–19, 130; politics, 2–3, 4, 6–7, 10–11; poststructuralism, 22, 23, 33; professional networks, 18–19; psychology, 20; race, 21; repositories for, 19; of Russian and Soviet women (*see* Russian and Soviet women's history); scientific understanding of women's nature, 20; second-wave feminism, 4, 19, 20; sources, 170; transnational nature of, 2, 27–29 (*see also* transnational feminist history); U.S. history, 22–23, 33; "women on top," skepticism toward research about, 130–131; "women worthies," 117–118, 130; world history, 8
Women's International Democratic Federation (WIDG), 241
women's political activism: African women's history, 69–75; Chinese women's history, 215, 217–219; Egyptian women's history, 137, 156; Indian women's history, 163–164; Russian and Soviet women's history, 4
women's property rights: Russian and Soviet women's history, 47
women's rights: British women's history, 123–124, 127, 129; Chinese women's history, 218–219; Indian women's history, 164
Women's Silence, Men's Violence (Clark), 5, 95
Women's studies, 24, 237
Woolf, Virginia, 246, 247
Worries of the Heart (Mutongi), 78–79
working class: feminist historians, 103; gender, 96; masculinity, 96; sexual antagonism, 96
"Working Women in Colonial Bengal" (Banerjee), 169–170
World Health Organization, 251
world history: area studies, 190–191, 198–199; empire in, 203; Eurocentrism, upending of, 193; European expansion, 201; gender history, 188–193; masculinity, 8, 197–203; sexuality, 188–190; women's history, 8
World Women's Christian Temperance Union, 250
World YWCA, 251
Wylie, Diana, 63

Xiaoyuan Liu, 213–214

Yang Nianqun, 224
YWCA, 249

Zaydan, Jurji, 149–150, 157
Zeleza, Tiyambe, 63
Zhang, Hong, 219–220